www.wadsworth.com

www.wadsworth.com is the World Wide Web site for Thomson Wadsworth and is your direct source to dozens of online resources.

At *www.wadsworth.com* you can find out about supplements, demonstration software, and student resources. You can also send email to many of our authors and preview new publications and exciting new technologies.

www.wadsworth.com
Changing the way the world learns®

CAREERS IN CRIMINAL JUSTICE

AND RELATED FIELDS:

FROM INTERNSHIP TO PROMOTION

Fifth Edition

J. Scott Harr
Concordia University St. Paul

Kären M. Hess
Normandale Community College, Bloomington, Minnesota

THOMSON

WADSWORTH

Australia • Canada • Mexico • Singapore • Spain
United Kingdom • United States

THOMSON
™
WADSWORTH

Careers in Criminal Justice and Related Fields: From Internship to Promotion, Fifth Edition
J. Scott Harr and Kären M. Hess

Acquisitions Editor: *Carolyn Henderson-Meier*
Assistant Editor: *Jana Davis*
Editorial Assistant: *Rebecca Johnson*
Technology Project Manager: *Susan DeVanna*
Marketing Manager: *Terra Schultz*
Marketing Assistant: *Annabelle Yang*
Marketing Communications Manager: *Stacey Purviance*
Project Manager, Editorial Production: *Rita Jaramillo*
Art Director: *Vernon Boes*

Print Buyer: *Doreen Suruki*
Permissions Editor: *Sarah Harkrader*
Production Service: *Buuji, Inc.*
Copy Editor: *Linda Ireland*
Design and Graphics: *Christine Hess Orthman*
Cover Designer: *Chris Wallace*
Cover Printer: *Coral Graphic Services*
Compositor: *Interactive Composition Corporation*
Printer: *Globus Printing Company*

Printed in the United States of America
1 2 3 4 5 6 7 09 08 07 06 05

For more information about our products, contact us at:
Thomson Learning Academic Resource Center
1-800-423-0563

For permission to use material from this text or product,
submit a request online at
http://www.thomsonrights.com.
Any additional questions about permissions
can be submitted by email to
thomsonrights@thomson.com.

Library of Congress Control Number: 2004115405

ISBN 0-534-62620-3

Thomson Higher Education
10 Davis Drive
Belmont, CA 94002-3098
USA

Asia (including India)
Thomson Learning
5 Shenton Way
#01-01 UIC Building
Singapore 068808

Australia/New Zealand
Thomson Learning Australia
102 Dodds Street
Southbank, Victoria 3006
Australia

Canada
Thomson Nelson
1120 Birchmount Road
Toronto, Ontario M1K 5G4
Canada

UK/Europe/Middle East/Africa
Thomson Learning
High Holborn House
50-51 Bedford Row
London WC1R 4LR
United Kingdom

Dedicated to the pursuit of dreams.

We look forward to hearing from our readers who call with the exciting message, "I got the job!" This book is for you. Good luck!

We also wish to provide a special dedication to Henry Wrobleski, former coordinator of the law enforcement department, and Pam Reierson, former media specialist, Normandale Community College, both of whom have contributed a great deal to the advancement of criminal justice and private security as true professions.

BRIEF CONTENTS

Figures/Tables   xvii
Foreword   xviii
Acknowledgments   xix
Introduction   xxi
About the Authors   xxiv

SECTION ONE: THE CHALLENGE   **1**

Chapter 1   Employment Trends: The World of Work   2
Chapter 2   First Responders: Careers in Law Enforcement, Public Safety and Related Fields   16
Chapter 3   Careers in the Courts, Corrections and Related Fields   51
Chapter 4   Careers in Private Security   70
Chapter 5   On Choosing a Career: Knowing the Job and Yourself   89
Chapter 6   Internships: Testing the Waters   109

SECTION TWO: MEETING THE CHALLENGE: PREPARING   **127**

Chapter 7   Physical Fitness and Testing   128
Chapter 8   Other Forms of Testing   146
Chapter 9   Attributes of Successful Candidates   165
Chapter 10   The Résumé: Selling Yourself on Paper   183
Chapter 11   Preparing for Not Getting the Job   205

SECTION THREE: JOB-SEEKING STRATEGIES   **217**

Chapter 12   The Application Process: Finding and Applying for Jobs   218
Chapter 13   Your Job-Seeking Uniform: Presenting Yourself as *THE* One to Hire   239
Chapter 14   The Interview: A Closer Look   255

SECTION FOUR: YOUR FUTURE IN YOUR CHOSEN PROFESSION   **277**

Chapter 15   At Last! You've Got the Job! Congratulations!!!   278
Chapter 16   The Career Ladder: Insights into Promotion and Job Change   288
Chapter 17   Job Loss and Change: The Road Less Traveled   305

Epilogue   319
Appendixes   320
Author Index   334
Subject Index   336

CONTENTS

═══════════

Figures/Tables   xvii
Foreword   xviii
Acknowledgments   xix
Introduction   xxi
About the Authors   xxiv

SECTION ONE: THE CHALLENGE   **1**

Chapter 1   Employment Trends: the World of Work   2
               Introduction, 2
               The Importance of Work, 2
               What's Important on the Job, 4
               A Brief History, 4
               Our Changing Work World, 5
                   Demographic Trends, 6
                   Vital Communication and Technical Skills, 7
               A Look at Jobs of the Future—Where Will You Fit In?, 8
                   Growth in the Service Industries, 8
                   A Need for More Education, 10
               Keeping Up-to-Date, 11
               Conclusion, 12
               Introducing the Insiders' Views, 12
               An Insider's View: "What You'll Need to Succeed in the 21st Century"
               (*Erickson*), 13
               Insider's View Online, 14
               Mind Stretches, 14
               References, 15

Chapter 2   First Responders: Careers in Law Enforcement, Public Safety and Related Fields   16
               Introduction, 16
               Is Law Enforcement for You?, 16
               Employment Requirements, 18
               Employment Outlook, 19
               Law Enforcement—Up Close, 19
               Where Opportunities Exist, 20
                   Local Agencies, 20
                   County Agencies, 21

Tribal Agencies, 22
State Agencies, 22
Federal Agencies, 24
Jurisdictions Compared, 30
Salaries, 31
Local, County and State Salaries, 32
Federal Salaries, 32
Fringe Benefits, 33
Promotions and Transfers, 33
Advanced Jobs and Specialization, 34
The Juvenile Officer, 35
Medicolegal Death Investigator (MDI), 36
Crime Scene Investigator (CSI), 37
Armed Sky Marshals, 37
Mint Police, 38
Humane Law Enforcement (HLE) Officer, 38
Other Venues Requiring Law Enforcement, 39
International Jobs, 39
Nonsworn Career Options Related to Law Enforcement, 40
Community Crime Prevention Specialists, 40
Juvenile Specialists, 41
Animal Control Officers, 40
Dispatchers, 41
Fire Service, 41
Emergency Medical Technicians (EMTs) and Paramedics, 44
Conclusion, 44
An Insider's View: "It's Not Like on TV" (*Conroy*), 45
Insider's View Online, 46
Mind Stretches, 47
References, 47
Helpful Websites, 48
Other Resources, 50

Chapter 3   Careers in the Courts, Corrections and Related Fields   51
Introduction, 51
Opportunities in Our Judicial System—the Courts, 52
Lawyers, 52
Judges, Magistrates and Other Judicial Workers, 54
Legal Assistants and Paralegals, 54
Court Reporters, 55
Bailiffs, 56
Clerks, 57
Other "Helping" Professions Necessary to the Justice System, 57
Opportunities in Our Judicial System—Corrections, 59
Corrections Officers, 60
Probation and Parole Officers, 62
Community Corrections—Alternatives to Incarceration, 63
Juvenile Corrections, 64
Other Careers in Corrections, 65

Conclusion, 65
An Insider's View: "Lawyers Wear Many Hats: Is One Right for You?"
(*Halberg*), 66
Insider's View Online, 67
Mind Stretches, 67
References, 68
Helpful Websites, 69
Other Resources, 69

Chapter 4   Careers in Private Security   70
Introduction, 70
Public versus Private Officers, 71
Public/Private Cooperation, 72
Privatization of Public Justice, 73
Private Corrections, 74
Private Sector Involvement in Juvenile Justice, 74
Private Security—Up Close, 74
Types of Jobs Available, 76
Employment Requirements, 79
Job Outlook, 81
Salaries, 82
Fringe Benefits, 84
Promotions, 84
Conclusion, 84
An Insider's View: "Career Opportunities in Private Security"
(*Iannone*), 85
Insider's View Online, 86
Mind Stretches, 86
References, 87
Helpful Websites, 88
Additional Contacts and Sources of Information, 88

Chapter 5   On Choosing a Career: Knowing the Job and Yourself   89
Introduction, 89
Selecting and Developing a Career, 90
Charting Your Future Course, 92
Career Coaches and Counselors, 93
Brainstorming Possibilities, 93
"Just the Facts," 94
Age, 94
Physical Requirements, 94
Education, 95
Background, 96
Experience, 97
Develop a Positive Attitude, 97
What Do You Want from a Career?, 98
Moving Toward Your Career Goal, 101

Acquire What You Need, 102
Internships, 102
Alternatives, 102
To Risk or Not to Risk—That Is the Question, 103
Get Going!, 104
It's Just a Job . . . , 104
Conclusion, 105
An Insider's View: "The Private Security Alternative" (*Green*), 105
Insider's View Online, 107
Mind Stretches, 107
References, 108
Additional Contacts and Sources of Information, 108

Chapter 6   Internships: Testing the Waters   109
Introduction, 109
Nothing New Here!, 110
On Interns and Internships, 110
Locating Internship Opportunities, 112
School-Related Internships, 112
Locating Internships Online, 113
Start Early! Stay Organized!, 114
Service Learning, 114
What Is Expected of You?, 114
Making the Most of the Experience, 116
When Good Internships Go Bad, 118
What If You Are Told to "Get Out"?, 120
Being Evaluated, 120
Internships Throughout Your Career, 121
A Recap—The Do's and Don'ts of Internships, 121
Conclusion, 124
An Insider's View: "The Benefits of Learning while Serving" (*Hendricks*), 124
Mind Stretches, 125
References, 126

SECTION TWO: MEETING THE CHALLENGE: PREPARING   127

Chapter 7   Physical Fitness and Testing   128
Introduction, 128
What Is Fitness?, 128
Why Is Fitness Important?, 129
Physical Fitness Testing, 130
The Medical Examination, 132
Self-Assessment, 133
Cardiovascular Tests, 133
Balance Test, 134
Flexibility Tests, 134
Agility Test, 135

Strength Tests, 135
Power Tests, 135
A Basic Physical Fitness Program, 136
Tips, 136
Sticking to Your Fitness Program, 136
The Challenge of Maintaining Fitness, 137
Fitness and Stress, 138
The Upside of Stress, 139
Fitness and Nutrition, 139
Obesity, 140
Fitness and Lifestyle, 140
Smoking, Alcohol and Other Drugs, 141
Benefits of Being Physically Fit, 141
Conclusion, 142
An Insider's View: "Fitness: The Most Important Weapon You Will Ever Carry"
(*Nierenhausen*), 142
Insiders' Views Online, 144
Mind Stretches, 144
References, 144

Chapter 8   Other Forms of Testing   146
Introduction, 146
Test Anxiety, 146
Testing Knowledge, 147
General Knowledge, 148
Specific Knowledge, 149
Memory and Observation Tests, 151
Strategies for Taking Tests, 151
Assessment Centers, 154
Psychological Testing, 154
Purposes of Psychological Testing, 155
Testing Methods, 156
Specific Psychological Tests, 156
Integrity Tests, 158
Polygraph Testing, 159
Background Checks, 160
On Being Dishonest, 161
Conclusion, 162
An Insider's View: "Preparing to Do Your Best" (*Conroy*), 162
Insider's View Online, 163
Mind Stretches, 163
References, 163
Recommended Test Preparation Books, 164

Chapter 9   Attributes of Successful Candidates   165
Introduction, 165
How Do You Appear on Paper?, 166

Personal Attributes, 166
    Past General Employment, 168
    Volunteer Community Service, 169
    Work-Related Experience, 169
    Military Service, 170
    Education, 170
    Communication Skills, 173
    Computer, Keyboarding and Word Processing Skills, 174
    Interning, 174
Painting a Picture, 175
Making the Best of Bad Situations, 175
Criminal Justice, Private Security and Ethics, 177
    Values, 178
Conclusion, 179
An Insider's View: "Getting Your Foot in the Door" (*Stein*), 179
Insider's View Online, 181
Mind Stretches, 181
References, 181

Chapter 10   The Résumé: Selling Yourself on Paper   183
Introduction, 183
What Is a Résumé?, 183
The Purposes of the Résumé, 184
Steps in Creating a Résumé, 185
Compile Information, 185
    Personal Identifying Information, 186
    Education, 187
    Work Experience, 187
    Position Desired or Employment Objective, 188
    Other Information, 188
    References, 188
    Photograph, 188
    What *Not* to Include, 189
Select the Type of Résumé, 190
    Historical/Chronological Résumé, 190
    Functional Résumé, 191
    Analytical Résumé, 191
    What about Creativity?, 192
Format the Résumé, 192
Write the Résumé, 192
    Preparing an E-Résumé, 194
    Preparing a Scannable Résumé, 195
    Tailoring Your Résumé, 195
Edit and Polish Your First Draft, 196
Evaluate and Revise, 196
Print Your Résumé, 196
Making It a "10", 197
The Cover Letter, 197
Sending Your Résumé, 199
    Electronic Submission and Faxing of Résumés, 200

Hand Delivering Your Résumé, 200
Following Up, 200
For More Help, 201
Conclusion, 201
An Insider's View: "The Résumé: A Balance of Modesty
and Self-Confidence" (*Kerlikowske*), 201
Insider's View Online, 202
Mind Stretches, 203
References, 203
Helpful Websites, 204

Chapter 11   Preparing for Not Getting the Job   205
Introduction, 205
Handling Rejection, 205
Remaining Positive, 208
Learning from the Process, 209
Normal Reaction to Loss, 209
Conclusion, 212
An Insider's View: "Each Failure Is One Step Closer to Success "
(*Thompson*), 213
Insider's View Online, 215
Mind Stretches, 215
References, 215

SECTION THREE: JOB-SEEKING STRATEGIES   **217**

Chapter 12   The Application Process: Finding and Applying for Jobs   218
Introduction, 218
Developing Your Job-Search Strategy, 219
Where to Look for Job Openings, 220
Newspapers, 220
Specialty Periodicals and Other Publications, 221
The Internet, 222
Government Employment and Educational Placement Offices, 223
Networking, 224
Personal Inquiries, 224
Telephone Inquiries, 224
On Being Your Best, 225
Contacts by Mail, 226
Networking Basics, 228
On Burning Bridges, 229
You've Found an Opening and They've Asked You to Apply, 229
The Application, 230
Remember the Magic Words—Thank-You, 231
Warning, 232
Testing Your Careering Competencies, 232
Conclusion, 234

An Insider's View: "Law Enforcement Jobs: Learning How to Get Them Takes the Same Skills Required to Do Them" (*Lombardi*), 234
Insider's View Online, 238
Mind Stretches, 238
References, 238
Additional Contacts and Sources of Information, 238

Chapter 13   Your Job-Seeking Uniform: Presenting Yourself as *THE* One to Hire   239
Introduction, 239
The Employer's Investment, 240
Elements of Your Job-Seeking Uniform, 240
The Primacy Effect and the Five-Minute Barrier, 241
Difficult Inquiries, 242
Getting to Know Each Other, 242
Before the Interview, 242
Initial Contact, 244
Clothing and Grooming, 244
Physical Condition, 246
Grammar and Speech, 247
Body Language, Composure and Personality, 248
Manners, 248
Enthusiasm, 249
Knowledge, 249
Follow-Up, 250
Planning Your Interview Strategy, 251
Conclusion, 252
An Insider's View: "Presenting Yourself as *THE* One to Hire" (*Maples*), 252
Insider's View Online, 253
Mind Stretches, 253
References, 253

Chapter 14   The Interview: A Closer Look   255
Introduction, 255
Purposes of the Job Interview, 256
The Purposes—Up Close, 256
Types of Interviews, 260
Informational Interviews, 260
Mass Interviews, 260
Stress Interviews, 261
"Unnecessary" Interviews, 262
Courtesy Interviews, 262
Teleconferencing and Video Interviews—A New Twist, 262
Typical Questions, 264
Practice, Practice, Practice, 269
Negotiating, 269
Closing the Interview, 270

Follow-Up, 270
Making a Decision, 271
A Quick Review, 272
Conclusion, 273
An Insider's View: "Your Turn to Star" (*Chaffee*), 273
Insider's View Online, 275
Mind Stretches, 275
References, 275
Additional Contacts and Sources of Information, 276

SECTION FOUR: YOUR FUTURE IN YOUR CHOSEN PROFESSION 277

Chapter 15   At Last! You've Got the Job! Congratulations!!! 278
Introduction, 278
Keep Trying, 279
Be Appropriate, 279
Know Nothing, 280
Wait Until You Are Asked, 280
Understand Politics, 281
Accept Criticism Maturely, 282
Be Yourself, 283
Maintain Yourself, 283
Conclusion, 285
Your Game Plan for Excelling on the Job, 285
An Insider's View: "Surviving Probation" (*Miller*), 285
Insider's View Online, 286
Mind Stretches, 286
References, 287

Chapter 16   The Career Ladder: Insights Into Promotions and Job Change 288
Introduction, 288
Promotions: What They Are and Where They Are, 289
Motivations for Seeking Change, 289
Similar Skills, 290
Increasing Your Chances for Promotion—Preparation Is Key, 291
    A Final Note on Broadening Your Experience and Education, 294
Networking and Other Valuable Promotion-Seeking Tools, 295
Advancement in the Other Protective Services, 296
Improving Promotional Exam Performance, 296
Improving Promotional Interview Performance, 299
Conclusion, 301
An Insider's View: "Making the Most of Your Law Enforcement Career" (*Beckman*), 301
Insiders' Views Online, 303
Mind Stretches, 303
References, 303

Chapter 17   Job Loss and Change: The Road Less Traveled   305
                Introduction, 305
                The Identity Crisis, 306
                Why Is Having a Strategy So Important?, 307
                The Myths and Hard Truths About Work, 307
                        The Myths, 307
                        The Hard Truths, 309
                Developing a Strategy, 309
                The Sequential Reaction to Job Loss and Change, 310
                        Managing the Responses, 311
                Dealing with Depression, 312
                Gotta Get Working, 313
                To Sue or Not to Sue, 314
                Conclusion, 315
                An Insider's View: "Job Loss and Grief" (*Obershaw*), 315
                Insiders' Views Online, 316
                Mind Stretches, 317
                References, 317
                Additional Contacts and Sources of Information, 317

Epilogue   319

Appendixes
        A   IACP Police Code of Conduct, 320
        B   ASIS Security Code of Ethics, 322
        C   Résumé Worksheets, 324
        D   Sample Résumés, 329
        E   Sample Cover Letter and Follow-Up Letter, 332

Author Index   334
Subject Index   336

FIGURES

1–1	Maslow's Hierarchy of Human Needs	3
1–2	Percent Change in Total Employment by Major Occupational Group, Projected 2002–2012	9
1–3	Number of Jobs Due to Growth and Replacement Needs by Major Occupational Group, Projected 2002–2012	10
5–1	The Career Development Process	91
7–1	POWER Chart (Chicago Police Department Fitness Test Standards)	131
9–1	SCANS Skills	171
9–2	Law Enforcement Code of Ethics	178
11–1	Sequential Reaction to Loss and Change	210
11–2	The Transition Curve	212
S3	Job-Search Steps	217
12–1	Typical Employment Process	230

TABLES

2–1	2002 Salaries for Sworn Local and County Law Enforcement Personnel	32
4–1	2002 Hourly Wage Ranges for Security Officers, Console Operators and Investigators	83
4–2	2002 Annual Average Salary of Security Managers, as Related to Several Factors	83
6–1	Comparing Passive and Active Interns	111
6–2	Comparing Positive and Negative Traits of Interns	116

FOREWORD

Abraham Lincoln once said, "Prepare yourself for the day opportunity presents itself, and you will be rewarded." The process of entering a career in criminal justice or private security usually consists of several steps to "prepare yourself."

Philosophical questions regarding your goals must be resolved by practical approaches. As an applicant, you will be seeking to reach one of your most important goals in life. Whatever the situation, you are more likely to realize success if you are prepared to present yourself in the best possible manner to a prospective employer. Different expectations are held by employers and future employees in a situation where there is the beginning of a career.

This book is a genuine contribution to the future of young Americans seeking employment in such careers as law enforcement, juvenile justice, corrections or any of the numerous areas within the private security profession. J. Scott Harr and Kären M. Hess have been heralded by many as being the best in providing information, guidance and direction to those seeking a career in the public or private sectors of the criminal justice system. The authors give applicants a realistic, factual approach in conveying to the reader "this is what it's all about."

The past and present dynamics of seeking employment projected into the future suggest great optimism for applicants who pursue careers and job hunting with a positive attitude. This book goes as far as our knowledge takes it today. It is the best resource for the 21st century and gives the aspirant an enlightened, positive approach to job seeking in these highly competitive fields.

Henry M. Wrobleski
Former Coordinator of Law Enforcement
Normandale Community College

ACKNOWLEDGMENTS

We wish to personally express appreciation to the criminal justice, security and other professionals who have contributed to this book, which is richer because of their personal sharing:

Russell M. Anderson, Field Supervisor and Investigator, Wisconsin Alliance for Fair Contracting;

Richard D. Beckman, Sergeant, Cloverdale (California) Police Department;

Brian Beniek, Officer, Plymouth (Minnesota) Police Department;

Jack R. Cahall, Past Chair, Crime Abatement Committee, New Orleans, Louisiana;

Jim Chaffee, Director of Security, Walt Disney Pictures and Television;

Jim Clark, Chief, Eden Prairie (Minnesota) Police Department;

Dennis L. Conroy, PhD, Sergeant and Director of the Employee Assistance Program, St. Paul (Minnesota) Police Department;

John H. Driggs, Licensed Clinical Social Worker, St. Paul, Minnesota;

Timothy E. Erickson, Assistant Professor, Metropolitan State University;

Lawrence J. Fennelly, Sergeant and Crime Prevention Specialist, Harvard University Police Department;

Bill B. Green, Manager, Security Services, Rosemount, Inc.;

Joe Guy, Officer, Roseville (Minnesota) Police Department;

Marsh J. Halberg, Attorney, Thomsen & Nybeck, P.A.;

Sheldon T. Hess, MD, General Internist, Health Partners;

Robert B. Iannone, CPP, President, Iannone Security Management, Inc.;

Gil Kerlikowske, Police Commissioner, Buffalo (New York) Police Department;

Molly Koivamaki, Emergency Management Coordination, Eden Prairie (Minnesota) Police Department;

John Lombardi, Professor of Criminal Justice and Criminology, Albany State College;

John J. Maas, Deputy Chief, U.S. Probation/Pretrial Services Officer, South Dakota;

Brenda P. Maples, Lieutenant, Memphis (Tennessee) Police Department;

Robert Meyerson, Trooper I, Minnesota State Patrol;

Linda S. Miller, former Sergeant, Bloomington Police Department and Executive Director, Upper Midwest Community Policing Institute;

Ron Nierenhausen, Sergeant, Elk River (Minnesota) Police Department;

Richard J. Obershaw, Grief Center, Burnsville, Minnesota;

Marie Ohman, Executive Director, Minnesota Board of Private Investigators and Protective Agents;

Penny A. Parrish, Public Information Officer, Minneapolis (Minnesota) Police Department; Parrish Institute of Law Enforcement and Media;

Richard W. Stanek, Sergeant, Minneapolis (Minnesota) Police Department;

Michael P. Stein, Chief, Escondido (California) Police Department;

Albert J. Sweeney, Captain Commanding, Training and Education Division, Boston (Massachusetts) Police Department;

Timothy J. Thompson, Director of Safety and Security, University of St. Thomas;

Kenneth S. Trump, Assistant Director, Tri-City Task Force Comprehensive Gang Initiative; Director of Safety and Security, Parma (Ohio) City School District; National School Safety Consultant;

Luis Velez, Captain, Colorado Springs (Colorado) Police Department;

Henry Wrobleski, Former Coordinator, Law Enforcement Department, Normandale Community College; *and*

Monte D. Zillinger, Special Agent in Charge, Burlington Northern Railroad.

We also wish to thank the reviewers of this text and its various editions for their helpful comments and suggestions:

Frank P. Alberico, Joliet Junior College;
Tim Apolito, University of Dayton;
DeWhitt Bingham, Heartland Community College;
Jerald C. Burns, Alabama State University;
Robert H. Burrington, Georgia Police Academy;
Dean J. Champion, Minot State College;
Paul V. Clark, Community College of Philadelphia;
Dana C. DeWitt, Chadron State College;
Marge Faulstich, West Valley College;
William J. Halliday, Brookdale Community College;
Debbie Hansen, Oregon Youth Authority;
William E. Harver, Widener University;
Robert Ives, Rock Valley College;
Vivian Lord, University of North Carolina—Charlotte;
Joseph Macy, Palm Beach Community College;
Charles E. Myers; Aims Community College;
James E. Newman, Rio Honda College;
Daniel W. Nolan, Gateway Technical College, Kenosha;
John M. Paitakes, Seton Hall University;
Carroll S. Price, Penn Valley Community College;
Heidi Samuels, Mountain State University;
Dave Sexton, Clatsop Community College;
Gregory B. Talley, Broome Community College;
Joy Thompson, University of Wyoming;
    and
Rosalie Young, State University of New York at Oswego.

We wish to acknowledge Christine Hess Orthmann for her research, writing and careful, accurate manuscript preparation; Dr. Diane Harr for her assistance reviewing the initial manuscript; Sara Dovre Wudali, our production editor at Buuji, Inc.; and Wadsworth Publishing Company editors Sabra Horne and Elise Smith for their encouragement and assistance.

Both authors would like to thank Henry Wrobleski for his influence on both of their careers and professional endeavors. Henry is the kind of friend, colleague and mentor whom everyone should experience, and the kind we should strive to be to others.

Scott would like to thank the following colleagues from Concordia University St. Paul: President Robert Holst, Vice President Carl Schoenbeck, Dean Thomas Hanson, Associate Dean Michael Walcheski, Dr. Robert DeWerff, Jim Ollhoff, Dr. Kay Madson, Dr. David Bredehoft and Associate Dean Jean Rock. Thank you also to Richard and Marie Lacy and Reed S. Harr. Scott would also like to acknowledge the support of his wife, Diane, and children, Kelsey and Ricky, with whom he has always shared his dreams. They provide more support than they realize, and their continued interest in these projects and contributions throughout help make them happen. Their smiles, laughter and demands that he put the work down and listen to their piano practice or attend their soccer or paintball games helps keep priorities in check.

Kären would like to acknowledge the support of her husband, Sheldon, and children, Christine and Timothy.

Without the patience and encouragement of our families, efforts such as this text could never come to be.

INTRODUCTION

"The longest journey begins with but a single step."

—*Anonymous*

There isn't much about job seeking that is simple. It's difficult to come to grips with just what career you are best suited for, and it's tough to get a job. It can be equally challenging to keep a job, and dealing with job changes or job loss can be particularly difficult. Why? Because work is such an important part of our lives . . . and this is why it is even more important to have a strategy to find meaningful work.

Webster's Dictionary defines *strategy* as "a careful plan or method . . . the art of devising or employing plans . . . toward a goal." Your goal is TO GET A NEW JOB! Whether it is to enter into a profession or to advance within your current profession, it all sounds so simple. Most of us have had no trouble getting work—flipping burgers, washing dishes, baby-sitting. Do not let this lull you into a false sense of security as so many others have. Assuming that getting a job—any job—is easy is a disastrous mistake.

You are interested in a field that has become exceptionally popular; however, opportunities abound in the areas of law enforcement and criminal justice as well as the private sector. Not everyone will qualify to work every job. The world of work is constantly changing, and with change comes opportunity. But it still takes significant effort and preparation to get the job you want. No one would expect to walk into an agency or department with little or no preparation and expect to be offered a job. A carefully planned job-search strategy has become more important than ever. Anyone seeking a job must prepare themselves to succeed in this endeavor.

In addition to the vast number of applicants who possess the minimum qualifications, many applicants have excellent experience. Applicants may have worked out of state as law enforcement officers, corrections officers or as private security officers. Military experience has also proven to be very beneficial in the job search, as has advanced college education.

In fact, some agencies and departments require applicants to have a bachelor's degree. And some applicants have master's degrees, law degrees, PhDs and myriad specialty certifications. In addition, many people have taken advantage of volunteer opportunities related to the field, such as police reserves, volunteer rescue/firefighting and civilian police support jobs. Such work not only provides valuable experience but also demonstrates that the individual can be trusted in a field demanding unqualified ethics. Other vocational and volunteer positions show the applicant is truly well rounded. In short, many applicants begin their job search with exceptional qualifications, making them most attractive candidates.

Do not get discouraged. While all of this may be overwhelming, it should not cause you to give up. You *will* eventually get a job. When and what that job will be depends on your job-hunting strategy. While job hunting sometimes takes longer than anticipated and has occasional discouragements, it is also challenging, exciting and eventually fruitful.

Reflecting on what little was required not too many years ago of those seeking employment in law enforcement, corrections or security work, it is amazing what is expected of job candidates today. Communication skills, computer knowledge, business sense—all are necessities now.

This book addresses both the public and the private sector. It discusses career opportunities throughout the criminal justice system, including law enforcement, the practice of law, courts, corrections and related local, state and federal agencies. It also discusses career opportunities within private security because private security and law enforcement are complementary professions. A private security job can be a stepping stone into a police job. Many students majoring in law enforcement have jobs in private security. Even entry-level security jobs are becoming harder to obtain. Additionally, private security is recognized as an attractive field. Pay, hours and assignments at the management level often are better than in the public sector. Conversely, a police job can lead to a position as a security director or numerous other jobs in criminal justice. Because the fields of criminal justice and private security have so many specific jobs, you can pursue whatever type of position appeals to you, whether it's on the line or in administration. Further, lateral transfers between both professions are occurring more often. You have an opportunity to position yourself for any number of truly rewarding jobs.

This book also addresses promotions and the career ladder. Traditionally, these professions have promoted from within. The ability to advance through the ranks requires many of the same attributes that apply to the entry-level job seeker. But, it also requires an effective strategy. The skills discussed here apply equally to getting a new job in a new field and to getting promoted. Finally, this book examines job loss and change. Many leave a job because they choose to; others leave because they're forced to. To be sure, everyone will eventually leave every job they ever have. Change = Growth. For those dismissed from a job, for deserved reasons or not, this change can be difficult. For those seeking something more than a particular job is providing, this change can be liberating.

Keep in mind that this book was written for individuals throughout the country and is, therefore, general. Each state has different laws you must be aware of, for example, laws regarding licensure requirements, use of polygraph testing and the like. In addition, every employing agency will have its own requirements, for example, what areas in a background investigation will be of particular concern or what types of physical agility testing will be given. Find out what your state and the agency you are interested in require and expect of applicants.

Recognize that searching for a job actually becomes a job in itself. The first step is to develop a personal job-hunting strategy. Always remember, however, your job-hunt strategy should not control you—you should control it. A planned strategy will make the entire process more tolerable, successful and even enjoyable.

Helping you develop such a strategy to get the job you seek is the purpose of this book. The first section gives a general overview of the world of work (Chapter 1). This is followed by a discussion of career opportunities as first responders in law enforcement, public safety and related fields, the most visible components of the criminal justice system (Chapter 2), opportunities in courts and corrections (Chapter 3), opportunities in private security (Chapter 4) and factors to consider when selecting a career (Chapter 5). The section concludes with a look at internships and how to test the waters (Chapter 6).

The second section focuses on preparing for the job search, including physical fitness and testing (Chapter 7), other tests that might be encountered (Chapter 8), desirable attributes to develop and present (Chapter 9) and the résumé (Chapter 10). The section concludes with a critical component of being prepared—facing the risks of failure and building upon them should they occur (Chapter 11).

Section Three presents very specific job-seeking strategies to help you land your "dream job." These strategies are important during the application process (Chapter 12), when presenting yourself (Chapter 13) and during an interview (Chapter 14).

The fourth and final section discusses how you can succeed on the job once you get it, including making it through probation (Chapter 15) and enhancing your chances for promotion (Chapter 16). The final chapter addresses job loss and change and how you move through such setbacks (Chapter 17).

Throughout the book you will be asked to become actively engaged with the topic being discussed, to write down your ideas and plans. Such instances will be indicated like this:

 You are strongly encouraged to keep a journal for this purpose. The more you interact with the content in this book, the more you will get out of it and the more effective your job-search strategy is likely to be.

Each chapter has relevant *Insiders' Views*—brief, personal essays written by individuals in the field. Additional *Insiders' Views* are found on the website. The *Insiders' Views* are based on experience and give a variety of perspectives on what is or might be important in seeking a career in law enforcement, corrections, private security or related fields in criminal justice, as well as learning how others have succeeded. The idea for these personal contributions resulted from the enthusiastic reception of speakers sharing similar ideas at our job-seeking seminars. Most job seekers never get a chance to find out what really goes on in the minds of those doing the hiring. The *Insiders' Views* fill this void. Repetition occurs within these personal essays. Although the individuals were asked to write about their experience with the topic of the chapter, many felt compelled to add information and advice about other areas as well. As areas are repeated, you will come to realize how critical certain aspects of the job-seeking process are. Every contributor talks about them. You may also find some contradictions with what is said in the text. Use your own judgment as to whose advice you feel suits *you* best. Often no "right" answer exists.

 Each chapter concludes with a series of *Mind Stretches* to get you thinking about the topic as it relates to your particular interests and talents. Again, to get the most out of this book, *do* take time to work through these Mind Stretches, either mentally or in your journal. We have been impressed by our students who have organized job-hunting support groups that discuss issues pertaining to their efforts, including reviewing these Mind Stretch questions together.

Let your first reading be only the beginning. As you get into your job search, use the book as a reference. Also, libraries and bookstores have a tremendous amount of information on the many important aspects of job seeking. Keep practicing your skills such as working up great responses to those "most commonly asked" interview questions. Look at interviews that do not result in a job as opportunities to practice your interviewing skills. Continue to role-play interviews whenever you get the chance.

Experts say that most people will have between *five* and *twenty* careers—not just jobs, *careers*—during a lifetime. The job-hunting process is, indeed, never-ending, so become skilled at it. No one should feel trapped in a job they dislike. Pursue a new one. Or grow in your present job.

We wish you the best of luck in your job search. Here's to developing the skills and a strategy that will get you the job you really want!

J. Scott Harr
Kären M. Hess

ABOUT THE AUTHORS

The authors of this book are committed to the advancement of the professionalism of criminal justice and related fields. Both Scott and Kären have been teaching college-level law enforcement classes for many years and have a number of other criminal justice-related texts on the national market. Their joint publications with Wadsworth include *Criminal Procedure* and *Constitutional Law for the Criminal Justice Professional*, 3rd edition.

Scott has been employed in various areas of the law for more than 28 years. He has been a social worker and a youth worker. For over 11 years he served as the chief law enforcement officer and public safety director for a suburb of the Twin Cities and served as a police officer for two other cities before that. In addition, Scott has served as a firefighter and emergency medical technician. He is licensed as a lawyer, police officer and private investigator, and founded Scott Harr Legal Investigations in 1985. Having taught as community faculty at Normandale Community College, and served as resident faculty at Metropolitan State University School of Law Enforcement and Criminal Justice, he is presently the Criminal Justice Chair for the College of Graduate and Continuing Studies at Concordia University St. Paul (Minnesota).

Kären is the executive director of Innovative Programming Systems, Inc., and president of the Institute for Professional Development. She holds a PhD in English and a second PhD in criminal justice. Kären conducts in-house workshops on writing effective reports. She has also published extensively. Wadsworth publications include *Community Policing: Partnerships for Problem Solving* (4th edition), *Criminal Investigation* (7th edition), *Criminal Procedure, Introduction to Law Enforcement and Criminal Justice* (8th edition), *Juvenile Justice* (4th edition), *Management and Supervision in Law Enforcement* (3rd edition), *Police Operations* (3rd edition) and *Private Security* (4th edition).

SECTION ONE

THE CHALLENGE

========

There are two things to aim at in life;
first, to get what you want; and,
after that, to enjoy it.
Only the wisest . . . achieve the second.

—*Langdon Smith*

Nothing great was ever achieved without enthusiasm.

—*Ralph Waldo Emerson*

Before beginning your job search, you should fully understand what you are getting into. Work is so vitally important that choosing a career deserves far more effort than many people give. By taking an educated look at the actual world of work, you begin a *realistic* job search. You've probably read startling statistics about the rate of change facing employees and the job market. These dramatic changes are directly affecting, and will continue to affect, the service sector, including employment in criminal justice and private security services. Chapter 1 addresses how these changes have affected the job market and what the career you're seeking might look like in the 21st century.

Chapter 2 discusses careers in law enforcement—the most visible and familiar component of the criminal justice system—and other first responder positions, examining where employment opportunities exist on the federal, state, county and local levels. Chapter 3 looks at careers in the courts and corrections. The field of corrections is rapidly expanding due to a growing intolerance of repeat offenders, the "three strikes and you're out" approach and the mandatory serving of sentences. Included in this chapter is information on careers in probation and parole.

Chapter 4 explores careers in the private sector. Privatization is a continuing trend, with private security growing much faster than any segment of the criminal justice system. Numerous career opportunities are found in the private security profession, including not only the familiar security officer but alarm services, armed courier services, executive protection services, private corrections and the like. Chapter 5 examines the steps for choosing a career and what factors to consider. It helps you look at the entrance requirements in light of your background, experience, and personal likes and dislikes. Finally, Chapter 6 explores the topic of internships and the benefits that come from trying on the job before you invest yourself 100 percent in the pursuit of a particular career.

If after reading this section you are convinced that a career in criminal justice, private security or a related field is for you, read on. The rest of the book provides strategies and techniques to help you get the job you seek. These fields are demanding, and so is the road to employment.

You have made an important decision by taking this step to develop your job-search strategies. Let's get started!

CHAPTER 1

EMPLOYMENT TRENDS: THE WORLD OF WORK

===

Most of our adult lives are spent working. Taking into account commuting time, overtime, thinking about our jobs, and worrying over work, we spend more of our waking hours in the office, at the factory, on the road, behind the desk, than we do at home.

—*The Joy of Working, p. ix*

Do You Know:

➤ What the "hierarchy of needs" is?
➤ What role work has in meeting our needs?
➤ How many job and career changes the average person will make in a lifetime?
➤ How our labor force is changing in terms of gender and race?
➤ Why it is crucial to keep current with technology?
➤ What job areas will expand?
➤ What the projections look like for jobs in criminal justice and security?
➤ What factor education will play in future work?

INTRODUCTION

Work. For most of us, work is a large part of who we are, occupying a vast amount of our time and, to a great degree, shaping how we view ourselves. The fact that you have invested your time, energy and money into working with this book says it is important to you too.

This chapter examines why work is so important to people, what needs it fulfills and how these needs may change. It then presents a brief history of how work has evolved to its present state and some of the massive changes that have occurred, including the impact of technology. This is followed by a look at the changing job market and jobs of the future, including growth trends in the service sector and the need for more education. The chapter concludes with a discussion on keeping up-to-date.

THE IMPORTANCE OF WORK

Working *is* important. It provides you with income, but work is so much more than just a paycheck. Work helps form your identity, and it makes a statement about who you are. Well-known psychologist Abraham H. Maslow developed a hierarchy of needs ranging from the most basic physical needs to the most complex self-actualization needs (Figure 1–1). Once people's needs are satisfied at the lowest level, they

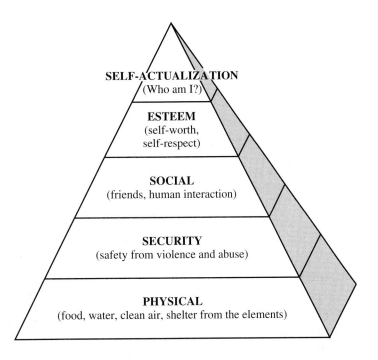

FIGURE 1–1   Maslow's Hierarchy of Human Needs

are able to move up the hierarchy to the next level. According to this rather simplistic hierarchy, work meets *all* five levels.

According to Maslow's simplified "hierarchy of needs," physical needs are the most basic of human needs and self-actualization needs are the most complex. Security, social and esteem needs fall in between.

These needs and their job-related counterparts in a *satisfying* job are often as follows:

➢   Physical: Good working conditions, rest periods, labor-saving equipment, sufficient income, heating/air conditioning

➢   Safety: Safe working conditions, good supervision, job security, training in survival

➢   Social: Feeling of belonging to a "job family," agency/department/organization spirit, after-hours get-togethers, picnics and softball games

➢   Esteem: Challenging job, promotions, titles, community recognition, awards

➢   Self-Actualization: Opportunity for growth and development, discretion/decision-making authority, contributing to society/organization

Work has the potential to meet all five levels of human needs; however, only truly *satisfying* jobs will actually fulfill every level.

Think for a few minutes about what's important to **you** in the career you select. Which level(s) of need will influence you the most? Jot down your responses in your journal.

WHAT'S IMPORTANT ON THE JOB

What's important to you as you consider your career? Several factors are listed below. Rank them yourself, using 1 for most important, 17 for least important.

_____ Amount of feedback given about your job performance

_____ Amount of freedom you have on your job

_____ Amount of fringe benefits

_____ Amount of job security

_____ Amount of pay

_____ Amount of praise you get for a job well done

_____ Chance for getting a promotion

_____ Chance for taking part in making decisions

_____ Chance to accomplish something worthwhile

_____ Chance to do something that makes you feel good about yourself

_____ Chance to do things you do best

_____ Chance to learn new things

_____ Friendliness of people you work with

_____ How you are treated by your supervisor

_____ Opportunities to develop your skills and abilities

_____ Resources available to do your job

_____ Respect you receive from people you work with

Think carefully about your top rankings and how well they would be met in your chosen field. Again, record your thoughts in your journal.

Work satisfies so many human needs that those who find themselves without meaningful employment usually experience a sense of loss. If your work is unfulfilling, your needs must be met elsewhere or anxiety, frustration or even depression may result. If you are suddenly unemployed, as in the case of an unexpected layoff, your lifestyle may become seriously disrupted. Losing a job and being unable to find other work has driven some to such self-destructive behaviors as alcoholism and other substance abuse and even suicide. Truly, work is important as something positive to do to meet your needs—not only your financial needs, but also your identity and self-esteem needs.

For these reasons it is important to give careful thought to what work you pursue. This book will help you decide what you want to do with your working life. You will have a chance to look at what is important to you and what you have to offer employers. Many people spend more time planning their next vacation than they do planning what they're going to do for the rest of their lives. To do so is risky.

A brief look at the evolution of work in the United States is revealing.

A BRIEF HISTORY

You may be familiar with Toffler's "three waves" theory, which compares ocean waves to sweeping major changes in society:

➢ The Agricultural Revolution

➢ The Industrial Revolution

➢ The Technological Revolution

The first wave, the Agricultural Revolution, occurred about 8,000 B.C., sweeping aside 45,000 years of cave dwelling. The second wave, the Industrial Revolution, came around 1760, turning our landscape from "amber waves of grain" into smokestacks. This second wave was not without its resistors. A group of workers, called Luddites, systematically destroyed machinery they saw as a threat to manual laborers. But the wave engulfed America, forcing many farmers into factories as blue-collar workers in the new era of industrialization.

Pulley (1997, pp. 15–16) notes that the Industrial Revolution had an impact on more than just how and where people worked—it changed the way people identified with each other and how they viewed themselves. Whereas the Agricultural Age saw family members working in the fields together, the Industrial Age separated families, sending its members, young and old, into the factories to labor as nameless "cogs" in the massive machine: "As people spent more time in the factory than with the family, the importance of work grew. Increasingly it became the princip[al] source of people's identity. . . . The workplace became the main organizing feature of our life and the source of our identity, status, income, and affiliations. And by the 20th century, identity became specifically tied to *organizations*."

Over time, these organizations became increasingly "paternalistic," taking care of their employees by providing benefits such as health care insurance and retirement pensions as well as rewards for company loyalty, such as bonuses, watches, plaques and dinners. Pulley (p. 16) contends: "Out of this grew the implicit and pervasive understanding between workers and organizations that is now coming apart at the seams—the belief that hard work and loyalty will be exchanged for promotions and job security."

Gradually, the dominance of factories and industrialized business ebbed and a new era was born—the "information age." This third wave, the Technological Revolution, began in the mid-1950s and again changed the face of the American workplace. Brains rather than brawn became important, and white-collar workers began displacing blue-collar workers. Again, resistance occurred. Many people, like the Luddites, have rebelled against computers, fax machines and voice mail. But the third wave *is* here.

OUR CHANGING WORK WORLD

One result of this third wave has been the virtual end to the one-company career path so common in previous generations. No longer does the American workforce toil under the assumption that hard work and loyalty will be rewarded with job security. The job turnover rate is at an all-time high, and news of mass layoffs seems perpetually present in the media. Su (2004, p. 23) observes: "After the boom of the 1990s, the U.S. economy suffered a number of serious setbacks, including: the bursting of the technology bubble; the September 11, 2001, terrorist attacks; significant losses of stock market wealth; a stagnant job market; corporate accounting scandals; and uncertainties related to the war in Iraq."

According to Su (p. 25): "During the recession of 2001, the unemployment rate rose from a 30-year low of 4.0 percent in 2000 to 4.7 percent in 2001 and jumped further to 5.8 percent in 2002. The unemployment rate reached an 8-year-high of 6.0 percent in 2003." These recent fluctuations in employment and economic statistics have left many with feelings of collapse and insecurity. Others, however, believe this "instability" has a positive impact on contemporary workers as they strive to continuously advance into better and more challenging positions. Regardless of perception, these trends have led to an increasing number of job changes for American workers over the past several decades.

According to a Bureau of Labor Statistics news release dated August 25, 2004: "The average person born in the later years of the baby boom held 10 jobs from age 18 to 38. . . . More than two-thirds of these jobs were held in the first half of the period, from ages 18 to 27." This trend appears to hold for younger generations as well.

Statistics indicate the average person is likely to make more than 10 job changes and 5 career changes in a lifetime.

The Bureau of Labor Statistics (BLS), under the U.S. Department of Labor, is a valuable resource for anyone keeping tabs on the changing face of the American workforce. The BLS is the principal fact-finding agency for the federal government in the broad field of labor economics and statistics, and data regarding employment in the United States is accessible through the BLS website at http://www.bls.gov. The *Occupational Outlook Handbook,* referred to from this point on as the *OOH,* is a biannual publication prepared by the BLS, available online at http://www.bls.gov/oco, that provides career information to individuals making decisions about their future work lives, including descriptions of what workers do on the job, working conditions, training and educational requirements, earnings and anticipated job prospects in a wide range of occupations.

Demographic Trends

As the U.S. population continues to grow, increasing by an estimated 24 million between 2000 and 2012, an important trend affecting employment is the growing proportion of minorities and immigrants. This increasingly diverse population has not only required an expanded range of goods and services, but it also has produced corresponding changes in the size and demographic composition of the labor force. According to the *OOH* (2004):

> The U.S. workforce will become more diverse by 2012. White, non-Hispanic persons will continue to make up a decreasing share of the labor force, falling from 71.3 percent in 2002 to 65.5 percent in 2012. . . . Hispanics are projected to account for an increasing share of the labor force by 2012, growing from 12.4 to 14.7 percent. By 2012, Hispanics will constitute a larger proportion of the labor force than will blacks, whose share will grow from 11.4 percent to 12.2 percent. Asians will continue to be the fastest growing of the four labor force groups.

The gender composition of the U.S. workforce is also changing: "The numbers of men and women in the labor force will grow, but the number of women will grow at a faster rate than the number of men. The male labor force is projected to grow by 10 percent from 2002 to 2012, compared with 14.3 percent for women. As a result, men's share of the labor force is expected to decrease from 53.5 to 52.5 percent, while women's share is expected to increase from 46.5 to 47.5 percent" (*OOH*).

The labor force in America is undergoing many changes, including an increasing percentage of minorities and immigrants, and an increasing percentage of women.

Important demographic changes have also resulted from shifts in basic societal values, norms and conditions. For example, prior to the Technological Revolution, American families were generally categorized as warm, secure units with both parents living at home with their children. However, as the 20th century progressed, divorce rates soared and an increasing number of families became categorized as blended or single-parent families. The disintegration of the "traditional" family and weakening of family values have been credited with contributing to numerous social ills, including crime, increased drug use, and a diminished sense of connection with and responsibility to the community and society in general. Another trend observed throughout the 20th century was the declining view of childhood as a carefree time and an increasing rate of children committing violent crimes and being victimized.

Americans have paid tremendous attention to crime and expect it to be contained. And despite the *decrease* in crime in the past few years, the fear of crime and violence continues to be a primary quality-of-life issue for the American public. In fact, in a Gallup Poll conducted on October 6–8, 2003, that asked, "Is there more crime in the U.S than there was a year ago, or less?" 60 percent of respondents stated their belief that there was *more* crime (The Polling Report, 2004). This perception, combined with the trends and demographic changes just mentioned, has produced myriad opportunities for everyone interested in criminal justice and security careers, particularly those who understand and prepare to address these changes.

Vital Communication and Technical Skills

One of the best ways to prepare for job success in today's rapidly evolving work environment is to develop critical skills, particularly communication and technical skills. As Bayer (2000) stresses: "Employees are realizing a very critical fact in this rapidly changing labor market: the greatest danger to your career is 'skill obsolescence.'"

As discussed, the U.S. population in general is becoming increasingly diverse, with language barriers presenting a formidable challenge in many professions, particularly those geared toward service to the public. The ability to speak more than one language is a quality many employers now actively seek in job applicants.

Many of the other emerging "critical skills" are the direct result of technological advances. Technology is changing so fast it is almost impossible to keep up, much less predict what is ahead. More than ever, successful job seekers will position themselves to showcase their computer knowledge and skills. This is definitely true for all areas of criminal justice and security employment.

It is strongly recommended that you bring your computer skill level up as high as possible. Professor Laurel Forsgren of Concordia University Saint Paul (Minnesota) asserts that it is no longer enough to know answers: "Educated people are those who have the information literacy skills to know how and where to seek answers using technology and how to present their findings professionally." Today's successful job applicant needs more than the "keyboarding skills" recommended in previous editions. You simply must be technologically competent.

Technology is a powerful, rapidly changing force in today's working world. To stay competitive and ensure your value in the workforce, keep current with technology.

Technology is not the only driving force behind the changing job market, however. Economic and political forces also have influenced the job market.

A LOOK AT JOBS OF THE FUTURE—WHERE WILL YOU FIT IN?

In the 21st century, interest has heightened in looking ahead at what our world of work might be like. Certain trends, some of which have already been discussed, are pointed out repeatedly:

➢   The labor force will continue to grow.

➢   Women and minorities will account for a greater share of the workforce.

➢   Blue-collar jobs will decline slightly.

➢   Rapid growth will occur in jobs in the *service sector* (which includes criminal justice and security).

➢   More education will be needed for more jobs.

Growth in the Service Industries

The *OOH* reports: "Total employment is expected to increase from 144 million in 2002 to 165 million in 2012, or by 14.8 percent. The 21 million jobs that will be added by 2012 will not be evenly distributed across major industrial and occupational groups. Changes in consumer demand, technology, and many other factors will contribute to the continually changing employment structure in the U.S. economy."

Figure 1–2 illustrates the projected percent change in total employment by major occupational group from 2002 to 2012; Figure 1–3 depicts the projected number of jobs that will exist by 2012 in each major occupational group, created either through growth or replacement needs.

I didn't know!

As these two figures show, many of the new jobs created in the next decade will be in the service industries, which include the protective services of law enforcement, corrections, firefighting, private investigation and security. According to Hecker (2004, p. 88), protective services occupations are projected to increase 24.7 percent between 2002 and 2012, adding a total of 769,000 new jobs in this sector. He (p. 99) notes: "Half of the growth is projected for government, and nearly two-fifths is projected for rapidly growing investigation and security services." As observed in the BLS's *Career Guide to Industries* (2004): "The attacks of September 11, 2001, will increase demand for police, firefighters, and other emergency personnel; however, budgetary constraints may force spending cuts in other areas, slowing overall employment growth."

Farr and Shatkin's compilation of the *Best Jobs for the 21st Century* (2004, p. 124) analyzes a variety of job factors, such as annual earnings, percent job growth and annual openings, and lists the following as the "Best Jobs for People Interested in Law, Law Enforcement and Public Safety":

> lawyers; correctional officers and jailers; paralegals and legal assistants; security guards; highway patrol pilots; police and sheriff's patrol officers; police patrol officers; sheriffs and deputy sheriffs; nuclear monitoring technicians; emergency medical technicians and paramedics; first-line supervisors/managers of correctional officers; private detectives and investigators; first-line supervisors/managers of police and detectives; forest fire fighting and prevention supervisors; municipal fire fighting and prevention supervisors; child support, missing persons, and unemployment insurance fraud investigators; criminal investigators and special agents; detectives and criminal investigators; immigration and customs inspectors; police detectives; police identification and records officers; and arbitrators, mediators, and conciliators.

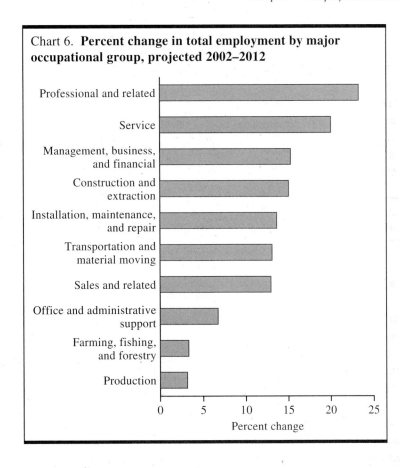

FIGURE 1–2   Percent Change in Total Employment by Major Occupational Group, Projected 2002–2012

SOURCE: *Occupational Outlook Handbook, 2004–05 Edition.* Washington, DC: Bureau of Labor Statistics, 2004, Chart 6. Online: http://www.bls.gov/oco/images/ocotjc06.gif

The Top 100: The Fastest Growing Careers for the 21st Century (2001) includes police officers, detectives, corrections officers, paralegals, and security consultants and technicians. According to this document (p. 141):

> The employment outlook for police detectives is expected to increase faster than average for all other occupations through 2008. U.S. Department of Labor estimates call for an increase of approximately 90,000 detectives, but this number also includes police officers and special agents. . . . An area of particular growth is the investigation of the various forms of computer fraud.

Regarding corrections officers (p. 115):

> The prison population has more than doubled in the past 10 years, and this growth is expected to be sustained for the near future. The increasing number of prisoners means there will be a strong need for new corrections officers. Employment in this field is expected to increase much faster than the average for all jobs. . . . The ongoing war on drugs, new tough-on-crime legislation, and increasing mandatory sentencing policies will create a need for more prison beds and more corrections officers.

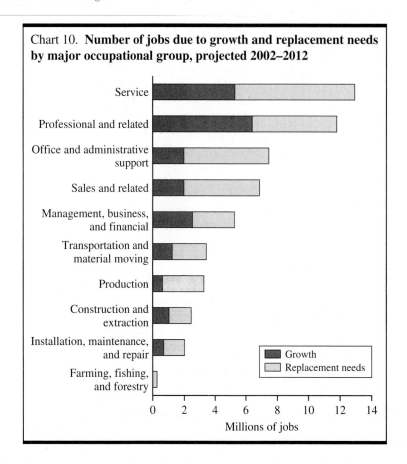

FIGURE 1–3   Number of Jobs Due to Growth and Replacement Needs by Major Occupational Group, Projected 2002–2012

SOURCE: *Occupational Outlook Handbook, 2004–05 Edition*. Washington, DC: Bureau of Labor Statistics, 2004, Chart 10. Online: http://www.bls.gov/oco/images/ocotjc10.gif

The employment outlook is equally positive for security consultants and technicians (pp. 331–332):

> Employment for guards and other security personnel is expected to increase faster than the average through 2008, as crime rates rise with the overall population growth. The highest U.S. Department of Labor estimates call for more than 1.25 million guards to be employed by 2008. . . . A factor adding to this demand is the trend for private security firms to perform duties previously handled by police officers, such as courtroom security and crowd control in airports.

> Trends in the changing workforce show service-producing industries, including criminal justice and security, will account for much of all job growth. Furthermore, protective services will remain one of the fastest-growing industries throughout the next decade.

A Need for More Education

New service industry jobs will require enhanced skills and proficiencies, and many will demand successful applicants possess college degrees and other certifications. According to the *OOH:* "Education is essential in getting a high-paying job. In fact, for all but 1 of the 50 highest paying occupations, a college degree or higher is the most significant source of education or training." Indeed, as Dohm and Wyatt (2002, p. 3) assert: "When it comes to work, having a college degree is one of the best ways to gain and maintain a competitive edge. On average, college graduates enjoy advantages—ranging from more job opportunities to better salaries—over their non-college-educated counterparts."

Fleetwood and Shelley (2000, p. 4) observe that most jobs in the service field are classified as non–college-level jobs, with the exception of police and detectives: "Training and educational requirements are especially ambiguous and may be changing for a small number of occupations, including police and detective [occupations]." Dohm and Wyatt (p. 13) note that while the number of full-time wage and salary workers with college degrees increased 33 percent between 1992 and 2000, some occupations experienced greater-than-average increases in the number of college graduates. They call this increasing level of educational attainment in specific occupations *educational upgrading:*

> Educational upgrading has been particularly noticeable in the health and protective service occupations. . . . There are many reasons for educational upgrading, including the need for more highly skilled workers to compete in an increasingly complex global economy. Growing competition has forced companies to emphasize . . . customer service and, thus, to seek employees with strong communication skills. Employers often feel that, compared to non-college-educated workers, college graduates are more motivated, learn tasks more quickly, are better able to meet deadlines, and have better problem-solving and communication skills.

Dohm and Wyatt (p. 14) report that 14 percent of workers aged 25 to 34 in protective service occupations held bachelor's degrees or higher in 1992; by 2000 that figure had risen to 21 percent. The reality is that a high-school diploma, while perhaps meeting the bare requirements for some jobs, will seldom be sufficient to ensure career advancement opportunities.

It is projected that more than half of the new jobs created over the next decade will require an educational level beyond high school. Criminal justice and security agencies nationwide are also raising applicants' educational requirements. To stay competitive, you must seek higher education.

The importance of education is discussed more fully in Chapters 8 and 9.

KEEPING UP-TO-DATE

As discussed, savvy job seekers must have sharp information technology skills. Never overlook the power of the Internet to enhance your job- or promotion-seeking strategy.

To this end, an excellent source for keeping current on jobs and employment trends is the *Occupational Outlook Handbook (OOH),* already mentioned and available online at http://www.bls.gov/oco/. Completely revised every two years by the U.S. Department of Labor, this resource covers more than 200 occupations and, for each career, describes work activities and environment, earnings, number of jobs and their location, and types of education, training and personal qualifications needed to have the best prospects. BLS projections of employment to the year 2012 are used to assess what kind of job opportunities future entrants to each occupation should encounter. It also includes a listing of sources of state and local job information. The *Handbook* is available in paper, hard cover and CD-ROM and can be purchased at any U.S. government bookstore or by calling the office of the Superintendent of Documents in Washington at (202) 783-3238.

write about sources covered

BLS supplements to the *OOH* include the *Career Guide to Industries* and *Occupational Projections and Training Data.* The *Career Guide* covers 42 diverse industries and highlights some occupations not covered by the *Handbook*, discussing the nature of the work, job qualifications and advancement opportunities, job outlook and earnings. *Occupational Projections and Training Data* provides the statistical data supporting the information presented in the *Handbook.* Education and training planners, career counselors and job seekers can compare more than 700 occupations on factors such as employment change, self-employed workers, earnings and the most significant source of education or training. Users will also find awards and degree data by field of study.

Another valuable source for finding help in planning careers that require college or technical degrees is Danga's (2002) *Professional Careers Sourcebook,* published by Gale Research Publishing, Detroit. It contains job descriptions and the names and addresses of associations able to provide further information on career possibilities.

You might also want to check with your local library, state agencies and employment offices, as well as your state department of education, state job services agencies and state labor departments.

CONCLUSION

The days of picking one career and sticking with it for 40 years are over. Statistics show the average person is likely to make more than ten job changes and five career changes in a lifetime. Trends in the changing workforce show service-producing industries, including criminal justice and security, will account for much of all job growth. Furthermore, these services will remain one of the fastest-growing major industries during the next decade. It is also projected that more than half of the new jobs created over the next decade will require an educational level beyond high school. Criminal justice and security agencies nationwide are raising applicants' educational requirements. Therefore, to stay competitive, you must seek higher education and keep current with technology.

INTRODUCING THE INSIDERS' VIEWS

A supplement to this book is a collection of short articles written by men and women whose careers have intersected with criminal justice and related fields. Each guest writer's contribution, called *An Insider's View*, presents a unique perspective about jobs in criminal justice or related fields and how to obtain them. The backgrounds and credentials of the contributors are quite varied, including police officer, sergeant, captain and chief; railroad police agent; probation/parole officer; private security manager; crime prevention specialist; gang task force member; director of safety for public schools; attorney; professor; medical doctor; and businessman. They also include perspectives from both sides of the interview table— those looking to be hired and those doing the hiring. Whichever angle a particular writer pursues, think about the important insights you are being given from those "on the inside."

At the end of each chapter, you will be directed to two or three *Insiders' Views* with relevance to the topic(s) just covered. One *Insider's View* will be included in each chapter of this book; the remaining supplemental *Insider's Views* can be found online under the Student Resources section at http://www.wadsworth.com/criminaljustice_d/.

For this first chapter we've selected articles by Timothy Erickson (in print) and Dr. Jack Cahall (online) to introduce you to the "World of Work" as it applies to criminal justice and security professionals.

AN INSIDER'S VIEW

WHAT YOU'LL NEED TO SUCCEED IN THE 21ST CENTURY

Timothy E. Erickson

Assistant Professor
Metropolitan State University

In the early 1900s August Vollmer, Chief of Police in Berkeley, California, had a vision that included a place for college-educated peace officers within law enforcement. Since the days of Vollmer, this vision has been revisited periodically through such events as the *Wickersham Report* of the 1930s and the *President's Commission on Law Enforcement and Administration of Justice* in the 1960s. In fact, the cry for college-educated peace officers has come from several quarters, but until rather recently, few real efforts have occurred to make this vision a reality.

During the 1970s substantial amounts of money were spent by the federal government in LEAA grants to help working peace officers attain postsecondary education. In 1977 Minnesota became the first state to require as a state standard, a minimum level of postsecondary education as an entry requirement for the peace officer position. In 1989 two separate proposals were introduced at the congressional level which would provide resources directed toward programs designed to provide college-level education for peace officers.

While these efforts are laudatory, the law enforcement profession has only been slowly nudged to the precipice. It is time for individual practitioners to take proactive steps to ensure this vision for themselves. In other words, peace officers need to "fish or cut bait."

The increasing complexity of the issues in our society—issues individual peace officers must address—has become an incredible burden. Rapid advances in theory, knowledge and technology, rapidly changing demographics, and newly developing and evolving social problems ranging from ecology to global political realities—all point toward the need for continual growth in peace officer education.

In addition, peace officers interact daily with other professionals in the criminal justice system, all of whom have at least one undergraduate degree. Most have graduate-level educational experiences. Add to this the fact that the educational level of all citizens is increasing dramatically (approximately 40 to 60 percent of current high-school graduates will go on to some form of postsecondary education experience), and it becomes clear that if peace officer education does not at least keep pace with these changes, individual officers will be "left in the dust."

All of the preceding information aside, individuals entering law enforcement professions owe it to themselves to aspire to higher educational levels and to make a commitment to lifelong learning. This is important for several reasons.

First, broadly based, postsecondary liberal arts education prepares individuals for a wide range of professional opportunities both within and outside the law enforcement profession. Recent research indicates that most adults will have the opportunity to make major career changes anywhere from three to six times during their life spans. It would be tragic if those choosing law enforcement as one of their careers were not in a position to have similar opportunities.

Second, although no scientific or empirical evidence indicates that increased education results in increased performance levels of peace officers, numerous recent perceptual studies report that citizens have more confidence in and esteem for more highly educated officers.

Third, law enforcement executives are constantly expressing the need for more officers who have:

➤ Well-developed verbal and written communication skills
➤ Excellent critical-thinking and decision-making skills
➤ Highly developed ethical and moral standards
➤ The ability to analyze complex public policy issues and social trends

Such attributes are developed in the broad-based, interdisciplinary liberal arts curriculum available through postsecondary educational experiences.

Finally, and perhaps most important, postsecondary education will prepare peace officers to grow personally. If allowed to, the law enforcement environment can become a narrow, isolated, cynical place, not unlike a prison. Postsecondary education, continuing education, commitment to lifelong learning and an appreciation for diversity can help peace officers keep the walls from closing in on them.

We in law enforcement do not have the luxury to wait for our agencies or our governments to provide education for us. We must recognize that education is as important to our "officer survival skills" as our firearms and other weapons training. Education does not need to be a state mandate or a department policy. It can be our individual choice, a gift to ourselves. No group of professionals is more deserving.

Timothy E. Erickson *is a returning professor at Metropolitan State University in Minnesota. He has been employed in the field of criminal justice for over 30 years, serving as a police officer, police sergeant and sergeant investigator for the St. Paul (Minnesota) Police Department and as the chief of police for the Arizona Western College, Campus Police Department. He also served as the education coordinator for the Minnesota POST Board. Mr. Erickson is also a licensed secondary education teacher and holds both MAT (broad-area social science) and MSE (educational counseling) degrees.*

INSIDER'S VIEW ONLINE

An additional *Insider's View* for this chapter is "New Orleans—'The Good, the Bad and the Ugly!'" by Dr. Jack R. Cahall, found on the Wadsworth website: http://www.wadsworth.com/criminaljustice_d/.

 MIND STRETCHES

1.   Imagine you have a crystal ball—what changes do you see in the world of work five years from now? Ten years from now? Fifty years from now?

2.   What role do you think education will play in the future?

3.   Do you think work will become more specialized or more generalized in the future? Why? How will your job goals be affected?

4.   What do you think will happen to current age limitations on jobs? Why?

5.   What jobs do you think will become more necessary in the future? Less necessary?

6.   Is your community changing? How? What about neighboring communities?

7.   Why do you think more people don't pursue advanced education or specialized training? Are these reasons legitimate?

8.   Recognizing that our entire society is always changing, what importance will you place on continuing to grow and change yourself?

9.   Is always striving to improve yourself important to you? Is there a danger in not continuing to grow and change?

10.   Can you think of jobs that do not now exist but will within the next 10 or 20 years?

REFERENCES

Bayer, Richard. "The U.S. Labor Market: Three Key Issues." *The Five O'Clock Club News,* November 2000. On the Internet at http://www.fiveoclockclub.com/articles/2000/11-00-USLabor.htm

Bureau of Labor Statistics. "Number of Jobs Held, Labor Market Activity, and Earnings Growth among Younger Baby Boomers Results from More than Two Decades of a Longitudinal Study." On the Internet at http://www.bls.gov/news.release/archives/nls04-08252004.pdf (USDL 02-497)

Career Guide to Industries, 2004–05 Edition. Washington, DC: Bureau of Labor Statistics, U.S. Department of Labor, 2004. On the Internet at http://www.bls.gov/oco/cg

Danga, Amy, ed. *Professional Careers Sourcebook: Where to Find Help Planning Careers That Require College or Technical Degrees,* 7th ed. Detroit: Thomson Gale, June 2002.

Dohm, Arlene and Wyatt, Ian. "College at Work: Outlook and Earnings for College Graduates, 2000–10." *Occupational Outlook Quarterly,* Fall 2002, pp. 3–15. On the Internet at http://www.bls.gov/opub/ooq/2002/fall/art01.pdf

Farr, Michael and Shatkin, Laurence. *Best Jobs for the 21st Century,* 3rd ed. Indianapolis: JIST Publishing, Inc., 2004.

Fleetwood, Chad and Shelley, Kristina. "The Outlook for College Graduates, 1998–2008: A Balancing Act." *Occupational Outlook Quarterly,* Fall 2000, pp. 3–9.

Forsgren, Laurel. Concordia University Saint Paul (Minnesota). Personal interview, February 25, 2004.

Hecker, Daniel E. "Occupational Employment Projections to 2012." *Monthly Labor Review,* February 2004, pp. 80–105.

Occupational Outlook Handbook (OOH), 2004–05 Edition. Bureau of Labor Statistics, U.S. Department of Labor. Washington, DC: U.S. Government Printing Office, 2004. On the Internet at http://www.bls.gov/oco/

The Polling Report, Inc. "Crime." 2004. On the Internet at http://www.pollingreport.com

Pulley, Mary Lynn. *Losing Your Job—Reclaiming Your Soul.* San Francisco: Jossey-Bass Publishers, 1997.

Su, Betty W. "The U.S. Economy to 2012: Signs of Growth." *Monthly Labor Review,* February 2004, pp. 23–36.

The Top 100: The Fastest Growing Careers for the 21st Century, 3rd ed. Chicago: Ferguson Publishing Company, 2001.

CHAPTER 2

FIRST RESPONDERS: CAREERS IN LAW ENFORCEMENT, PUBLIC SAFETY AND RELATED FIELDS

The opportunity for public service through law enforcement work is attractive to many because the job is challenging and involves much personal responsibility.

—*Occupational Outlook Handbook*

Do You Know:

➤ What percentage of time is spent on patrol or doing routine paperwork and how much time is actually taken up with chases and shoot-outs?

➤ What local agencies you might consider when seeking employment in law enforcement or a related field? County agencies? Tribal agencies? State agencies? Federal agencies?

➤ Where the greatest employment potential is usually found?

➤ How common promotions in law enforcement are?

➤ Why specialization within the law enforcement profession is important?

➤ How specialized training or expertise may benefit a law enforcement professional?

➤ How job prospects look for those interested in the field of juvenile justice?

➤ What the availability of international jobs in law enforcement is?

➤ What nonsworn civilian career options exist for those interested in law enforcement?

➤ What other careers are available to those interested in public safety and first response?

INTRODUCTION

This chapter discusses the largest, most visible component of criminal justice—law enforcement, beginning with what law enforcement entails in reality as opposed to what is often seen in movies and on television. Next, employment requirements and the outlook for careers in this field are discussed, followed by an up-close look at the variety of employment available in law enforcement and an explanation of where specific opportunities exist at the local, county, tribal, state and federal levels. Salaries for various law enforcement positions, as well as fringe benefits and promotional opportunities, are presented next, followed by a look at advanced jobs and specialization within the field, international job opportunities and a variety of nonsworn civilian jobs that support law enforcement. The chapter concludes with a look at other first responders and a discussion of public safety career opportunities in fire services and emergency response.

IS LAW ENFORCEMENT FOR YOU?

To make informed decisions about your career, you must gather facts. Some of this information comes from within. Do you possess the personal attributes needed to be a police officer? Can you give orders? Can you take orders? Can you remain calm under stress? Can you treat people professionally and apply the law equally? Can you work the hours under the conditions required by the job?

You also need to consider objective, external data. Much of what happens within law enforcement is not common knowledge. Consequently, many people considering employment in law enforcement may find themselves relying on inaccurate data. Unless you have a personal friend or relative in law enforcement, you are likely to obtain what you know about the field from where most people do: television or the movies.

Because of the popularity of police investigators and detectives, movies and television shows about them abound. But the primary goal of such shows is to entertain, not to educate. Sensationalism is much more likely than realism. A major public misconception about police work is that it is primarily oriented toward catching criminals. *NYPD Blue, CSI, Cold Case* and other television dramas about law enforcement depict police continuously involved in high-speed chases, exciting and dangerous shoot-outs and other dramatic criminal-catching activities.

> The law enforcement profession is grossly misrepresented in television shows and movies. In reality, about 80 percent of duty time is spent on patrol and doing routine paperwork. "Action" such as investigations, high-speed chases, shoot-outs and other dramatic criminal-catching activities consumes only about 20 percent of duty time.

To select a career based on fiction is to set yourself up for disappointment. No one knows better than those in the profession that television shows and movies don't exactly "tell it like it is." The uniforms, the cars, the equipment, the apparent prestige and the legal authority combine to make for a romantic ideal. Don't be fooled. Take a hard look at the law enforcement profession as you make realistic, informed decisions about your future career.

The *Occupational Outlook Handbook* (*OOH;* 2004) notes 40-hour workweeks are typical for law enforcement officers, although paid overtime is common. Because most communities require round-the-clock police protection, officers (typically junior officers) are needed to work the night, weekend and holiday shifts. Also, keep in mind that you will not begin your career as a detective—it may be a goal that requires many years to achieve. Other significant points to consider when exploring a career as a police officer, detective or special agent include:

➢ Police work can be dangerous and stressful.

➢ Competition should remain keen for higher-paying jobs with state and federal agencies and police departments in affluent areas.

➢ Opportunities will be better in local and special police departments that offer relatively low salaries or in urban communities where the crime rate is relatively high.

➢ Applicants with college training in police science or military police experience should have the best opportunities.

Large, urban departments may offer the widest variety of positions, as well. According to *The Top 100: The Fastest Growing Careers for the 21st Century* (2001, p. 287):

> In very large city police departments, officers may fill positions as police chiefs, precinct sergeants and captains, desk officers, booking officers, police inspectors, identification officers, complaint evaluation supervisors and officers, and crime prevention police officers. Some officers work as plainclothes detectives

in criminal investigation divisions. Internal affairs investigators are employed to police the police. Other specialized police officers include police reserves commanders; police officer commanding officers III, who act as supervisors in missing persons and fugitive investigations; and police officers III, who investigate and pursue nonpayment and fraud fugitives. Many police departments employ police clerks, who perform administrative and community-oriented tasks.

The possibility of officer assaults and fatalities is one aspect of the job many prefer to not think about. Nonetheless, grim statistics attest to the danger law enforcement officers may face on the job. According to the National Law Enforcement Officers Memorial Fund (NLEOMF) website, 148 law enforcement officers across the nation were killed in the line of duty in 2002, down from the decade-long average of 165 deaths annually and a major drop from 2001, when 234 officers were killed (including 72 officers in the September 11 attacks). This same website reports law enforcement officers suffer an average of 51,265 assaults per year and another 15,750 injuries annually.

Another hazard of police work involves communicable diseases. Officers called to the scene of an accident may come in contact with blood or other bodily fluids. Officers attempting to arrest or contain drunken, high, violent, excited or otherwise "altered" individuals may be bitten, scratched, spit on or worse, increasing their chances of contracting diseases, some of which may be fatal. Many agencies now make hepatitis vaccinations available and have regular HIV testing for officers involved in needle pricks and other high-risk incidents. Furthermore, police work often takes an emotional and psychological toll on officers, who routinely witness death and suffering resulting from accidents and criminal behavior. Officers' private lives may also suffer under such stress.

This information is presented not to discourage you from considering a career in law enforcement but to raise your awareness about some potential hazards of a very worthwhile profession. Caution, alertness and good judgment are critical, possibly lifesaving, qualities every good officer should possess. Other personal characteristics such as honesty, integrity and a sense of responsibility are especially important in law enforcement. You must also consider the level of education, training and other qualifications necessary to apply for a law enforcement position.

EMPLOYMENT REQUIREMENTS

According to the *OOH*:

> Civil service regulations govern the appointment of police and detectives in practically all States, large municipalities, and special police agencies, as well as in many smaller ones. Candidates must be U.S. citizens, usually at least 20 years of age, and must meet rigorous physical and personal qualifications. In the Federal Government, candidates must be at least 21 years of age but less than 37 years of age at the time of appointment. Physical examinations for entrance into law enforcement often include tests of vision, hearing, strength, and agility. Eligibility for appointment usually depends on performance in competitive written examinations and previous education and experience. In larger departments, where the majority of law enforcement jobs are found, applicants usually must have at least a high school education. Federal and State agencies typically require a college degree.

Law enforcement agencies are encouraging applicants to complete college-level courses in criminal-justice related subjects: "Many entry-level applicants for police jobs have completed some formal postsecondary education and a significant number are college graduates. Many junior colleges, colleges, and universities offer programs in law enforcement or administration of justice. Other courses helpful in preparing for a career in law enforcement include accounting, finance, electrical engineering, computer science, and foreign languages" (*OOH*). The International Association of Chiefs of Police (IACP) website states:

> The minimum education level for the majority of police departments is a high school diploma, or equivalent. However, the current trend is for applicants to have college credit equal to two years:
>
> - 16% of state police agencies require a two-year college degree; 4% require a four-year degree.
> - 13% of county police agencies require a two-year degree.
> - 9% of local agencies require a two-year degree; 2% require a four-year degree.

EMPLOYMENT OUTLOOK

The outlook for jobs in law enforcement is positive, although continuing budgetary constraints may keep the field from growing as much as is needed: "The level of government spending determines the level of employment for police and detectives. The number of job opportunities, therefore, can vary from year to year and from place to place. Layoffs, on the other hand, are rare because retirements enable most staffing cuts to be handled through attrition. Trained law enforcement officers who lose their jobs because of budget cuts usually have little difficulty finding jobs with other agencies. The need to replace workers who retire, transfer to other occupations, or stop working for other reasons will be the source of many job openings." Furthermore:

> Law enforcement officers in many agencies may retire with a pension after 20 or 25 years of service, allowing them to pursue a second career while still in their 40s. Because of relatively attractive salaries and benefits, the number of qualified candidates exceeds the number of job openings in Federal law enforcement agencies and in most State police departments—resulting in increased hiring standards and selectivity by employers. Competition should remain keen for higher paying jobs with State and Federal agencies and police departments in more affluent areas.

The *OOH* states: "Employment of police and detectives is expected to *grow faster than the average* for all occupations through 2012. A more security-conscious society and concern about drug-related crimes should contribute to the increasing demand for police services." The Bureau of Labor Statistics (BLS) projects a 31 percent increase in employment for police and sheriff's patrol officers between 2002 and 2012, raising their numbers from approximately 618,786 to 771,581 (Horrigan, 2004, p. 19).

Some aspects of law enforcement require careful, realistic consideration. But these fields continue to draw people to them. Ask a hundred officers why they're in it, and you'll hear a hundred different responses. And, yes, police officers complain a lot—about the hours, the pay and the administration. But there is something about law enforcement that gets in your blood.

LAW ENFORCEMENT—UP CLOSE

The public generally believes that being a police officer means wearing a uniform and pushing a squad car around town. Few people outside the field have any idea of the variety of employment available. Consider the vocational spectrum shown by the following partial listing of positions, many obtained by reviewing the 2004 *International Association of Chiefs of Police Membership Directory*:

Animal Control Worker	Bailiff	Campus Police
Arson Investigator	Ballistics Expert	Chaplain
Attaché	Booking Officer	Chief of Police

Chief of Staff
Commander of Field
    Operations
Commissioner
Communications Officer
Community Safety Coordinator
Community Service Officer
Computer Crime Specialist
Conservation Officer
Crime Lab Technician
Crime Prevention Specialist
Customs and Border Protection
    Officer
Data Processing Specialist
Deputy
Deputy Chief
Detective
Detention Officer
Director of Research and
    Development
Director of Scientific Service
Director of Standards and
    Training
Document Specialist
Drug Recognition Expert
Emergency Management
    Coordinator

Evidence Technician
Explosives Technician
FBI Special Agent
Fingerprint Technician
Firearms Instructor
Forensic Scientist
Gaming Enforcement Agent
Gang Investigator
Inspector
Instructor
Insurance Fraud Investigator
Intelligence Officer
Investigator
Jailer
Juvenile Specialist
K-9 Handler
Narcotics Agent
Operations Specialist
Patrol Officer
Personnel Specialist
Photographer
Pilot
Police Attorney/Legal Advisor
Police Psychologist
Police Surgeon
Polygraph Operator
Professor

Psychiatric Advisor
Public Information Officer
Public Relations Officer
Public Safety Director
Radio Communications
Railroad Police
Records Management
    Director
School Resource Officer
Scientist
Secret Service Agent
Security Specialist
Serology Specialist
Sheriff
Street Crimes Specialist
Superintendent of Police
S.W.A.T.
Traffic Officer
Training Director
Transit Police
Treasury Agent
Trooper
Undercover Operative
Undersheriff
U.S. Marshal
Water Patrol
Witness Protection Agent

WHERE OPPORTUNITIES EXIST

To begin your look at law enforcement, consider the basic jurisdictions in which you might work. Jurisdiction in this sense basically addresses both *where* particular agencies work and *what* their enforcement emphasis is. The primary jurisdictional levels are local, county, state and federal.

Different levels of law enforcement agencies have different jurisdictions and areas of responsibility. For example, while Secret Service agents are law enforcement officers, they do not do traffic enforcement. Similarly, local law enforcement officers are seldom called on for diplomatic protective service. The following descriptions of local, county, state and federal law enforcement positions are adapted from *Introduction to Law Enforcement and Criminal Justice,* 7th edition (Wrobleski and Hess, 2003, pp. 15–20. Reprinted by permission) and the *OOH.*

Local Agencies

According to Reaves and Hickman (2002a, p. 1), 12,666 general purpose local police departments were operating throughout the United States as of June 2000. Hickman and Reaves (2003a, p. iii) also report: "As of June 2000, local police departments had 565,915 full-time employees, including about 441,000 sworn personnel. Local police employment was up an average of about 2% per year since 1990."

Local agencies and offices with law enforcement responsibilities include (1) township and special district police, (2) the constable, (3) the marshal and (4) municipal police.

Township and Special District Police. The United States has thousands of townships, which vary widely in scope of governmental powers and operations. Most townships provide a limited range of services for predominantly rural areas. Some townships, often those in well-developed fringe areas surrounding a metropolitan complex, perform functions similar to municipal police.

The Constable. Several states have established the office of constable, especially in New England, the South and the West. The constable is usually an elected official who serves a township, preserving the peace and serving processes for the local justice court. The constable also may be the tax collector or be in charge of the pound, execute arrest warrants and transport prisoners.

The Marshal. In some parts of the United States, a marshal serves as a court officer, serving writs, subpoenas and other papers issued by the court and escorting prisoners from jail or holding cells in the courthouse to and from trials and hearings. The marshal also serves as the bailiff and protects the municipal judge and people in the court. In some jurisdictions, the marshal is elected; in other jurisdictions, the marshal is appointed.

Municipal Police. The United States has, again, thousands of municipal police jurisdictions employing hundreds of thousands of police officers, all with similar responsibilities but with limited geographical jurisdictions. The least uniformity and greatest organizational complexity are found at the municipal level due to local autonomy. The majority of these police forces consist of fewer than 10 officers, yet this is what most people think of when they think of law enforcement.

County Agencies

Hickman and Reaves (2003b) state: "As of June 2000, sheriffs' offices had 293,823 full-time employees, including about 165,000 sworn personnel. Employment was up an average of about 4% per year since 1990." In addition to sheriffs, law enforcement at the county level includes county police and the county coroner or medical examiner.

County agencies with law enforcement responsibilities include (1) the county sheriff, (2) the county police and (3) the county coroner or medical examiner.

The County Sheriff. Many state constitutions designate the sheriff as the chief county law enforcement officer. The sheriff is usually elected locally for a two- or four-year term and may appoint deputies to help provide police protection as well as to (1) keep the public peace, (2) execute civil and criminal process throughout the county, (3) maintain and staff the county jail, (4) preserve the court's dignity and (5) enforce court orders.

The hundreds of sheriff's departments vary greatly in organization and function. In some states, the sheriff is primarily a court officer; criminal investigation and traffic enforcement are delegated to state or local agencies. In other states, notably in the South and West, the sheriff and deputies perform both traffic and criminal duties. The sheriff's staff ranges from one (the sheriff only) to several hundred, including sworn deputies and civilian personnel. A major difference between sheriffs' and municipal police departments is that sheriffs often place greater emphasis on civil functions and operating corrections facilities.

The County Police. The county police are often found in areas where city and county governments have merged and are headed by a chief law enforcement officer.

The Coroner or Medical Examiner. The coroner's principal task is to determine the cause of death and to take care of the remains and personal effects of deceased persons. The coroner need not be a medical doctor or have any legal background to be elected. In some jurisdictions, however, the coroner has been replaced by the medical examiner, a physician, usually a pathologist who has studied forensic science. Still other jurisdictions are using medicolegal death investigators or deputy coroners, discussed shortly.

Tribal Agencies

Somewhere between the county level and the state level of law enforcement lies the tribally operated agency. According to Hickman (2003, p. 1): "As of June 2000, American Indian tribes operated 171 law enforcement agencies that employed the equivalent of at least 1 full-time sworn officer with general arrest powers. In addition, the Bureau of Indian Affairs (BIA) operated 37 agencies providing law enforcement services in Indian country." He (p. 1) adds that the broad range of public safety services and functions provided by tribally operated agencies includes responding to calls for service, engaging in crime prevention activities, executing arrest warrants, performing traffic law enforcement, serving court papers, providing court security, conducting search-and-rescue operations and operating jails. Hickman (p. 2) further reports:

> While tribally operated agencies and other general purpose police agencies provide a similar range of services, a major difference between them is the land area served. . . . In terms of land area, some tribally operated agencies may be more like county or regional police departments.

> Criminal jurisdiction is another major difference between tribally operated agencies and their State and local counterparts. Jurisdiction over offenses in Indian country may lie with Federal, State, or tribal agencies depending upon the particular offense, the offender, the victim, and the offense location.

> Tribal law enforcement agencies provide a broad range of public safety services and functions.

State Agencies

> State agencies with law enforcement responsibilities include (1) state investigative agencies, (2) state fire marshal divisions, (3) departments of natural resources, (4) driver and vehicle services divisions, (5) departments of human rights and (6) state police and highway patrol agencies.

State Investigative Agencies. State investigative agencies place investigators throughout the state to help investigate major crimes, organized criminal activity, and the illegal sale or possession of narcotics and prohibited drugs; conduct police science training courses for peace officers; provide scientific examination of crime scenes and laboratory analysis of evidence; and maintain a criminal justice information and telecommunications system.

State Fire Marshal Division. Designated state fire marshals investigate suspicious and incendiary fire origins, fire fatalities and large-loss fires; tabulate fire statistics; and provide education, inspection and training programs for fire prevention.

State Department of Natural Resources (Fish, Game and Watercraft). Conservation officers investigate complaints about nuisance wildlife, misuse of public lands and waters, violations of state park rules and unlawful appropriation of state-owned timber. They also dispose of big-game animals struck by motor vehicles, assist state game managers on wildlife census projects and assist in identifying needed sites for public access to lakes and streams. The department also issues resident and nonresident boat licenses and licenses for hunting, fishing and trapping.

Driver and Vehicle Services Division. The *Motor Vehicle Section* registers motor vehicles, issues ownership certificates, answers inquiries, licenses motor vehicle dealers, supplies record information to the public and in some states, registers bicycles. The *Driver's License Section* tests, evaluates and licenses all drivers throughout the state; maintains accurate records of each individual driver including all violations and crashes occurring anywhere in the United States and Canada; interviews drivers whose records warrant possible revocation, suspension or cancellation; records the location of every reported crash; assists in driver education efforts; and administers written and road tests to applicants.

Department of Human Rights. The Department of Human Rights enforces the Human Rights Act, which prohibits discrimination on the basis of race, color, creed, religion, national origin, sex, marital status, status with regard to public assistance, or disability in employment, housing, public accommodations, public service and education.

State Law Enforcement—State Police and Highway Patrol. Some state police enforce all state laws; others enforce primarily traffic laws on highways and freeways and are usually designated as state highway patrol. A major difference between the two officers is that state police generally have more investigative duties than do the highway patrol.

Usually, *state police* work within jurisdictions on request or in following up on their own cases. State police typically have specialized units of special agents or criminal investigators, plainclothes detectives who investigate various violations of state law such as drug trafficking.

Most *state patrol* agencies enforce state traffic laws and all laws governing operation of vehicles on the state's public highways. Officers usually work in uniform and drive marked cars and motorcycles. Duties include (1) maintaining preventive patrol on the highways, (2) regulating traffic movements and relieving congestion, (3) investigating traffic crashes and (4) making surveys and studies of crashes and enforcement practices to improve traffic safety. (NOTE: *Highway patrol,* while still used, is becoming less common, with many states replacing the term with *state patrol.* While their training emphasizes traffic-related matters, state patrol officers are trained in all areas of professional law enforcement.)

State officers seeking additional specialization should research their state's specialized units, such as canine units, aircraft units, special response and tactical teams, investigation units and executive protection teams. Sources of further information regarding state law enforcement careers are provided at the end of this chapter.

Federal Agencies

Reaves and Bauer (2003, p. 1) report: "As of June 2002, Federal agencies employed more than 93,000 full-time personnel authorized to make arrests and carry firearms." In 2002, women and minorities accounted for 14.8 and 32.4 percent of federal officers, respectively.

Prior to September 11, 2001, the primary federal law enforcement agencies were housed under either the Department of Justice (DOJ) or the Department of the Treasury. Following the terrorist attacks of 9/11, however, President George W. Bush decided 22 previously disparate domestic agencies needed to be coordinated into one department to protect the nation against threats to the homeland, thus creating a new federal agency called the Department of Homeland Security (DHS; website).

The DHS now oversees a variety of law enforcement agencies that were previously within either the Department of Justice or the Department of the Treasury, such as the Bureau of Customs and Border Protection, the U.S. Secret Service, the Bureau of Citizenship and Immigration Services (formerly the Immigration and Naturalization Service, or INS) and the U.S. Coast Guard. Other DHS agencies with investigative and law enforcement roles include the Transportation Security Administration (TSA), the Office of Inspector General and the Federal Computer Incident Response Center.

The Department of Justice (DOJ) is the largest law firm in the country, representing U.S. citizens in enforcing the law. Numerous federal law enforcement agencies exist within the DOJ, including the Federal Bureau of Investigation (FBI), the Federal Drug Enforcement Administration (DEA), the U.S. Marshals Service; Federal Bureau of Prisons (BOP); Bureau of Alcohol, Tobacco, Firearms and Explosives; and Office of Justice Programs (Juvenile Justice, Office of Community Oriented Policing Services (COPS), Victims of Crime, Violence Against Women and more).

The Internal Revenue Service (IRS), under the Department of the Treasury, also has agents involved in law enforcement activities.

Federal agencies to consider when looking for a job in law enforcement or a related field include (1) the Bureau of Customs and Border Protection; (2) the U.S. Secret Service; (3) the U.S. Citizenship and Immigration Services; (4) the U.S. Coast Guard; (5) the Transportation Security Administration; (6) the Office of Inspector General; (7) the Federal Computer Incident Response Center; (8) the Federal Bureau of Investigation; (9) the Federal Drug Enforcement Administration; (10) the U.S. Marshals Service; (11) the Federal Bureau of Prisons; (12) the Bureau of Alcohol, Tobacco, Firearms and Explosives; (13) the Office of Justice Programs; and (14) the Internal Revenue Service. Other federal career avenues to pursue include (15) the Federal Aviation Administration; (16) the Bureau of Diplomatic Security; (17) the U.S. Mint; (18) Postal Inspectors; (19) the Bureau of Indian Affairs Office of Tribal Justice; (20) the Forest Service; (21) the National Park Service; (22) military services; and (23) the Federal Law Enforcement Training Center.

In addition to changing the placement of several agencies on the government's organizational chart, the emphasis of many agencies has changed. For example, fighting terrorism has replaced drug enforcement as the U.S. Customs Service's first responsibility.

The Bureau of Customs and Border Protection (CBP). The CBP is charged with protecting the more than 8,000 miles of international land and water boundaries surrounding the United States and has agents stationed along various points of entry to the United States (ports and along the Mexican and Canadian borders). On a typical day, CBP agents perform many diverse tasks to ensure homeland security, flow of trade and compliance, inspections at ports of entry, and seizures of illegal drugs and contraband. CBP enforces, in addition to its own statutes, more than 400 provisions of law for 40 other federal agencies.

The U.S. Border Patrol is the mobile uniformed law enforcement arm of the Department of Homeland Security (DHS) responsible for combating illegal entries into the country and the growing business of alien smuggling. The Bureau of Immigration and Customs Enforcement (ICE) brings together the enforcement and investigative arms of the Customs Service, the investigative and enforcement functions of the former Immigration and Naturalization Service (INS) and the Federal Protective Service (FPS) as part of the DHS.

The U.S. Secret Service. The Secret Service was established in 1865 to fight currency counterfeiters. In 1901 it was given the responsibility for protecting the president and vice president, their families, heads of state and other designated individuals; investigating threats against these protectees; protecting the White House, vice president's residence, Foreign Missions and other buildings within Washington, DC; and planning and implementing security designs for designated National Special Security Events. The Secret Service also investigates violations of laws relating to counterfeiting of obligations and securities of the United States; financial crimes that include, but are not limited to, access device fraud, financial institution fraud, identity theft and computer fraud; and computer-based attacks on our nation's financial, banking and telecommunications infrastructure.

The U.S. Citizenship and Immigration Services (USCIS). USCIS officers are responsible for adjudicating and processing various applications and forms, such as petitions for the immigration of relatives and workers, work authorizations, adjustments of status, requests for asylum, and naturalization, necessary to ensure the legal immigration of people and their families to the United States, from initial stages through their transition, to permanent residence and finally to citizenship.

The Coast Guard. The Coast Guard helps local and state agencies that border oceans, lakes and national waterways. The Coast Guard's mission is multifaceted and involves maritime safety (search and rescue, recreational boating safety, international ice patrol), maritime mobility (aids to navigation, icebreaking services, vessel traffic/waterways management), maritime security (drug interdiction, alien migrant interdiction, protection of fisheries resources, general maritime law enforcement, law/treaty enforcement), national defense (homeland security, port and waterway security) and protection of natural resources (marine pollution education, prevention, response and enforcement; foreign vessel inspections; and living marine resources protection).

The Transportation Security Administration (TSA). The TSA is responsible for security relating to civil aviation, maritime and all other modes of transportation (including transportation facilities) and is the lead agency for security at airports, ports and on the nation's railroads, highways and public transit systems. The TSA National Explosives Detection Canine Program (NEDCP) exists to deter and detect the introduction of explosive devices into the transportation system. TSA-certified explosives detection canine teams are stationed at each of the nation's largest airports and are used daily to search aircraft and terminals, to check out suspect bags or cargo, and to deter terrorist activities.

The Office of Inspector General (OIG). The OIG's mission is to protect the integrity of Department of Health and Human Services (HHS) programs, as well as the health and welfare of program beneficiaries. The Office of Investigations (OI) is responsible for investigating a variety of crimes committed against over 300 departmental programs. A primary responsibility of a Special Agent for the OIG is to detect and investigate Medicare/Medicaid fraud, child support enforcement matters, internal investigations, and grant and contract fraud. Agents conduct interviews, serve search and arrest warrants, and use surveillance and undercover operations during their investigations. Agents also ensure the protection and safety of the Secretary of HHS.

The Federal Computer Incident Response Center (FedCIRC). FedCIRC, working with the United States Computer Emergency Readiness Team (US-CERT), is a collaboration of computer incident response, security and law enforcement professionals working together to handle computer security incidents and to provide both proactive and reactive security services for the federal government. The primary purposes of the FedCIRC are to provide the means for federal agencies to work together to handle security incidents, share related information, solve common security problems and to collaborate with the National Infrastructure Protection Center (NIPC) for the planning of future infrastructure protection strategies and dealing with criminal activities that pose a threat to the critical information infrastructure.

The Federal Bureau of Investigation (FBI). The FBI is the primary investigative agency of the federal government. Its special agents are responsible for investigating violations of more than 260 statutes and conducting sensitive national security investigations. Agents may conduct surveillance, monitor court-authorized wiretaps, examine business records, investigate white-collar crime, track the interstate movement of stolen property, collect evidence of espionage activities, or participate in sensitive undercover assignments. The FBI investigates organized crime, public corruption, financial crime, fraud against the government, bribery, copyright infringement, civil rights violations, bank robbery, extortion, kidnapping, air piracy, terrorism, espionage, interstate criminal activity, drug trafficking and other violations of federal statutes.

The FBI also provides valuable services to law enforcement agencies throughout the country. The *Identification Division* is a central repository for fingerprint information, including the automated fingerprint identification system (AFIS), which greatly streamlines the matching of fingerprints with suspects. The *National Crime Information Center* (NCIC-2000) is a computerized, electronic data exchange network developed to complement computerized systems already in existence and those planned by local and state law enforcement agencies. The *FBI Laboratory*, the world's largest criminal laboratory, is available without cost to any city, county, state or federal law enforcement agency in the country. The *Uniform Crime Reports* (UCR) is a national clearinghouse for U.S. crime statistics.

The Federal Drug Enforcement Administration (DEA). DEA agents seek to stop the flow of drugs at their source, both domestic and foreign, and to assist state and local police in preventing illegal drugs from reaching local communities. Not only is the DEA the lead agency for domestic enforcement of federal drug laws, but it also has sole responsibility for coordinating and pursuing U.S. drug investigations abroad. DEA agents are involved in surveillance, undercover operations, raids, interviewing witnesses and suspects, searching for evidence and seizing contraband. Positions within the DEA include special agent, intelligence research specialist, forensic chemist, diversion investigator and attorney.

The U.S. Marshals. In 1789 Congress created the office of U.S. Marshal. Marshals are appointed by the president and are responsible for protecting the federal courts and ensuring the effective operation of the judicial system. Duties of U.S. marshals include (1) seizing property in both criminal and civil matters to satisfy judgments issued by a federal court, (2) providing physical security for U.S. courtrooms, (3) transporting federal prisoners and (4) protecting government witnesses whose testimony might jeopardize their safety. They enjoy the widest jurisdiction of any federal law enforcement agency and are involved to some degree in nearly all federal law enforcement efforts. In addition, U.S. marshals pursue and arrest federal fugitives.

The Bureau of Prisons (BOP). The BOP is responsible for the care and custody of persons convicted of federal crimes and sentenced to federal penal institutions. The Bureau operates a nationwide system of 104 maximum-, medium- and minimum-security institutions, 6 regional offices, a Central Office (headquarters), 2 staff training centers and 28 community corrections offices. Community corrections offices oversee community corrections centers and home confinement programs. The Bureau is responsible for the custody and care of more than 174,000 federal offenders. Over 147,000 of these inmates are confined in Bureau-operated correctional institutions and detention centers. The rest are confined in privately operated prisons, detention centers, community corrections centers and juvenile facilities, as well as some facilities operated by state or local governments.

The Bureau of Alcohol, Tobacco, Firearms and Explosives (ATF). The ATF is primarily a licensing and investigative agency involved in investigating violations of federal alcohol and tobacco tax regulations and violations of federal firearms and explosives laws. The Firearms Division enforces the Gun Control Act of 1968 and the Arms Export Control Act. Domestic and foreign investigations involve the development and use of informants, physical and electronic surveillance, and examination of records from importers/exporters, banks, couriers and manufacturers. Agents conduct interviews, serve on joint task forces with other agencies, and get and execute search warrants.

Office of Justice Programs (OJP). The OJP is a conglomerate of bureaus, offices and programs directed to provide federal leadership in developing the nation's capacity to prevent and control crime, improve the criminal and juvenile justice systems, increase knowledge about crime and related issues, and assist crime victims.

The five OJP bureaus are the *Bureau of Justice Assistance* (BJA), which provides funding, training, and technical assistance to state and local governments to combat violent and drug-related crime and to help improve the criminal justice system; the *Bureau of Justice Statistics* (BJS), the principal criminal justice statistical agency in the nation; the *National Institute of Justice* (NIJ), the principal research and development agency in the Department of Justice, responsible for conducting demonstrations of innovative approaches to improve criminal justice, developing and testing new criminal justice technologies, evaluating the effectiveness of justice programs and disseminating research findings to practitioners and policy makers; the *Office of Juvenile Justice and Delinquency Prevention* (OJJDP), which provides federal leadership in preventing and controlling juvenile crime and improving the juvenile justice system at the state and local levels, in addition to administering the Missing and Exploited Children's program, four programs funded under the Victims of Child Abuse Act, and the Coordinating Council on Juvenile Justice and Delinquency Prevention; and the *Office for Victims of Crime* (OVC), which provides federal leadership in assisting victims of crime and their families, administers two grant programs created by the Victims of Crime Act of 1984 (VOCA), and sponsors training for federal, state, and local criminal justice officials and other professionals to help improve their response to crime victims and their families.

OJP offices include the *Corrections Program Office* (CPO); the *Drug Courts Program Office* (DCPO); the *Violence Against Women Office* (VAWO); the *Office of State and Local Domestic Preparedness Support* (OSLDPS); the *Office of the Police Corps and Law Enforcement Education* (OPCLEE); the *American Indian and Alaskan Native Affairs Office* (AI/AN); and the *Executive Office for Weed and Seed* (EOWS).

The Internal Revenue Service (IRS). The Internal Revenue Service, established in 1862, is the largest bureau of the Department of the Treasury. Its mission is to encourage the highest degree of voluntary compliance with the tax laws and regulations. IRS Criminal Investigation (CI) Special Agents are the premier financial investigators for the federal government and investigate potential criminal violations of the Internal Revenue Code and related financial crimes such as willful tax evasion, tax fraud and the activities of gamblers and drug peddlers. IRS-CI Special Agents use accounting and law enforcement skills to investigate financial crimes and "follow the money." No matter what the source, all income earned, both legal and illegal, has the potential of becoming involved in crimes that fall within the investigative jurisdiction of the IRS.

The Federal Aviation Administration (FAA). The Federal Aviation Administration (FAA) is responsible for the safety of civil aviation. In 1970, President Nixon began a sky marshal program as part of the Customs Service. Following the 1985 hijacking of TWA Flight 847, this elite team of sharpshooters re-formed under the FAA.

Technically called Civil Aviation Security Specialists, Federal Air Marshals fly on selected high-risk routes to deter hijacking attempts and thwart terrorist attacks with minimum endangerment of passengers and crew. Dressed in civilian clothes to maintain a low profile, air marshals board flights at random or in response to specific threats. They are authorized to carry firearms on planes and make arrests without warrants with the objective of using minimum force to achieve maximum security. They receive intensive, highly specialized law enforcement training, followed by recurrent training and recertification. This is an intensely stressful position requiring exceptional judgment. Having limited contact with family members during missions, agents can be deployed at any time and anywhere in the world. Agents must be comfortable working independently and be willing to travel extensively, as missions often involve long flights cross-country or overseas.

Bureau of Diplomatic Security. Part of the U.S. Department of State, these special agents investigate passport and visa fraud, conduct personnel security investigations, issue security clearances and protect the Secretary of State and foreign dignitaries. Overseas, they advise ambassadors on all security matters and manage a complex range of security programs designed to protect personnel, facilities and information. They also train foreign civilian police and administer counterterrorism and counternarcotics rewards programs. Their numbers are expected to grow rapidly as the threat of terrorism increases and the battle against it intensifies.

The U.S. Mint. Mint Police possess expertise in high-level security, and officers' primary duty is protecting the country's $100 billion of gold, silver and coins at the nation's six Mint facilities, 24/7. Each mint is typically staffed with firearm instructors, field training officers, an emergency response team, a hostage negotiator and a detective specializing in areas such as cyber-fraud. Mint Police also safeguard Mint employees, visitors and tourists, and guard the Declaration of Independence, the U.S. Constitution, the Articles of Confederation and Lincoln's Gettysburg Address. The agency is currently expanding its mission to include offering consulting services to foreign governments on how best to protect their gold and precious metals, and offering assistance to other federal agencies in protecting and transporting valuable assets.

Postal Inspectors. Postal inspectors protect the mails and recipients of mail by enforcing federal laws pertaining to mailing prohibited items such as explosives, obscene matter and articles likely to injure or cause damage, including biological and chemical agents sent with intent to kill and terrorize, such as anthrax and cyanide. Any mail that may prove to be libelous, defamatory or threatening can be excluded from being transported by the postal service. They also investigate any frauds perpetrated through the mails such as chain letters, gift enterprises and similar schemes.

Bureau of Indian Affairs (BIA) Office of Tribal Justice. From its earliest days, the United States has recognized the sovereign status of Indian tribes as "domestic dependent nations." Our Constitution recognizes Indian sovereignty and establishes Indian affairs as a unique area of federal concern. Consequently, Indian country has been allowed to develop and perpetuate its own justice system in line with Indian customs and laws. However, while some tribal governments have developed strong law enforcement programs, many others have encountered significant difficulty in doing so, with great numbers of Indian citizens receiving police, investigative and detention services that lag far behind those existing in non-Indian territory. The BIA's Office of Law Enforcement Services (OLES) works in conjunction with the DOJ to train and certify the criminal investigators and uniformed officers needed to serve our nation's Indian population.

The U.S. Forest Service. The Forest Service employs over 600 rangers to patrol federal lands, protect various cultural and natural resources, and investigate criminal activity. Crimes may involve anything from simple vandalism and theft of Forest Service property, such as chainsaws or solar panels, to timber theft, contract fraud, narcotics production on federal lands, theft of archeological artifacts, bombings and personal assaults on Forest Service personnel.

National Park Service (NPS). The NPS comprises 379 areas in nearly every state and U.S. possession, from the Hawaii Volcanoes National Park to the Statue of Liberty National Monument. NPS positions with law enforcement duties include the U.S. Park Police, Park Rangers and Guard Force.

The primary duty of the *U.S. Park Police* is to protect lives. Park Police Officers preserve the peace; prevent, detect and investigate accidents and crimes; aid citizens in emergency situations; arrest violators; and often provide crowd control at large public gatherings. The Park Police force includes horse-mounted, motorcycle, helicopter and canine units; a special equipment and tactics team; and investigations and security details.

Park Rangers supervise, manage and perform work in the conservation and use of resources in national parks and other federally managed areas. Park Ranger duties include forest or structural fire control; protection of property; enforcement of laws and regulations; investigation of violations, complaints, trespass/encroachment and accidents; search and rescue; and management of historical, cultural and natural resources such as wildlife, forests, lakeshores, seashores, historic buildings, battlefields, archaeological properties and recreation areas.

The *uniformed guard force* protects federal property and buildings. Guards either may serve at fixed posts or patrol assigned areas to prevent and protect them from hazards of fire, theft, accident, damage and trespass. Most guards are located in the National Capitol Region, as a subunit of the Park Police, for which they work as permanent part-time employees. A few are located in other regions, and some have full-time positions.

The Military Services. The armed forces also have law enforcement responsibilities. The uniformed divisions are known as the Military Police (Army), the Shore Patrol (Navy) and the Security Police (Marine Corps and Air Force). The military police are primarily concerned with the physical security of the various bases under their control. Within each operation, the security forces control criminal activity, court-martials, discipline, desertions and the confinement of prisoners. Military law enforcement assignments such as the military police provide exceptional experience. Other non–law enforcement assignments, however, also provide proof that the individual can take orders, assume responsibility and successfully accept challenges.

Even if you are not interested in the military as a career, it is a great background when job seeking. The military is particularly well suited for those who are younger and less certain as to what career direction to take. Any military experience is better than just throwing those years away aimlessly wandering from job to job. Military experience is usually directly applicable to successful employment in law enforcement.

Federal Law Enforcement Training Center (FLETC). New recruits with most federal law enforcement agencies throughout the country receive their initial training at the Federal Law Enforcement Training Center (FLETC) in Glynco, Georgia. FLETC's mission is to serve as the federal government's leader for and provider of world-class law enforcement training and to prepare new and experienced law enforcement professionals to fulfill their responsibilities in a safe manner and at the highest level of proficiency. Of more than 250 programs taught each year, most of the 40,000-plus students that are trained annually receive basic instruction in rules and principles of law, investigation, detention, arrest, and search and seizure. Basic and advanced training also includes fingerprinting, photography, physical conditioning, interviewing skills, firearms use, radio communication procedures, high-speed pursuit and protection, undercover investigations, advanced computer crime detection, advanced fraud detection and advanced marine law enforcement.

JURISDICTIONS COMPARED

Each agency level has its own particular benefits. Federal work may be considered prestigious and dynamic, and usually has the best pay and benefits. However, it also usually has high standards and often requires relocating, which can substantially interfere with today's common two-profession families. Because of the large number of people employed by the federal system, the bureaucracy can be frustrating, with a possibility of feeling lost or engulfed in the numbers. Age also may be a drawback; you cannot be older than 35 at the time you are hired due to laws governing retirement in the federal law enforcement system.

Employment with local law enforcement has its own benefits, frequently associated with being part of a more concentrated law enforcement effort. One community benefit to a local police department is local identity and control. Many officers enjoy being a recognized part of a smaller community. Smaller agencies may have fewer transfer or promotional opportunities, but may also permit officers to assume more responsibilities on the job.

Usually, the larger the geographic jurisdiction and population size, the greater the number of employment opportunities. According to Reaves and Hickman (2002a, p. 3): "Although State and local agencies with 100 or more full-time sworn officers accounted for just 6% of all agencies, they employed 63% of all State and local full-time sworn personnel." They (2002b, p. 2) further note: "From 1990 to 2000, the average number of full-time personnel in police departments serving cities with a population of 250,000 or more increased by 20%. . . . From 1990 to 2000, the average number of full-time sworn personnel among police departments in large cities increased by 17%. . . . In 2000, these agencies employed 310 full-time sworn personnel per 100,000 residents. This represented an increase of 21 per 100,000, or 7%, compared to 1990." In considering where you might find your best employment potential, consider which governmental agencies have the greatest number of employees because with numbers comes advancement potential.

Some departments are also more aggressive in hiring women and minorities, although the general employment outlook has improved tremendously for both groups over the last quarter century. Reaves and Hickman (2002b, p. 3) report: "Minority representation among local police officers in large cities increased from 29.8% in 1990 to 38.1% in 2000. . . . The percentage of female officers rose from 12.1% in 1990 to 16.3% in 2000."

Local police departments offer more than half the jobs available, including many civilian opportunities. Bureau of Justice Statistics (BJS) data show: "State and local agencies had 708,022 full-time sworn personnel and 311,474 full-time civilian employees in 2000" (Reaves and Hickman, 2002a, p. 1), indicating more than 30 percent of full-time employees at local police departments were nonsworn civilians. Similarly: "As of June 2000, sheriffs' offices had 293,823 full-time employees, including about 165,000 sworn personnel," meaning roughly 44 percent of all full-time positions were filled by civilians (Hickman and Reaves, 2003b, p. iii).

> To find the greatest employment potential, consider agencies that have the greatest number of employees. Remember, more than half of all law enforcement positions are found in local police departments, and civilian opportunities exist at all three levels—local, state and federal.

Since the number of employees at various jurisdictional levels changes from year to year, the most current available data can be found at http://www.ojp.usdoj.gov/bjs/. We encourage you to reference this site for valuable and timely information regarding careers in law enforcement.

SALARIES

Simply put, government work will never share the nearly limitless compensation potential of private employment. This is not to say that law enforcement personnel are destined to be destitute. On the contrary, pay at the local, county, state and federal levels is certainly comfortable. Considering the benefits associated with government work—pensions, medical coverage, vacation and sick time, and greater job security than that found in the private sector—a career in law enforcement is well compensated. Deferred compensation and generous retirement plans may allow for excellent early retirement. The advice here: Start early and contribute the most you possibly can.

In many agencies, additional opportunities may make law enforcement employment more attractive. For example, most jurisdictions allow for some part-time work. This may include overtime work (usually paying more than the 40-hour-per-week pay scale) or moonlighting for local businesses doing security work, traffic control for special events and so on. While it is usually something other than money that motivates the law enforcement officer, salary is an important consideration. Different jurisdictions pay differently, and advancement offers pay incentives.

Local, County and State Salaries

Salaries for police officers and detectives vary greatly, depending on location and the size of the population served. *The Top 100* (p. 290) observes: "Police departments in the West and North generally pay more than those in the South." Table 2–1 contains salary information for sworn local and county law enforcement personnel in 2002. For the most current figures, check the Bureau of Labor Statistics (BLS) website: http://www.stats.bls.gov.

Federal Salaries

Federal jobs in law enforcement fall under the *General Schedule,* or *GS,* system. This salary scale has 15 grades (GS-1 to GS-15), defined according to level of responsibility, type of work and required qualifications. Salary increases as the grade increases. Each grade has 10 steps, also with increasing salary. The 2004 Salary Table for federal law enforcement officers is posted online at the U.S. Office of Personnel Management (OPM) website: http://www.opm.gov/oca/04tables/html/491.asp. For those interested in salaries in a particular geographic area, a complete set of locality pay tables is also available at this website.

The *OOH* adds:

> Federal special agents and inspectors receive law enforcement availability pay (LEAP)—equal to 25 percent of the agent's grade and step—awarded because of the large amount of overtime that these agents are expected to work. For example, in 2003 FBI agents [entered] Federal service as GS-10 employees on the pay

TABLE 2–1   2002 Salaries for Sworn Local and County Law Enforcement Personnel

Rank	2002 Median Annual Salary	Lowest 10% Earned . . .	Middle 50% Earned . . .	Highest 10% Earned . . .
Police & Sheriff's Patrol Officers	$42,270	< $25,270	$32,300 − $53,500	$65,330+
Detectives & Criminal Investigators	$51,410	< $31,010	$39,010 − $65,980	$80,380+
Police & Detective Supervisors	$61,010	< $36,340	$47,210 − $74,610	$90,070+

SOURCE: *Occupational Outlook Handbook, 2004–05 Edition.* Bureau of Labor Statistics, 2004. Online: http://www.stats.bls.gov/oco

scale at a base salary of $39,115, yet earned about $48,890 a year with availability pay. They can advance to the GS-13 grade level in field nonsupervisory assignments at a base salary of $61,251, which is worth $76,560 with availability pay. FBI supervisory, management, and executive positions in grades GS-14 and GS-15 [paid] a base salary of about $72,381 or $85,140 a year, respectively, and equaled $90,480 or $106,430 per year including availability pay.

Fringe Benefits

As civil service employees, police officers typically receive generous benefits, including health insurance, life insurance, paid sick leave and paid vacation. The *OOH* notes: "In addition to the common benefits . . . most police and sheriffs' departments provide officers with special allowances for uniforms."

With a growing emphasis placed on advanced education, more departments are now picking up the costs associated with keeping their officers up-to-date on the latest police science techniques. According to *The Top 100* (p. 290): "Most city police departments offer various types of in-service study and training programs. . . . Training courses are provided by police academies, colleges, and other educational institutions. Some of the subjects offered are civil defense, foreign languages, and forgery detection. Some municipal police departments share the cost with their officers or pay all educational expenses if the officers are willing to work toward a college degree in either police work or police administration."

A further benefit, as stated in *The Top 100* (p. 290), is granted to officers when they leave their law enforcement careers: "In addition, most police departments offer retirement plans and retirement after 20 or 25 years of service, usually at half pay."

Promotions and Transfers

Law enforcement has definite upward salary limitations, but the main frustration for most is that promotions are limited, corresponding to the number of officers in the particular department.

> Advancement in [law enforcement] occupations is determined by several factors. An officer's eligibility for promotion may depend on a specified length of service, job performance, formal education and training courses, and results of written examinations. Those who become eligible for promotion are listed on the promotional list along with other qualified candidates. Promotions generally become available from six months to three years after starting, depending on the department. . . . Advancement to the very top-ranking positions, such as division, bureau, or department director or chief, may be made by direct political appointment. Most of these top positions are held by officers who have come up through the ranks (*The Top 100*, p. 289).

Larger city departments usually offer greater numbers of advancement opportunities, whereas police forces in smaller communities are typically more limited by the rank and number of law enforcement personnel needed (*The Top 100*, pp. 289–290). The fact is, most police officers will retire at the employment level at which they were hired. While intermediate supervisory positions between patrol officer and chief exist, there are far fewer of these than there are officers. A major contributing factor to police "burnout" is that many officers consider lack of promotion as a lack of recognition.

> Promotions in law enforcement are limited. Most police officers retire at the employment level at which they were hired.

Promotions and transfers generally come from within a department. Not only does the administration know the individual, but the promotion bolsters morale by serving as recognition for that officer's work. There are, however, benefits to bringing in an outsider, particularly if no one from within the department is qualified or if internal problems require someone without prior ties to the department. Lateral and promotional opportunities outside one's department are occurring more often.

Like other professions, getting ahead in law enforcement requires time and commitment—sometimes combined with luck. People do make sergeant, lieutenant, captain and chief. But you can't rise to the top without landing that first entry-level position. From there, your job-seeking skills become job-advancing skills.

Many other employment opportunities exist in specialty positions within a department. Becoming a specialist in such areas as traffic enforcement, crash investigation/reconstruction, juvenile, narcotics enforcement, K-9 handling or internal affairs may prevent officers from falling into a rut.

ADVANCED JOBS AND SPECIALIZATION

While a majority of officers do, and possibly should, begin their careers as generalists, most upwardly mobile, successful police professionals will specialize at some point in their careers: juvenile specialists, crime prevention specialists, polygraph specialists—the list goes on.

As technology continues to develop, specialists in these areas will be sought. As society's demographics change, becoming older and more culturally diverse, other needed specialties will emerge as well. In fact, *The Top 100* (p. 291) states: "The opportunities that become available [in law enforcement] . . . may be affected by technological, scientific, and other changes occurring today in police work. . . . New approaches in social science and psychological research are also changing the methodology used in working with public offenders. These trends indicate a future demand for more educated, specialized personnel."

> A need exists for specialization within the law enforcement field. While a majority of officers begin as generalists, those who wish to progress up the ladder of responsibility and salary will usually need to specialize.

This does not mean that the day of the generalist police officer on patrol is nearing an end. It is highly likely that patrol officers will continue as the backbone of any law enforcement agency. However, the reality is that every aspect of our world is becoming more complex and specialized, and the people putting themselves in a good position for future advancement will be those who anticipate and prepare for change by learning and honing specific skills.

Criminal justice involves many areas requiring special expertise in such diverse fields as training and firearms instruction, handwriting and fingerprint identification, or forensic sciences such as chemical and microscopic analysis. Others work as part of special units such as mounted, motorcycle, bicycle, harbor patrol or K-9 units, or as part of special weapons and tactics (SWAT) or other emergency response teams.

Other specialists needed in the criminal justice system include psychologists, physicians, scientists and accountants. The FBI, for example, specifically seeks people with very specialized training. Police officers with degrees in law, psychology or medicine are of great value to their departments. In addition, the many skills that can be taken into the private sector not only fill important departmental needs, but also create attractive and lucrative specialty positions. A law degree, for instance, is an excellent education for any area of law enforcement, whether the person wants to use it in a courtroom or "in the trenches." This topic is discussed further in Chapter 3. Expertise in such areas as drawing, photography, computers, firearms, flying or even public relations can help any police professional on the move. Almost *any* specific area of interest you have can be successfully woven into a satisfying and advancing career.

Specialized training or expertise, whether in the form of a law degree, a talent for drawing or the ability to pilot an aircraft, can benefit any law enforcement professional seeking advancement.

Preparing for advancement may be as basic as obtaining a generalized advanced education to effectively interact with those of similar educational levels in other professions. It may be acknowledging the increasing cultural diversity of the United States and learning a foreign language or two. It may be acquiring a degree in management, computer science or public relations. It's your call. *Anything* you can do to set yourself positively apart from others is important. If you have the chance to acquire specialized skills, take that chance. Don't merely keep up with the others. Take advantage of the myriad opportunities available to meet the challenge and forge ahead.

Working in law enforcement with specialized degrees can provide attractive pay and benefits. The downside, however, is that your work may not vary and travel may be a requirement. In particular, federal agencies may require a number of relocations throughout a career, which can be seen as exciting opportunities or extreme inconveniences. To illustrate the wide variety of career options within law enforcement, following is a brief look at six specialty areas: juvenile justice officer, medicolegal death investigator (MDI), crime scene investigator (CSI), armed sky marshal, U.S. Mint Police and humane law enforcement (HLE) officer.

The Juvenile Officer

For those who enjoy working with youths and families, the juvenile system provides very satisfying employment. With the growing amount of juvenile delinquency and serious, violent offenses committed by youths, the juvenile justice system is expanding at a phenomenal rate and should be a major employer of personnel in the years ahead.

Work in the juvenile justice system is very challenging, and the need for juvenile officers is growing.

The juvenile officer faces a particular challenge in that the system "lumps" youths who are violent criminals together with youths who commit relatively minor offenses (such as smoking) and youths who are victims of neglect or abuse. According to Hess and Drowns (2004, p. 72): "An extreme challenge facing the juvenile justice system is the one-pot approach to youths evident throughout history. The one-pot approach lumps children and youths who are abused and neglected, those who commit minor offenses and those who commit vicious, violent crimes into the same judicial 'pot.'"

In most departments, juvenile work is considered a promotion after three to five years as a patrol officer. In addition, many departments have school resource officers (SROs) who work within local schools and whose roles include the multiple duties of law enforcement officer, teacher and counselor. According to

Burke (2001, p. 73): "The tragedies that have occurred in schools in the recent years combined with the Department of Justice dedicating millions of dollars to hiring SROs for schools have made SROs the fastest growing field in law enforcement."

Medicolegal Death Investigator (MDI)

More than 3,100 death investigation jurisdictions are scattered across the country. The two primary systems used by these jurisdictions to investigate deaths, particularly sudden deaths, are the elected sheriff-coroner system and the appointed medical examiner (ME) system. Whichever system is used, it is becoming more common for these professionals to be referred to as medicolegal death investigators (MDIs), a term indicating the requisite combination of medical and legal knowledge often required to successfully resolve a death investigation.

The American Board of Medicolegal Death Investigators (ABMDI) was created in 1998, with support from the U.S. Centers for Disease Control and Prevention, by veteran, practicing medicolegal death investigators from throughout the United States who were involved in the development of standards supported by the National Institutes of Justice. The ABMDI stresses that those interested in this field must have a combination of education and skills encompassing the areas of medicine and law.

A "Medicolegal Death Investigation Course," offered three times each year at the St. Louis University School of Medicine, pools investigators, law enforcement officers, forensic scientists and physicians (not forensic pathologists)—anyone who investigates deaths for medical examiner/coroner offices—into the same class, despite their varied educational and professional backgrounds, because the particular skill set required for MDIs is the same.

In addition to studying basic death and homicide investigation, medicolegal training academies teach investigators how to deliver death notification and deal with the grief process. Other responsibilities include collecting evidence and taking photographs, which are sent to the state police forensic science lab for examination. The lab, in turn, issues a report back to the investigator who then tries to recreate the scene.

The Amador County, California, Sheriff-Coroner's website (http://www.sheriff.co.amador.ca.us/coroner.htm) states:

> The mission of the Coroner's Office is to serve and protect the interests of Amador County residents by determining the circumstances, manner, and cause of sudden or unexplained deaths in the county, while simultaneously ensuring that decedents and their families are treated with the utmost dignity and respect.
>
> This mission is accomplished by a team of peace officer deputy coroners, forensic pathologists, support staff, as well as administrative and clerical personnel who contribute to the investigation of all deaths within Amador County. . . . This investigative process includes: death scene review, body identification, and a wide range of forensic science examinations and testing, notification of the decedent's next of kin, preparation or authorization of the issuance of death certificates and disposition of the remains of the deceased.

A job posting in the ABMDI Newsletter (2003, p. 5) for a Forensic Investigator reads:

> The Forensic Investigator position involves all aspects of medicolegal death investigations. The Forensic Investigators working in this office are responsible for a wide variety of death investigations, including responding to and conducting scene investigations on non-natural deaths.

The Forensic Investigators interact with numerous law enforcement agencies, hospitals, government agencies, attorneys, and the residents of the community. This position requires the ability to handle stressful situations, excellent critical thinking and problem solving skills, competence, and the desire to be involved with a professional organization. . . . The compensation for this position will be commensurate with education and experience, at a minimum of $37,000/year, plus overtime.

Crime Scene Investigator (CSI)

Popularized by recent television shows, this is an intriguing job to consider. As further discussed in this book, the vast majority of people doing crime scene work were promoted to it from law enforcement positions rather than "just getting the job." While it can occur, the likelihood of doing this specialized work without the beneficial experience of "coming up through the ranks" is highly improbable.

If you've watched the shows, you have an idea of what people in this career do. However, the job is not nearly as glamorous as the entertainment industry leads us to believe. Weisberg (2001, p. 45) describes the role of the Crime Scene Investigations Unit (CSU):

> The CSU provides support services in the form of crime scene processing, fingerprint identification, and forensic photography. The CSU responds to major crime scenes to detect, preserve, document, impound and collect physical evidence.
>
> The Unit assists in the identification of unknown subjects, witnesses, and victims involved in criminal investigations. . . . The CSU will work closely in conjunction with the Detective Bureau in providing assistance in follow-up investigations, as well as subject apprehension and arrest. Members of the CSU can be either sworn or nonsworn.

The increased interest in CSI can be seen in some colleges offering a degree in crime scene technology. Capsambelis (2002, p. 119) notes that, in addition to general education requirements (including applied ethics), major course requirements include crime scene technology, photography, fingerprint classification, biological evidence, crime scene safety and courtroom presentation of scientific evidence.

Armed Sky Marshals

Until the deadly September 11, 2001, airborne terrorist attacks on the World Trade Center and the Pentagon, most Americans had never heard of the Federal Air Marshals. Hawley (2001) notes: "The FAA has always been secretive about the air marshals, refusing to divulge their number, how they work or what they look like. The assault teams wear masks when giving rare public demonstrations." In the wake of the attacks, however, several congressional leaders and members of the Air Transportation Association, the trade organization for the U.S. airlines, have strongly urged expansion of the air marshal program, and it is likely this "shadowy force" will be strengthened in the coming years.

Among other skills, sky marshals must be very comfortable with firearms. An FAA spokesperson states: "They have some of the highest, if not the highest, firearms qualifications in the federal government. They don't miss" (Hawley). Each agent spends at least three hours a week in shooting practice at their training base near Atlantic City, NJ, which includes a five-story simulated control tower, three outdoor shooting ranges with moving targets and two retired airliners.

Mint Police

Established in 1792, the U.S. Mint Police is one of the nation's oldest police forces. Mint Police are responsible for protecting the country's gold, silver and coins located at Mint facilities in Fort Knox, Denver, San Francisco, West Point, Philadelphia and Washington, DC. Hanson (2001, p. 66) states:

> Currently, each mint is staffed with firearms instructors, field training officers, an emergency response team, a hostage negotiator and a detective specializing in areas of cyber-fraud. These officers have backgrounds in the Secret Service, FBI, Defense Department and local police departments. Maintaining a full roster, however, has been difficult due to a 20 percent turnover rate and the fact that the Mint Police have maintained a low profile in the past, making applications somewhat sparse.

Humane Law Enforcement (HLE) Officer

The American Society for the Prevention of Cruelty to Animals (ASPCA), headquartered in New York City, staffs a Humane Law Enforcement (HLE) Department of 15 uniformed and plainclothes officers, dedicated to investigating crimes against the city's animal population. As part of its original charter from the state of New York in 1866, the ASPCA was given the legal authority to investigate and make arrests for crimes against animals. For three seasons, cable TV's Animal Planet channel has aired *Animal Precinct,* an award-winning reality series that takes viewers on patrol with HLE agents.

While not a requirement, many of the officers have backgrounds in law enforcement. For example, the vice president of the HLE Department was a 27-year veteran of the New York City Police Department prior to joining the ASPCA. Three of the current special agents are former NYPD officers, and another agent has held a variety of criminal justice positions, including federal police officer with the U.S. Veteran Affairs Department, park ranger and private investigator. The ASPCA's website (http://www.aspca.org) suggests:

> When preparing for a career in Humane Law Enforcement, your choice of schooling is really up to you. Prior experience as police officer, park ranger, or peace officer may help make you a more attractive candidate. Many states offer specific training for humane law enforcement. In addition, classes in criminology and animal sciences will also complement a career in an humane law enforcement division.

Furthermore:

> As mandated by the New York State Municipal Police Council, Humane Law Enforcement gives new agents a 40-hour Peace Officer training class and a 47-hour firearms class. After the agents complete the courses, they are assigned to take complaints from members of the public for a period of two weeks. This gives them an opportunity to learn about the different kinds of cases that are reported and develop basic interviewing skills. When the two weeks are over, agents are assigned to work with a training officer for a period of six months. During this time, they are shown how to handle the animals and people they encounter while responding to complaints. Humane Law Enforcement also provides training for police officers and employees of other humane organizations. This training consists of on- or off-site classes and accompanying agents on investigations, when appropriate.

In 2003, the HLE department received approximately 45,000 complaints of suspected animal cruelty that resulted in the investigation of 3,809 cases and 277 arrests. Following the September 11, 2001, attacks on the World Trade Center, HLE agents and investigators rescued over 200 animals left homeless and/or injured by the event. In addition to investigating abuse and other animal-related issues, many humane officers perform community education services, taking their expertise into schools, talking with students about pet care and answering their questions. Humane officers also train police officers in the skills needed to handle situations in the field where animals are involved, such as guard dogs at drug "labs." Animal control officers may accompany police officers on raids when an informant has warned of a guard dog in the house. Animal control may tranquilize or otherwise contain a threatening animal until police are able to complete their duties, making sure no one gets bitten in the process.

The Humane Society of the United States (HSUS), Investigative Services, works to expose animal fighting, the fur trade, greyhound racing and the Norwegian whaling industry, among other issues. HSUS investigators handle national and international animal exploitation and abuse issues. Primary responsibilities include conducting (primarily undercover) field investigations, researching, analyzing and providing input on strategy for proposed investigations. Investigators document acts of cruelty, neglect and exploitation through still and video photography and write reports on the investigations. HSUS lists as qualifications a bachelor's degree and five or more years of experience in major undercover criminal investigations, with the ideal candidate having experience at a major metropolitan police force or federal agency. Frequent travel is required. Salary is in the mid to high $40s with excellent benefits (http://www.hsus.org).

The HSUS and the Law Enforcement Training Institute (LETI) at the University of Missouri have collaborated to develop the National Cruelty Investigations School to train animal cruelty investigators at the federal, state and local levels; humane society cruelty investigators; animal control officers; and police officers and sheriff's deputies responsible for the investigation of animal cruelty complaints.

Other Venues Requiring Law Enforcement

In addition to the more traditional police agencies, you might consider working in a more specialized environment. Many institutions, facilities and industries operate their own police forces. Examples include college and university campus police and transportation/transit police for railroads and airports.

INTERNATIONAL JOBS

The vast majority of career areas have a new emphasis on international employment. Law enforcement is no exception. Many people are eager to travel, and if it can be part of their job, all the better.

International jobs are available in law enforcement, but obtaining them is not easy. Most overseas positions are classified jobs with special requirements such as security clearances and confidentiality. Because of such factors as jurisdiction, these jobs tend to be covert. Federal agencies such as the FBI, DEA and Secret Service have agents around the world. Although it is not part of the criminal justice or law enforcement field, the Central Intelligence Agency (CIA) also offers opportunities for excitement and travel. Again, travel can be a perk as well as a potential difficulty.

As the field of law enforcement expands, so does the geographic availability of jobs. International job opportunities in law enforcement are slowly increasing, but obtaining them is still difficult.

In addition to the multitude of sworn positions, both domestic and abroad, you may also find a nonsworn position in a career field related to law enforcement.

NONSWORN CAREER OPTIONS RELATED TO LAW ENFORCEMENT

Positions traditionally filled by sworn personnel are now often being filled by nonsworn personnel. The simple reason for this trend is economic—nonsworn personnel may be every bit as qualified and yet need not be paid at the salary level of sworn, often unionized, personnel. More regular hours, the varied and interesting assignments, and the relative lack of danger are just a few factors that might motivate you to consider some exciting careers that *support* law enforcement. These positions also may serve as a "stepping stone" to a sworn job. You can work out of a police station or sheriff's office without being subjected to some of the less desirable aspects of police work.

> Civilians are becoming more common in various careers that support traditional law enforcement, including crime prevention specialists, juvenile specialists, animal control officers and dispatchers.

Community Crime Prevention Specialists

The last decade has seen an increasing interest in and reliance on community crime prevention. While some law enforcement agencies have sworn officers conduct such work, others assign civilians. Crime prevention specialists have the luxury of working with the community in a positive effort *before* crisis occurs, with the hope of *preventing* crime. Or, they may be the contact that lends valuable assistance after a crisis.

Crime prevention specialists educate the community about such issues as locks, lighting, alarms and personal safety. It is an excellent opportunity to be creative because much of crime prevention involves developing programs, designing brochures, presenting speeches and even directing videos and slide presentations. Salaries vary, but the more regular schedule and the opportunity to step into the private sector make this an area worth considering.

Juvenile Specialists

As previously discussed, the juvenile justice system is expanding at a phenomenal rate and is projected to be a major employer of personnel in the future. In addition to jobs with police agencies, careers in juvenile justice include group home childcare workers and counselors, as well as intake officers and childcare workers in juvenile detention facilities or correctional facilities, such as boot camps, juvenile probation and so on.

If you enjoy working with youths, a career in the juvenile justice system may be right for you. If you think you might be interested in this area of law enforcement, start volunteering with some youth groups to gain experience working with youths and to confirm that this is, indeed, an area of special interest to you. Some suggest this area offers the greatest opportunity to affect the community.

Animal Control Officers

Animal control is one area within the realm of community service that can effectively serve as both an entry-level stepping stone to a job in law enforcement or as a specialty area that many find rewarding in itself. If you have a special interest in animal welfare, this is an area where you can get paid for doing what you love. In recent years, there has been a strong push to professionalize animal control and humane investigations. While some jurisdictions have police officers or sheriff's deputies handle these tasks, others are turning to civilians to fulfill this role.

Dispatchers

Police, fire and ambulance dispatchers, also called public safety dispatchers, monitor the location of emergency service personnel within their jurisdiction. The *OOH* states:

> These workers dispatch the appropriate type and number of units in response to calls for assistance. Dispatchers, or call takers, often are the first people the public contacts when emergency assistance is required. If certified for emergency medical services, the dispatcher may provide medical instruction to those on the scene of the emergency until the medical staff arrives.

> Police, fire, and ambulance dispatchers work in a variety of settings: a police station, a fire station, a hospital, or, increasingly, a centralized communications center. In many areas, the police department serves as the communications center. In these situations, all emergency calls go to the police department, where a dispatcher handles the police calls and screens the others before transferring them to the appropriate service.

> When handling calls, dispatchers question each caller carefully to determine the type, seriousness, and location of the emergency. The information obtained is posted either electronically by computer or, with decreasing frequency, by hand. . . .

> When appropriate, dispatchers stay in close contact with other service providers—for example, a police dispatcher would monitor the response of the fire department when there is a major fire. In a medical emergency, dispatchers keep in close touch not only with the dispatched units, but also with the caller. They may give extensive first-aid instructions before the emergency personnel arrive, while the caller is waiting for the ambulance. Dispatchers continuously give updates on the patient's condition to the ambulance personnel and often serve as a link between the medical staff in a hospital and the emergency medical technicians in the ambulance.

Dispatchers held 262,000 jobs in 2002, about one-third (86,460) of which were for police, fire and ambulance services. The majority of these dispatchers worked for state and local governments—primarily local police and fire departments.

Employment of public safety dispatchers is expected to grow about as fast as average for all occupations through 2012. The *OOH* states: "The growing and aging population will increase demand for emergency services and stimulate employment growth of police, fire, and ambulance dispatchers. Many districts are consolidating their communications centers into a shared areawide facility. Individuals with computer skills and experience will have a greater opportunity for employment as public-safety dispatchers."

FIRE SERVICE

Because many communities have a public safety department, encompassing both law enforcement and firefighting responsibilities, a look at careers in the fire service seems appropriate for this chapter.

> As with police work, a career in the fire service attracts many applicants seeking a position that combines challenging, action-oriented work and excitement with the chance to perform an essential public service.

Some communities have full-time, paid firefighters while others maintain a staff of volunteers, also referred to as *paid-on-call,* because almost all "volunteer" departments provide some, albeit minimal, pay. The *OOH* reports: "According to the United States Fire Administration, nearly 70 percent of fire companies are staffed by volunteer firefighters. Paid career firefighters held about 282,000 jobs in 2002. First-line supervisors/managers of firefighting and prevention workers held about 63,000 jobs; and fire inspectors held about 14,000." Some communities have experimented with private fire companies. Their responsibilities are generally the same—to protect the public against the dangers of fire and other emergencies:

> Firefighters have assumed a range of responsibilities, including emergency medical services. In fact, most calls to which firefighters respond involve medical emergencies, and about half of all fire departments provide ambulance service for victims. Firefighters receive training in emergency medical procedures, and many fire departments require them to be certified as emergency medical technicians.
>
> Firefighters work in a variety of settings, including urban and suburban areas, airports, chemical plants, other industrial sites, and rural areas like grasslands and forests. In addition, some firefighters work in hazardous materials units that are trained for the control, prevention, and cleanup of oil spills and other hazardous materials incidents (*OOH*).

Between extinguishing fires and responding to medical emergencies, firefighters clean and maintain equipment, conduct practice drills and fire inspections, and participate in physical fitness activities. They also prepare written reports on fire incidents. Fire service officers are often involved in prevention efforts including community education aimed at public assemblies, school groups and civic organizations.

Some firefighters become certified fire inspectors, checking existing structures for fire code compliance and working with developers and planners to ensure new buildings meet those codes. Other firefighters specialize in fire investigation, becoming involved when the cause of a fire is suspicious, perhaps criminal negligence or arson. These investigators collect evidence, interview witnesses, write fire reports and, if necessary, testify in court.

Working conditions are often strenuous, dangerous and complex. Firefighting involves risk of injury or death from structural collapse, exposure to flames and smoke, and the increased potential for traffic crashes when responding to alarms. As witnessed during the tragic unfolding of events on September 11, 2001, when terrorists attacked the World Trade Center and Pentagon, firefighters (and other first responders) are expected to run *into* a situation that all others are running *away from*. Firefighters may also be exposed to poisonous, flammable or explosive gases or chemicals, as well as radioactive or other hazardous materials, presenting immediate and/or long-term negative health impacts.

Shift hours are longer and vary more widely than hours of most other workers. Many full-time firefighters work shifts that last several days in a row, requiring them to eat and sleep at the fire station. In addition, many work more than 50 hours a week, and sometimes they may work even longer. In some agencies, they are on duty for 24 hours, then off for 48 hours, and receive an extra day off at intervals. In others, they work a day shift of 10 hours for 3 or 4 days, a night shift of 14 hours for 3 or 4 nights, have 3 or 4 days off, and then repeat the cycle. In addition, firefighters often work extra hours at fires and other emergencies and are regularly assigned to work on holidays. Fire lieutenants and fire captains often work the same hours as the firefighters they supervise. Duty hours include time when firefighters study, train and perform fire prevention duties.

In 2002, the median hourly earnings of firefighters were $17.92 in local government, $13.58 in state government and $15.96 in the federal government. First-line supervisors/managers of firefighting and prevention workers employed in local government earned about $56,390 a year in 2002, and fire inspectors and investigators employed in local government earned about $46,820 a year (*OOH*).

Benefits typically include medical and liability insurance, pension plans, vacation time, sick leave and some paid holidays. Nearly all fire departments provide necessary uniforms and equipment. Firefighters are generally covered by pension plans, often providing retirement at half pay after 25 years of service or if disabled in the line of duty.

The job outlook for firefighters is projected to remain keenly competitive, with employment expected to grow about as fast as the average for all occupations through 2012. Turnover in this field is unusually low and layoffs are uncommon. According to the *OOH:*

> Applicants for municipal firefighting jobs generally must pass a written exam; tests of strength, physical stamina, coordination, and agility; and a medical examination that includes drug screening. Workers may be monitored on a random basis for drug use after accepting employment. Examinations are generally open to persons who are at least 18 years of age and have a high school education or the equivalent. Those who receive the highest scores in all phases of testing have the best chances for appointment. The completion of community college courses in fire science may improve an applicant's chances for appointment. In recent years, an increasing proportion of entrants to this occupation have had some postsecondary education.
>
> As a rule, entry-level workers in large fire departments are trained for several weeks at the department's training center or academy. Through classroom instruction and practical training, the recruits study firefighting techniques, fire prevention, hazardous materials control, local building codes, and emergency medical procedures, including first aid and cardiopulmonary resuscitation. They also learn how to use axes, chain saws, fire extinguishers, ladders, and other firefighting and rescue equipment. After successfully completing this training, they are assigned to a fire company, where they undergo a period of probation.

Personal qualities necessary for firefighting include mental alertness, self-discipline, courage, mechanical aptitude, endurance, strength and a sense of public service. Continuing education is also part of the job, as firefighters must stay current with new technology and equipment and must continuously practice their skills and coordination with others on their team. The *OOH* adds:

> Most experienced firefighters continue studying to improve their job performance and prepare for promotion examinations. To progress to higher level positions, they acquire expertise in advanced firefighting equipment and techniques, building construction, emergency medical technology, writing, public speaking, management and budgeting procedures, and public relations.
>
> Opportunities for promotion depend upon written examination results, job performance, interviews, and seniority. Increasingly, fire departments use assessment centers, which simulate a variety of actual job performance tasks, to screen for the best candidates for promotion. The line of promotion usually is to engineer, lieutenant, captain, battalion chief, assistant chief, deputy chief, and finally to chief. Many fire departments now require a bachelor's degree, preferably in fire science, public administration, or a related field, for promotion to positions higher than battalion chief. A master's degree is required for executive fire officer certification from the National Fire Academy and for State chief officer certification.

The *OOH* also notes: "A number of fire departments have accredited apprenticeship programs lasting up to 5 years . . . [that] combine formal, technical instruction with on-the-job training under the supervision of experienced firefighters. Technical instruction covers subjects such as firefighting techniques and equipment, chemical hazards associated with various combustible building materials, emergency medical procedures, and fire prevention and safety. . . . Some States also have extensive firefighter training and certification programs. In addition, a number of colleges and universities offer courses leading to 2- or 4-year degrees in fire engineering or fire science. Many fire departments offer firefighters incentives such as tuition reimbursement or higher pay for completing advanced training."

EMERGENCY MEDICAL TECHNICIANS (EMTs) AND PARAMEDICS

As discussed, many jurisdictions have a public safety department combining law enforcement, fire service and emergency medical response activities. The medical response component may be assigned to the police, to the fire department or to an entirely separate entity.

> Emergency medical technicians (EMTs) and paramedics respond to a variety of incidents where people are in need of immediate medical attention, including automobile crashes, heart attacks, drownings, childbirths and gunshot wounds.

EMTs and paramedics provide stabilizing medical care on site and transport the sick or injured to a medical facility. Some EMTs work as part of a flight crew that transports critically ill or injured patients to hospital trauma centers via helicopter. At medical facilities, EMTs and paramedics help transfer patients to the emergency department and report their observations and actions to emergency room staff. After each run, EMTs and paramedics replace used supplies and check equipment. If a transported patient had a contagious disease, EMTs and paramedics decontaminate the interior of the ambulance and report the case to the proper authorities. Formal training and certification is required of all EMTs and paramedics. All 50 states possess a certification procedure.

Working conditions of these professionals vary but are usually physically strenuous and fast-paced. EMTs and paramedics work both indoors and outdoors, in all types of weather. Their jobs involve considerable kneeling, bending and heavy lifting. EMTs and paramedics should be emotionally stable and have good dexterity, agility and physical coordination. They also need good eyesight (corrective lenses may be used) with accurate color vision. They come in regular contact with bodily fluids and face increased exposure to diseases, some of which may be fatal. They may also be attacked or assaulted when responding to calls involving people who are high on drugs or psychologically disturbed.

Earnings of EMTs vary based on employment setting, geographical location, training and experience. The median annual salary of EMTs and paramedics was $24,030 in 2002, with the lowest-paid EMTs earning less than $15,531 annually and the highest-paid earning more than $41,980. EMTs who are part of fire or police departments receive the same benefits as firefighters or police officers.

EMTs and paramedics held approximately 179,000 jobs in 2002, not including the thousands of volunteers who supplement these services. Employment of EMTs is projected to grow faster than average for all occupations through 2012. According to the *OOH:*

> Most opportunities for EMTs and paramedics are expected to be found in private ambulance services. Competition will be greater for jobs in local government, including fire, police, and independent third-service rescue squad departments, in which salaries and benefits tend to be slightly better. Opportunities will be best for those who have advanced certifications, such as EMT-Intermediate and EMT-Paramedic, as clients and patients demand higher levels of care before arriving at the hospital.

CONCLUSION

A multitude of agencies exist for those considering a career in law enforcement or related fields, including federal agencies, state agencies, county agencies and local agencies. To find the greatest employment potential, consider agencies that have the greatest number of employees. Remember, more than half of all law enforcement positions are found in local police departments, and civilian opportunities exist at all three levels—local, state and federal.

Keep in mind a need exists for specialization within the law enforcement field. While a majority of officers begin as generalists, those who wish to progress up the ladder of responsibility and salary will usually need to specialize. Specialized training or expertise, whether in the form of a law degree, a talent for drawing or the ability to pilot an aircraft, can benefit any law enforcement professional seeking advancement. Also consider that as the field of law enforcement expands, so does the geographic availability of jobs. International job opportunities in law enforcement are slowly increasing, but obtaining them remains difficult.

Civilians are becoming more common in the various careers that support traditional law enforcement, including crime prevention specialists, juvenile specialists, animal control officers and dispatchers.

Other public safety careers that routinely interface with law enforcement include firefighting and emergency medical response. As with police work, a career in the fire service attracts many applicants seeking a position that combines challenging, action-oriented work and excitement with the chance to perform an essential public service. Emergency medical technicians (EMTs) and paramedics respond to incidents where people need immediate medical attention, including automobile crashes, heart attacks, drownings, childbirths and gunshot wounds.

AN INSIDER'S VIEW

IT'S NOT LIKE ON TV

Dennis L. Conroy, PhD

Former Director of the Employee Assistance Program
St. Paul (Minnesota) Police Department

It is crucial for those anticipating a career in law enforcement or private security to realize they will get a view of the world no one else has. They will do and see things that are boring, exciting and amusing. They will also do and see things that are painful, tragic and sometimes terrifying. Careers in law enforcement and private security can be rewarding, but the applicant must also remember there may very well be a "price to pay."

Very few, if any, people entering law enforcement know what they are getting into. *It's not like on television.* The endings aren't always successful, and officers don't always get respect. Those entering law enforcement look forward to becoming a police officer and intend to wear the uniform with pride. The lessons these new officers learn are often very difficult to accept and frequently result in alcoholism, physical problems, divorce and even suicide.

The first lesson new officers learn is that not everyone respects police officers simply because *they are police officers.* Officers soon learn that a large number of people they deal with do not even want them around most of the time. Some will call officers names like "Pig," lie to them, fight with them and even spit on them—just because they are officers. Officers subjected to such treatment discover they are not even permitted to respond except to defend themselves from the most grievous physical harm. Even in that response, they will frequently be challenged on the level of force used and will have to justify such actions later.

The next step in the discovery process occurs when officers learn they are *expected* not to respond when spit on. Being spit on is considered "part of the job." Officers learn that everyone else in the criminal justice system demands respect and inflicts sanctions on those refusing to comply. Can you imagine a defendant spitting on a prosecutor or a judge in a courtroom with impunity? But officers are prohibited from imposing their own sanctions.

New officers are usually shocked at the amount of pain and suffering in the world. Most police officers have grown up without exposure to situations requiring police intervention. They have not seen young children, or even babies, who have been beaten or killed simply for crying. They have not had to talk with and console an elderly couple whose house has been burglarized by teenage vandals, their world invaded and destroyed for no apparent reason. They have probably never had to console a rape victim and tell her that her "hell" may only be starting because if she wants to prosecute the offender she will have to relive the experience time and again and defend her own morality each time.

As new officers learn these lessons, they respond, they change. Officers learn that to work with these problems day after day, they must build a suit of armor to protect themselves. They build this armor by (1) becoming less personally involved and (2) not believing in anyone or anything. While such armor protects officers from work-related issues, it also changes them as individuals.

Many officers find they become cynical and isolated. They lose the capacity to believe in anything or anybody because they have seen or experienced so much disappointment in performing their duties. They see humanity at its worst and the system in almost constant failure. It becomes increasingly difficult to believe in successful outcomes. This cynicism is not only an "at work" attitude, but soon pervades every aspect of the officers' lives.

As officers become more and more cynical, they believe less and less in successful outcomes and begin to invest less and less in personal relationships. This can lead to isolation and loneliness. Officers in the end may have no one but themselves, and they are not sure that they can even believe in themselves.

If applicants know they are likely to experience change, this change can be monitored and, along with the law enforcement career, have a positive outcome. Officers will find rewards in the little things they can do to help individuals they come in contact with. They can brighten a small child's life with just a smile or brief "Hello." They can make an elderly couple feel a bit more secure by driving by and taking the time to wave, showing them that someone cares. As a result, the officers feel better knowing that they made even the smallest difference in the lives of those they have sworn to "protect and serve."

Dr. Dennis Conroy, *licensed psychologist, has recently retired after 30-plus years of service with the St. Paul (Minnesota) Police Department. During his career, he had such diverse assignments as patrol officer, juvenile officer, patrol supervisor, vice/narcotics investigator, director of the Professional Development Institute, director of the Field Training Program and director of the Employee Assistance Program. His clinical experience spans more than 20 years and includes working with children, adolescents and adults. Dr. Conroy has also taught upper-level college courses blending the fields of psychology and law enforcement, including Adolescent Psychology, Human Behavior in Law Enforcement, Police Stress, Peer Counseling in Law Enforcement and The Psychology of Victims.*

INSIDER'S VIEW ONLINE

An additional *Insider's View* for this chapter is "A Wealth of Opportunities" by Molly Koivamaki, found on the Wadsworth website: http://www.wadsworth.com/criminaljustice_d/.

MIND STRETCHES

1. What do most people think of when they think of a "police job"? Where did you acquire the information on which you base your answer?

2. Do you see law enforcement changing to respond to new challenges?

3. Why might you *not* want to consider a job as a police officer "on the street"?

4. Do "nonsworn" law enforcement positions, such as civilian crime prevention specialists, have career benefits not available to police officers? What negatives would you want to be aware of in considering a career such as a community service officer?

5. What other vocational or avocational skills could blend well with a police career? Can you think of unique skills that could make a candidate for a job more attractive to a hiring agency?

6. Why might someone interested in a career in policing fail to consider other jobs in the security or criminal justice fields?

7. Can law enforcement continue as it has been in serving communities, or is some change inevitable? What change do you foresee, if any? What can you begin doing right now to meet the challenge?

8. Why do you think the entertainment field is so obsessed with law enforcement? Do you think this obsession helps or hurts the profession? Why?

9. What is your favorite television police show? Why? Do you think television and the movies have influenced your career choice?

10. Are police salaries more or less than you had anticipated? Does salary affect your decision as to what field of employment you will eventually pursue? Why or why not?

REFERENCES

American Board of Medicolegal Death Investigators. *A.B.M.D.I. News*. October 2003, p. 5.

American Society for the Prevention of Cruelty to Animals. 2004. On the Internet at http://www.aspca.org

Burke, Sean. "The Advantages of a School Resource Officer." *Law and Order,* September 2001, pp. 73–75.

Capsambelis, Christopher B. "So Your Student Wants to Be a Crime Scene Technician?" *Journal of Criminal Justice Education,* Spring 2002, pp. 113–124.

Department of Homeland Security. On the Internet at http://www.dhs.gov

Hanson, Marce. "U.S. Mint Police." *Police,* August 2001, pp. 66–67.

Hawley, Chris. "Armed Sky Marshals May Increase." *Associated Press,* as reported on LATimes.com (*Los Angeles Times*), September 15, 2001.

Hess, Kären M. and Drowns, Robert W. *Juvenile Justice,* 4th ed. Belmont, CA: Wadsworth Publishing Company, 2004.

Hickman, Matthew J. *Tribal Law Enforcement, 2000.* Washington, DC: U.S. Department of Justice, Bureau of Justice Statistics Fact Sheet, January 2003. (NCJ 197936)

Hickman, Matthew J. and Reaves, Brian A. *Local Police Departments, 2000.* Washington, DC: U.S. Department of Justice, Bureau of Justice Statistics, January 2003a. (NCJ 196002)

Hickman, Matthew J. and Reaves, Brian A. *Sheriffs' Offices, 2000.* Washington, DC: U.S. Department of Justice, Bureau of Justice Statistics, January 2003b. (NCJ 196534)

Horrigan, Michael W. "Employment Projections to 2012: Concepts and Context." *Monthly Labor Review,* February 2004, pp. 3–22.

International Association of Chiefs of Police. On the Internet at http://www.theiacp.org

National Law Enforcement Officers Memorial Fund. On the Internet at http://www.nleomf.com

Occupational Outlook Handbook, 2004–05 Edition. U.S. Department of Labor, Bureau of Labor Statistics. Washington, DC: U.S. Government Printing Office, 2004. On the Internet at http://stats.bls.gov/oco

Reaves, Brian A. and Bauer, Lynn M. *Federal Law Enforcement Officers, 2002.* Washington, DC: Bureau of Justice Statistics Bulletin, August 2003. (NCJ 199995)

Reaves, Brian A. and Hickman, Matthew J. *Census of State and Local Law Enforcement Agencies, 2000.* Washington, DC: U.S. Department of Justice, Bureau of Justice Statistics Bulletin, October 2002a. (NCJ 194066)

Reaves, Brian A. and Hickman, Matthew J. *Police Departments in Large Cities, 1990–2000.* Washington, DC: Bureau of Justice Statistics Special Report, May 2002b. (NCJ 175703)

The Top 100: The Fastest Growing Careers for the 21st Century, 3rd ed. Chicago: Ferguson Publishing Company, 2001.

Weisberg, Michael W. "Recent Directions in Crime Scene Investigations." *Law Enforcement Trainer,* March/April 2001, pp. 44–48.

Wrobleski, Henry M. and Hess, Kären M. *Introduction to Law Enforcement and Criminal Justice,* 7th ed. Belmont, CA: Wadsworth Publishing Company, 2003.

HELPFUL WEBSITES

Air Force Office of Special Investigations (AFOSI)
http://www.afpc.randolph.af.mil/osi

American Board of Medicolegal Death
Investigators (ABMDI)
http://www.slu.edu/organizations/abmdi

American Federation of Police and Concerned Citizens
http://www.aphf.org/afp-cc.html

American Society for the Prevention of Cruelty to
Animals (ASPCA)
http://www.aspca.org

Association of Public Safety Communications
Officials (dispatch)
http://www.apcointl.org

Bureau of Alcohol, Tobacco, Firearms and
Explosives (ATF)
http://www.atf.gov

Bureau of Diplomatic Security (DS), U.S.
Department of State
http://www.state.gov/m/ds/career

Bureau of Indian Affairs (BIA)
http://www.doi.gov/bureau-indian-affairs.html

Bureau of Justice Statistics (BJS)
http://www.ojp.usdoj.gov/bjs

Bureau of Labor Statistics (BLS), U.S. Department of Labor
http://www.bls.gov

Drug Enforcement Administration (DEA)
http://www.usdoj.gov/dea

Federal Air Marshals
http://www.faa.gov

Federal Bureau of Investigation (FBI)
http://www.fbi.gov

Federal Bureau of Prisons (BOP)
http://www.bop.gov

Federal Computer Incident Response Center (FedCIRC)
http://www.us-cert.gov/federal/

Federal Law Enforcement Training Center (FLETC)
http://fletc.gov

Humane Society of the United States (HSUS)
http://www.hsus.org

Internal Revenue Service (IRS)
http://www.jobs.irs.gov/mn-LawEnforcement.html

International Association of Chiefs of Police (IACP)
http://www.theiacp.org

International Association of Firefighters
http://www.iaff.org

International Union of Police Associations (IUPA)
http://www.iupa.org

INTERPOL (International Law Enforcement)
http://www.usdoj.gov/usncb

National Association of Emergency Medical Technicians (NAEMT)
http://www.naemt.org

National Association of Investigative Specialists (NAIS)
http://www.pimall.com/nais/nais.menu.html

National Association of Police Organizations (NAPO)
http://www.napo.org

National Cruelty Investigations School (Animal Cruelty)
http://www.missouri.edu/~letiwww/animal3.htm

National Fire Academy, U.S. Fire Administration
http://www.usfa.fema.gov/nfa

National Highway Transportation Safety Administration (NHTSA)
http://www.nhtsa.dot.gov

National Law Enforcement Officers Memorial Fund (NLEOMF)
http://www.nleomf.com

National Park Service
http://www.nps.gov

National Police Officers Association of America
http://www.npoaa.tripod.com

National Registry of Emergency Medical Technicians (NREMT)
http://www.nremt.org

Occupational Outlook Handbook
http://www.bls.gov/oco

Office of Inspector General (OIG), Department of Health and Human Services (HHS)
http://www.oig.hhs.gov

Office of Juvenile Justice and Delinquency Prevention (OJJDP)
http://ojjdp.ncjrs.org

Office of Tribal Justice (OTJ), U.S. Department of Justice
http://www.usdoj.gov/otj

Transportation Security Administration (TSA)
http://www.tsa.gov

U.S. Citizenship and Immigration Services (USCIS)
http://www.dhs.gov/dhspublic/

U.S. Coast Guard (USCG)
http://www.uscg.mil

U.S. Customs and Border Protection (CBP)
http://www.cbp.gov

U.S. Department of Homeland Security (DHS)
http://www.dhs.gov

U.S. Department of Justice (DOJ)
http://www.usdoj.gov

U.S. Mint Police
http://www.usmint.gov/about_the_mint/mint_police

U.S. Forest Service
http://www.fs.fed.us/fsjobs

U.S. Office of Personnel Management (OPM)
http://jobsearch.usajobs.opm.gov

U.S. Intelligence Community
http://www.intelligence.gov

U.S. Postal Inspector
http://www.usps.com/websites/depart/inspect

U.S. Marshals Service
http://www.usmarshals.gov

U.S. Secret Service
http://www.secretservice.gov

OTHER RESOURCES

http://www.officer.com

http://www.911hotjobs.com

http://www.lawenforcementjobs.com

http://rehiredbadge.com

http://www.policeemployment.com/

http://www.federaljobsearch.com

Applying for Federal Jobs—A Guide to Writing Successful Applications and Resumes for the Job You Want in Government.
     By Patricia B. Wood. May be ordered from: Workbooks, Inc., 9039 Sligo Creek Parkway, #316, Silver Springs, MD 20901
          Phone/FAX (301) 565-9467
          Also available: *The 171 Reference Book*
                    The 171 Writing Portfolio
                    *Promote Yourself! How to Use Your Knowledge, Skills and Abilities . . . and Advance in the
                    Federal Government*

The Top 100: The Fastest Growing Careers for the 21st Century, 3rd ed. Chicago: Ferguson Publishing Company, © 2001.
     http://www.fergpubco.com

Best Jobs for the 21st Century, 3rd ed. By Michael Farr and Laurence Shatkin.
     Indianapolis: JIST Publishing, Inc., © 2004.
     http://www.jist.com

CHAPTER 3

CAREERS IN THE COURTS, CORRECTIONS AND RELATED FIELDS

The pessimist complains about the wind; the optimist expects it to change; the realist adjusts the sails.

—Anonymous

Do You Know:

- ➤ How a law degree may be useful to someone not seeking to become a lawyer?
- ➤ Besides lawyers, what other professionals work in our nation's courts?
- ➤ What the purpose of corrections is in our criminal justice system?
- ➤ What the primary difference between adult corrections and juvenile corrections has traditionally been and whether this is still the case?
- ➤ Who the majority of corrections employees are?
- ➤ What corrections officers do and how the future looks for those seeking this job?
- ➤ What the primary difference is between probation and parole?
- ➤ How the job outlook is for probation and parole officers?
- ➤ What impact home detention and electronic monitoring have on jobs in corrections?

INTRODUCTION

As you learned in Chapter 2, an incredible variety of jobs are available within the law enforcement profession—everything from patrol officer to police surgeon—assuring a niche for almost every interest. Beyond that, the criminal justice field offers even more than you may have ever considered. You may be destined for a job you have never thought of or even knew existed—until now.

Directing your career toward one of these other areas could open a whole new world of employment satisfaction. The criminal justice system is so complex it needs a tremendous number of participants. While many of these jobs may not appear as glamorous as those frequently depicted on television, they are extremely important and provide exceptional opportunities.

This chapter presents the numerous job opportunities within the other two components of the criminal justice system—the courts and corrections. It begins with a discussion of the judicial system in the United States and the critical role played by lawyers. It also discusses numerous other careers within this system that might interest those wishing to become part of criminal justice. The chapter then discusses corrections in the United States, including the adult and juvenile systems as well as careers at the local, state and federal levels.

OPPORTUNITIES IN OUR JUDICIAL SYSTEM—THE COURTS

Before exploring the various jobs within the judicial system, briefly review the nature of our legal system. It is highly complex and, by design, adversarial—accuser versus the accused. The entire affair is presumed to involve a challenge of the individuals as well as a challenge to the system. While this process has been criticized for being too complicated, full of loopholes and technicalities, one thing is certain: The system requires a lot of employees.

Lawyers

When you think of job opportunities within the legal system, you usually begin by thinking of attorneys. And if you are like a lot of other people, you may not think too highly of lawyers. However, lawyers are essential in our courts, acting both as advocates and advisers.

The judicial process generally requires at least two lawyers, one representing each side. In criminal cases, one lawyer (or a team of lawyers) represents the state, or "the people" (the prosecutor), and another lawyer (or legal team) represents the defendant (the defense attorney). Civil cases also involve prosecutors and defense lawyers, but the clients are generally private individuals. Lawyers must represent their clients aggressively within the boundaries of the law.

Many people who don't understand the system look down on defense lawyers because of what their clients have been accused of doing when, in actuality, these lawyers are simply doing their job— providing the constitutionally guaranteed right to legal representation. In addition, some people may feel the system is unfair because it seems to favor the wrongdoer with such rules as prohibiting certain evidence from being admitted. Although some attorneys find this side of the system unappealing and may prefer to be a prosecutor, many attorneys find working for the defense a great challenge.

The practice of law requires a law degree, otherwise known as a doctor of law or a juris doctorate (JD). To obtain this degree you must complete three to four years of intense study beyond your bachelor's degree. The competition for getting into law school is intense, requiring a strong academic background and experience. The demands of obtaining a law degree are both difficult and expensive. Law school is very competitive, and the level of student ability is extremely high. Kasanof (2000, p. 48), a police lieutenant who also holds a law degree, offers this advice:

> Know that a law degree is *not* an automatic ticket to big money and status. While partners at big law firms, and lawyers who sue tobacco companies or do big personal injury cases, may make a lot of money, many lawyers do not. Some lawyers who work for non-profit organizations, or for some government agencies, may make less than police officers. A lot of legal work is not very glamorous: it's reading, writing, talking on the phone, etc. Even trial lawyers don't spend most of their time actually *in* court.

He (p. 49) further suggests:

> If you plan to work primarily in law enforcement, in certain other government agencies, as a solo practitioner or in many smaller law firms, you may be able to get by with a solid record from a typical state law school, or from a less prestigious private law school. . . . If you want to work at a large law firm, you will need top grades, usually from a prestigious law school. While big law firms may pay a lot of money, they can be very unpleasant places to work. And you *will* work long and hard.

Other realities of law school are that it takes a significant amount of time (three years if you go full-time and take summers off for internships/clerkships; four years for part-time/night school) and a significant amount of money (tuition alone runs anywhere from $6,000/year to $34,000/year). Such sacrifices require you to consider this avenue carefully and discuss it with those important to you—spouse, significant other, family—because you will need their support.

Attorneys can practice in many areas besides criminal law, such as corporate, probate and personal injury law. Some lawyers specialize in bankruptcy, divorce or environmental law, while others are committed to working with the poor and disadvantaged. The *Occupational Outlook Handbook (OOH)* notes:

> Some lawyers concentrate in the growing field of intellectual property, helping to protect clients' claims to copyrights, artwork under contract, product designs, and computer programs. Still other lawyers advise insurance companies about the legality of insurance transactions, writing insurance policies to conform with the law and to protect companies from unwarranted claims. When claims are filed against insurance companies, these attorneys review the claims and represent the companies in court.

Some law school graduates use their law degrees in their current jobs as their employers discover it helpful to have people knowledgeable about the law on staff. Others simply enjoy the academic challenge of attaining this level of degree and continue in their present line of work.

As law schools themselves have marketed their degrees as being more "generic" and applicable to career development beyond merely lawyering, the number of students applying to law schools has increased. Business leaders, community leaders and criminal justice practitioners are finding a JD to be a viable degree for professional development. This trend, however, has generated a sufficient number of attorneys that salaries have tended to decrease.

A career option for those seeking active employment in our nation's courts is that of law. In fact, many already employed in the field of criminal justice are pursuing law degrees to help them achieve their professional goals, even if they do not include the traditional practice of law.

Someone considering law school as an option would be well advised to talk with others who have taken this route and learn from their experience. There are many issues to consider. For example, some criminal justice agencies might view someone with a law degree as "overqualified" for a patrol position, while some colleges and universities (other than law schools) consider a juris doctorate more on par with a master's degree and not a "terminal degree" for tenure track positions. Neither of these are the case all the time but exemplify why it is important to be a wise consumer of educational options.

Lawyers held about 695,000 jobs in 2002. According to the *OOH*: "Employment of lawyers is expected to grow about as fast as the average through 2012, primarily as a result of growth in the population and in the general level of business activities. Employment growth of lawyers also will result from growth in demand for legal services in such areas as elder, antitrust, environmental, and intellectual-property law. In addition, the wider availability and affordability of legal clinics and prepaid legal service programs should result in increased use of legal services by middle-income people."

About 75 percent of lawyers are in private practice; most of the remaining 25 percent hold positions in government (mainly at the local level) and with corporations and nonprofit organizations. According to the *OOH,* the median annual earnings of all lawyers was $90,290 in 2002. In 2001, the median salaries of lawyers six months after graduating from law school varied significantly by the type of work obtained:

All law school graduates–$60,000 (median)

Private practice–$90,000   Academe–$40,000

Business/industry–$60,000   Judicial clerkship and government–$40,300

Many lawyers advance to become judges or other judicial workers.

Judges, Magistrates and Other Judicial Workers

The *OOH* states:

> Judges, magistrates and other judicial workers apply the law and oversee the legal process in courts according to local, State, and Federal statutes. They preside over cases concerning every aspect of society, from traffic offenses, to disputes over management of professional sports, to issues concerning the rights of huge corporations, to questions over disconnecting life-support equipment connected to terminally ill persons. All judicial workers must ensure that trials and hearings are conducted fairly and that the court administers justice in a manner which safeguards the legal rights of all parties involved.

Judges' duties and powers are dictated by the jurisdictional levels over which they preside—general trial court, municipal court, county court, appellate court, federal district court, circuit court, state supreme court and U.S. Supreme Court are some of the jurisdictional levels. Federal and state judges are generally required to have first been lawyers, although nearly 40 states allow nonlawyers to hold limited jurisdiction judgeships. Opportunities are better, however, for those with law experience.

Judges, magistrates and magistrate judges held 27,000 jobs in 2002, primarily in state and local government. Administrative law judges, adjudicators and hearing officers held about 19,000 jobs; and arbitrators, mediators and conciliators held another 6,100 jobs. The *OOH* reports the job outlook for judges and magistrates is expected to grow more slowly than average through 2012 but that "employment of arbitrators, mediators, and conciliators is expected to grow as fast as the average for all occupations through 2012 . . . [and] administrative law judges are expected to experience little to no change in employment, due to a slowing of growth in the Federal sector."

All judicial positions are government positions—local, state or federal. Earnings of judicial workers vary greatly by jurisdiction, with the Chief Justice of the U.S. Supreme Court earning $198,600 in 2002 to state judges of general jurisdiction trial courts earning between $82,600 and $150,000. Overall, however: "Judges, magistrate judges, and magistrates had median annual earnings of $94,070 in 2002. The middle 50 percent earned between $44,970 and $120,390. The top 10 percent earned more than $138,300, while the bottom 10 percent earned less than $24,250" (*OOH*).

Many fascinating, lucrative and very satisfying nonlawyer job opportunities also exist within our judicial system. In fact, most people are not aware of the multitude of other careers within the courts.

Legal Assistants and Paralegals

Whether they are called legal assistants or paralegals, these occupations have generated a great deal of interest recently. They require considerably less schooling than a law degree and often pay very well.

Many in this field feel they get the opportunity to do almost as much as the lawyers—they investigate the facts of the case; research precedent case law; and help lawyers prepare for closings, hearings, trials and corporate meetings. Because they often interact with the clients and witnesses and are actively involved in working up the cases, there can be a great deal of job satisfaction. All states require a license to actually practice law; thus, legal assistants and paralegals must work under a supervising lawyer. The *OOH* states:

> There are several ways to become a paralegal. The most common is through a community college paralegal program that leads to an associate's degree. The other common method of entry, mainly for those who have a college degree, is through a certification program that leads to a certification in paralegal studies. . . . Some employers train paralegals on the job, hiring college graduates with no legal experience or promoting experienced legal secretaries. Other entrants have experience in a technical field that is useful to law firms, such as a background in tax preparation for tax and estate practice, criminal justice, or nursing or health administration for personal injury practice.

> Formal paralegal training programs are offered by an estimated 600 colleges and universities, law schools, and proprietary schools. Approximately 250 paralegal programs are approved by the American Bar Association (ABA). Although this approval is neither required nor sought by many programs, graduation from an ABA-approved program can enhance one's employment opportunities.

Paralegals held about 200,000 jobs in 2002, 70 percent of which were with private law firms (*OOH*). These jobs are projected to be among the fastest-growing occupations through 2012 because, in part, of the cost-effectiveness of their services. Paralegals generate much of the information and documentation needed by lawyers but at a fraction of the cost. In 2002, the median annual earnings of paralegals were $37,950 (*OOH*). Paralegals and legal assistants employed by the federal government had median annual earnings of $53,770 in 2002, whereas those working for state government had median annual earnings of $34,750 that same year.

Court Reporters

You've seen them on TV or in the movies. As testimony and questioning swirls about the courtroom, the court reporter sits before a tiny typewriter, nearly motionless, except for her fingers, which seem to be moving considerably slower than the words being spoken by others in the room. Yet the entire proceeding is captured verbatim. According to the *OOH:* "Court reporters play a critical role not only in judicial proceedings, but at every meeting where the spoken word must be preserved as a written transcript. They are responsible for ensuring a complete, accurate, and secure legal record."

> Although many court reporters record official proceedings in the courtroom, others work outside the courtroom. For example, they may take depositions for attorneys in offices and document proceedings of meetings, conventions, and other private activities. Still others capture the proceedings taking place in government agencies at all levels, from the U.S. Congress to State and local governing bodies (*OOH*).

In addition to preparing and protecting the legal record, many court reporters assist judges and trial attorneys in such ways as organizing and searching for information in the official record or making suggestions to judges and attorneys regarding courtroom administration and procedure.

In many courtrooms, evolving technology has changed the way courtroom proceedings are recorded. The *OOH* states:

> There are two main methods of court reporting: Stenotyping and voice writing. Using a stenotype machine, stenotypists document all statements made in official proceedings. The machine allows them to press multiple

keys at a time to record combinations of letters representing sounds, words, or phrases. These symbols are then recorded on computer disks or CD-ROM, which are then translated and displayed as text in a process called computer-aided transcription. In all cases, accuracy is crucial because there is only one person creating an official transcript. . . .

The other method of court reporting is called voice writing. Using the voice-writing method, a court reporter speaks directly into a stenomask—a hand-held mask containing a microphone with a voice silencer. As the reporter repeats the testimony into the recorder, the mask and silencer prevent the reporter from being heard during testimony. Voice writers record everything that is said by judges, witnesses, attorneys, and other parties to a proceeding, including gestures and emotional reactions.

Some voice writers produce a transcript in real time, using computer speech recognition technology. Other voice writers prefer to translate their voice files after the proceeding is over, or they transcribe the files manually, without using speech recognition at all.

The amount of training required to become a court reporter varies with the type of reporting chosen. According to the *OOH:* "It usually takes less than a year to become a voice writer. In contrast, the average length of time it takes to become a stenotypist is 33 months. Training is offered by about 160 postsecondary vocational and technical schools and colleges. The National Court Reporters Association (NCRA) has approved about 82 programs, all of which offer courses in stenotype computer-aided transcription and realtime reporting. NCRA-approved programs require students to capture a minimum of 225 words per minute, a Federal Government requirement as well."

Court reporters must have excellent listening skills, as well as good English grammar, vocabulary and punctuation skills. An expert knowledge of legal terminology and criminal and appellate procedure is essential. Additionally, because capturing proceedings requires the use of computerized stenography or speech recognition equipment, court reporters must be knowledgeable about computer hardware and software applications.

What may appear to be a rather mundane job is, in fact, a very rewarding one. Not only are court reporters right in the middle of very interesting events, but the pay is fairly good. The *OOH* states that court reporters had median annual earnings of $41,550 in 2002, with the highest paid 10 percent earning more than $73,440. Many court reporters work a standard 40-hour week, although part-time work is also common. According to the *OOH:*

Both compensation and compensation methods for court reporters vary with the type of reporting job, the experience of the individual reporter, the level of certification achieved, and the region of the country the reporter works in. Official court reporters earn a salary and a per-page fee for transcripts. Many salaried court reporters supplement their income by doing additional freelance work. Freelance court reporters are paid per job and receive a per-page fee for transcripts.

The *OOH* projects overall employment of court reporters to grow about as fast as average for all occupations through 2012.

Bailiffs

Bailiffs are officers, usually deputy sheriffs, who are assigned to facilitate the court process. While some are sworn, armed law enforcement officers, others are not. Duties of the bailiff include maintaining order in the court; providing security for those in the courtroom, including the judge, staff and others in attendance; helping to move those involved with the court process, including defendants and the jury; and assisting in the administration of other court functions as directed by the judge and the clerk.

If a particular assignment requires a sworn officer, all the regular requirements for any police officer apply. Nonsworn bailiffs may require less education or experience. Common requirements for sheriff's deputy-bailiffs include being a U.S. citizen, meeting physical requirements for the position, passing written and physical agility tests, passing a background investigation and completing requisite academy courses.

Clerks

Court clerks play many roles that assist the administration of justice. The role of the clerk includes maintaining accurate records and ensuring that court schedules are made and kept. The system, whether criminal or civil, revolves around records and paperwork, and it is the duty of the clerks to see that all records are properly generated during the processing of a case and maintained indefinitely following final disposition. This may include filing indictments, informations and verdicts. The clerk may also be responsible for preparing appellate records; filing, securing and disposing of all evidence entered by the court; jury selection; and receiving and disbursing money for fees and fines, court costs, forfeitures and victim restitution. While many of these positions are clerical, those who work their way up to be *the* Clerk of Court attain a position that is both prestigious and well paying.

Other "Helping" Professions Necessary to the Justice System

One of the wonders of the criminal justice field is the number and types of jobs available. Psychologists, social workers and case managers are involved with both the adult and juvenile systems. Chemical dependency and domestic abuse counselors work hand-in-hand with financial, marriage and vocational counselors. If you are interested in criminal justice as a career path, you should be able to find a niche that suits you.

Because our legal system seeks to help people who become involved with the system, including those who are being punished, almost every job that people have in the helping professions outside the legal system can be found within the system. These jobs provide an opportunity to positively affect the lives of those who find themselves in the legal system that appeals to those who enjoy being a part of it. The *OOH* states:

> Social and human service assistant is a generic term for people with a wide array of job titles, including human service worker, case management aide, social work assistant, community support worker, mental health aid, community outreach worker, life skill counselor, or gerontology aide. . . . Social and human service assistants . . . assess clients' needs, establish their eligibility for benefits and services . . . and help to obtain them.

The *OOH* also reports:

> Social work is a profession for those with a strong desire to help improve people's lives. Social workers help people function the best way they can in their environment, deal with their relationships, and solve personal and family problems. . . . These problems may include inadequate housing, unemployment, serious illness,

disability, or substance abuse. Social workers also assist families that have serious domestic conflicts, including those involving child or spousal abuse. . . .

Most social workers specialize. Although some conduct research or are involved in planning or policy development, most social workers prefer an area of practice in which they interact with clients.

Child, family, and school social workers provide social services and assistance to improve the social and psychological functioning of children and their families and to maximize the family well-being and academic functioning of children. Some social workers . . . help find foster homes for neglected, abandoned, or abused children. In schools, they address such problems as teenage pregnancy, misbehavior, and truancy. They also advise teachers on how to cope with problem students. . . .

Mental health and substance abuse social workers assess and treat individuals with mental illness, or substance abuse problems, including abuse of alcohol, tobacco, or other drugs. Such services include individual and group therapy, outreach, crisis intervention, social rehabilitation, and training in skills of everyday living. They may also help plan for supportive services to ease patients' return to the community. Mental health and substance abuse social workers are likely to work in hospitals, substance abuse treatment centers, individual and family services agencies, or local governments. These social workers may be known as clinical social workers.

According to the *OOH,* job opportunities for social and human service assistants are expected to be excellent, with numbers projected to grow much faster than the average for all occupations between 2002 and 2012, particularly for applicants with appropriate postsecondary education. In particular: "Employment of substance abuse social workers will grow rapidly over the 2002–12 projection period. Substance abusers are increasingly being placed into treatment programs instead of being sentenced to prison. As this trend grows, demand will increase for treatment programs and social workers to assist abusers on the road to recovery."

Median annual earnings of child, family and school social workers were $33,150 in 2002, with the top 10 percent earning more than $54,250. Median annual earnings of mental health and substance abuse social workers were $32,850 in 2002, with the top 10 percent earning more than $52,240. And median annual earnings of social and human service assistants were $23,370 in 2002, with the top 10 percent earning more than $37,550 and the lowest 10 percent earning less than $15,420 (*OOH*).

Counseling is another occupation projected to grow faster than average through 2012. Counselors help people with a variety of issues, ranging from personal and family matters to educational problems, mental health concerns, addictions, substance abuse, stress and anger management. Counselors are employed by various social agencies, correctional institutions and residential care facilities, such as halfway houses for criminal offenders. According to the *OOH*:

Demand is expected to be strong for substance abuse and behavioral, mental health, and marriage and family therapists and for rehabilitation counselors, for a variety of reasons. For one, California and a few other States have recently passed laws requiring substance abuse treatment instead of jail for people caught possessing a drug. This shift will require more substance abuse counselors in those States. Second, the increasing availability of funds to build statewide networks to improve services for children and adolescents with serious emotional disturbances and for their family members should increase employment opportunities for counselors.

The *OOH* also suggests: "Counselors must possess high physical and emotional energy to handle the array of problems they address. Dealing daily with these problems can cause stress."

In addition to becoming a lawyer, many other career alternatives exist for those wishing to work in a courtroom setting. Possibilities to consider include a job as a legal assistant or paralegal, court reporter, bailiff, clerk, psychologist, social worker, case manager or a variety of counseling positions.

The judicial system provides work for people of all levels of education, experience and background. In fact, some people who were "on the wrong side" of the law earlier in their lives are now playing valuable roles in the criminal justice field. Some believe that those who have been in trouble themselves, and possibly even served jail or prison time, can address the issues and concerns of those presently involved better than those who have merely read about it. Similarly, some exceptional chemical dependency and domestic abuse counselors have police records dating back to before they received treatment. Such experiences give them valuable insight for helping those currently needing treatment. So, whether you like to work with the young or the old, those accused of committing a crime or those victimized by it, or even if you enjoy administrative work, the legal system has a place for you.

OPPORTUNITIES IN OUR JUDICIAL SYSTEM—CORRECTIONS

The corrections portion of our criminal justice system serves several purposes:

➢   To punish offenders

➢   To rehabilitate wrongdoers

➢   To make society safer for the public

The purpose of corrections is to punish and rehabilitate offenders while protecting the public and making our society safer.

Like law enforcement and the courts, corrections is divided into an adult and a juvenile system. Traditionally, the adult system has tended to be more punitive and punishment-oriented while the juvenile system has emphasized treatment and rehabilitation. Typical of state statutes regarding *adult offenders* is Chapter 609 of the *Minnesota Statutes,* which states that the purpose of the adult criminal code is:

> To protect the public safety and welfare by preventing the commission of crime through the deterring effect of the sentences authorized, the rehabilitation of those convicted, and their confinement when the public safety and interest requires.

In contrast, typical of state statutes regarding *juveniles* is Chapter 260 of the *Minnesota Statutes:*

> The purpose of the laws relating to children alleged or adjudicated to be delinquent is to promote the public safety and reduce juvenile delinquency by maintaining the integrity of the substantive law prohibiting certain behavior and by developing individual responsibility for lawful behavior. This purpose should be pursued through means that are fair and just, that recognize the unique characteristics and needs of children, and that give children access to opportunities for personal and social growth.

The trend of punishing adults and "treating" juveniles seems to be reversing itself to some extent. More emphasis is being placed on the *treatment* of adult offenders while, at the same time, more traditional penalties, such as incarceration and even manual labor, are being used more frequently as "treatment" for juvenile offenders. Nonetheless, some people prefer working with juveniles because the system remains more treatment-oriented, and our society retains the belief that youths are generally more capable than adults in redirecting their lives. It is particularly satisfying to see young people straighten out their lives.

The primary difference between adult corrections and juvenile corrections has traditionally been the *punishment* of adults and the *treatment* of juveniles, although this difference seems to be reversing itself to some extent.

Is corrections as exciting as being in on the action-packed arrest? (Remember, that's only 20 percent of police work.) Maybe not. But then, police work doesn't offer the long-range benefits of really helping people to change. Many police officers are frustrated by seeing only the misery caused by crime and not having a positive influence on people, as those who work in corrections often do, particularly those in probation and parole, as will be discussed shortly. But first, look at the most prevalent professional in corrections—the corrections officer, or CO.

Corrections Officers

Corrections begins after the arrest and involves everything from the initial "booking" to long-term "guarding." Some positions involve counseling inmates, while others are limited to an armed position in a watchtower. For some, work in corrections is a step toward getting somewhere else, a legitimate "stepping stone" to other jobs in law enforcement. It is also, however, an opportunity to be part of a whole other world of the criminal justice system, which many find appealing and very satisfying.

As noted by the *OOH:* "Correctional officers are responsible for overseeing individuals who have been arrested and are awaiting trial or who have been convicted of a crime and sentenced to serve time in a jail, reformatory, or penitentiary. They maintain security and inmate accountability to prevent disturbances, assaults, or escapes." The *OOH* reports an estimated 476,000 correctional officer jobs existed in 2002, about 60 percent of which were in state correctional institutions such as prisons, prison camps and youth correctional facilities. Most of the remaining jobs were in city and county jails or other institutions run by local governments.

It is worth making the distinction here between corrections officers and detention officers. Though they both perform their functions behind bars, and their jobs are similar in some ways, their jobs are also different in several critical ways. One major distinction is the different constitutional justifications for doing what they do. Individuals held in detention have not yet appeared before the court and, therefore, retain the presumption of innocence. Consequently, any punitive aspect of the correctional environment is not justified with such "inmates." The officer's duty regarding such individuals is to keep them safe and secure until they can be brought before a judge.

Working conditions in correctional institutions may be stressful and occasionally dangerous. COs may be assaulted, injured or even killed by inmates. As with police work, officers in correctional facilities must provide security 24/7. Most COs work 8 hours a day, 5 days a week, but the shifts usually rotate and will typically include nights, weekends and holidays at some point. Paid overtime is also common. The *OOH* notes:

> Most institutions require that correctional officers be at least 18 to 21 years of age and a U.S. citizen; have a high school education or its equivalent; demonstrate job stability, usually by accumulating two years of work

experience; and have no felony convictions. Promotion prospects may be enhanced through obtaining a postsecondary education.

Correctional officers must be in good health. Candidates for employment are generally required to meet formal standards of physical fitness, eyesight, and hearing. . . . Good judgment and the ability to think and act quickly are indispensable. Applicants are typically screened for drug abuse, subject to background checks, and required to pass a written examination.

Snyder (2002, p. 93) notes the findings of a study aimed at identifying essential job duties of correctional officers and the physical abilities and capacities required to perform them:

Job tasks can include walking or standing for several hours, climbing flights of stairs, searching areas that are not easily accessible, running to an emergency scene, lifting and carrying heavy objects such as property boxes, physically subduing or restraining a violent inmate with the help of another officer, applying restraints to a resisting inmate, defending oneself against an armed inmate, disarming and subduing that inmate, using force to move a hostile inmate, and handling and firing weapons.

The Top 100 (2001, p. 115) adds: "Corrections officers need physical and emotional strength to cope with the stress inherent in dealing with criminals, many of whom may be dangerous or incapable of change. A correctional officer has to remain alert and aware of the surroundings, prisoners' movements and attitudes, and any potential for danger or violence."

Rackleff (2002, p. 76) observes: "Choosing a career in corrections has never been for the fainthearted." As a former prison warden contends: "It takes a certain kind of person to be a correctional officer—a person not easily intimidated." Riley and Wilder (2002, p. 90) elaborate:

Agencies are not only seeking people who can clearly set and maintain limits, but also those who have the self-confidence, maturity and integrity to demonstrate the value of pro-social choices in the way they perform their work duties. People who understand the strengths as well as limitations of the offender population with whom they work, and who possess intelligence, flexibility and interpersonal skills to deal with individual offenders differently but consistently will be successful.

Skills in stress management, CPR/first aid, self-defense, public relations and the use of prison tools and equipment are also advantageous to those seeking employment as a correctional officer.

Corrections is considered a growth industry, and the outlook for CO jobs at all levels—local, state and federal—is very favorable over the next decade, given the projected increases in the number of individuals incarcerated across the country. According to *The Top 100* (p. 115): "Employment in this field is expected to increase much faster than the average for all jobs. . . . The ongoing war on drugs, new tough-on-crime legislation, and increasing mandatory sentencing policies will create a need for more prison beds and more corrections officers." Indeed, as Harrison and Karberg (2003, p. 2) report, the national prison incarceration rate continues to rise: "Between 1995 and midyear 2002, the incarcerated population grew an average of 3.8 percent annually. . . . In the 12 months before midyear 2002, the number of inmates in prison and jail rose an estimated 54,933 inmates, or 1,056 inmates per week."

However, Kiekbusch (2001, p. 1) warns: "Corrections in America soon will be confronted by a serious manpower problem: the severe shortage of properly trained and highly motivated correctional officers to staff the nation's correctional facilities." According to Farr and Shatkin (2004, p. 281), the projected growth in jobs for correctional officers and jailers through the year 2010 is 32.4 percent, with an estimated 30,000 openings annually for such jobs to meet the rising needs of correctional facilities across the country.

Salaries vary greatly across the country for all positions and personnel of all experience levels. In 2002, the median annual earnings of correctional officers and jailers were $32,670:

> Median annual earnings in the public sector were $40,900 in the Federal Government, $33,260 in State government, and $31,380 in local government. In the management and public relations industry, where the relatively small number of officers employed by privately operated prisons are classified, median annual earnings were $21,390. According to the Federal Bureau of Prisons, the starting salary for Federal correctional officers was about $23,000 a year in 2003. Starting Federal salaries were slightly higher in selected areas where prevailing local pay levels were higher (*OOH*).

Benefits commonly available to corrections officers include uniforms or a clothing allowance to buy their own work clothes, medical and dental insurance, disability and life insurance, vacation, sick leave and retirement pensions. *The Top 100* (p. 114) adds: "Officers who work for the federal government and for most state governments are covered by civil service systems or merit boards."

A career in corrections, while demanding and challenging, can be extremely rewarding. Furthermore, the trend toward new generation prisons and direct supervision gives COs more involvement with inmates and more control over the populations they supervise, which translates into enhanced professionalism and greater job satisfaction.

A career option for those seeking work in corrections is that of a corrections officer. Corrections officers make up over half of all employees in corrections today. Duties include maintaining the security and safety of persons being held within the correctional facility, enforcing rules and regulations and possibly providing a degree of counseling to inmates. Present and predicted increases in inmate populations mean more corrections officers will be needed in the future.

For prospective criminal justice applicants interested in long-term personal interaction, the fields of probation and parole are worth considering.

Probation and Parole Officers

Careers in probation and parole are other options for those seeking employment in corrections. Like COs, probation and parole officers (POs) counsel offenders, but they also evaluate the progress of offenders in becoming productive members of society. Unlike corrections officers, probation and parole officers usually work outside the steel bars and high brick walls, in the community corrections environment. The *OOH* notes:

> Many people who are convicted of crimes are placed on probation, instead of being sent to prison. During probation, offenders must stay out of trouble and meet various other requirements. *Probation officers,* who are called community supervision officers in some States, supervise people who have been placed on probation. *Correctional treatment specialists,* who may also be known as case managers, counsel prison inmates and help them plan for their release from incarceration.
>
> *Parole officers* and *pretrial services officers* perform many of the same duties that probation officers perform. However, parole officers supervise offenders who have been released from prison on parole to ensure that they comply with the conditions of their parole. In some States, the job of parole and probation officer is combined. Pretrial services officers conduct pretrial investigations of criminal suspects when they are arrested by police. Their findings help to determine whether a suspect should be released before their trial. When

suspects are released before their trial, pretrial services officers have the responsibility of supervising them to make sure they adhere to the terms of their release and that they show up for their trial. Occasionally, in the Federal courts system, probation officers perform the functions of pretrial services officers.

> The primary difference between probation and parole is that probation is an alternative to incarceration, while parole is supervised release from incarceration before the expiration of the sentence. Both probation and parole officers have considerable interaction with offenders.

According to the *OOH:*

> The number of cases a probation officer or correctional treatment specialist handles at one time depends on the needs of offenders and the risks they pose. Higher risk offenders and those who need more counseling usually command more of the officer's time and resources. Caseload size also varies by agency jurisdiction. Consequently, officers may handle from 20 to more than 100 active cases at a time.
>
> Computers, telephones, and fax machines enable the officers to handle the caseload. Probation officers may telecommute from their own homes. Other technological advancements, such as electronic monitoring devices and drug screening, also have assisted probation officers and correctional treatment specialists in supervising and counseling offenders.

Most states require at least a bachelor's degree for probation and parole officers. These positions require good active listening, speaking and reading comprehension skills; the ability to make sound judgments and decisions; and a service orientation.

There were approximately 84,000 probation officers and correctional treatment specialists in 2002. Farr and Shatkin (p. 543) list these careers among the best jobs for the 21st century, noting an estimated growth rate of 23.8 percent through 2010 and a projected 14,000 annual job openings. The *OOH* notes: "Most jobs are found in State or local governments. In some States, the State government employs all probation officers and correctional treatment specialists; in other States, local governments are the only employers. In still other States, both levels of government employ these workers. Jobs are more plentiful in urban areas." Furthermore:

> Median annual earnings of probation officers and correctional treatment specialists in 2002 were $38,360. The middle 50 percent earned between $30,770 and $50,550. The lowest 10 percent earned less than $25,810, and the highest 10 percent earned more than $62,520. In 2002, median annual earnings for probation officers and correctional treatment specialists employed in State government were $38,720; those employed in local government earned $39,450. Higher wages tend to be found in urban areas (*OOH*).

Careers in the correctional field are quite different from those in law enforcement, but probation officers can take defendants from the crisis point at which they enter the criminal justice system and work with them to help them alter their lives. This long-term payoff makes probation and parole work rewarding.

> Probation and parole officers are professionals with vital roles in our corrections system. The job outlook for those interested in becoming probation and/or parole officers is positive, as the entire area of corrections is expanding rapidly.

Community Corrections—Alternatives to Incarceration

Because of increasing jail populations, both the adult and juvenile systems are being forced to examine community alternatives to incarceration. Some of these options are residential facilities such as halfway houses, prerelease centers, transition centers, work furlough and community work centers, community treatment centers and restitution centers. These facilities employ a wide range of staff, including probation/parole officers, counselors, caseworkers, educators, health care workers and numerous administrative, management and support/clerical personnel. Nonresidential correctional alternatives, such as day reporting centers, require similar personnel.

Another option that eases overcrowded jails and prisons is to allow offenders to remain in their own homes under house arrest.

> **Electronic Monitoring and House Arrest.** Used in conjunction with *electronic monitoring* (EM), house arrest or home detention offers an effective, inexpensive method of supervising probationers. A typical electronic monitoring system (EMS) consists of a bracelet worn on the offender's wrist or ankle. The bracelet contains a transmitter that emits a signal that is continuously monitored, enabling authorities to know the whereabouts of the offender at all times. The increasing use of home detention and electronic monitoring is creating new work opportunities for those who implement and manage these programs.

As house arrest and electronic monitoring gain popularity and grow in use, new job opportunities are created for those who implement and manage such programs.

Ramsey County (Minnesota) PO, Joe Arvidson, elaborates (2004):

> The trend in community corrections work is no longer in simply finding alternatives to incarcerating the offender. That only begins to address the issues of cost savings and offender re-integration. Community corrections agencies continue to refine their risk/needs assessment tools. The goal is to ensure that the most serious offenders are getting the closer attention they warrant. . . . Although it has been used by correctional agencies for over 20 years, electronic monitoring, specifically GPS- (Global Positioning Satellite) based monitoring, is gaining tremendous ground as an implemented innovation. . . . Today's technology not only can determine that an offender is speeding on his way home from work, but can also send him a text page instructing him to slow down. That is just one example of how much the job has changed and will certainly continue to change. Twenty years ago you could cite the responsibilities of a PO and have a list of 10 or 12 things. With today's specialty caseloads, that list doesn't end.

Juvenile Corrections

If you're interested in working with youths, the same positions needed in adult corrections can generally be found in the juvenile justice system. In fact, considering the historical focus of juvenile justice has been treatment and rehabilitation, this area of corrections is heavily dependent on probation officers, counselors, case workers, social workers, educators and those interested in providing "surrogate" families for troubled youths.

As Gondles (2004, p. 6) observes: "Kids today may be maturing physically earlier than before, but mentally they still require teaching, training, loving, skill-building and learning through years of maturity. Bodies may be growing faster, but no child is born with morals, with judgment, or with remorse; they learn these and other emotions and controls."

In answering the question, "Why would anyone want to work in the business of juvenile corrections?" Frank Alarcon (2004, pp. 8–9), Deputy Secretary of the Florida Department of Juvenile Justice, asserts:

> We have the wonderful opportunity to help change people's lives in positive ways. As we have embraced restorative principles and practices, we continue to improve public safety. We assist victims of juvenile crime, help communities strengthen families and neighborhoods, and give young people opportunities to reduce deficits and develop the skills necessary to make it in the real world. . . .
>
> Our work takes us to every nook and cranny of our communities—poor and affluent, rural and urban, diverse and homogeneous. We run small six-bed group homes and large 1,000-bed facilities. We see courtrooms and boardrooms and visit the YMCA and jail.

Other Careers in Corrections

Although corrections officers make up the largest number of those with careers in corrections, numerous other careers are available, including administrative, clerical, educational, professional/technical, treatment-oriented, medical, religious, recreational and maintenance/food service positions.

Many departments of corrections now employ public information officers (PIOs) to interface with the media and perform other functions. In California, for example, the PIOs also serve as administrative assistants to the warden: "He or she has other duties in addition to working with the media. PIOs often schedule certain days of the week for media tours and visits" (Harry, 2001, p. 114). According to Scott (2001, p. 102): "PIOs should educate the public, particularly about treatment and conditions of inmates, to positively promote the department. Through news articles, broadcasts or letters to the editor, one can tout the benefits of inmate rehabilitation programs and taxpayer costs involved." Furthermore (p. 103): "In today's information age, PIOs also have to concern themselves with the Internet and its abundance of websites that foster inmate propaganda."

Furthermore, those facilities involved in prison labor must also staff personnel knowledgeable in the specific industry and the products being produced. Finally, bear in mind that as more correctional facilities are built, an increasing number of staff in *all* these categories must be hired to keep the institutions operating effectively and constitutionally.

CONCLUSION

Many career options exist for those seeking work in our nation's courts and corrections. One of the most popular career choices is that of law. Many other alternatives exist for those wanting to work in a courtroom setting, including jobs as a legal assistant or paralegal, court reporter, bailiff, clerk, psychologist, social worker, case manager or a variety of counseling positions.

The field of corrections is experiencing phenomenal growth. Possible career options for those seeking work in corrections include corrections officers in both adult and juvenile facilities, probation officers and parole officers. The job outlook for those interested in becoming corrections officers and probation/parole officers is positive, as the entire area of corrections is expanding rapidly.

While government agencies are being challenged to "do more with less" to appease the very vocal "no new taxes" constituency, the less traditional fields of employment will expand. Even the areas providing alternatives to more expensive imprisonment that can lessen the burden on taxpayers, including probation and parole work, will flourish. Beyond government employment, all areas of the system will continue to take advantage of private responses. No doubt a "partnership" will develop, allowing people to move from one area to another, with new possibilities always on the horizon.

AN INSIDER'S VIEW

LAWYERS WEAR MANY HATS: IS ONE RIGHT FOR YOU?

Marsh J. Halberg

Attorney at Law
Edina, Minnesota

The dilemma most students face, whether in college or law school, is trying to envision a job they will enjoy when they enter the workforce. Each of you knows that the "real world" is far different from that which you learn about in books.

When I was going to law school, the most common question people would ask me was what type of law I intended to practice. My standard answer at that time was, "I don't know. It could be anything except criminal law." Reflecting back on that, for the past 20 years over 90 percent of my practice has involved criminal law. I laugh at my poor prediction of what lay ahead for future employment!

What I discovered, upon looking more closely at the practice of law, was that a great number of lawyers spend their days sitting behind a desk and pushing papers, whether it be drafting corporate documents, preparing real estate papers or drafting wills. I recognized that I was very much a "people person" and that it would be a slow, agonizing death for me to sit behind a desk all day, staring at four walls.

This meant that I wanted to practice in an area of law that involved interacting with people and getting out of the office. Criminal law, more than any other area, allows an attorney to interact with many different people daily and to also spend a great deal of time in the courtroom.

While corporate or commercial legal battles can drag on for many years, a criminal case is typically charged soon after the alleged crime occurs. The defendant has a right to a speedy trial, which may occur within several months after the case is charged. As such, criminal law involves a high-volume, fast-turnover type of workload.

Because of the high volume of criminal cases, most matters (over 95 percent) never go to trial. As such, the attorneys involved for both the prosecution and defense become professional negotiators, required to make quick decisions and move on to the next case. This is necessitated by the pure volume of cases in the system. We have all heard the saying, "It's not *what* you know but *who* you know." To a certain extent this is true in the state criminal court system. Because so many case negotiations occur, the practice of criminal law is very relationship-oriented. Attorneys work together over and over on a weekly, if not daily, basis negotiating, if not trying, cases. A level of confidence, respect and friendship develops between lawyers when that much contact occurs. As such, a relatively small band of criminal defense attorneys practice the lion's share of the criminal work.

Where I live, most of the municipal communities contract with private law firms to represent them on city prosecution matters because it is more cost-effective than hiring full-time government employees. The city attorneys prosecute all of the lesser crimes (i.e., everything short of felony cases). This might involve DWI, forgery, assault, prostitution and so on. The "big cases" (murder, robbery, etc.) are handled by a full-time county attorney's office.

The same private lawyers who handle the city prosecution matters on a contract basis are free to practice criminal defense work outside of the communities for which they prosecute. Therefore, it is very common to see an attorney being a prosecutor in a courtroom one morning and, that afternoon, being a defense attorney in a separate courtroom. This is an ethical and recognized course of practice. Frankly, it allows attorneys who are both prosecutors and defense attorneys to better serve both of their clients. That is, prosecutors know all of the defense tricks and vice versa. I think it also prevents attorneys from becoming too jaded by working on only one side of the fence. Specifically, attorneys see that police officers are not always right, nor are defendants always falsely accused. It gives the attorney a far better perspective of the tough job on both sides.

I work as both a city prosecutor and do private defense work for cases occurring outside the city. I am currently a prosecutor for a suburb of Minneapolis. Although the city is relatively small, we generate in excess of 10,000 charges per year. Many of the minor traffic matters are simply handled by the violator paying the fine and never going to court. Many cases, however, whether traffic charges or criminal charges, involve the defendants making a required court appearance. Another part-time prosecutor and I handle thousands of criminal prosecution files each year. I typically spend approximately 50 percent of every day in the courtroom. It is not uncommon, on a typical day, to work through in excess of 100 separate cases.

When I am retained as a defense attorney, I tell my clients that much of what they are paying for are my relationships with others within the system—it is my ability to be a professional negotiator rather than Clarence Darrow in the courtroom. More deals are done over the water cooler than standing in front of the judge in the courtroom.

I would encourage you to do internships for various lawyers to get a better feel for what the practice of law is actually like before making the dive into law school.

Marsh J. Halberg *has been employed in the legal profession for 25 years, during which he has served as an assistant county attorney, a city prosecutor and a defense attorney. He currently works for the law firm of Thomsen & Nybeck, P.A. in Edina, Minnesota.*

INSIDER'S VIEW ONLINE

An additional *Insider's View* for this chapter is "The Path to a Career in Corrections" by John J. Maas, found on the Wadsworth website: http://www.wadsworth.com/criminaljustice_d/.

 MIND STRETCHES

1.   How do you feel about lawyers?

2.   If you were to become a criminal lawyer, would you rather be a prosecutor or a defense attorney?

3.   Do you think judges should be elected public officials or appointed by members of local and state government?

4.   What do most people think of when they think of a "correctional officer job"? Where did you acquire the information on which you base your answer?

5.   What benefits would you find in a job in corrections that may not exist in a street police job?

6.   What negatives would you want to be aware of in considering a job as a correctional officer?

7.   Can you think of unique skills that could make a job candidate more attractive to a hiring agency?

8.   Is there a danger in pursuing a specific job that "really excites" you, to the point you do not believe any other job would be worthwhile?

9.   What corrections jobs do you think will become more necessary in the future? Less necessary?

10.   How do you predict corrections will change? Why?

REFERENCES

Alarcon, Francisco "Frank" J. "Juvenile Corrections: Why Would Anyone Want to Work in This Business?" *Corrections Today,* June 2004, pp. 8–9.

Arvidson, Joe. Probation officer, Ramsey County, Minnesota. Personal interview, February 25, 2004.

Farr, Michael and Shatkin, Laurence. *Best Jobs for the 21st Century,* 3rd ed. Indianapolis: JIST Publishing, Inc., 2004.

Gondles, James A., Jr. "Kids Are Kids, Not Adults." *Corrections Today,* June 2004, pp. 6–7.

Harrison, Paige M. and Karberg, Jennifer C. *Prison and Jail Inmates at Midyear 2002.* Washington, DC: Bureau of Justice Statistics Bulletin, April 2003. (NCJ 198877)

Harry, Jennifer L. "An Interview with Margot Bach: Information Officer II for the California Department of Corrections." *Corrections Today,* June 2001, pp. 114–119.

Kasanof, Adam. "Is Law School Right for You?" *Police,* July 2000, pp. 48–49.

Kiekbusch, Richard G. "The Looming Correctional Work Force Shortage: A Problem of Supply and Demand." *Corrections Compendium,* April 2001, pp. 1–3, 24–25.

Occupational Outlook Handbook, 2004–05 Edition. Bureau of Labor Statistics, U.S. Department of Labor. Washington, DC: U.S. Government Printing Office, 2004.

Rackleff, Jo Ellyn. "Florida's Recruitment Methods: Attracting and Retaining Valuable Employees." *Corrections Today,* June 2002, pp. 76–79, 119.

Riley, Frank E., III and Wilder, Beverly A. "Hiring Correctional Staff with the Right Stuff." *Corrections Today,* June 2002, pp. 88–91.

Scott, Gerges. "So, You Want to Be a Public Information Officer for a Corrections Department." *Corrections Today,* June 2001, pp. 102–104.

Snyder, Donald H., Jr. "Recruitment and Retention Programs: Important during Economic Ups and Downs." *Corrections Today,* June 2002, pp. 92–95.

The Top 100: The Fastest Growing Careers for the 21st Century. Chicago: Ferguson Publishing Company, 2001.

HELPFUL WEBSITES

American Bar Association (ABA)
http://www.abanet.org

American Correctional Association (ACA)
http://www.corrections.com/aca

American Jail Association (AJA)
http://www.corrections.com/aja/index.html

American Probation and Parole Association
e-mail: appa@csg.org

Federal Bureau of Prisons (BOP)
http://www.bop.gov

International Corrections and Prisons Association
http://www.icpa.ca/

Law School Admission Council
http://www.lsac.org

National Court Reporters Association
http://www.verbatimreporters.com

Standing Committee on Legal Assistants
http://www.abanet.org/legalassts

United States Court Reporters Association
http://www.uscra.org

OTHER RESOURCES

American Correctional Association Publications – Call (800) 222-5646, extension 1860
    Correctional Officer Resource Guide, 3rd ed.; Item #631-CC01; $29.95
    Correctional Law for the Correctional Officer, 3rd ed., by William C. Collins, JD; Item #630-CC01; $19.95
    Mental Health in Corrections: An Overview for Correctional Staff, by Wesley Sowers, MD, Kenneth Thompson,
        MD and Stephen Mullins, MD; Item #210-CC01; $15.00
    Staff Supervision Made Easy, by Scott D. Hutton, PhD; Item #194-CC01; $19.95

CHAPTER 4

CAREERS IN PRIVATE SECURITY

Private security is the invisible empire of criminal justice.

—*Christopher A. Hertig*

Do You Know:

➢ The difference between proprietary, contractual and hybrid security?
➢ The difference between public and private policing?
➢ Why cooperation between public law enforcement and private security is necessary and what some examples of such cooperation are?
➢ What areas of public justice are being affected by privatization?
➢ What trend is occurring in corrections?
➢ Why many law enforcement officers desire jobs as private security directors?
➢ What typical entry-level, mid-level and top-level positions exist in private security?
➢ How common licensing and registration requirements are for private security professionals? Where to obtain information about such requirements?
➢ What qualities employers seek in private security applicants?
➢ What the outlook is for jobs in private security?
➢ Where job opportunities in private security are most likely? Least likely?
➢ What kind of salary you might expect from a job in private security?
➢ How available promotions are in private security?

INTRODUCTION

Security. Since September 11, 2001, the word has taken on new meaning and unprecedented importance to most, if not all, Americans. Its significance was captured in the creation of an entirely new government agency—the Department of Homeland Security. And no area in the criminal justice system is growing as rapidly as careers in private security.

A trend that was well underway a decade before the terrorist attacks of 9/11, private security *is* big business and a protective presence that continues to get bigger every year. The American Society for Industrial Security (ASIS) (n.d., p. 2) notes that all businesses, regardless of size, have numerous security concerns relating to fraud, theft, computer hacking, industrial espionage, workplace violence and, now, terrorism:

> Security is one of the fastest growing professional careers worldwide. A career in the security field provides a multitude of opportunities. These opportunities range from entry level security officer positions to investigators specializing in specific areas and managers and directors of security at major corporations and organizations around the world. The demand for heightened security is being increased by theft of information, workplace violence, terrorism and white-collar crime.

Harowitz (2003) observes:

> Security is now a rising star in the corporate firmament. The people responsible for security "have become much more visible to the top of the business," says [AT&T CEO Mike] Armstrong, "and much more important to the business itself." The shift in business attitudes is also evident in a market report on the security industry by Lehman Brothers. In that report, analyst Jeffrey Kessler writes that the global security industry "has moved from a peripheral activity to center stage."
>
> A further sign of the maturing nature of corporate security is that Boyden Global Executive Search saw a market need for a formalized "Chief Security Officer" (CSO) job description. The ASIS International Guidelines Commission is now in the process of helping to develop that description as a guide for companies looking to fill the top security position.

This chapter begins with a comparison of the private security officer and the public law enforcement officer. It then examines the relationship between these two fields; the criticality of cooperation between them, particularly in post-9/11 homeland security efforts; and the expanding privatization of public justice. This is followed by an up-close look at career opportunities within the security profession, including salaries and the potential for growth in this field.

PUBLIC VERSUS PRIVATE OFFICERS

Because public policing and private security are closely related, and because people employed in one field often become involved at some time in the other, start by looking at how the two fields basically differ.

A primary difference between public policing and private security, as the names imply, is who you work for. Who pays your salary? Individuals in public policing are paid with tax dollars and, consequently, are accountable to the tax-paying citizens, whether on a local, county, state or federal level. They are under constant scrutiny by both the public and the politicians charged with overseeing expenditures of public funds, and their incomes are heavily influenced by the tax dollars allocated to policing. Private security positions, in contrast, are funded by business, industry or any entity in the private sector wanting protection beyond what public law enforcement provides.

Another basic difference between public policing and private security is the essential goals of each. Public law enforcement has traditionally been quite reactive, operating as a service to the jurisdiction that pays for it (although the move toward community policing is leading officers to take a more proactive approach to jurisdictional issues). Ideally, public police serve everyone within the jurisdiction equally, without a profit motive. People call, and the police are expected to respond. Private security is proactive, seeking to prevent problems and limit losses for a particular private employer. Whether a private security operation is *proprietary* (the security officers are actual employees of the company) or *contractual* (the security officers are hired from an independent security company), the private security profession is profit-oriented and serves the employer paying for such service. The current trend is *hybrid security,* which combines contractual and proprietary security.

Proprietary security officers are actual employees of the company they guard. Contractual security officers work for an independent security company and are assigned to guard a company without its own internal security staff. The trend is toward using hybrid security, combining both proprietary and contractual security services.

A third basic difference between public and private policing is in the statutory power involved. Public police officers are an arm of the government and act with its full authority, including the authority of arrest. Although police powers of arrest are awesome, public officers may be denied access to private facilities that are accessible to those facilities' security officers. Without a warrant, public police could well be denied access to an industrial facility that relies on its own security department to deal with such concerns as industrial espionage.

Private security officers have no more power than that of private citizens. However, as citizens, they can carry weapons, conduct investigations, defend property and make arrests. And they may, in fact, *appear* to have more authority than regular citizens as a result of wearing a uniform, carrying a weapon and having the approval and support of the organization to defend the property.

Differences between public police and private security officers include:
1. Where the paycheck comes from (public tax dollars versus private sector budgets)
2. Whether the response is reactive or proactive
3. The statutory power involved

Frequently public policing and private security have been viewed as being competitors. Additionally, some people in public law enforcement have looked down on security officers, calling them "wanna-bes," that is, individuals who really want to be police officers but didn't make it. But these attitudes have changed—private security as a profession has come of age.

PUBLIC/PRIVATE COOPERATION

Private security has become a major player in safeguarding Americans and their property. As our increasing elderly and business populations are likely to continue their inhabitation of high-rise condos and office buildings, their reliance on private security will also increase. The traditional police officer patrolling public roads or a beat officer on foot cannot practically be expected to patrol such structures. Unlike public police officers, private security officers can and do patrol specific buildings, even specific floors or rooms within buildings. It can be anticipated that the fields of public law enforcement and private security may tend to blend together as society recognizes the need for each and as these professions themselves learn how they can best work together—to the benefit of all. Samuels (2003, p. 8), former president of the International Association of Chiefs of Police (IACP), asserts:

> It is important to remember that law enforcement agencies are not the only protective force operating in towns and cities around the globe. Private-sector security represents a vast and vital resource, and we must strengthen our existing partnership with them.

> Current estimates of public-sector policing strength by the Bureau of Justice Statistics indicate that there are 16,661 state, local, and county law enforcement agencies in the United States, and they employ a total of 677,933 sworn officers. Studies on private security force staffing indicate there may be as many 10,000 private security agencies employing slightly less than 2 million private security officers in the United States.

These numbers illustrate the substantial contribution private officers make to safeguarding Americans and their property. Hertig (2001, p. 28), who advocates using the term *protection officer* instead of *security guard,* contends liaison with law enforcement is a key issue for private security forces:

> Private security can also be harnessed to combat major criminal activity and terrorism. Terrorist groups often rob banks, shoplift, commit credit card fraud and engage in other theft offenses as "fund raisers." Private protection officers are therefore in a position to help uncover serious terrorist threats. Protection officers are on the front lines in the fight against crime. They often feed intelligence and preliminary investigative information to public law enforcement entities. In many cases, security officers at retail stores, shopping centers, colleges, healthcare facilities and parks apprehend criminals and turn them over to police.

In the wake of the 2001 terrorist attacks, states have been directed to organize their own homeland security efforts and take steps to assess and enhance the security of their local resources. Gips (2002, p. 108) reports that in Iowa, for example, approximately 1,000 critical sites and assets have been identified, 90 percent of which are in the private sector: "With the help of the proprietary security departments at these facilities, vulnerabilities have been targeted."

Another reason for cooperation is that individuals often move from one field to the other. Some individuals use private security as a stepping stone into public policing. Likewise, some individuals in public policing enter private security, sometimes as a consultant, sometimes after retiring from public policing, sometimes as a part-time job while working as a public police officer and sometimes as a highly paid corporate security director. As Samuels (p. 8) notes: "One retired FBI agent, an expert in counterintelligence, now works for a detective agency specializing in employee background checks. A former director of a state police agency now runs the security division for a major bank." According to ASIS (http://www.asisonline.org): "ASIS International is comprised of more than 33,000 security management professionals worldwide. Many hold senior security positions with major corporations, and they often have military and/or law enforcement backgrounds including work with the CIA, ATF and FBI." Samuels (p. 8) concludes:

> Clearly, we have enough information on hand to know that private-sector security could bring a substantial level of skills and resources to bear on issues such as public disorder and terrorism prevention and response. Many private security agencies are very sophisticated in their application and use of high-end technologies. In addition, they also possess large amounts of critical intelligence information. We also know that partnerships between the private and public sectors have made huge improvements in other areas of policing—in the investigation of computer-related crimes, for example. Operation Cooperation, a joint venture between the IACP and the American Society for Industrial Security, helped illustrate the potential value found in public-private partnerships.

Cooperation between public law enforcement and private security can benefit both sides and is an important step toward enhanced safety for all. Examples of cooperation between the public and private sector include combined efforts at the sites of natural disasters, common initiatives in controlling and securing large public events and cooperation in preventing and handling neighborhood crime.

PRIVATIZATION OF PUBLIC JUSTICE

The privatization trend has extended to more than just police officers. It is working its way into other areas of the justice system as well.

The trend toward private justice can also be found in the areas of corrections and juvenile justice.

Private Corrections

The privatization of corrections is controversial. Critics fear the quality of inmate care will be compromised as private facilities focus on generating a profit and raise concerns about the degree of control the government will have over the nation's criminals if they are housed in privately operated facilities. Nonetheless, the privatization of corrections has been slowly gaining ground since the 1980s.

Segal (2003) notes that three-fifths of all U.S. states host private prisons, most of them contracting with private companies to house prisoners. According to Bayer and Pozen (2003, p. 1): "At year-end 2001 privately operated facilities held over 6.5 percent of America's total adult correctional facility population—representing more than 90,000 adult offenders. And at year-end 1999 privately operated facilities held almost 30 percent of all juveniles in residential placement—representing more than 30,000 juvenile offenders." Texas has the most facilities (42, as of September 4, 2001), followed by California (22) (*Sourcebook of Criminal Justice Statistics,* 2002, p. 97). Numerous companies are capitalizing on the expanding niche for private corrections, some of the largest companies being the Corrections Corporation of America, Wackenhut Corrections Corporation, Management and Training Corporation and Cornell Corrections, Inc. (*Sourcebook,* p. 96).

> The privatization of corrections has been increasing since the 1980s.

Factors to consider in the private sector, however, concern staffing levels and the resultant impact on staff security. Private prisons, concerned about the bottom line, often reduce expenditures by having smaller staffs or paying employees less: "The survey of private prisons showed that they have 'significantly lower staffing levels' than comparable public prisons . . . —28 staff members per 100 inmates in private facilities, as opposed to 32 staff members per 100 inmates in public prisons" ("Privatization Can Save . . . Money," 2001, p. 4). Furthermore: "Major incidents of violence were more common in private prisons. . . . The rate of inmate assaults on staff members was 12.2 per 1,000 inmates in private prisons, and 8.2 per 1,000 in public prisons" (p. 4).

Private Sector Involvement in Juvenile Justice

Some juvenile justice agencies, finding their jurisdictions lack adequate services and expertise, are also contracting with private sector vendors to meet their clients' needs. A survey by Levinson and Chase (2000, p. 158) found the most common private sector services and programs provided to juvenile justice agencies involved health/mental health programs, programs for special needs juveniles, services for females, residential (secure) programs, community-based programs and inpatient substance abuse programs. The survey (p. 159) also showed the private sector to be a growth area for juvenile correctional programs and services.

PRIVATE SECURITY—UP CLOSE

Because private security is profit-oriented, opportunities exist that are not available in the public sector. With corporate America recognizing that security and loss prevention are as critical to a successful business as management and marketing, an increasing number of very appealing job opportunities are developing.

The stereotype of the retiree sitting at a guard desk overnight is no longer an accurate portrayal of what has become a profession in every sense of the word. Like law enforcement, much of what happens in this profession is not common knowledge. Consequently, many people considering employment in private security may find themselves relying on inaccurate data. Unless you know someone in the field, you probably obtained what you know about security work where most people do: television or the newspaper. Television may lead you to believe *security work* consists primarily of solving crimes the police cannot or will not deal with. Television shows about private detectives frequently do two injustices to the profession. First, they unrealistically glamorize it. Second, they fail to explain what a lucrative and necessary area of business it is.

Law enforcement officers are able to do only so much, and their work may not cover all aspects necessary to other participants in the criminal justice system, such as lawyers. Remember, the role of the police is to investigate *crimes*. Once they have done this, their job is over. But what about facts surrounding a civil, noncriminal negligence case such as a car accident which falls short of criminal activity but which might spawn significant litigation? Even if it *is* a police matter, police don't always put as much emphasis on obtaining evidence as a defense attorney might like—evidence that could help exonerate the accused. Furthermore, the police have little interest in personal matters such as infidelity investigations or even workers' compensation violations. Here are excellent opportunities for the private investigator.

When you consider that the private sector may provide more advancement potential and more overall control of one's professional and personal life, it is easy to see why many law enforcement officers set eventual goals to become private security directors.

> Employment in the private sector usually provides more advancement potential and greater control over one's professional and personal life, explaining why many law enforcement officers desire jobs as private security directors.

While many individuals who have enjoyed a successful career in law enforcement will enjoy a "second career" in private security, many people successfully use work in the private sector as a "stepping stone" into the public sector. Law enforcement is a popular career, and jobs as police officers are difficult to come by. Having worked in security at any level says a number of things about an applicant for a police job:

➢ The applicant has been successfully employed.

➢ The applicant has worked in a position of trust.

➢ Unusual hours do not present a problem.

➢ The uniform does not create a power-hungry person.

➢ The applicant can keep cool under stressful circumstances.

Those seeking careers in private security may also wish to consider public security positions as well as those of special deputies, code enforcement officers and others with limited law enforcement authority. Many government agencies hire "special deputies" who possess law enforcement authority while on duty. These special deputies perform many of the same functions carried out by private security forces but do so for the government. At the local level, special deputies may be under the direct authority of the sheriff, or they may constitute a security department within a government organization. In New York, for example, security officers working for local governments are called *peace officers* to distinguish them from their public police officer counterparts.

Special deputies are also found in the federal government. For example, the U.S. Marshals assign special deputy marshals to courthouses. Such deputies are often contract employees who possess law enforcement authority only while on duty and only at their assigned venue. The Department of Energy (DOE), through its contractors, employs hundreds of individuals to perform security and safeguard responsibilities related to classified documents and materials. While such individuals are not DOE inspectors and lack law enforcement authority, they do work closely with local police departments and the FBI to investigate all levels of security breaches, thefts of government property and other crimes affecting government property and issues. Furthermore, compensation in this area can be quite lucrative.

Types of Jobs Available

The continuously evolving complexity of our society is necessitating specially trained private security officers in all phases of life. Businesses need individuals who can effectively use high-tech surveillance equipment. They rely on private suppliers of search dogs and strike/civil disobedience response teams. Some businesses need 24-hour surveillance. Services commonly identified as candidates for privatization include animal control, court security, funeral escorts, parking enforcement, patrolling of public parks, prisoner transport, public building security, public housing development patrol and special event security.

An ASIS survey of security professionals found them handling a variety of specific responsibilities, including physical security; loss and crime prevention; fraud and economic crime investigation; information security; background investigations; fire and life safety; business continuity, contingency planning and disaster management; executive protection; human resources–related functions; general management and administrative functions; and computer/Internet/network security ("Comp and Circumstance," 2001, p. x).

With the enhanced function of private security has come the opportunity for specialization. As the private security profession has expanded, so have the kinds of jobs available. ASIS lists the following as security specialties with career opportunities (http://www.asisonline.org):

Corporate Security	High-Rise Facilities Security	Risk Assessment
Cyber Security	IT Security	Strategic Intelligence
Executive Protection	Loss Prevention	Terrorism (including bioterrorism
Financial Services Security	Physical Security	and agro-terrorism)
Government Security	Private Security Management	Workplace Violence & Legal Liability
Health Care Security		

Regardless of the specific security discipline or specialty, opportunities in the private sector are typically categorized as entry-level, mid-level and top-level positions.

Entry-Level Positions. Typical entry-level jobs include private security guards and private patrol officers. Private security guards control access to private property; protect against loss through theft, vandalism or fire; enforce rules; maintain order and lower risks of all kinds. The *Occupational Outlook Handbook* (*OOH*; 2004) states:

> In department stores, guards protect people, records, merchandise, money, and equipment. They often work with undercover store detectives to prevent theft by customers or store employees and help in the

apprehension of shoplifting suspects prior to arrival by police. . . . In office buildings, banks, and hospitals, guards maintain order and protect the institutions' property, staff, and customers. At air, sea, and rail terminals and other transportation facilities, guards protect people, freight, property, and equipment. They may screen passengers and visitors for weapons and explosives using metal detectors and high-tech equipment, ensure nothing is stolen while being loaded or unloaded, and watch for fires and criminals.

Guards who work in public buildings such as museums or art galleries protect paintings and exhibits by inspecting people and packages entering and leaving the building. . . . Armored car guards protect money and valuables during transit. In addition, they protect individuals responsible for making commercial bank deposits from theft or bodily injury.

Most guards wear a uniform, and some carry a baton or other weapon, such as a gun. Security guards may work inside and/or outside, patrolling the interior of buildings or the exterior grounds. They may be stationed at a desk to monitor security cameras and to check the identification of people coming and going. As with many other jobs, a typical guard shift lasts eight hours, although many guards work at night, and many work alone. Because of the flexible hours and limited formal training requirements, this occupation is attractive to those seeking a second or part-time job.

Private patrol officers are similar to patrol units of the public police force. They move from one location to another, on foot or in a vehicle, protecting property and preventing losses. Some patrol officers work for a single employer; others have several employers.

> Typical entry-level jobs include private security guards and private patrol officers. Private security guards control access to private property; protect against loss through theft, vandalism or fire; enforce rules; maintain order and lower risks of all kinds. Private patrol officers, similar to patrol units of the public police force, move from one location to another, on foot or in a vehicle, protecting property and preventing losses.

In 2002, security guards and gaming surveillance officers held more than 1 million jobs. More than half of the guard jobs were in investigation and security services, including guard and armored car services. Most other security officers were employed directly by educational services, hospitals, food services and drinking establishments, hotels, lessors of real estate (residential and nonresidential buildings), department stores, manufacturing firms and governments. Gaming surveillance officers worked primarily in gambling industries; traveler accommodations, which includes casino hotels; and local government.

Security guard jobs exist throughout the country but are most common in metropolitan areas. Gaming surveillance officers are employed only in those states and Indian reservations where gambling has been legalized. More than 25 percent of guards worked part-time: "A significant number of law enforcement officers work as security guards when off-duty to supplement their incomes. Often working in uniform and with the official cars assigned to them, they add a high profile security presence to the establishment with which they have contracted" (*OOH*).

Mid-Level Positions.   Mid-level jobs in private security include private investigators, detectives, armed couriers, central alarm respondents and consultants. Private investigators and detectives may "freelance" or may work for a specific employer. Often the work involves background checks for employment, insurance and credit applications, civil litigation and investigation of insurance or workers' compensation claims. Sometimes investigators are brought in to work undercover to detect employee dishonesty, shoplifting or illegal drug use:

Private detectives and investigators offer many services, including executive, corporate, and celebrity protection; pre-employment verification; and individual background profiles. They also provide assistance in civil liability and personal injury cases, insurance claims and fraud, child custody and protection cases, and premarital screening. Increasingly, they are hired to investigate individuals to prove or disprove infidelity. . . .

Private detectives and investigators often specialize. Those who focus on intellectual property theft, for example, investigate and document acts of piracy, help clients stop the illegal activity, and provide intelligence for prosecution and civil action. Other investigators specialize in financial profiles and asset searches. Their reports reflect information gathered through interviews, investigation and surveillance, and research, including review of public documents (*OOH*).

According to the *OOH,* private detectives and investigators held about 48,000 jobs in 2002. Nearly one-third were self-employed, including those who held a secondary job as a self-employed private investigator: "Almost a fifth of jobs were found in investigation and security services, including private detective agencies, while another fifth were in department or other general merchandise stores. The rest worked mostly in State and local government, legal services firms, employment services, insurance carriers, and credit intermediation and related activities, including banks and other depository institutions."

Mid-level jobs in private security include private investigators, detectives, armed couriers, central alarm respondents and consultants. Top jobs in security include loss prevention specialists, security directors, risk managers and chief security officers (CSOs).

Top-Level Positions. Top jobs in security include managing a private security company or heading up security for a private concern. Common titles include loss prevention specialist, security director, risk manager and chief security officer (CSO).

As with guard positions, higher-level security positions are most likely to exist in urban regions with higher populations. International jobs are also available in security, but obtaining them is not easy. Many businesses and establishments, such as hotels, are opening facilities in foreign countries. Often the security director of such businesses and establishments are sent to set up the security system.

While top jobs in security involve managing people and budgets, companies are not necessarily looking to hire people with master's of business administration (MBA) degrees to fill their CSO slots. Harowitz notes:

[While] a knowledge of business remains important . . . corporate executives are requesting that their CSOs have intelligence capabilities or experience, and they want people with more investigative skills. Consequently, . . . many of [the] top spots go to people from federal law enforcement, the intelligence community, certain areas of the military, and investigative areas within an agency like the U.S. Department of Treasury.

An example is Larry L. Cockell, who was hired . . . to be the senior vice president and CSO at AOL Time Warner, Inc., a business with 90,000 employees and seven distinct global companies. In the aftermath of 9-11, management wanted someone with strong international experience and a strategic approach to structuring the security function. . . . They did not put the emphasis on business skills. . . .

George Campbell, president of the International Security Management Association (ISMA), which has members holding top security slots in multinational corporations, says he sees that theme play out repeatedly on ISMA's list of available jobs. "When you look at the experience profile that they are after," he says, "it's around law enforcement. . . . It's not saying they want an MBA."

Lehman Brothers' Kessler has seen a similar trend. "There are about five companies in our immediate one-block-to-two-block radius here in New York City that have all hired ex-security people from places ranging from the New York City Police Department to the FBI to the CIA," he says.

Internet Security Specialists. As technology advances, the types of security jobs available also expand. One of the newest arenas of security involves cyber-crime. *The Top 100* (2001, p. 223) notes:

> An *Internet security specialist* is someone who is responsible for protecting a company's network, which can be accessed through the Internet, from intrusion by outsiders. These intruders are referred to as hackers (or crackers), and the process of breaking into a system is called hacking (or cracking). . . . Internet security specialists are sometimes known as Internet security administrators, Internet security engineers, information security technicians, and network security consultants.
>
> The duties of an Internet security specialist vary depending on where he or she works, how big the company is, and the degree of sensitivity of the information that is being protected. . . .
>
> Primarily, Internet security specialists are in charge of monitoring the flow of information through the firewall [a system set up to act as a barrier of protection between the outside world of the Internet and the company]. Security specialists must be able to write code and configure the software to alert them when certain kinds of activities occur. . . . Logs are kept of all access to the network. Security specialists monitor the logs and watch for anything out of the ordinary. If they see something strange, they must make a judgment call as to whether the activity was innocent or malicious. Then they must investigate and do some detective work—perhaps even tracking down the user who initiated the action. In other instances, they might have to create a new program to prevent that action from happening again. . . .
>
> Secondary duties can include security administrative work, such as establishing security policies for the company, or security engineering duties, which are more technical in nature. For example, some companies might deal with such sensitive information that the company forbids any of its information to be transmitted over email. Programs can be written to disallow transmission of any company product information or to alert the specialist when this sensitive information is transmitted. The security specialist also might be in charge of educating employees on security policies concerning their network.

Obviously, this type of security work requires a specialized skill and degree of technical knowledge. While such technical knowledge is not a prerequisite for most security positions, employment requirements in the growing field of private security are becoming increasingly higher.

Employment Requirements

Private security is joining the trend of other fields that stress the importance of achieving certain basic professional requirements. Employers with proprietary forces usually set their own standards for security officers. Contractual security companies often are regulated by state law. Individuals who wish to provide security services on their own may need to be licensed by their state. Requirements vary, so it is important to check on your local situation.

While some states require few, if any, qualifications to be met by those wishing to work in private security, other states are very strict as to who may practice in this field, either as an individual or a company supplying security services. Of the three professional licenses author Harr holds, his private detective license required more comprehensive administrative requirements and was more expensive to initially obtain than his licenses as a police officer or a lawyer. Minnesota statutes stipulate who needs to be licensed as a private investigator in the state, what the application consists of and what must accompany the application, including:

➢   A surety bond for $5,000

➢   Verified certificates of at least five citizens not related to the signer who have known the signer for more than five years, certifying that the signer is of "good moral character"

➢   Two photographs and a full set of fingerprints for each signer of the application

A majority of states now recognize that some controls have to be in place to ensure responsible involvement by those operating in this field: "Most States require that guards be licensed. To be licensed as a guard, individuals must be at least 18 years old, pass a background check, and complete classroom training in such subjects as property rights, emergency procedures, and detention of suspected criminals. Drug testing is often required, and may be random and ongoing" (*OOH*). The *OOH* also reports:

> There are no formal education requirements for most private detective and investigator jobs, although many private detectives have college degrees. . . .
>
> The majority of the States and the District of Columbia require private detectives and investigators to be licensed. Licensing requirements vary widely, but convicted felons cannot receive a license in most States and a growing number of States are enacting mandatory training programs for private detectives and investigators. Some States have few requirements, and 6 States—Alabama, Alaska, Colorado, Idaho, Mississippi, and South Dakota—have no statewide licensing requirements while others have stringent regulations. For example, the Bureau of Security and Investigative Services of the California Department of Consumer Affairs requires private investigators to be 18 years of age or older; have a combination of education in police science, criminal law, or justice, and experience equaling 3 years (6,000 hours) of investigative experience; pass an evaluation by the Federal Department of Justice and a criminal history background check; and receive a qualifying score on a 2-hour written examination covering laws and regulations. There are additional requirements for a firearms permit.

Be sure to investigate the requirements of the state(s) in which you want to work. Some county and city governments also require certification or licensure of those working in private security positions within their jurisdiction. Because many duties of private security officers can have consequences as critical as those of the law enforcement officer—for example, using firearms, K-9s and other weapons; arresting people; rendering emergency medical assistance and the like—it makes sense to have basic requirements in place. Most common are regulations regarding background checks, certain minimal knowledge and posting some sort of bond. Some states have a residency requirement; many have policies on autos and uniforms.

> Nearly every state now has licensing or registration requirements for guards who work for contract security agencies. Some states have a residency requirement, and many states have regulations concerning autos and uniforms. Be sure to investigate these employment requirements by contacting the appropriate regulatory agency.

Training requirements and other qualifications vary among different agencies; however, some applicant qualities are fairly common. Most employers prefer guards who are high school graduates. Some jobs require a driver's license. Some employers seek individuals who have had experience in the military police or in state and local police agencies. Furthermore: "Applicants are expected to have good character references, no serious police record, and good health. They should be mentally alert, emotionally stable, and physically fit in order to cope with emergencies. Guards who have frequent contact with the public should communicate well." The *OOH* notes:

> For private detective and investigator jobs, most employers look for individuals with ingenuity, persistence and assertiveness. A candidate must not be afraid of confrontation, should communicate well, and should be able to think on his or her feet. Good interviewing and interrogation skills are also important and usually are acquired in earlier careers in law enforcement or other fields.

Because competition for prime security positions is increasing, applicants should strive to increase their marketability by gaining knowledge of the field through education and other types of experiences. According to ASIS (p. 2): "Students seeking careers in security should pursue course work in security, computer science, electronics, business management, law, police science, personnel and information management."

In addition, some individuals may want to be certified by the ASIS through their *Certified Protection Professional (CPP)* program. This program, organized in 1977, is designed to recognize individuals meeting specific criteria of professional protection knowledge and conduct. To be eligible to take the examination, candidates must either have ten years of experience with no degree, eight years of experience and an associate's degree, five years of experience and a bachelor's degree, four years of experience and a master's degree or three years of experience and a doctoral degree. At least half the experience must be in "responsible charge" of a security function. The examination takes a full day, with the morning devoted to general security knowledge and the afternoon devoted to a choice of four specialty tests selected from a wide variety of areas.

Most employers seek security applicants with high school diplomas and some experience in the military police or in state- or local-level police work. Other important qualities include good character references, good health, good personal habits and no police record. A valid driver's license may also be required. Eligible individuals may benefit by becoming a Certified Protection Professional, or CPP.

Job Outlook

As referenced earlier, private sector security is clearly a critical protective resource today, and the job outlook for those choosing this career path is positive. According to *The Top 100* (p. 330): "Security services is one of the largest employment fields in the United States." Furthermore (pp. 331–332):

> Employment for guards and other security personnel is expected to increase faster than the average through 2008, as crime rates rise with the overall population growth. The highest U.S. Department of Labor estimates call for more than 1.25 million guards to be employed by 2008. . . . A factor adding to this demand is the trend for private security firms to perform duties previously handled by police officers, such as courtroom security and crowd control in airports.

Given the enhanced state of alert within the United States following recent terrorist attacks, it seems safe to say the demand for security forces will most certainly remain high in the foreseeable future.

The private security field is expected to grow more rapidly through 2008 than the average for all occupations, requiring the hiring of many employees to meet the increasing security needs.

Certain areas within the security industry are also projected to grow more rapidly than others, for example, computer security and information technology. *The Top 100* (p. 226) states:

> Employment for Internet security specialists will grow much faster than the average. The number of companies with a presence on the Internet is exploding. As these companies connect their private networks to the public Internet, they will need to protect their confidential information. Currently, the demand for Internet security specialists is greater than the supply, and this trend is expected to continue as the number of businesses connecting to the Internet continues to grow.

The CERT® Coordination Center (2004) asserts:

> The need to address security within organizations is growing in the public awareness. Customers are demanding it as concerns about privacy and identify theft rise. Business partners, suppliers, and vendors are

starting to require it from one another, particularly when providing mutual network access. There is a wide range of current and pending US national and international legislation that calls for organizations to exercise due diligence and demonstrate an acceptable standard of due care in how they manage their computing infrastructures and the information that such networks and systems create, transmit, and store, particularly when connected to the Internet.

Another area of growth is contract security and investigations, as more companies outsource these positions in an effort to improve cost-effectiveness.

> Job opportunities in private security are greater in metropolitan areas. Security jobs are more difficult to obtain in foreign countries and in less populated areas of the United States.

Political Trends. Politics influence the job market. Just as politics can restrict tax dollars available to hire more public police officers, thus stimulating the market for private sector security-related jobs, national and international politics can cause shifts in the job market. Unquestionably the world politics since September 11, 2001, have caused increased attention to be paid to security here and abroad. In fact, since the last edition of this book was published, an entire new realm of travel-related security work at airports and elsewhere has evolved. Both public and private sectors have needed to reevaluate the importance and staffing of security-related divisions, creating many new and previously underconsidered or not-even-considered jobs. This includes front-line security, risk management and emergency response. These areas are among those with the best job outlook and highest growth potential for future career opportunity and development.

Salaries

Overall, as expressed by Anderson (2004): "Security professionals did well in 2002." Yet it is difficult to provide an accurate listing of "average" pay in private security because the range is extreme. Entry-level jobs may start at the minimum wage, but the upper wage is virtually unlimited. Owners of successful private security or investigation firms and upper-level security directors can expect lucrative salaries, with perks like bonus plans and company cars.

The *OOH* reports median annual earnings of guards were $19,140 in 2002, while median annual earnings of salaried private detectives and investigators were $29,300 that same year. The *OOH* also notes:

> Earnings of private detectives and investigators vary greatly depending on their employer, specialty, and the geographic area in which they work. According to a study by Abbott, Langer & Associates, security/loss prevention directors and vice presidents had a median income of $77,500 per year in 2002; investigators, $39,800; and store detectives, $25,000.

The Top 100 (p. 331) adds:

> Earnings for security consultants vary greatly depending on the consultant's training and experience. Entry-level consultants with a bachelor's degree commonly start at $26,000 to $32,000 per year. Consultants with graduate degrees begin at $34,000 to $41,000 per year, and experienced consultants may earn $50,000 to $100,000 per year or more. Many consultants work on a per-project basis, with rates of up to $75 per hour.

In an interesting twist, while the earning potential of private security professionals generally exceeds that of public police officers, private security managers working in publicly held companies typically earn

TABLE 4–1   2002 Hourly Wage Ranges for Security Officers, Console Operators and Investigators

	HOURLY WAGE RANGES	
	Low End	*High End*
Security Officers		
Contract – Unarmed	$10/hour	$14/hour
Proprietary – Unarmed	$13/hour	$17/hour
Contract – Armed	$17/hour	$19/hour
Proprietary – Armed	$15/hour	$21/hour
Console Operators		
Contract	$12/hour	$15/hour
Proprietary	$12/hour	$15/hour
Investigators		
Contract	$31/hour	$56/hour
Proprietary	$24/hour	$31/hour

SOURCE: Adapted from Teresa Anderson. "The Key to Earnings." *Security Management Online,* January 2004.

more than security managers in privately owned enterprises: "The highest paid security professionals manage multiple facilities for publicly owned global enterprises and work in the fields of information technology, manufacturing, and retail. . . . Security managers working for public companies earned $96,116, 11 percent more than their counterparts in private companies, who earned $85,708. Also, those in public companies earned 26 percent more than those in other organizations, such as academic institutions or nonprofit groups, who earned $76,408" (Anderson). Tables 4–1 and 4–2 show earnings data for security officers, console operators, investigators and security managers.

When considering potential salaries in the private sector, changing economic times must be factored in. While some private sector jobs will pay less than public positions, the increased awareness and reliance on private sector protection means the salaries may not be as limited as in the public arena.

TABLE 4–2   2002 Annual Average Salary of Security Managers, as Related to Several Factors

NUMBER OF LOCATIONS		SIZE OF SECURITY BUDGET MANAGED		CERTIFICATION AND EDUCATION	
One location (building or facility)	$65,700	$500,000 and under	Low $60,000	CPP designation	$98,332
Two or more locations within one state	$75,300	$1,000,001 to $2,500,000	$89,049	No CPP certification	$80,485
Two or more locations in more than one state	$95,800	More than $2,500,000	$126,116	Master's degree	$102,600
Two or more locations in more than one country	$132,500			Four-year degree	$89,954
				No degree	$74,100

SOURCE: Adapted from Teresa Anderson. "The Key to Earnings." *Security Management Online,* January 2004.

Salaries in the field of private security vary greatly, ranging from around $17,000 a year for unarmed contract security officers to $150,000 or more a year for corporate security managers working for large public companies.

Fringe Benefits

Most security professionals receive benefits from their employers, although various surveys indicate different percentages of employees are receiving certain benefits (Anderson; "Comp and Circumstance . . .,"; "2001 Salary Survey," 2001). Nonetheless, most security employees receive paid vacation time, paid holidays, health care coverage, life insurance, dental insurance, sick leave, a 401(k) plan and a long-term disability plan. Other benefits frequently provided include tuition reimbursement, childcare support, a pension plan, personal time off, vision insurance, short-term disability, cellular/airtime usage, trade show/convention expenses and association memberships.

In addition to these benefits, nearly half of security employees receive performance bonuses and many are offered stock options or stock purchase plans and allowed to participate in a profit sharing plan. The "2001 Salary Survey" (p. S7) reports security professionals employed by transportation/utility firms received the greatest number of benefits of any industry surveyed, while government workers received the fewest.

Promotions

Like law enforcement, security careers can meet a stumbling block not as prevalent in other careers. Promotions can come few and far between—if at all. The problem is that jobs in the security field tend to be at one end of the spectrum or the other. At the entry level, security jobs can be minimum-wage jobs, with minimal raises. "Middle management" positions are usually few in number. The money is in top management jobs, either for a corporation or for one's own business. At these levels there is literally no upward limit.

As in law enforcement, promotions in private security may be scarcer than in other professions, particularly into middle management where positions are limited.

Those aspiring to become security managers must also possess critical technical and computer skills, as asserted by Wilson (2001, p. 37):

> Security managers are no longer able to concern themselves solely with the physical access or perimeter security of a facility or campus. Today's security managers also must deal with securing a company's computer network, preventing e-mail viruses, restricting employee access to computer databases, and protecting and facilitating the flow of corporate information from facility to facility. Successful security professionals need to be able to incorporate traditional security skills with the IT skills now required.

CONCLUSION

Private security is a critical protective resource in our nation today. The private security field is expected to grow rapidly through the year 2008, requiring the hiring of a large number of employees to meet the increasing security needs. A security job can serve as a stepping stone to other employment or a chance to obtain supplemental income as a second job or while attending school. Whether you seek employment in private security as a chance to acquire valuable training to help gain future employment in law enforcement or because the security field has exceptional future potential, private security can provide satisfying work.

AN INSIDER'S VIEW

CAREER OPPORTUNITIES IN PRIVATE SECURITY

Robert B. Iannone

Certified Protection Professional
President, Iannone Security Management, Inc.

Preparing yourself for employment in any field should include achieving competency through pursuing three factors: (1) training, (2) education and (3) experience. Training includes attending security seminars, conferences and on-the-job training. Education refers to achieving a college degree in the security field or a related field. Gaining experience, of course, requires working in your chosen field. These elements apply no matter what field you pursue.

In private security, formal education can be obtained from the numerous colleges and universities throughout the United States that offer associate of arts degrees, bachelor's degrees and graduate degrees in security. Core courses in these curricula may include such subjects as Introduction to Security, Physical Security, Information Security, Information Technology, Ethics, Legal Aspects of Security, and Security Management and Administration. A degree in a related field might include a curriculum in business or management.

Following graduation, experience can be achieved by obtaining an entry-level position. To help prospective security applicants obtain the entry-level experience necessary, colleges and universities may offer a core security internship. Internships allow students to be employed in industry and perform actual security-related functions while earning credits toward graduation. In many instances, employers have retained interns following graduation.

Security-related training can be gained through professional security organizations such as the American Society for Industrial Security (ASIS), the International Security Conference (ISC), Research Security Administrators (RSA) and the National Classification Management Society (NCMS). Security-related training courses offered through the ASIS, ISC, RSA and NCMS include virtually all aspects of the security profession. In addition, numerous periodicals published by security organizations such as the ASIS and ISC address a variety of security-related subjects. Full advantage of the services offered by professional security organizations can be gained through becoming a member. Services offered through membership range from newsletters, periodicals and announcements to sponsored seminars and conferences. There is no membership to ISC and RSA; however, there are mailing lists.

Employment opportunities in the security field have increased in recent years. Some factors causing this increase include (1) the doubling of personnel working in the field over the past 30 years, (2) a current shortage of qualified personnel, (3) technological advances, (4) higher salaries, (5) a shift from the law enforcement image and (6) the availability of two-year, four-year and graduate degrees. Employment opportunities available in the security industry include government service (military and civilian), banking/finance, retail, health care, airport/airline, campus, lodging, computer, aerospace and the security services.

Although employment opportunities in the aerospace industry have decreased in recent years, the security services industry has increased significantly. The security services include providers of security-related hardware such as intrusion detection systems and devices, access control systems and devices, closed-circuit television, fire detection systems and devices, lock and key control, physical barriers and identification systems. Other security service providers include suppliers of contract security officers. With the increase in the use of personal computers, there are also suppliers of computer software for a variety of applications such as wireless technology, data management and material accountability systems.

Salaries in the security field vary, depending on the industry. In addition, salaries vary within specific industries depending on such factors as training, education and experience. Salaries also differ between geographic areas and policy-making and non–policy-making positions.

In summary, career development begins with each individual; therefore, individuals who prepare themselves by acquiring job-specific training, formal education and field-related experience will obtain the best positions. In addition, regardless of the security discipline, they will be assured of higher salaries.

Robert B. Iannone, *CPP, is the President of Iannone Security Management, Incorporated, located in Fountain Valley, California. He has over 30 years' experience as a security practitioner, manager, author, consultant, expert witness, lecturer, educator and advisor to security book publishers. Mr. Iannone has been a member of the American Society for Industrial Security since 1966, and has been conferred a Lifetime Certified Protection Professional (CPP). He is also a member of the International Association of Professional Security Consultants and a member of the Board of Directors, Research Security Administrators.*

A consultant since 1989, he provides objective, independent studies and surveys of a security organization's personnel, systems and equipment. He also provides consulting and expert witness services to the legal profession. For more than two decades, Mr. Iannone has been an adjunct professor of security-related courses at the California State University, San Marco; California State University, Long Beach; and Golden West College, Huntington Beach, California. He holds a Bachelor of Science degree in Criminal Justice (Security Management) from California State University, Long Beach, and a Master of Science degree in Management from the University of LaVerne. He has been married 42 years to Theresa; they have one married daughter and one grandson. His hobbies include spectator sports and working with personal computers.

INSIDER'S VIEW ONLINE

An additional *Insider's View* for this chapter is "The Changing Face of Private Security" by Marie Ohman, found on the Wadsworth website: http://www.wadsworth.com/criminaljustice_d/.

 ## MIND STRETCHES

1.   Why do you think the entertainment field is obsessed with depicting private security? Do you think this obsession helps or hurts the profession? Why?

2.   Do you personally know any security officers? Are they like the private investigators depicted on television?

3.   What is your favorite private detective show? Why?

4.   Do you think television and the movies have influenced your career choice?

5.   Do you think security work will become more specialized or more generalized in the future? Why? How will your job goals be affected?

6.   What stereotype do you think private security officers have? Why? Is it justified?

7.   Why do you think the trend to license all professions exists? Do you think it is helpful?

8.   Are security salaries more or less than you had anticipated? Does salary affect your decision as to what field of employment you will eventually pursue? Why or why not?

9.   How do you predict the field of private security will change? Why?

REFERENCES

American Society for Industrial Security (ASIS). Online: http://www.asisonline.org

Anderson, Teresa. "The Key to Earnings." *Security Management Online,* January 2004. Online: http://www.securitymanagement.com/library/001549.html

ASIS International. *Career Opportunities in Security.* Alexandria, VA: ASIS International, no date.

Bayer, Patrick and Pozen, David E. *The Effectiveness of Juvenile Correctional Facilities: Public versus Private Management.* Yale University, Economic Growth Center Discussion Paper No. 863, July 2003. Online: http://www.econ.yale.edu/growth_pdf/cdp863.pdf

CERT® Coordination Center. "Governing for Enterprise Security." May 28, 2004. Online: http://www.cert.org/

"Comp and Circumstance: ASIS International 2000 Employment Survey." *2001 Security Industry Buyers Guide,* 2001, pp. ix–xii.

Gips, Michael A. "On the Front Lines: How State and Local Governments Battle Crime and Terrorism." *Security Management,* August 2002, pp. 100–108.

Harowitz, Sherry L. "The New Centurions." *Security Management Online,* January 2003. Online: http://www.securitymanagement.com/library/001363.html

Hertig, Christopher A. "The Evolving Role of Protection Officers." *Access Control and Security Systems,* November 2001, pp. 28–29.

Levinson, Robert B. and Chase, Raymond. "Private Sector Involvement in Juvenile Justice." *Corrections Today,* April 2000, pp. 156–159.

Occupational Outlook Handbook, 2004–05 Edition. Bureau of Labor Statistics, U.S. Department of Labor. Washington, DC: U.S. Government Printing Office, 2004.

"Privatization Can Save Money in Prison Construction, Study Says." *Criminal Justice Newsletter,* May 25, 2001, pp. 3–4.

Samuels, Joseph, Jr. "Building Partnerships between Private-Sector Security and Public-Sector Police." *The Police Chief,* September 2003, p. 8.

Segal, Geoffrey F. "Private Prisons Save Money, Boost Productivity, Study Finds." *The Heartland Institute,* November 1, 2003. Online: http://www.heartland.org

Sourcebook of Criminal Justice Statistics 2002. Online: http://www.albany.edu/sourcebook

The Top 100: The Fastest Growing Careers for the 21st Century. Chicago: Ferguson Publishing Company, 2001.

"2001 Salary Survey." Supplement to *Access Control and Security Systems Integration,* 2001, pp. S1–S7.

Wilson, Jeff M. "Money Matters." *Security Products,* May 2001, pp. 36–40.

HELPFUL WEBSITES

American Society for Industrial Security (ASIS)
http://www.asisonline.org

CERT® Coordination Center
http://www.cert.org

CSO Informer
http://csoinformer.com

National Association of Legal Investigators (NALI)
http://www.nalionline.org

Security Magazine
http://www.securitymagazine.com

Security, Police and Fire Professionals of America (SPFPA)
http://www.spfpa.org

ADDITIONAL CONTACTS AND SOURCES OF INFORMATION

Professional Training Resources
PO Box 439
Shaftsbury, VT 05262
(802) 447-7832 or (800) 998-9400
Publishes: *Cashing In on Consulting for the Private Security Professional,* by Jim R. Matison and Kären M. Hess, © 1997

CHAPTER 5

ON CHOOSING A CAREER:
KNOWING THE JOB AND YOURSELF

Life is to be lived. If you have to support yourself, you had bloody well better find some way that is going to be interesting. And you don't do that by sitting around wondering about yourself.

—*Katharine Hepburn*

Do You Know:

➢ Why job satisfaction is so important?
➢ The best way to avoid job dissatisfaction?
➢ What the four steps of the career development process are?
➢ What specific requirements and limitations you should consider when choosing a career?
➢ How your background could prevent employment in the criminal justice or security fields?
➢ What an *inventurer* is? If you are one?
➢ What five essential parts of a dream job must be considered before it can become a reality?
➢ The importance of taking risks?

INTRODUCTION

Previous chapters discussed some realities of careers in criminal justice and security. As you consider these professions, understand what they are—and what they are *not*. Also, take a serious inventory of your abilities and interests to determine if your career goals are realistic.

In this chapter you'll combine knowledge about your chosen field with an honest look at yourself, to make certain you are, indeed, on a road that will take you where you want to be. How often would you get into your car and just drive with no thought of where you want to go? Yet many people launch themselves toward a career with very limited forethought—or with unrealistic dreams. Many job seekers have dreams—dreams of a successful career and a carefree, pleasurable lifestyle. However, as Leider and Shapiro (2002, pp. 100–101) state:

> The "perfect job" isn't really about enjoyment. Instead, it's one that mirrors perfectly the person who holds it. And people do find, or invent, or create these jobs. They do it by working a process . . . that links who you are with what you do. The process involves developing a clarity about your talents, passions, and values—looking inside yourself to discover what you do best, what you like to do best, and the type of working environment that supports what you care about most. And then combining all three to develop a clear vision of the kind of work that links who you are with what you do. . . .
>
> The perfect job isn't a standard of living—it's a state of mind and state of being. In the perfect job, you're applying the talents you enjoy most to an interest you're passionate about, in an environment that fits who you are and what you value.

The romanticized dream of a successful career becomes even more problematic when it involves the fields within criminal justice. Many people are intrigued by such employment because they want to be like the TV undercover police officer or private investigator they watch week after week. You must enter your career search with a much more open mind. Realistically, what *is* the job you are seeking?

SELECTING AND DEVELOPING A CAREER

Carelessly pursuing a career can be costly. First, selecting a career is extremely important because the vast majority of your waking hours will be spent working—why spend so much time being unhappy and unfulfilled? Perhaps even worse is that job frustrations may manifest themselves in unpleasant, if not dangerous, ways. People who dislike their work show it. For people employed by the criminal justice system, job dissatisfaction can seriously affect job performance. At best, they may appear as unfeeling individuals, expressing little concern for anyone, including victims. At worst, inappropriate physical force, even brutality, may be evidence of something going on "inside." Such behavior can result in nationwide antipolice publicity, as seen in the beating of Rodney King.

> Career dissatisfaction can lead to unhappiness, negativity and cynicism in the individual and to a decrease in productivity and morale for the unit in which the individual works. The impact may be felt by coworkers and may affect their work attitudes as well.

The best ways to prevent career dissatisfaction are to research the field carefully before applying for employment, ask questions of those already in the field, and carefully evaluate the positive and negative aspects of the occupation *as they apply to your values and expectations.* Rather than jumping into a career you know little about, including how well suited to it *you* are, look objectively at the whole picture. Consider the job. Consider yourself. Is it a "match"? Or is it the frustrating pursuit of a fantasy? There is a story about a woman who loved everything about being an engine mechanic—except getting dirty. Absolutely nothing could prevent her from leaving work each night grimy and greasy, and it was causing her to consider a career change. The simple fact was that an inherent part of her work was to get dirty. Determining whether getting dirty was worth it was an issue that had to be addressed.

Similarly, facts about working in criminal justice and private security must be faced. The relatively mediocre pay, difficult hours, odd days off, public's perception of the job, limited opportunity for promotions and inherent danger are issues that may make the job unacceptable to some. For other job seekers, this field remains attractive for reasons that go far beyond the motivations for other fields of work, including the desire to play a helping role in society, to have an exciting career or to have a job with significant power over others (good or bad). Take a realistic look at these issues now, examining why you want to work in this field and what your true expectations are.

> The best way to avoid career dissatisfaction is to thoroughly research the field you are interested in and to carefully and realistically address issues concerning the nature of the work, the hours, the pay—any and all positives *and* negatives. Go in with your eyes wide open, free from unrealistic expectations.

While this text is specifically directed at helping you develop your own job-seeking strategy, there is much more to the process than merely learning to write a résumé. If you are not heading in a direction that will really work for you, your work will not be fulfilling.

Career coaches and counselors help people develop the ability to examine their motivations, a skill that applies to people seeking to enter a certain career as well as those considering getting out. Nathan and Hill (1992, p. 2) view career counseling as a process that enables clients to become more aware of their own resources to lead a more satisfying life as well as to "take into account the interdependence of career and non-career considerations" (p. 3). They cite the approach advocated by Parsons (1909) nearly a century ago:

> In the wise choice of vocation, there are three factors:
>   1. A clear understanding of yourself
>   2. A knowledge of the requirements and prospects in different lines of work
>   3. True reasoning on the relations of these two groups of facts

In Figure 5–1, Krannich (1995, p. 100) illustrates how the first two factors are critical to career development (see steps 1 and 2 in the figure). The next section of this book focuses on steps 3 and 4.

Krannich identifies the four steps of the career development process as (1) self-assessment, (2) career exploration, (3) job-search skill development and (4) implementation of the job-search steps.

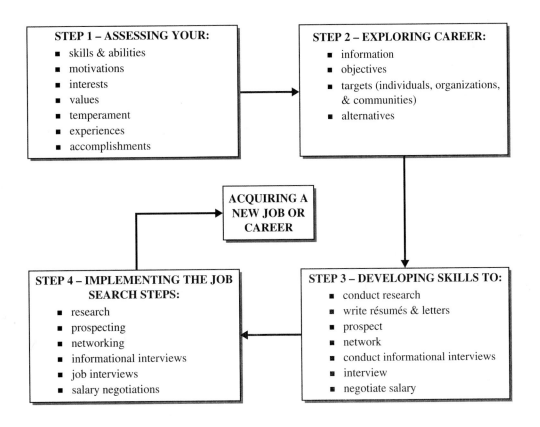

FIGURE 5–1   The Career Development Process

SOURCE: Ronald L. Krannich. *Change Your Job, Change Your Life,* 5th ed. Manassas Park, VA: Impact Publications, 1995, p. 100. Reprinted by permission.

Interesting changes have occurred in what motivates job seekers. It is likely that as the baby boomers have become well entrenched in the workforce, they have brought with them a degree of their "me-generation" mentality that includes a certain self-centeredness resulting in an expectation that everything should be perfect . . . at least for them! The question is, then, can work be . . . perfect?

Indeed, many Americans become encumbered by an ideal of the perfect job. But as Leider and Shapiro (p. 100) note: "Every job has its good parts and its bad parts. It's hard to imagine any kind of work that would be enjoyable 100 percent of the time. Even sports heroes and movie stars have their bad days."

Unrealistic expectations of work may be a natural evolution of American society. Post-Depression work, followed by post–World War II work, really did help satisfy the American dream. The economy was strong and growing; opportunities were everywhere, and work itself provided so much to so many. Even as people expected more and more, the workplace was able to keep up . . . at least for awhile. Increasing salaries, benefits and new types of jobs seemed limitless. But they weren't. And as time passed, jobs became more scarce, upward mobility more challenging and the seemingly "unlimited potential" noticeably more limited.

The world of work, including why people seek the jobs they do, has come back to where it arguably began: to provide for our more basic needs. Personal, perhaps selfish, needs take precedence over the broader things that work provides. The benefits a job directly provides is only one aspect of how satisfying a job can be. Now the important question that needs to be asked is whether a job provides the leisure time for individuals to achieve their goals beyond just being successful on the job.

Charting Your Future Course

It's difficult to consider the future without becoming philosophical. No one *knows* what the future will bring, so all you can do is speculate about what might occur. Of course, you can make some pretty darned good guesses based on what has occurred in the past combined with what is happening right now.

Here's what is known for sure: Technology demands that successful job candidates have certain skill levels, and work affects your life to the degree that careful thought must be invested in future job considerations. The future of *your* work will be dictated by the decisions you make about it. Even if you make no decision and let yourself be blown about the job market like a tumbleweed, you have, indeed, made that decision.

Not only is the rapid development of technology influencing the working world, so too are the reasons people pursue certain jobs. The job you seek *does* influence how you feel about yourself and those around you. You must have a balance of interests and activities, a sense of identity, a realistic sense of your capabilities and reasonable goals for your life. It is also important to feel in control of your destiny. By examining yourself and your goals, together with a realistic idea of what expectations are truly important to you, you place yourself in control of your future.

One way to find out your true career interests *before* committing to a particular line of work is to volunteer with a potential employer, request a ride-along or interview some officers or other employees. Visit agencies you think you'd like to work for and see what a typical workday is like. Local colleges and universities can often supply the names of recent graduates working in your field. Call them to find out what they are doing and how they like it.

Career Coaches and Counselors

A variety of tools exist to help you better understand your own aptitudes and interests. You are encouraged to take such interest inventories and aptitude tests to help highlight career areas that might satisfy your many needs. There may even be job options you have never heard about or considered. A great place to start is the counseling department at your school or career counselors in the private sector.

Bolles (2004, pp. 393–404) offers advice on selecting a coach or counselor, beginning with collecting three names of career counselors in your geographical area. Starting places include your friends, the yellow pages (under such headings as "Aptitude and Employment Testing" or "Career and Vocational Counseling"), local schools and community organizations, where you may receive recommendations on qualified counselors. Next, Bolles (p. 396) recommends: "Once you have three names, you need to go do some comparison shopping. You want to talk with all three of them face-to-face, and decide which of the three (if any) you want to hook up with." In searching for a good career counselor, Bolles (p. 397) suggests asking the following questions:

➢   What is your program?

➢   Who will be doing it with me? And how long has this person been doing it?

➢   What is your success rate?

➢   What is the cost of your services?

➢   Is there a contract up front? If so, may I see it please, and take it home with me?

Bolles (p. 398) contends: "As you look over your notes, you will realize there is no definitive way for you to determine a career counselor's expertise. It's something you'll have to *smell out,* as you go along." He also cautions: "If they [the career counselors] give you the feeling that everything will be done for you, by them . . . rather than asserting that you are going to have to do almost all of the work, with their basically assuming the role of coach, give them 15 bad points." For more information about career counselors or a list of certified counselors in your area, contact one of the agencies listed at the end of this chapter.

Finally, don't overlook the resources readily at hand who already know you well: family and friends. Ask their opinions about what they think you'd be good at and whether they can see you in the work you're considering.

The steps to understanding yourself and your career goals have a beginning but never an end! Here's the beginning.

BRAINSTORMING POSSIBILITIES

Even if you are fairly certain about what you want to do with your life, it is worthwhile to consider other alternatives. These may be similar jobs, or they may be different altogether. Choices are what life is about, so start developing some.

Of all the exercises you will complete, this will be one of the easiest. Sit down with a clear mind and list in your journal the jobs that appeal to you. Don't analyze what you think you will or won't be qualified for. Simply write down the jobs that intrigue you.

> ➤ Do any general patterns emerge?
> ➤ Are the jobs you listed more in the service fields? The academic fields?
> ➤ Are they jobs that stress physical skills? Mental ability? Both equally?
> ➤ Do they stress working with people or alone? Indoors or outdoors?
> ➤ Why do you think you picked these jobs?

"JUST THE FACTS"

Having generated some career choices, next determine the facts about these alternatives.

> In deciding which career is best suited to you and your needs, you must consider age requirements, physical requirements, educational requirements, background limitations and experience requirements.

Age

A common question asked is "Am I too old" to consider law enforcement or criminal justice as a career? Frankly, a better question is "Am I too *young*?" Criminal justice hiring can be both fickle and cyclical, with hiring authorities more interested, at times, in young people they can "mold" and, at other times, favoring older candidates with more experience and maturity. More than ever, maturity is playing a very important part in who gets hired. Increased public scrutiny, increased liability concerns and the departure from the traditional paramilitary perspective make people with more life experience more attractive to employers. All that is recommended is that people be realistic about age desirability for various jobs.

Some jobs are better suited for young adults; others are ideal for retirees. Some positions, including certain law enforcement and security jobs, have age limitations. For example, most states require police officer recruits to be at least 21 years old. While the majority of policing jobs do not have an upward age limit for applicants, the federal system usually will not accept applicants older than 35. While the majority of criminal justice jobs do not have an upward age limit, federal agencies and others may. It is important to learn about any restrictions prior to applying.

Corrections and private security are open to an even greater variety of ages. On one hand, either field is exceptional for entry-level people seeking experience to help them eventually obtain jobs as police officers. On the other hand, corrections and security work can be great fields in their own right or ideal jobs for retired police officers or others.

Physical Requirements

The jobs you are interested in likely have physical requirements. Most agencies or companies set minimum vision and hearing requirements. One young man went through law school to be an FBI agent, only to learn later that his vision disqualified him from even taking the entrance test. Check with the agencies to find out what they require.

Most agencies want height and weight to be proportionate, even if they do not follow a specific chart. If you need to lose weight, start an exercise program now, preferably one you can continue throughout your career. An increasing number of agencies are requiring physical "stress tests" to assess candidates' vascular health. You can prepare for this by participating in a regular exercise program.

Most departments or companies will ask if you have any physical or health restrictions that will interfere with job performance. Be realistic with yourself and honest with the employer. While occasional back pain may not be a problem, an inability to lift heavy items might be. Various medical conditions will not necessarily eliminate you either. For instance, controllable diabetes should not be a problem for most jobs. Again, be honest with yourself and the employer regarding any health problems you have.

Education

Different states have different requirements regarding what schooling is needed. Similarly, different employers have different standards. Employers in either the private or public sectors may require at least a high school diploma or general equivalency diploma (GED). Some states, Minnesota for example, require at least two years of college. Some agencies, particularly in the federal system, may require graduate credits or even a graduate degree, such as a law degree.

The more education you have, the better. This can include specialized training such as first-aid courses, first-responder courses, CPR and the like. Knowing a foreign language, knowing how to "sign" to hearing-impaired people, having skills in photography—any specialized knowledge is likely to be a plus as you pursue your career.

Dohm and Wyatt (2002, p. 3) contend: "When it comes to work, having a college degree is one of the best ways to gain and maintain a competitive edge. On average, college graduates enjoy advantages—ranging from more job opportunities to better salaries—over their non-college-educated counterparts." They (pp. 13, 15) also note:

> [The] increasing level of educational attainment in specific occupations is called educational upgrading. Educational upgrading has been particularly noticeable in the health and protective service occupations. . . .
>
> There are many reasons for educational upgrading, including the need for more highly skilled workers to compete in an increasingly complex global economy. . . . Employers often feel that, compared to non-college-educated workers, college graduates are more motivated, learn tasks more quickly, are better able to meet deadlines, and have better problem-solving and communication skills.

According to the FBI's Web page, the agency is interested in people with the following backgrounds: law, accounting, foreign language and "generalist." Many believe getting a degree in a field besides criminal justice might "set them apart" from other applicants, since they will eventually learn what they need to know about being an officer by attending a police academy. It is further noted that a recent trend regarding hiring practices of the FBI and some other federal law enforcement agencies is to *not* hire students directly out of college, but rather to seek college graduates with two or three years of local law enforcement experience.

While it is possible to find an initial or entry-level job with the minimum-required high school diploma or some college courses, for those seeking promotions and other advancement, higher education becomes a "must have." According to Polk and Armstrong (2001, p. 97): "Although the literature review revealed that there are inconclusive findings in prior studies about whether or not increased education caused an increase in the ability of law enforcement officers to perform their duties, this study showed no ambiguity in finding agencies are responding as if there are benefits if employees are more educated." From their research, Polk and Armstrong (p. 97) conclude: "Those persons who hold higher levels of education, regardless of what other traits or personality characteristics they may possess, are more likely to hold higher rank and progress more quickly through their career path."

Background

Most private security companies, corrections facilities and certainly all law enforcement agencies will thoroughly investigate applicants' backgrounds. You should know what facts about your past will and won't affect your employment potential. Most police departments and security agencies will not accept applicants with a felony conviction on their adult record. Depending on the nature of the crime, a misdemeanor may not automatically eliminate you. Be prepared to honestly explain the situation to the employer.

While it will be difficult to deal with any criminal record, it is much easier to explain a petty shoplifting charge when you were 18 than a conviction when you were 28. Unfortunately, some students make serious errors in judgment while studying to become police or security officers—errors that ruin their chances at a career in criminal justice. Act responsibly.

Traffic records, like lesser criminal records, may or may not be a hindrance. While they generally won't be grounds for automatic elimination from the application process, they will be strikes against you. Be up-front and honest about the circumstances. Many applicants make the mistake of saying they have no traffic record when, in fact, they do. It is easier to explain why you got a ticket 10 years ago than why you lied on your application. *Lying is justification to eliminate an applicant.* A traffic record may not be.

Juvenile records may also be a factor. Although the record may be sealed, an agency may likely find out about it during a background check. When police do a neighborhood check during the course of a background check, a neighbor may recall an incident involving the applicant and the police, where the applicant ended up leaving in the back seat of a patrol car.

Drug use is also considered. Experimental drug use within a year or so of applying may be cause for disqualification. Current drug use will most certainly eliminate you from the candidate pool.

Other situations need to be thought out honestly. Past counseling, or even institutionalization, may not be sufficient grounds for eliminating you from the running, but lying about it would be. Some agencies may be more likely to consider applicants who helped themselves by going through Alcoholics Anonymous or other self-help programs.

Most police departments and security agencies will not accept applicants with a felony conviction on their adult record. A misdemeanor may not automatically eliminate you. Traffic records, like lesser criminal records, may or may not be a hindrance. Past counseling, or even institutionalization, may not be sufficient grounds for eliminating you from the running, but lying about it would be. *Always be honest* about such background circumstances.

Experience

Some agencies, such as the U.S. Bureau of Prisons and state probation and parole agencies, require previous experience in some related field. You should be aware of these requirements before applying for positions in these agencies. But remember, employers will be interested not only in direct experience (work similar to that you are applying for) but also "indirect" experience or *life experience*. Have you had some variety in your life, personally and professionally? Were you willing to take an entry-level job to work your way through school? Have you had jobs interacting with the public? Have you been enthusiastic enough to travel? Involved enough to participate in school activities and organizations? In other words, do you have some experience in life that contributes to you being unique enough to stand out from the competition? Experience is not just having held a job in that particular field; rather, it's the background you bring with you as an individual.

Develop a Positive Attitude

Seeking employment and promotion can be frustrating. Be certain your attitude is not contributing to this frustration. Bolles (p. 146) asserts: "Your attitude is the first (and last) thing everyone notices about you." He (p. 147) adds:

> Your attitude shows, the minute you walk in the employer's office. If you have been unjustly let go at your previous job, your first great need is to let go of your righteous anger at how different the world of work is from what you thought it would be; otherwise, that anger will cripple your job-hunting efforts. You will reek of it to every employer you go see, even as a drunk reeks of strong drink. You may love or hate what's happening to the job market since the Nasdaq meltdown and the terrorist attacks on September 11th. But you've got to make your peace with it. In this arena, as in others, your attitude is *crucial,* and every employer will notice it.
>
> That's important because employers will hire someone with lesser skills, who has the right attitude, before they will hire a more-experienced and more-skilled person with a bad attitude.

Nathan and Hill (p. 69) list several attitudes and beliefs that are often unconsciously held and may be self-defeating:

- ➤ I don't need anyone's help.
- ➤ I'll fail.
- ➤ It's so competitive, I'd never get in.
- ➤ Everything will be okay when I get a new job.
- ➤ I can't change anything—I don't have any power.
- ➤ If I wait long enough, things will change.
- ➤ Life is so unfair to me.
- ➤ I can't help the way I am—it's just the way I'm made.
- ➤ "X" will sort it all out for me.
- ➤ I can't live on less than I earn now.
- ➤ It's undignified to have to promote yourself.
- ➤ Somewhere there's the perfect job.
- ➤ It's too late.
- ➤ I'm too old/young/overqualified/underqualified.
- ➤ I won't be good enough.
- ➤ It's safer not to try than to risk failure.

(Reproduced from Robert Nathan and Linda Hill, *Career Counseling,* p. 69, copyright © 1992 by Sage Publications. Reprinted by permission of Sage Publications, Inc.)

WHAT DO YOU WANT FROM A CAREER?

A career is different from a job. A job is a short-term means to an end: money. High school and college students have jobs during the summer. People get jobs between careers to pay their bills. A career is more long-term, with more serious implications. Too many people find their jobs dull, laborious and repetitive—a necessity of life, like death and taxes. Most people are afraid to make changes—to take risks—and yet this is what is needed to be happy. One who risks nothing usually gains nothing.

Many people are trapped in jobs they dislike—even hate. This trapped feeling may be hard for younger job seekers to understand, especially those who are single. But as you get older, changing jobs becomes less attractive. The benefits associated with seniority—acquired sick time, vacation time and preferential scheduling—can make it difficult to consider leaving an "old" job.

A primary reason people find themselves in a rut is that they fell into it. The deeper the rut, the easier it is to feel trapped. Rather than allowing yourself to fall into the job rut and become trapped, plan what you want out of life and then go after it. Nathan and Hill (p. 129) describe several "career drivers" to consider:

➤   Material rewards—seeking possession, wealth and a high standard of living

➤   Power and influence—seeking to be in control of people and resources

➤   Search for meaning—seeking to do things believed to be valuable for their own sake

➤   Expertise—seeking a high level of accomplishment in a specialized field

➤   Creativity—seeking to innovate and be identified with original input

➤   Affiliation—seeking nourishing relationships with others at work

➤   Autonomy—seeking to be independent and make key decisions for oneself

➤   Status—seeking to be recognized, admired and respected by the community at large

➤   Security—seeking a solid and predictable future

(Reproduced from Robert Nathan and Linda Hill, *Career Counseling*, p. 129, copyright © 1992 by Sage Publications. Reprinted by permission of Sage Publications, Inc.)

In *The Inventurers*, Hagberg and Leider (1982, p. 6) provide an "Excursion Map" to help people identify what is important to them and how to get there, thus enabling them to plan their own destiny rather than falling prey to a rut. They (p. 106) encourage readers to examine five important career issues.

 Take time to do so now. In your journal, record your answers to the following career issues:
➤   What are my present skills?
➤   What values are important to me?
➤   What lifestyle do I wish to lead?
➤   What work conditions are important to me?
➤   What interests do I have?

Take an introspective look at yourself and apply the information learned to answer this question: "Will this job allow me to get what I want from life?" By answering honestly, you are being an "inventurer, one of those special breed of people who take charge and create your own challenges to get yourself moving."

> You are an inventurer if you are willing to take a long look at yourself and consider new options, venture inward, and explore. You are an inventurer if you see life as a series of changes, changes as growth experiences, and growth as positive. You are inventuring on life's *excursions* and learning about yourself as a result. You may feel lonely at times, and get discouraged for a while. But you are willing to risk some disappointments and take some knocks in your quest because you are committed to a balanced lifestyle and to more than just making a living. You are part of a unique group of people who want to make a living at work. If you have these qualities, you are an inventurer.
>
> Inventurers are people who choose to take a fresh look in the mirror to renew and perhaps recycle their lifestyle and careers. Some inventurers, seemingly snug in life and career patterns, are exploring their "greener pasture" . . . in search of their own personal Declaration of Independence: the pursuit of happiness. Other inventurers are planning second careers or early retirements. Some are underemployed and seeking careers more integrated with their abilities and lifestyle. They are female and male, old and young, and in between (Hagberg and Leider, pp. 3–4).

According to Hagberg and Leider (p. 6): "These inventurers prove what wise teachers have said for ages: *'The knowledge is right in us—all we have to do is clear our minds and open ourselves to see the obvious.'*"

Inventurers are people who take charge and create their own challenges to get themselves moving. They are willing to take a long look at themselves and consider new options, venture inward and explore. They see life as a series of changes, changes as growth experiences and growth as positive.

One important step is to look at what you love to do. As Boldt (2004, pp. xxviii–xxix) observes:

> Discovering your creative passion, the work you love, not only brings greater personal fulfillment but also gives you a leg up in the new economy. Mere interest in a career may have been enough when you could settle into a job and stay there for years. Today, you need the sustained motivation that comes from having a real passion for your work, and that requires a self-defined sense of purpose.

Boldt (p. 12) further notes: "Since you probably spend more waking hours working than doing anything else, your work must be something that you can be proud of, be creative in, and enjoy—if you are to have a happy and fulfilling life." He (pp. 13–14) adds: "People who are truly dedicated to their work— Buckminster Fuller, Albert Schweitzer, Mahatma Gandhi, Mother Teresa, and Pablo Picasso were excellent examples—continue to thrive on into old age."

You might want to keep a "values journal" to help identify what is personally important and what is not. Write down how you spend your time. What problems do you encounter? What makes you happy, angry, sad, up, down? After keeping the journal for awhile, review it, looking for patterns to such issues as the following:

➤ How do I, on an average day, generally spend my time?

➤ What are five or ten things that really interest me?

➤ What conflicts or problems do I have? Which ones have I created for myself, and which ones have stemmed from outside factors?

➤ What short-range and long-range goals can I identify?

➤ What, ultimately, do I want to accomplish?

Also consider the "human equation" to answer the question, "How important is time with family and friends?" An involved family life may not be compatible with a career requiring 60-hour workweeks, a lot of traveling and hectic scheduling. Consider also where you want to live. Is climate important to you?

At this point in your self-inquiry, look at yourself and the world around you in relatively general terms. As you develop a sense of what is important to you, apply these ideas to the specific job choices that came out of the earlier brainstorming exercise. Ask yourself: Are my needs compatible with that particular job? Don't fool yourself. No one is watching to make certain you are honest. You will have only yourself to blame if you kid yourself now. Begin to apply some of your answers to the previous questions to the overall requirements of the jobs listed at the start of this chapter. Can you get what you need from the jobs that interest you? Consider the following:

➤ Am I old enough? Mature enough?

➤ Do I have a background that will prohibit me from any certain work?

➤ Am I healthy enough for such work?

➤ Does the job coincide with my personal values?

➤ Do I have the skills for this work?

➤ Will I be able to achieve my long-term goals (e.g., financial, promotional) through such work?

➤ Can my family goals be achieved with this job (considering such issues as travel and time commitments)?

Bolles (p. 329) encourages people to pursue their "ideal" jobs by creating a visual depiction of the essential parts of that work through an exercise he calls "the flower exercise":

> In order to hunt for your ideal job, or even something close to your ideal job, you must have a picture of it, in your head. The clearer the picture, the easier it will be to hunt for it. . . . We have chosen a "Flower" as the model for that picture. . . . Skills are at the center of the Flower, even as they are at the center of your mission, career, or job. They are listed in order of priority. Surrounding them are six petals . . .

- Geography
- Interests (Fields of Fascination)
- People Environments
- Values, Purposes, and Goals
- Working Conditions
- Salary & Level of Responsibility

 Consider each of these "essential parts" for your "ideal work" and record your responses:

➤ **Geography**—Where would you most like to live and work, if you had a choice? In what kind of setting do you see yourself working? "Setting" means both physical location and invisible places your heart, mind and soul most often yearn to be—values and the like.

➤ **Interests**—What are your favorite subjects? If you were stuck on a desert island with a person who had the capacity to speak on only a few subjects, what would you pray those subjects were? What kinds of tasks, using what kinds of skills, do you see yourself doing? With what kind of style?

➤ **People Environments**—The people you are surrounded by have great importance in job satisfaction. Dr. John Holland describes six principal people environments among which, he theorizes, everyone has three preferred groups (your "Holland Code"):

   ➤ *Realistic (R):* people who like nature, or athletics, or tools and machinery

   ➤ *Investigative (I):* people who are very curious, liking to investigate or analyze things

   ➤ *Artistic (A):* people who are very artistic, imaginative and innovative

   ➤ *Social (S):* people who are bent on trying to help, teach or serve people

   ➤ *Enterprising (E):* people who like to start up projects or organizations, and/or influence or persuade people

   ➤ *Conventional (C):* people who like detailed work, and like to complete tasks or projects

➤ **Values, Purposes and Goals**—What guides you through every day, every task, every encounter with another person? What qualities do you want people to remember you for? What goals do you hope to accomplish before you die?

➤ **Working Conditions**—Under what circumstances do you do your most effective work? Degree of supervision? Autonomy? Discretion? Pressure to meet deadlines? Public eye? Desk job or out in the field? Loud, crazy and chaotic? Quiet, calm and orderly?

➤ **Salary and Level of Responsibility**—What kind of salary or other types of compensation do you want to have? What rewards do you hope your work will bring you?

You might also consider taking an occupational preference test such as "Discovery II" to see how your interests and preferences match up with different occupations. Such tests are programmed so that computers can match your answers with answers given by representatives of different occupations. The computer compares your answers and indicates which occupational fields best match your interests.

> Essential parts for your ideal work, besides skills, are geography; interests; people environments; values, purposes and goals; working conditions; and salary and level of responsibility. These parts must be considered if your dream job is to become a reality.

MOVING TOWARD YOUR CAREER GOAL

Perhaps some jobs you considered in the brainstorming exercise were eliminated after you thought about what you need from a career to be fulfilled in life. Perhaps you are still considering whether the career field or a specific career is right for you.

Be honest in considering a career because, as stressed, the very nature of the work in many areas of criminal justice and security is disruptive to what many consider a "normal work routine." Scheduling; having days off in the middle of the week; working nights, holidays and weekends; seeing people at their worst; having your professionalism and honesty challenged in court—all are realities of the criminal justice and security fields. Also be aware of the areas on which the various levels of government are spending their resources. If you know you want to work in corrections but are unsure about where the majority of jobs are or how the payrolls compare, research the current available data.

In the final equation, do your goals, needs and desires balance with the realities of the job? Only you can make this determination. For example, if you were to enroll in an introductory course in law enforcement, where do you fit among the three groups of "typical" students enrolled in such classes?

➢   Students who have known since they were very young that they were destined to be police officers

➢   Students who are considering the career, but have yet to make the commitment

➢   Students who are fascinated by the subject, not the career

If you have the chance to take an introductory course in law enforcement, corrections, private security or criminal justice, consider doing it. It's one good way to better understand what the careers involve and if they are right for you. Some students who have always wanted to go into law enforcement become troubled when they learn more about the field and begin to question whether or not it is right for them. This is an appropriate benefit of exposure to new knowledge and experiences, for it is far better to learn such things *before* you (and the agency that hires you) have spent the time and resources needed to get through the police academy. While many students end up feeling alone following this discovery, they are not. These fields are not for everyone.

Acquire What You Need

As you continue to assess whether your career goals are compatible with your needs and interests, you will also learn what else is required to get into the field. If you need college, register. If you need a physical fitness regime, begin one. If you need experience, get it.

As mentioned earlier, do some investigative research by visiting agencies and interviewing those working in the field(s) you are considering. Volunteer and get involved in short-term experiences with potential employers—step into the shoes and walk around in them for awhile to make sure they fit *before* you commit to buying them. Plodding along an uncharted path will get you, at best, nowhere, and at worst, somewhere you don't want to be. *NOW* is the time to develop your own realistic, exciting career map.

Internships

Internships are an excellent way to discover if a specific area of criminal justice is a good fit for you. An internship is an opportunity to receive supervised, practical, on-the-job training in a specific area. Many law enforcement agencies and correctional institutions offer internships, usually without pay, for those interested in learning about a specific area of employment while acquiring skills that make them more employable in that area. Internships are the focus of discussion in Chapter 6.

ALTERNATIVES

Look around and contemplate the almost infinite number of jobs that make up the criminal justice system and its related fields. It is truly amazing. Even if one job is not for you, another will be. Don't be afraid to change your mind, to take some risks. For many people, taking risks is more frightening than facing a gun. Facing a gun lasts only an instant—a wrong career choice lasts much longer!

Our culture does not encourage risk taking. Even during the 1960s and 1970s, when a different cultural climate prevailed, a conservative work-ethic encouraged people to stay where they were. A successful career was often defined as a long career with one employer.

Then came a shift toward looking for a more satisfying career, which meant exploring work options and being open to changing employers and jobs. Even employers found benefits to hiring someone who had worked elsewhere. Rather than someone asking, "Why did you change jobs?" employees began wondering why someone didn't.

Today, change has become a fact of life in the world of work. Regardless of whether you ever want to change jobs, it is likely you will have to at some point. Change *is* intimidating. But stagnation is even more frightening. The greatest hazard in life is to risk nothing. It has often been said: "Those who risk nothing, do nothing, have nothing, are nothing." Don't let it be engraved on your headstone, *Here lies John Doe, his potential fully intact.*

> Risk taking is important because it exposes you to challenges and prevents you from getting stuck in a rut. Ruts lead to stagnation, which leads to job dissatisfaction and other adverse effects.

A certain amount of risk taking is important because it exposes you to challenges, keeps you flexible and prevents personal and professional stagnation, which can lead to job dissatisfaction and burnout, which in turn affect one's personal life. As world-renowned counseling expert Richard Obershaw succinctly puts it, "A rut is a grave with the ends knocked out."

TO RISK OR NOT TO RISK—THAT IS THE QUESTION

Like everything else, risk carries with it a certain amount of . . . well, risk. Change is all well and good, but there isn't always a rainbow at the end of every trail. Particularly now, when job security isn't guaranteed, maintaining a job that meets your needs may prove to be every bit as important, if not more so, as leaving for the sake of leaving, or changing just for the sake of change. While staying in a job that makes you miserable and negatively affects all other aspects of your life makes no sense, leaving a secure job "just because" may not either.

In the first place, "dream jobs" often do not live up to the fantasy. A friend recently shared that his newly acquired dream job, one he'd worked all his career to achieve, was now ruining his life because of the associated demands and stress. A colleague who quit a 17-year successful job to take a "calculated risk" with a startup venture found himself out of the new job after only three months because of the precarious financial times. In addition, it is wise to stay with a job for at least a minimum length of time to give yourself a chance to acclimate to a new environment and to avoid being thought of as a "job hopper."

Who Moved My Cheese? An Amazing Way to Deal with Change in Your Work and in Your Life, by Dr. Spencer Johnson, is a best-seller about how people respond and react to change. You are encouraged to get this book and read it now, and reread it from time to time. It's straightforward and whimsical but sends a powerful message: Whether you intend to change or not, you will find yourself confronting change, and so your strategy for dealing with it becomes as important as other life strategies you develop.

Is change always worth it? Probably not. Is change always an option? Absolutely! And it's nice to have options.

GET GOING!

An effective exercise for motivating yourself to change is the "last day of my life" test. Bolles suggests that you consider the statement "Before I die, I want to . . ." and then list the things you would like to do before you die. Or write on the topic: "On the last day of my life, what must I have done or been so that my life will have been satisfying to me?"

    As the concluding exercise in this chapter, take time to write your feelings on one of these two topics.

Picking Daisies

If I had my life to live all over again, I would pick more Daisies.
If I had my life to live over, I would try to make more mistakes next time.
I would be sillier than I have been this trip.
I would relax. I would limber up.

I know very few things I would take seriously. I would be crazier;
I would be less hygienic; I would take more chances;
I would take more trips, I would climb more mountains,
Swim more rivers, and watch more sunsets.
I would burn more gasoline. I would eat more ice cream and less meals.

I would have more actual troubles, and fewer imaginary ones.
You see, I am one of those people who lives prophylactically
and sensibly and sanely, hour after hour, day after day.
Oh, I have had my mad moments, and if I had it to do all over again,
I would have more of them; in fact, I'd try to have nothing else,
just moments, one after another, instead of living so many years ahead.

I have been one of those people who never go anywhere without a thermometer,
a hot-water bottle, a gargle, a raincoat and a parachute.
If I had it to live all over again I would go places and travel lighter than I have.
If I had my life to live over again, I would start barefoot earlier in the spring,
and stay that way later in the fall. I would play hookey more,
I would ride on more merry-go-rounds. I'd pick more Daisies.

(Reproduced from *Mindstyles/Lifestyles,* by Nathaniel Lande, published by Price Stern Sloan, Inc., Los Angeles, California. Copyright 1976 by Price Stern Sloan, Inc. Reprinted by permission.)

IT'S JUST A JOB . . .

Work and careers. Unquestionably important. But it is critical to bear in mind that this is only *part* of the balance that makes up anyone's life. Exploring careers should be an ongoing process that focuses on the questions: What am I doing now, and what do I want to do in the future? No law says you must stay in the same job or career forever. In fact, it's a crime when people do so to the detriment of themselves and their families, who then become casualties of the effects of work. And yet many people elect to stay in a job that is, quite literally, killing them.

This may sound extreme to a young person looking toward a career that can be as exciting as criminal justice. But things change, and so do priorities. It always pays to look ahead while assessing what's going on at the moment. Be prepared for change. It's going to happen. Control it, rather than letting it control you.

CONCLUSION

It is important to think carefully about what career you'd like to pursue *before* you jump into it. A hasty decision, or one based on rumor or television portrayals, will likely lead to disappointment and dissatisfaction. The four steps that comprise the career development process are (1) self-assessment, (2) career exploration, (3) job-search skill development and (4) implementation of the job-search steps. The first two steps are very important. In deciding which career is best suited to you and your needs, you *must* assess yourself and how your abilities and needs compare to the demands of the job.

Risk taking is important because it exposes you to challenges and prevents you from getting stuck in a rut, which could lead to stagnation and job dissatisfaction. Become an *inventurer,* someone who takes charge and creates their own challenges to get themselves moving. Be willing to take a long look at yourself and consider new options. Venture inward and explore. See life as a series of changes, changes as growth experiences and growth as positive.

AN INSIDER'S VIEW

THE PRIVATE SECURITY ALTERNATIVE

Bill B. Green

Security Manager
Dell, Inc.

My exposure to the security profession started during my sophomore year in college. While attending the university, I also worked full-time as a sales clerk for a large retailer. My declared major was criminal justice, and I became good friends with the store's detective and also its security manager. I increasingly found their daily work more interesting than what I was doing. Attending school full-time and working 50 hours a week caused my class work to suffer. Something had to give. I was persuaded to enter a company management training program and dropped out of college. The management program, however, proved unsatisfying. I was drawn back to the two mentors from my brief retail career. The store detective, who also owned a small contract security firm, offered me a job. I went to work for him, first as a night-shift security officer at an industrial complex, then as an account supervisor. I also again pursued college (this time much more successfully).

Another avenue I was drawn to was the military. Both mentors were retired military, and their stories piqued my interest. A year later, I enlisted in the Army. For a young man whose world had been confined within the boundaries of Arkansas, my specialty of Military Intelligence was a real eye-opener. Those three years in Military Intelligence proved extremely illuminating, both in terms of knowledge of the world as well as a career direction. After my three years in the military, I planned to return to civilian life, probably in law enforcement or something in the criminal justice system, gain experience and eventually return to the private sector. I began networking nine months before ending my tour of duty and was offered a parole officer position by the Department of Corrections in Arkansas. Three weeks before my release, however, an Army acquaintance called from Texas with another alternative. I interviewed for a security consulting position in Texas, withdrew from the parole officer position and was on my way into the field of private security.

That position opened my eyes wider, offering the chance to do in the private sector what I had just spent three years doing in the military sector—learning a lot by working with senior-level professionals and advising clients on how to improve their security posture. While this was a dream position for a young man at such an early career stage, changes in the company led me only a year later to consider other employment opportunities. A consulting assignment with a precious metals distributor led to my next job—security director for that small company. That position provided a rare opportunity to "do it my way." The young entrepreneurial firm hired me to build a security department from the ground up. A startup department is a tremendous, but extremely rewarding, challenge.

Two years later I found myself seeking bigger and better things. Note, however, that you cannot change jobs every couple of years (as I had been) without eventually paying a price, being labeled a *job hopper*. Few employers are interested in hiring someone who will stay only 12 to 24 months. Most positions take six months to a year to absorb the company's standards, culture, products and mode of operation. It simply does not pay employers to invest that time in you and then see you leave.

I knew my next position needed to be long-term. Pursuing a local newspaper ad, I applied for a position with a high-tech manufacturing firm and found myself in the interviewing process, then in the second interview, then the third, followed by a battery of psychological exams and eventual selection as a member of their management team. Again I had the good fortune, and great challenge, to be in another startup department—the first security professional ever hired by this firm of 1,900 employees.

Today that company has grown to a world leadership position in its market. Almost 14 years later I have assumed a variety of responsibilities along the way while remaining in charge of the overall security effort. You might sum up a career by looking at the titles held. Mine are as follows: security officer; security supervisor; intelligence analyst; security analyst; security coordinator; director of security; security administrator; safety, security, and environmental manager; and manager of security services. Today I manage a security department of both proprietary and contract employees, providing protective, investigative and customer services.

I'd like to offer some thoughts on developing your career, particularly if you decide on a career in corporate security:

➤ Join the American Society for Industrial Security (ASIS) as soon as you qualify. There are memberships for students as well as for those already in the field.

➤ All security is not the same. Many of the principles apply from one segment of business to another, but different facets of private security have significant, noteworthy differences—contract security services, investigations, consulting and training, financial services, manufacturing, retail and so on.

➤ Volunteer for an internship. It's good exposure for you and looks good on your résumé. *EVERYONE you meet is a potential employer or a potential lead to an employer.* A few personal examples include the mentor who gave me direction and eventually pointed me to the military to gain further experience, the good Army friend who recommended me for the Texas job and the client who saw my work and subsequently offered me a position. Show them all your very best—you never know which one may recommend you for your next position or promotion.

➤ Plan to pay your dues. If you decide to become a police officer, you won't start with the best shift or as a sergeant or lieutenant. In the military, private security or any other endeavor, you start at the bottom.

➤ In a smaller corporation, be prepared to do it all. Security managers are responsible for the physical security of the facility, protecting employees, staffing, scheduling, investigating, budgeting and always selling, selling, selling—themselves, their department and their security program.

➤ In a larger corporation, the security manager is likely to have more staff and more specialists to get the job done. In this capacity, you become more of a manager as opposed to the multitalented specialist of a smaller organization.

➤ Corporate security professionals are not "company cops." They are one of many specialists necessary to successfully operate a business. Their job is not to enforce laws (that's why you call the police). Instead, they protect corporate assets, which include people, property and information.

➢   Be honest with yourself about your likes, dislikes and emotional and physical makeup. Are you well suited for law enforcement work? Is your eyesight good enough? Do you have any other physical limitations that may hinder a particular career pursuit? Do you have any criminal history (including even "youthful" mistakes such as a DWI)? Talk to some police officers and security managers. Find out what they think about their work. Conduct your own surveys. Forget what you've seen on television or at the movies—find out what the jobs are really all about.

➢   For law enforcement jobs in most parts of the country, a two- or four-year college degree is or will soon be required. While you are working on that degree, get some experience. Get a job at least related to the field you are thinking of pursuing. A stable work history as a security officer at a reputable firm will look better on that fresh graduate résumé than some other totally unrelated experience.

➢   As you settle on a career path, keep in mind that numerous opportunities will permit you to achieve the same honorable goal—"to protect and to serve."

Bill B. Green *has been employed in the profession of criminal justice and security for over 25 years. Past positions include the director of security at Investment Rarities, Inc.; security analyst at International Security Group, Inc.; senior security consultant for Dell Computer Corp.; director of operations at Castletop Support Services, Inc.; and security manager at Dell, Inc. Mr. Green holds a BA in Public Administration (Criminal Justice).*

INSIDER'S VIEW ONLINE

An additional *Insider's View* for this chapter is "Searching Outside the 'Box'" by Kenneth S. Trump, found on the Wadsworth website: http://www.wadsworth.com/criminaljustice_d/.

 MIND STRETCHES

1.   What is your strategy for identifying a career path? Do you know anyone who has just "floated along" whichever way the current carried them? Are they happy? Why or why not?

2.   Do you think American workers are cynical? Why?

3.   How important is job security to you? Can you see it changing in five years? Ten years?

4.   How important is money to you? Will you be satisfied with an officer's pay? Can you see this need changing for you?

5.   Have you ever worked nights, holidays or weekends? What can you imagine would be good about such a schedule? Bad?

6.   What prevents people from accepting change? What keeps people from taking risks? Why do you think many people stick with a less-than-satisfactory job?

7.   What five jobs within the criminal justice field interest you? Why? What jobs in the field do not appeal to you? Why?

8.   What elements of your personal history might be negative factors in pursuing your career goals? How can you deal with these at the interview?

9.   Why do you think more people don't take an active role in their career choices?

10.   What are the five most important things you will consider when selecting a job? Are these under your control?

REFERENCES

Boldt, Laurence G. *How to Find the Work You Love,* 2nd ed. New York, Penguin Group, 2004.

Bolles, Richard Nelson. *What Color Is Your Parachute? A Practical Manual for Job-Hunters & Career-Changers.* Berkeley, CA: Ten Speed Press, 2004.

Dohm, Arlene and Wyatt, Ian. "College at Work: Outlook and Earnings for College Graduates, 2000–10." *Occupational Outlook Quarterly,* Fall 2002, pp. 3–15.

Hagberg, Janet and Leider, Richard. *The Inventurers: Excursions in Life and Career Renewal.* Reading, MA: Addison-Wesley Publishing Company, 1982.

Krannich, Ronald L. *Change Your Job, Change Your Life,* 5th ed. Manassas Park, VA: Impact Publications, 1995.

Lande, Nathaniel. "Picking Daisies." *Mindstyles/Lifestyles.* Los Angeles: Price Stern Sloan, Inc., 1976.

Leider, Richard J. and Shapiro, David A. *Repacking Your Bags: Lighten Your Load for the Rest of Your Life,* 2nd ed. San Francisco: Berrett-Koehler Publishers, Inc. 2002.

Nathan, Robert and Hill, Linda. *Career Counseling.* Newbury Park, CA: Sage Publications, 1992.

Parsons, F. *Choosing a Vocation.* Boston, MA: Houghton-Mifflin, 1909.

Polk, O. Elmer and Armstrong, David A. "Higher Education and Law Enforcement Career Paths: Is the Road to Success Paved by Degree?" *Journal of Criminal Justice Education,* Spring 2001, pp. 77–99.

ADDITIONAL CONTACTS AND SOURCES OF INFORMATION

National Board of Certified Counselors (NBCC)
3 Terrace Way, Suite D
Greensboro, NC 27403
(910) 547-0607
http://www.nbcc.org

National Career Development Association (NCDA)
5999 Stevenson Avenue
Alexandria, VA 22304
(703) 823-9800
http://www.ncda.org

CHAPTER 6

INTERNSHIPS: TESTING THE WATERS

People are always blaming their circumstances for what they are. I don't believe in circumstances. The people who get on in this world are the people who get up and look for the circumstances they want, and if they can't find them—make them.

—George Bernard Shaw

Do You Know:

➤ The difference between a passive intern and an active intern?
➤ What the two general types of internships are and how they differ?
➤ Where internship opportunities may be located?
➤ How much lead time may be needed to arrange for an internship?
➤ What service learning involves?
➤ How much employers want interns to talk, listen or participate in work activities?
➤ How to make the most of an internship opportunity?
➤ What to do if an internship does not work out?

INTRODUCTION

Dictionary.com defines *internship* as "A student or a recent graduate undergoing supervised practical training" and "to train or serve as an intern." Rubinstein (2002) further explains: "An internship is a trial run. It's a chance for you to explore a particular career field without making a long-term commitment. Whether you love it or hate it, your internship will put you one step closer to determining what you might want to do once you graduate from college." With Google promptly serving up well over three million hits on the term, internships are certainly an aspect of job searching *and* professional development worthy of understanding and taking advantage of.

In *The Internship Bible,* Oldman and Hamadeh (2003, p. xiii) suggest: "It's now accepted wisdom that if you don't do internships, you're at a competitive disadvantage when it comes to launching a career . . . that more than 89 percent of U.S. college seniors graduating in spring 2002 had completed at least one internship by graduation, and over 70 percent had done two or more." There are certain things employers expect to see on résumés, if for no other reason than that the majority of applicants possess them. It is very possible that internships are becoming one of these *expectations.*

Internships are an excellent way to discover if a specific area of criminal justice is a good fit for you. An internship is an opportunity to receive supervised, practical, on-the-job training in a specific area. Many law enforcement agencies and correctional institutions offer internships, usually without pay, for those interested in learning about a specific area of employment while acquiring skills that make them more employable in that area. Often individuals who complete an internship with a specific police department are hired by that department when they have completed their formal education. Or, conversely, the intern or the department may find that the fit is not good, and both are spared a difficult situation.

In this chapter you will explore the concept of internships—where they are rooted in history, the general kinds of interns and internships, how to find internship opportunities, what is expected of you as an intern, how to make the most of an internship and what to do if a good internship goes bad, being evaluated as an intern and participating in internships even after you land a job. The chapter concludes with a recap of the do's and don'ts of internships.

NOTHING NEW HERE!

The idea of interning is not new. In fact, the concept has a rich history rooted in apprenticeships dating back thousands of years before Christ. According to Oldman and Hamadeh (p. 398): "The Babylonian Code of Hammurabi, written in 2100 B.C., contains a provision requiring artisans to teach their handicrafts to their sons. Similarly, records of ancient Greece, Egypt, and Rome show that the young learned their trade under the supervision of skilled workers." They (p. 398) note some famous apprentices in history (and where they apprenticed):

> Benedict Arnold, famous "traitor" and military leader (apothecary's shop)
> Benjamin Franklin, scientist and politician (printer's shop of brother James, 1718–1723)
> Samuel Gompers, labor leader (shoemaker, 1860)
> Alexander Hamilton, Secretary of the Treasury and author of the Federalist Papers
>   (merchant on St. Croix)
> Thomas Hardy, author (architect, 1856)
> Andrew Johnson, 17th President of the United States (tailor in Raleigh, NC, 1820–1826)
> Alfred Nobel, Swedish philanthropist, originator of the Nobel prizes (Swedish ship
>   designer, 1860)
> Paul Revere, courier and political activist (gold and silversmith shop, 1753)
> Mark Twain, author and journalist (printer's shop, 1846, and riverboat, 1857)
> Martin Van Buren, 8th President of the United States (NY law offices of Francis Silvester,
>   1796–1801)

ON INTERNS AND INTERNSHIPS

In *Internships for Dummies,* Donovan and Garnett (2001, p. 18) describe two general kinds of interns: passive and active. Passive interns are those who "wait for opportunities to come to them . . . wait until an internship falls into their lap," whereas active interns take responsibility for their own internship—for their own work and learning and, ultimately, for their own future. Table 6–1 compares the skills of passive and active interns.

Passive interns *wait* for things to happen *to* them. Active interns *make* things happen *for* themselves.

Just as there are two basic types of interns, so too are there two types of internships. One is a *survey internship;* the other is a *practical internship*. While intended for different people at different times of their careers, both become exceptionally important.

TABLE 6–1   Comparing Passive and Active Interns

Skill	Passive Interns	Active Interns
Assessing needs and goals	Only casually think about their needs and goals if they do it at all.	Systematically reflect on their needs and goals for an internship.
Searching for internships	Wait for opportunities to come their way or only come up with a few leads through the obvious sources.	Explore a range of leads using a range of sources (not just the obvious ones) and compare those leads to their needs and goals.
Getting the internship	Submit one or two applications, wait for a response and take the first offer if they get one.	Submit a number of applications for internships that meet their needs and goals, follow up with prospective employers, don't automatically jump at the first offer and negotiate terms if feasible.
Orienting yourself to the workplace	Wait for a formal orientation and go through the motions during the orientation. If no orientation occurs, passive interns let the opportunity drop.	Take the initiative to get the most out of any organized orientation, but if none is arranged, they actively orient themselves and work to get an organized orientation.
Handling problems	Wait until problems occur during the internship and wait for the work supervisor, school intern advisor or someone else to solve these problems.	Anticipate the kinds of problems that might occur and work to avoid these problems. Actively seek appropriate help before a situation gets out of control.
Doing the work	Wait until assigned a task, fail to get essential information for completing that task and fail to keep supervisors informed of progress (or problems).	Energetically seek assignments, probe to get essential information about them and actively keep supervisors informed of progress and problems before they get out of hand.
Evaluating own performance	Wait until the end-of-the-internship evaluation to find out what they are doing well and poorly. If no formal evaluation exists, they write off this opportunity for feedback.	Conscientiously (but tactfully) seek informal feedback each week or with each task. They learn what the formal evaluations are and prepare for them.
Networking	Wait until coworkers or others contact them. If contact occurs, passive interns let the other person carry the relationship. If contact doesn't happen, they miss these chances to network.	Systematically and conscientiously contact other people to share experiences and to obtain advice about the immediate job and career. Active interns keep up their end of the professional relationship by helping mentors and others where possible.
Linking to a job or career	Sit back to see what happens at the end of the internship. If nothing happens, back to square one!	Conscientiously work toward parlaying their internship into full-time jobs or other opportunities by performing well during the internship, building a professional network and developing knowledge and skills for the next step.

SOURCE: Adapted from Craig P. Donovan and Jim Garnett. *Internships for Dummies.* New York: Wiley and Sons, 2001, pp. 19–20. Used with permission.

The survey internship is a relatively short-term experience during which the intern, most often a student, is permitted to observe work being done and ask questions pertinent to the profession and requisite tasks. It is a passive experience, as the intern does not actually participate in any work activities but merely watches them being done. Nonetheless, this kind of internship provides an excellent opportunity to learn about a job through observation and inquiry.

In criminal justice, a survey internship involves visiting the various divisions of a particular agency to watch people do their jobs. For example, a student might sit in the dispatch center and see how incoming calls are handled and personnel dispatched. Later the student may observe jail operations, watch evidence technicians, sit with the administrative division and even take a ride-along with a patrol unit. The result of such an experience is to see firsthand what really occurs in such an agency and how it differs from any preconceived notions the student may have.

The practical internship differs from the survey experience because, as the name implies, actual experience is the goal. The practical internship allows students to learn through hands-on involvement. These experiences tend to be longer than survey internships and can last months or more.

Practical internships in criminal justice can involve any number of activities, from entry-level tasks to actually working side-by-side with officers or other personnel. These experiences are not just for people exploring a career path or new to the field. It is not uncommon for more senior practitioners to participate in a practical internship with another agency that does things differently or specializes in something their home agency does not. It is also a way to cross-train employees and keep superiors in touch with the daily functions of their subordinates.

> Survey internships are passive, observation-based experiences best suited to people in the initial stages of career exploration. Practical internships are active, hands-on experiences intended primarily for people developing their experience (either as students or practitioners) in a particular area.

LOCATING INTERNSHIP OPPORTUNITIES

Much of what this book recommends regarding seeking employment in criminal justice can directly apply to internships as well, with some adjustments. While internships may be advertised, they are usually not advertised the way actual jobs are. That is, it is most unusual to see an internship opportunity in the newspaper. They are, however, posted, but you need a strategy to know where these postings are.

 List as many resources as you can to obtain information on where to find out about internships.

School-Related Internships

Many, if not most, schools have relationships with agencies that provide internships. Some programs are formally structured, with internships taking the format of actual courses for which the student receives credit. Other programs offer rather informal or unstructured internship opportunities where students receive no credit but are afforded an invaluable "inside look" at a career they are considering.

> A logical place to begin seeking internship opportunities is through school contacts.

Some school-coordinated internships are optional, most likely providing elective credits, while other internships are required. An example of this is a criminal justice and law enforcement school that requires students to complete 115 hours of interning at a social service agency, the primary purpose being to learn about resources available to criminal justice practitioners.

In addition to speaking with a counselor, teacher or program director, be sure you know when agencies may have recruiters on campus to engage potential interns. These people are often tapped to speak to classes, attend criminal justice/law enforcement club meetings and staff display tables at job fairs. And never forget networking with other students who may currently be interning, working or otherwise know of opportunities. It *always* pays to ask.

Credit versus Compensation. As seen, not all internships are created equal. It is worth noting that some programs, namely those coordinated through an academic institution, offer students a choice: an unpaid internship with credits toward graduation or a paid internship with no credits toward graduation. For example, the Department of Criminology and Criminal Justice at Florida Atlantic University (FAU) posts the following information on its website:

> Many students are confused about the difference between Field Experience internship (CCJ-4940) and the Cooperative Education course (CCJ-3949) offered by this department. While both courses are listed in the undergraduate catalog for 3 credits, the catalog also states that the credits for the Cooperative Education course do not count towards graduation. The credits for Field Experience do count towards graduation. The reason for this is that the student taking the Cooperative Education course is being paid by the agency, and a student cannot receive credit towards graduation and be paid at the same time. Students need to choose between receiving credit or being paid for their internship.

It behooves you to thoroughly understand the type of internship you are getting involved in and what, exactly, you will be credited or compensated for.

Locating Internships Online

With the proliferation of agency websites has come an enhanced ability to locate internship (as well as employment) opportunities at departments, quite literally, anywhere on earth. For example, the International Association of Chiefs of Police (IACP) home page (http://www.theiacp.org) offers an FAQ (frequently asked questions) link, which brings up a list of common queries, including: "Does the IACP accept interns?" The answer: "Yes. IACP seeks undergraduate and graduate students with a background in criminal justice, law enforcement, communications, public administration, or a related field for potential internship positions. See the Jobs Database for 'Jobs at IACP Headquarters.'"

Another example: Someone interested in a career in law enforcement at the federal level goes to the FLETC website (http://www.fletc.gov), does a search for "intern" and receives 15 results, the first one of which describes FLETC's college intern program. (Hint: When searching online, use "intern" instead of "internship" to maximize the number of results.)

The lesson: If you are interested in a particular area of criminal justice or want to explore a specific agency, a little Web surfing could go a long way in locating potential opportunities.

The Internet also provides an almost limitless resource for locating internships in criminal justice.

START EARLY! STAY ORGANIZED!

Internships, especially in the criminal justice field, require that you begin your search well before you are actually interested in beginning. As O'Connor (2004) asserts: "The best internship sites always require long-range planning, sometimes at least a year or more in advance." Many agencies require some sort of background check, so give yourself plenty of lead time when exploring internship options.

> Plan your internship well in advance.

Because many people will be looking for a limited number of internships, keep a notebook of contacts, just as you should as part of your job-seeking strategy, so you have a ready networking list to use now and in the future. In addition to the obvious benefits of internships, the process of seeking such an experience is great, too, because of the similarities to job seeking. It is all about developing a strategy to achieve what you want . . . and part of that strategy is to recognize the necessary time constraints.

 Begin compiling a list of the types of work you are interested in. These can be general positions, such as probation officer, police officer, corrections officer, forensics, investigation, armed sky marshal.

 Next consider which jurisdictional level(s) are most appealing to you right now (federal, state, local) and explore the reasons you feel this way.

SERVICE LEARNING

"Service learning" is gaining popularity in college programs. This concept integrates community service work with the objectives of a particular course, providing an even richer educational experience. According to Professor Carter Hendricks (2004), Hopkinsville Community College, Kentucky: "Service learning is a form of experiential learning that requires students to participate in service projects, or unpaid internships, while they apply knowledge and skills to meet real community needs. The key is to understand that service projects must, in some way, be connected to an intentional course objective and outcome and must, in some way, meet a real need in the 'community.'"

Hendricks goes on to explain:

> A course in Community Policing may integrate a service project with the curriculum in a number of different ways. For example, as students are discussing and learning about the various factors that influence public perception of law enforcement, they are instructed to develop a survey that they use to compile data and information on local perceptions of law enforcement. Once the data is collected and analyzed, the same group of students uses the data to present their findings to local law enforcement agencies. In this example, the students are learning valuable tools and skills to determine and understand public perception while providing a needed service by working to educate local law enforcement agencies of the current public perception of law enforcement.

> The most effective learning is *applied* learning, and service learning embraces this ideal.

WHAT IS EXPECTED OF YOU?

An intern is basically considered an entry-level member of the organization. This does not mean you are entitled to the same benefits as *bone fide* employees, but you are expected to behave similarly. In addition, it is probable the experience is linked to a school program you are involved with. Thus, you are playing two roles: that of someone with the agency you are interning with and that of a student.

If you have not previously interacted with the profession you are interning with, you will not likely know the culture, the jargon or the behavior expected (other than being polite and other commonsense factors). So *ask*. Before the internship even occurs, you should ask what manner of dress is appropriate. If you are doing a ride-along, ask the person you are with to tell you what to do. Do not just go running after them into a call. If they do not verbally express their expectations, ask, "Should I come with you or wait here?"

Among the reasons you don't want to interfere is because any criminal justice internship involves exposure to situations most people never consider, and certainly things you do not yet know about (that's why you are interning, after all). For starters, there is the issue of safety. You will be exposed to new, potentially dangerous situations where you may not necessarily know how to react. This may occur on an emergency police call, working in a correctional facility or interacting with people on probation. The professionals know what to do; you don't. And they will not expect you to, so you have nothing to prove by "knowing it all." Furthermore, pretending you do could be hazardous to your internship in any number of ways.

You could become a witness just by being present at an incident. You may even be asked to write down your observations or what you heard. You absolutely do *not* want to interfere with an investigation by touching anything, disturbing evidence or engaging in conversation you have no business engaging in. If another agency representative makes an assumption and asks you to do something, assert that you are an intern and identify the person you are accompanying. If a witness or suspect asks you a question, immediately defer to the person you are interning with. If anyone says anything to you, report it. Violations of these basic tenets are grounds for immediate termination of your internship and could cause the loss of a criminal case, even if due to an unintentional indiscretion.

If employers have one solid recommendation for most interns, it's two fairly simple words, followed by some encouragement. The words are *"quietly listen."* The encouragement is, when asked to, participate. Similar to our recommendations later in this book on how to keep a job once you get it, you want to be very careful in how you behave and what you say. One student couldn't keep quiet long enough to make it through her first ride-along before the officer returned her to the police station and simply said, "Get out." By the time she reached the station door the commander had already been advised she was no longer welcome as an intern. Her fault was not talking too much (although an irritation, to be sure); it was behaving inappropriately. The details are not important because there are plenty of similar stories: being a know-it-all, telling officers how to do their job, being critical of the agency or profession, getting in the way, behaving immaturely, wearing inappropriate clothing or anything else that would equate to "this person is not right for this internship . . . or profession."

Employers expect interns to *quietly listen* and to *participate only when asked*. Above all, interns are expected to *behave appropriately.*

Keep in mind you are the new person among people on their own turf. You don't want to pretend you know it all, make inappropriate jokes or cover any discomfort or anxiety you are experiencing with humor or behavior that just does not fit. Even if others exhibit such behavior, don't you. Just *quietly* soak in the experience to whatever degree others will permit it. Table 6–2 lists employer comments about desirable qualities in interns.

TABLE 6–2   Comparing Positive and Negative Traits of Interns

Positive Traits	Negative Traits
Asks a lot of questions	Fails to ask relevant questions
Follows directions well	Follows own agenda
Understands some "gofer" work is part of the job	Objects to routine work
Displays enthusiasm	Lacks energy and enthusiasm
Actively looks for things to do	Fails to display initiative
Follows rules and regulations	Disregards [department] rules and policies
Socializes appropriately with staff	Has poor interpersonal skills
Exhibits punctuality and dependability	Displays irresponsibility and lack of punctuality
Tries to understand organization	Tries to jump in too soon without knowing the organization
Checks out all projects with supervisor	Fails to keep supervisor informed about activities

SOURCE: Marianne Ehrlich Green. *Internship SUCCESS: Real-World, Step-by-Step Advice on Getting the Most Out of Internships*. New York: The McGraw-Hill Companies, 1997, p. 74. Reprinted by permission.

MAKING THE MOST OF THE EXPERIENCE

Whether a survey or practical internship, for credit or not, you want to make the most of the experience. Not only do you want to gain as much information as possible, but you want to take full advantage of the networking opportunities to develop contacts that may serve your future job-search efforts. You will be meeting people actively engaged in the profession you are interested in, many of whom may be potential points of contact when you are ready to seek employment. Furthermore, if you participate in an internship long enough, some individuals will likely readily allow you to list them as a reference. You may even find a mentor, someone who will be supportive of and helpful to you throughout your job-seeking efforts, or even your career.

Oldman and Hamadeh, in *The Internship Bible* (pp. xii–xiv), remind us that things are just beginning when an internship is obtained. They provide 10 suggestions to help make the most of an internship [From *The Princeton Review: The Internship Bible*, 2004, ed. by Mark Oldman, copyright © 2004 by Princeton Review Publishing, LLC. Used by permission of Princeton Review, a division of Random House, Inc.]:

➤ **Chart Your Course:** Before starting an internship, create a checklist. List the skills you hope to learn, people you want to meet, types of projects you'd like to work on, ideas you have about the company, etc. As the internship progresses, check off items on the list to ensure that you're making the most of your experience.

➤ **Expect Some Busywork:** All internships—and most jobs for that matter—involve some menial tasks like photocopying, faxing and filing. While your internship will hopefully involve substantive work beyond busywork, don't expect to be running the show. No one likes an intern with unrealistic expectations or delusions of grandeur.

➤ **Use Your "Intern-al Access":** Because interns tend to be viewed by employees as young, energetic visitors, they often have access to meetings and areas of the company that young employees don't. Make the most of this access to learn about the inner workings of the company and the people who work there.

➢ **Bond with Your Fellow Interns:** Be sure to meet and share ideas with the other interns at your company—even ones who are not in your particular department. Your fellow interns can be a powerful source of information about the company, letting you know, for example, which departments are hot and which are not.

➢ **Say Hello to Higher-Ups:** When passing executives in the hallway, don't hesitate to introduce yourself and chat with them about the company. Most interns are too intimidated to say hello to higher-ups, so by taking the initiative, you'll stand out as motivated and engaged.

➢ **Volunteer for Extra Assignments:** During slow periods, be sure to track down your supervisor and volunteer for extra assignments—something few interns bother to do. The more initiative and enthusiasm you show, the more responsibility you'll get.

➢ **Participate in "Extracurriculars":** If your company offers interns access to field trips, brown-bag luncheons with executives, barbecues, tickets to sporting events or other traditional internship "extracurriculars," by all means participate. Some interns' most memorable and rewarding experiences occur outside the direct scope of employment.

➢ **Be Nice to Everyone:** Many interns don't realize that gaining the respect of assistants, mail-room workers and other support staff can be as important as winning the appreciation of executives. When it comes time to be considered for a full-time position, how you treat support staff can make the difference in whether you get a job offer.

➢ **Get a Rec:** While your work is still fresh in the minds of your supervisor, make sure to ask him or her for a detailed letter of recommendation. Even if you have no immediate need for a recommendation, it is useful to have already secured one when you later search for a job or apply to graduate school.

➢ **Stay in Touch:** After your internship ends, keep in touch with coworkers with periodic calls or e-mails. This is an easy way to get company updates and keep your name fresh in the minds of employees when hiring decisions are made.

The "10 Commandments" of internships are:
➢ Chart Your Course
➢ Expect Some Busywork
➢ Use Your "Intern-al Access"
➢ Bond with Your Fellow Interns
➢ Say "Hello" to Higher-Ups
➢ Volunteer for Extra Assignments
➢ Participate in "Extracurriculars"
➢ Be Nice to Everyone
➢ Get a Recommendation
➢ Stay in Touch

 As the first "commandment" directs, create a checklist for your internship, if only hypothetical. In thinking about the type of agency or department you would like to explore job opportunities with (via an internship), list the skills you would be expected to gain proficiency in, the people you want to meet and the types of assignments or projects you would like to work on.

It is generally helpful, when embarking on a new experience, to know a little of what to expect. On his website, Dr. O'Connor familiarizes students with the world of interning by providing a list of what a criminal justice internship *is* and what it is *not*:

A Criminal Justice Internship is:

- An opportunity to get real exposure to a variety of agencies in the local Criminal Justice community
- A chance to meet professionals in the field who can advocate for your future employment
- An opportunity to explore a specific profession prior to committing yourself to it in a full-time capacity
- An appointment as a representative and ambassador of [your academic institution]
- A privilege
- An opportunity to broaden your educational experience with some real practical experience
- A huge responsibility—the vast majority of which falls upon the student
- Unpaid
- To be set up far in advance of starting—five to ten weeks before the internship semester begins
- To be completed by individuals who have declared Criminal Justice as their major and are of junior or senior standing
- To be granted at the complete and mutual discretion of the internship coordinator and the participating agency
- For students who have demonstrated adequate academic performance, and are in good academic standing with the department, any faculty committees and [the college/university]

A Criminal Justice Internship is NOT:

- To be taken for granted
- A filler because you can't find a class that you like
- Something to do because you can't think of anything else to do
- A "fast-track" to guaranteed post-graduation employment
- A blow-off course
- A right as a student (see "privilege" above)
- Required
- A guaranteed "A"—students are assessed as stringently as in most other courses in the Criminal Justice Criminology Department
- To be done at an agency or business where you already work, or have worked in the past
- For students who have any type of criminal history in their past (or present)—this would include outstanding traffic violations and other minor infractions that have turned into warrants

Some may think the worst thing to have happen with an internship is to select one that doesn't produce the anticipated results, whether that be a good grade, a strong letter of recommendation or a solid job offer. *Wrong.* The worst thing is to leave on a bad note—one that could haunt you during your future job-seeking efforts.

WHEN GOOD INTERNSHIPS GO BAD

No one thing is ever right for everyone, including internships. Reasons we have heard to explain why a particular placement did not work for someone include:

➢ There just was so little to do, it seemed like a waste of time.

➢ Expectations weren't made clear, so I didn't know what to do.

➢ The placement turned out to be of no interest to me whatsoever.

➤   The hours negatively affected things at home, work or school.

➤   I saw unethical, even illegal, behavior, and worse, was told to ignore it.

➤   I was placed in situations for which I had no training and that sometimes proved dangerous.

While an entry-level internship may not be the most exciting (okay, sometimes they are just downright boring), you are expected to complete it, barring any extreme circumstances. Just as "job hopping" does not look good on a résumé, neither does failing to finish an internship. Yes, criminal justice work can be monotonous at times, so there is something to be said for being able to fulfill a dull, even tedious, internship. There are times in any job, and criminal justice is no exception, that you will be directed to complete tasks you may not particularly like. Remember: Experiences lead to other, often better, experiences. Especially if you have little or no previous experience, you want to prove you have what it takes to survive the monotony on the bottom rung and to progress into something even better. This is exactly what the job world is like.

It is important to show courteous enthusiasm throughout the internship process, even if a particular opportunity does not work out. Whether you decide the placement is not for you, or the agency you are interning at makes that decision, you simply do not know what may be around the corner. Particularly in those instances when an internship goes less than smoothly, it is critical that you remain positive about the experience and take the time to personally and sincerely thank your contacts for the opportunity. It speaks volumes about your character—the kind of person you are, and the kind of employee you will be.

Any time an internship placement does not work, regardless of why, you must speak to someone about it. If it is a school or work-related internship (in other words, you are doing it as part of your school program or a part of another job), immediately discuss it with your academic advisor or job supervisor. While you may then be directed to discuss the issue with a supervisor at the internship site, always begin with your own supervisor.

It is crucial for you to listen carefully to your internal responses to the internship experience. Many students ignore their reactions or discount their "gut feelings," writing off negative responses as merely a sign of their inexperience or a need to develop a tougher hide. Some students decide, in error, that the agency they interned with is not truly representative of the field as a whole—that they just got stuck with a particularly boring department, the clientele was unusually "yucky" and "rude," the personnel were atypically unfriendly and that work in other agencies must be more exciting and more tolerable. If the internship does not measure up to your expectations, don't automatically assume you were handed a raw deal. Although every department is different, and maybe the personalities involved during your internship didn't quite mesh optimally, it could also be that the field was not the "fit" you actually need in your career. Be realistic.

Although not common, there are occasions when an internship truly is "no good." In these exceptions, such as when personal safety is at issue, or illegal or unethical behavior is occurring and you are told to "look the other way," it is definitely better that you honorably terminate the internship than to be terminated in any other way (e.g., caught up in the illegal acts of dirty cops or dishonest lawyers or, the ultimate termination, killed in the line of interning). It is a great sign of maturity to recognize what is not right and take proactive and decisive measures. You will be much further ahead when asked why you left an internship early if you can explain what occurred and the steps that went into your decision than to have to explain that you just quit going or, worse, were asked not to return.

What If You Are Told to "Get Out"?

Having an internship terminated is not just something you walk away from. It follows you. If the experience was part of a school program, it will be documented for background investigators to see for years to come. In the business, others will become aware of the event one way or another. Remember, like any profession, the local criminal justice community can be rather small. People know people, and people talk. Under no circumstances do you want to be talked about . . . except in a positive light.

If you think such a bad experience is easily concealed by simply "not mentioning it" to prospective employers, know that you will be asked about internships during your application process. If you lie, you will have quite possibly terminated any success at future job-seeking efforts in the field. Criminal justice employers will probably ask where else you have applied, and they will find out about your dishonesty. Do NOT put yourself in this position.

> If, for whatever reason, an internship does not work out, there is only one option: *Learn from it and be honest.*

BEING EVALUATED

Most schools and agencies with formal internship programs have some means of evaluating the intern. According to Donovan and Garnett (p. 203):

> Even if you don't get regular, ongoing feedback, you will almost certainly have a formal intern evaluation. Because you're a proactive intern, try to talk about your final evaluation as early as possible. How will it be done? When? What information will be used? From what sources will this information come?

While specific evaluation procedures and forms vary among organizations, many are completed by the intern's immediate supervisor and include the following elements (Donovan and Garnett, pp. 203–206):

➢   Name of the intern, date of internship and approximate number of hours worked

➢   Summary of intern's specific job duties and responsibilities

➢   Description of specific accomplishments and/or improvements made by intern while under supervision

➢   An evaluation of the intern's traits, usually on a scale of 1–5 or 1–10, with a low score being negative or unfavorable and a high score being positive or favorable (e.g., 1 = poor; 3 = average; 5 = outstanding):

Dependability	Pride in work	Verbal communication skills
Creativity	Speed	Written communication skills
Initiative	Accuracy	Professional skills
Professional appearance	Interest in job	Judgment skills
Self-confidence	Ability to learn	Contributes to the organization

Emotional maturity	Ability to organize	Understands procedures
Emotional stability	Ability to work with others	Follows procedures
Promptness	Ability to work alone	Accepts and makes use of criticism
Resourcefulness	Ability to work under pressure	Promise of future success

➤   What specific actions can you suggest to help interns improve their future performance?

Interns are often allowed to add comments to their evaluations and are usually required to sign them, confirming they have seen and discussed the evaluation with the supervisor who prepared it.

INTERNSHIPS THROUGHOUT YOUR CAREER

As you struggle and sweat to land that first job in criminal justice, it may seem hard to believe that, once "in," anyone would even consider leaving—but they do. We have observed professional five-year cycles that can lead people to want to do something different. After five years, give or take a year, you will know your job inside-out, and that is when people start to get tired of it, even burned out. This is one factor to keep in mind when considering what size agency you want to work for. The variety of positions increases with agency size, and it is typically much easier to transfer within a large agency than in a smaller one. However, even personnel in large departments may eventually get "stuck" and need a drastic change of scenery to find career satisfaction.

Interning when you already have a job serves similar purposes to interning before you get a job. These experiences help you learn. Many professionals pursue a practical internship to learn more about the work they do from people doing different or specialized work. For example, a colleague, already a successful police detective, completed several internships with different agencies that handle certain types of investigations differently than his. Similarly, professionals considering transferring or doing something altogether different may intern to learn whether it is really work they would like to do.

A word of caution: Do not assume that having an internship is always the best thing to have on your résumé. Internships are especially good for younger applicants with no experience in the field. Internships also provide something to add to a résumé when one has little else to include. But to quit another job altogether just because it isn't in a criminal justice–related field may be a mistake. For example, a 30-something law enforcement student was prepared to quit his 10-year well-paying position with an insurance company to take an entry-level nonsworn parking enforcement position "to get his foot in the door." While that particular department did use animal control and parking enforcement personnel as a pool from which to consider applicants, after discussing this move, he rethought the benefits. He had an excellent work record in a responsible position. This, combined with the other attributes he had in his résumé, made having his "foot in the door" not as critical as maintaining a stable work history, and he didn't have to take a massive pay cut. He had things going in his favor the younger, inexperienced applicants didn't, and he decided it was best to keep it that way. This isn't to say some departments do not rely on their entry-level personnel pool, which is why this is one more reason to learn about the agency you are applying to.

A RECAP—THE DO'S AND DON'TS OF INTERNSHIPS

Mistakes often happen because people simply have not taken time to think about what they would do *if* circumstances arose that had not been considered. It is a little like peer pressure in that if people think ahead of time how they would respond to situations, they may well not find themselves there in the first place, or at least handle them better. Here are some thoughts to help prepare you for those "what ifs" that have happened to others.

Do

➢   Explore internship options well ahead of when you want to intern.

➢   Apply for internships just as you would any other position (see chapters on résumés, cover letters, follow-up and thank-you letters, etc.).

➢   Maintain a clean record that will reflect positively on you when you apply for an internship, especially one in criminal justice that may well require a background check.

➢   Arrive on time, know who to report to, do what you're told and leave when instructed to ("I finished my work, so I just left" is not acceptable on-the-job behavior).

➢   Dress professionally, and ask ahead of time what the appropriate manner of dress is. Even if casual, dress smartly to make your best impression. You are better off overdressing the first day than finding yourself embarrassingly underdressed.

➢   Ask if you should go along on calls or exit the vehicle on stops. Do not assume that because you are riding along, you get to go everywhere and do everything. Never assume; always *ask*.

➢   Be prepared to make at least mental notes in the event something out of the ordinary is encountered. You may have become a witness to a significant event. The prepared intern will have a small notebook, pen and money for coffee or lunch stops.

➢   Speak up if you observe inappropriate actions by the person you are with or someone else. And under no circumstances go along with something illegal or unethical or be part of a cover up, even if told to. You do not want to end your career before it has even begun.

➢   If appropriate, ask for a general letter confirming you successfully participated in an internship. What would make it not appropriate to ask? Perhaps you only rode along for an hour or a day, or things did not go well. Then you are better off to let it go.

➢   Relax, enjoy the experience and leave on a good note. Thank-you's to the person or people you were with shows class and maturity, and a thank-you and good words to the supervisor of the person who accommodated you will be greatly appreciated—and remembered.

Don't

➢   Start looking for an internship too late.

➢   Submit a handwritten application or one that includes typos or grammatical errors.

➢   Keep getting traffic tickets or get yourself into trouble that would reflect poorly on you when being considered for an internship, *particularly* in the criminal justice field.

➤ Assume you know what to wear on the first day, and certainly don't show up in something altogether inappropriate.

➤ Be unfit. You should appear able to do the work you are interested in learning about.

➤ Be a know-it-all (remember, you are there to learn, not to teach senior personnel!).

➤ Do anything in excess, including talking (imagine what that's like for a patrol officer used to working alone).

➤ Assume it is permissible to jump out of your seat every time the person you are assigned to does (ask beforehand when you should accompany them).

➤ Talk to people you have no business talking to (victims, witnesses, suspects).

➤ Assume anyone else present knows who you are (when appropriate, introduce yourself, or answer at a hectic scene when someone challenges, "Who are you?").

➤ Assume you are invisible to all that is going on around you (you may have to provide a report on what you observed).

➤ Forget your manners when you arrive.

➤ Show up late or leave early—ever. If it is unavoidable, call.

➤ Do anything that would reflect poorly on the agency you are assigned to or the program you are from.

➤ Cover up any misdeeds you observe, even if asked to by anyone.

➤ Tell the person you are with how they should do their job, what kind of equipment they should be using or why anything they are doing is not correct (even if it is).

➤ Be critical of others in that profession.

➤ Be too passive. (Ask questions and show interest, but do so appropriately.)

➤ Leave on a negative note, no matter how the experience went.

Having successfully completed an internship, it is wise to ask for a "to whom it may concern" letter from someone at the agency. This letter will serve to document the experience, as well as explain you did a good job. Especially for younger people without a great deal of work history, letters like this contribute greatly to an application packet for future employment.

Internships are so much more than "just doing nothing there" or "only a program requirement." What internships provide is the opportunity to "try on" a profession before you get yourself in too deep and to get your foot in the door of a profession you are interested in. This is something *not* afforded everyone. Take it seriously.

CONCLUSION

Internships are all about people learning from others. They are among the most basic forms of active learning and should be taken advantage of whenever possible. Similarly, there is a resurgence of mentoring, with many employers assigning a more experienced mentor to new hires for the sole purpose of helping the new person learn faster and more effectively in the workplace. There is no question that internships offer many benefits, both for the person entering a career area as well as for those already employed in the field. Whether required, as in the medical profession, or as part of professional development at any level, interning returns greatly on the time invested.

As you continue to develop yourself for employment in the career of your choice, continue to ask yourself whether you are the kind of person you would want to hire. Interning makes a strong statement; that is, it shows that you have participated in the work outside of the school environment and that you are able to plan, behave appropriately, exercise your desire to learn and get along with people. Combined with your academic education, interning and service learning will help you present yourself as a very viable job candidate.

AN INSIDER'S VIEW

THE BENEFITS OF LEARNING WHILE SERVING

Carter Hendricks

Program Coordinator
Hopkinsville Community College, Kentucky

As an educator, my goal is to challenge each student to excel and strive to make a difference. I want my students to have new insights of their own knowledge and skills, as well as an ability to make an impact in their career and community. In the end, I want my students to be competent, caring and positive citizens. I want my students to have the desire and ability to apply their knowledge to improve society.

These qualities are desirable because of the impact they can have on our country and society. Our democracy is based on the premise that we will have an informed *and* active citizenry. We need citizens to seek knowledge and strive to make a difference if we are to maintain our status as the world's shining example of democratic governance. Therefore, I challenge my students to learn through experience. I challenge them to participate in service learning and internships because I know this will help prepare them to make a difference, to be competent and to be caring.

The benefits of experiential learning, like service learning and internships, are numerous. We know that we remember information if we apply it. We know that we remember information if we are engaged in discussing it. We know that we remember information if we have emotional responses to it. Consequently, with service learning and internships, we are asked to apply knowledge and skills to meet a real community need. We are engaged in discussions to reflect on our experience and learning. And, we are often emotionally connected as we work with other students and the community.

We must also remember that theory and lectures can do only so much to prepare us for the real world. Life outside of classrooms is quick and ever-changing. Therefore, we must engage in experiences that allow us to react and make decisions in the real world. This is especially important for professionals who work in fields that require frequent interaction with the community. From criminal justice to education, professionals who have experienced service learning and/or internships during their college coursework are far better prepared to excel once they have completed their college coursework. They are also able to establish a network base that can be helpful in the search for employment. Simply put, students who have successfully completed such experiential learning as part of their education make very viable candidates for employment.

Important to note is that the benefits of service learning and internships extend beyond self. When we engage in opportunities where we provide our services to meet real needs, then we bring benefit to our community. We extend a helping hand that might be the difference between success and failure for an individual, organization and community. All human service positions, including those in criminal justice, require people able to apply these real skills to the real world.

"Knowledge is power. Knowledge without action is wasted potential."

Carter Hendricks *is the former Service-Learning Specialist with the Minnesota Department of Education and a recognized leader in the service-learning field. He has conducted numerous workshops and presented nationally on service learning. Mr. Hendricks is currently Program Coordinator for the AAS in Education at Hopkinsville Community College. He holds a master's degree in education from Concordia University–Saint Paul and an undergraduate degree in history and political science from Western Kentucky University.*

 MIND STRETCHES

1. In what ways would an internship help you in your criminal justice job search?

2. If you were an employer, what kind(s) of interning completed by a prospective officer would impress you the most? Why?

3. What do you think would be the most difficult part of interning in criminal justice, and what could you do to plan for it?

4. Once you secure an internship, what things could you do to make it a success before you even begin?

5. What are some reasons an internship might not be a good fit for someone? What should be done in such cases?

6. Recognizing that an internship provides many opportunities to network, how would you go about taking full advantage of this?

7. How would you deal with a problem during an internship?

8. Brainstorm a list of how a good criminal justice internship could go "bad."

9. Create a "top 10" list of attributes that make for a good criminal justice intern.

10. In what ways do you think a criminal justice internship is similar to and different from a "job" in the same field?

REFERENCES

Donovan, Craig P. and Garnett, Jim. *Internships for Dummies.* New York: John Wiley & Sons, 2001.

Florida Atlantic University. Online: http://www.fau.edu/divdept/caupa/dcj/internship.html

Hendricks, Carter. Professor, Hopkinsville Community College, Kentucky. Direct correspondence for this text, June 2004.

O'Connor, Thomas R. Online: http://faculty.ncwc.edu/toconnor/421/intern.htm (last updated January 6, 2004).

Oldman, Mark and Hamadeh, Samer. *The Internship Bible.* New York: Random House, Inc. and Princeton Review Publishing, 2003.

Rubinstein, Ellen. *Scoring a Great Internship (Students Helping Students).* New York: Natavi Guides, Inc., 2002.

SECTION TWO

MEETING THE CHALLENGE: PREPARING

===

Even if you are on the right track, you'll still get run over if you just sit there.

—Will Rogers

Most people don't plan to fail—they fail to plan.

—Anonymous

Before everything else, getting ready is the secret of success.

—Henry Ford

For every officer who is hired, there are 250 applicants who are not. The secret to accomplishing your dream comes down to one objective—preparation.

—Larry R. Frerkes

The normal process in seeking a job is to find where job openings exist, apply, submit a résumé, undergo various kinds of testing, be interviewed and be hired! This section does not follow that order. Rather, it asks you to continue doing what you began in Chapter 5—looking at your own qualities, experiences and preferences and seeing how they fit with what criminal justice agencies and security departments are looking for. It also suggests ways to overcome any shortcomings you might find as you consider yourself in relation to the job requirements. This should be done *before* you actually begin looking for specific jobs. This section is written as though you were already actively engaged in testing and interviewing.

You'll begin by looking at the physical requirements of these fields and what tests you might have to pass (Chapter 7). One of the most important attributes of successful candidates is physical fitness—which doesn't happen overnight. Next you'll look at the educational and psychological requirements that might be considered and how they might be tested (Chapter 8).

This is followed by a discussion of the "beneficial attributes" of successful candidates in these fields, that is, who is most likely to be hired (Chapter 9), giving you a chance to realistically assess what attributes *you* have and how you might fare. The next chapter discusses how you can assemble the information you have collected about yourself thus far into that all-important document—your résumé (Chapter 10). The section concludes with a critical part of the job-hunting process—being prepared for rejection (Chapter 11). Each rejection must be seen as a learning situation, a chance to become better at presenting yourself and as being one step closer to that job you *will* eventually get.

These chapters should be reread at appropriate times during your actual job hunt. For example, if you are scheduled for a physical fitness test, reread Chapter 7 a few days before. If you don't even make it to the testing stage, reread Chapter 11. When you're ready, move on to Section Three, which presents specific job-seeking strategies to enhance your chances of getting a job in your chosen field.

CHAPTER 7

PHYSICAL FITNESS AND TESTING

"It's easier to maintain your health than to regain it."

—*Dr. Ken Cooper*

Do You Know:

➤ Why physical fitness is crucial for police, corrections or security officers?
➤ Why it is difficult for people in these fields to stay in shape?
➤ What five parameters are generally considered in evaluating physical fitness?
➤ What four things most physical fitness tests seek to measure?
➤ What three areas are of critical importance during the medical examination and what other tests might be conducted?
➤ What impact the ADA has had on medical examinations and inquiries about disabilities?
➤ How fitness and stress interrelate?
➤ How personality and stress interrelate?
➤ Why proper nutrition is important?
➤ Whether an unhealthy lifestyle is linked to premature death?

INTRODUCTION

An essential criterion for obtaining a job in criminal justice, security and related areas is physical fitness. The importance of having fit personnel goes without saying—the work is physically and emotionally taxing, and the job demands that those who pursue employment in these fields enter such work in shape and *remain* in shape.

This chapter examines how fitness is defined; the importance of fitness to those seeking employment in criminal justice; the nature of fitness testing and medical examinations; how you can assess your own fitness levels and design a program to improve and maintain your personal fitness; and the interplay between physical fitness and stress, nutrition and lifestyle.

WHAT IS FITNESS?

Fitness refers to a person's physical well-being or, to use the popular phrase, being "in shape." Blum (2000, pp. 12–13) notes:

> Fitness is generally defined as the ability to carry out daily physical tasks or leisurely pursuits with vigor and alertness, but without undue fatigue. Fitness may also refer to individual, but measurable levels of ability when completing physically demanding tasks associated with aerobic (running) and muscular (bench press, sit ups) events.

WHY IS FITNESS IMPORTANT?

According to Ebling (2002, p. 5): "Physical fitness for law enforcement officers is important not only for their personal well-being but also for their survival in a profession fraught with danger and high levels of stress." She notes: "The FBI has long held that the physical fitness of law enforcement officers ranks equal with their mental preparedness." Collingwood et al. (2003, p. 49) add:

> The public's expectation of a responding officer in a situation requiring physical effort, especially in a use of force situation, is the ability to provide the requisite service. They expect and deserve a fit officer because in a situation with injury and life and death consequences having those physical capabilities can minimize those threats.

Fitness can become a legal issue too. The people and property you are paid to protect will depend on your being able to do your job. If you cannot, you could be sued. In *Parker v. District of Columbia* (1988), the jury awarded $425,046 to a man shot by a police officer who was arresting him. As part of the case, the court noted: "Officer Hayes simply was not in adequate physical shape. This condition posed a foreseeable risk of harm to others." Oldham (2001, p. 77) notes: "Recent studies indicate officers who are in good physical condition are involved in far fewer uses of force than other, less fit officers."

Your future, your very life, may depend on your level of fitness. Ebling (p. 2) cites statistics that show, out of 149 professions, the law enforcement occupation ranks highest in rates of heart disease, diabetes and suicide. Blum (p. 13) reports: "More than 2000 officers have heart attacks and die each year in the line of duty."

Your future in criminal justice or security, your very life and the lives of the civilians you've sworn to protect, depend on your physical fitness. Being "out of shape" can even become a legal issue.

As noted, these professions, while appearing to be full of exciting chases and confrontations, are more likely to consist of extended periods of idle waiting, punctuated by immediate demands for extreme activity. Strandberg (2002, p. 38) states: "Law enforcement isn't a high activity job, unless you're in the bike patrol unit. It is essentially sedentary—sitting in a patrol car or riding a desk. The job does call for bursts of activity when there is action, so it's important for officers to be in tip-top condition or going from inactivity to full sprints will be too much to handle." Collingwood et al. (p. 44) bring the need for fitness into focus:

> The images are burned into our memories: Hundreds of New York/New Jersey Port Authority Police, New York City Police and Fire Department of New York Officers performing heroic tasks. Carrying people out of the towers, assisting the injured and eventually running for their lives when the collapse of the buildings began. Not one of those officers woke up on September 11, 2001, thinking that today would be the day he would be called on to exhibit levels of fitness beyond anything most of them had ever previously needed on the job.

What is particularly critical about physical fitness for criminal justice and security personnel is that the nature of their jobs can actually contribute to keeping them *out* of shape. As noted, most of these jobs involve a significant amount of inactivity with little opportunity for physical exercise. Combine this with odd working hours—often when only fast-food restaurants are open—and it becomes easy to understand why the stereotype of police, corrections and security officers is that of being overweight and out of shape.

The very nature of police and security jobs can contribute a great deal to officers being out of shape. The often-sedentary duties, such as driving a car or sitting at a desk, and the need to eat quick meals on the go—often fast food high in calories and fat—all contribute to the deterioration of physical fitness.

Ignoring physical fitness is little different from carrying a malfunctioning gun or driving a defective squad car. It could kill you. Employers know it is a challenge to keep their officers in shape. It is difficult for everyone to keep in shape as the years pass. This is good reason for employers to seek applicants who are physically fit.

Think about what being physically fit says about you to an employer. It says you are concerned about yourself. It also says you can project a positive image of the agency or institution you represent. For obvious reasons, employers do not want employees who would make their agency or institution look bad.

PHYSICAL FITNESS TESTING

Most candidates undergo some sort of physical fitness testing. Although specific fitness standards may vary from agency to agency, a typical well-balanced, comprehensive testing program will include five general parameters:

➢ Cardiorespiratory endurance or aerobic capacity (commonly measured by a 1.5-mile run)

➢ Abdominal and lower back strength (measured by sit-ups)

➢ Muscular strength and endurance (measured by push-ups)

➢ Flexibility (measured by a controlled sit and reach test)

➢ Body composition (percentage of body fat) or body mass index (BMI)

Physical fitness is often evaluated using five general parameters: cardiorespiratory endurance or aerobic capacity; abdominal and lower back strength; muscular strength and endurance; flexibility; and body composition or BMI.

An example of fitness standards in testing is provided by the U.S. Marshals Service (USMS), whose new deputies undergo a 10-week training program. According to the USMS website (http://www.usmarshals.gov):

> Prior to attending training, applicants must pass a physical fitness test given by USMS personnel. The test must be successfully passed within the six months prior to scheduled training. Students are *strongly* encouraged to be in top physical condition prior to attending training at the FLETC. The training program includes numerous hours of strenuous physical conditioning. Intense exercise in the warm, humid climate of southern Georgia can induce severe medical problems such as heat exhaustion and heat stroke.

> While in training, students will be required to participate in running distances from 1.5 to 10 miles in length. During lengthy runs, classes are also involved in periodic and repeated vigorous calisthenics (sit-ups, push-ups, "mountain climbers," etc.). Classes will run through obstacle courses, sprints and related other conditioning activities. Due to the intensity of physical activity, and the relatively short duration of the class, participating students *must* arrive at the FLETC in excellent physical condition.

During the last week of the Basic Training program, students are given another physical fitness test. Students must successfully pass the final FIT test to graduate training.

The required physical fitness test includes:
- 1.5 mile run
- Maximum push-ups in 60 seconds
- Maximum sit-ups in 60 seconds
- Stretch
- Body Composition

Another example is found in the Chicago Police Department's (CPD) fitness test standards (Krainik, 2003, p. 55): "Performance levels are dictated by gender and age. The tests are meant to examine cardiovascular health, strength and flexibility. The listed scores for the Maximum Bench Press Ratio are calculated by dividing the weight lifted by the officer's body weight." Figure 7–1 shows the acceptable fitness performance levels for CPD officers.

Regarding body composition, the trend is to look at the amount of body fat rather than weight as compared to height. The generally accepted percentage of fat for males is 14 to 16 percent of total body weight; for females, between 23 and 26 percent of body weight. A body mass index (BMI) is used to determine obesity and will be explained in more detail later in the chapter.

Another approach used by departments is having candidates perform "events," such as a Back Yard Pursuit, a Stretcher Carry, a Body Drag and a 300-Yard Sprint. In some agencies, multiple events are combined to form an obstacle course, through which candidates must maneuver within a set time limit. Ebling (p. 3) describes one such course used at the FBI National Academy:

> The Yellow Brick Road is the final test of the Fitness Challenge. Its wooded trails, 3 walls, 6 ropes, and 26 obstacles make it the ultimate challenge for everyone. Students either must run out to or back from the Yellow Brick Road for a total of 6.1 miles. . . .

> Once at the site, students face a bear trap, barbed wire, and numerous hills that wind through rough terrain. . . . Climbing over walls, running across creeks, jumping through simulated windows, and scaling sheer rock faces with the help of ropes present physically demanding tasks for the runners. . . .

	MALES				FEMALES			
Test	20–29	30–39	40–49	50–59	20–29	30–39	40–49	50–59
Sit and Reach	16.0	15.0	13.8	12.8	18.8	17.8	16.8	16.3
One minute Sit-Up	37	34	28	23	31	24	19	13
Maximum Bench Press Ratio	.98	.87	.79	.70	.58	.52	.49	.43
1.5 Mile Run	13.46	14.31	15.24	16.21	16.21	16.52	17.53	18.44

FIGURE 7–1   POWER Chart (Chicago Police Department Fitness Test Standards)

SOURCE: Peggy Wilkins Krainik. "Chicago's Fit Officers Count Their Benefits." *Law and Order,* February 2003, p. 55. Reprinted by permission.

Next comes the most well-known obstacle—the cargo net made famous in the motion picture *The Silence of the Lambs*. Flipping over the top of the net, approximately 10 to 12 feet above the ground, offers a tough but exhilarating test for everyone. After accomplishing this, . . . [students continue] the last three-quarters of a mile, which includes a combat crawl under barbed wire in muddy water, to the finish line.

> A wide variety of physical fitness tests may be administered, but they are all likely to measure the same things: endurance, agility, flexibility and strength.

Most police departments, correctional institutions or businesses hiring security personnel require that job applicants have a medical examination as well as a physical test of some sort to be certain they are physically fit.

THE MEDICAL EXAMINATION

Three areas of critical importance during the medical examination are vision, hearing and the condition of the cardiovascular-respiratory system. The vision test may include a test for colorblindness. Most agencies will accept applicants who have *corrected* vision and hearing problems, that is, those who wear a hearing aid and/or eye glasses or contact lenses or who have had laser eye surgery. If you think you may have problems in any of these areas, get checked out before you apply for a position.

The cardiovascular and respiratory systems play a critical role in fitness. To a large extent endurance, the ability to continue exertion over a prolonged period, is directly related to the ability of the cardiovascular-respiratory system to deliver oxygen to the muscles.

The medical exam may also include tests for determining blood pressure, smoking status, drug use, blood sugar level (for diabetes) and the ratio of total cholesterol to HDL cholesterol (to identify cardiovascular risk factors). If a physician finds that you have a functional or organic disorder, the recommendation may be made to disqualify you.

> Three areas of critical importance during the medical examination are vision, hearing and the condition of the cardiovascular-respiratory system. The medical exam may also include a cholesterol check, blood pressure check, inquiries about smoking status or lung capacity checks, drug tests and blood sugar level check for diabetes.

The use of medical examinations in hiring is governed by the Americans with Disabilities Act (ADA). According to Colbridge (2001, p. 25): "During the application/interview process, the ADA bars employers' disability-related inquiries (i.e., those that are likely to elicit information about disabilities)." In addition (p. 26):

> Medical examinations are prohibited during the application/interview stage. Tests for illegal drug use are not considered medical examinations under the ADA, so employers may test applicants for current illegal drug use. However, the EEOC has ruled that tests for alcohol use are medical in nature, and violate the ADA at this stage of the employment process.
>
> Two other kinds of tests may also be given at this stage. Physical agility tests that demonstrate the ability to do actual or simulated job-related tasks . . . are permissible if given to all applicants. . . . Employers may also require that applicants take physical fitness tests that measure their ability to do physical tasks

such as running and lifting, so long as all applicants must do so. Neither test is considered a medical examination under the ADA unless applicants' physiological or psychological responses to the tests are measured.

Colbridge (p. 27) further explains:

> Once employers have judged applicants based upon their non-disability related qualifications during the application/interview stage, found them qualified, and made bona fide job offers to them, the ADA permits employers to face the issue of disabilities. Employers may now inquire about disabilities, require medical examinations, and condition their employment offers on the results of these medical examinations.

The Americans with Disabilities Act (ADA) prohibits medical examinations or inquiries regarding mental or physical problems or disabilities *before* a conditional offer of employment has been made.

In other words, the employer makes the candidate a job offer provided the candidate passes the medical examination.

SELF-ASSESSMENT

It is important that you know how physically fit you really are. Just because you feel good does not necessarily mean that you are "in shape." The FBI's publication *Physical Fitness for Law Enforcement Officers* (n.d.) recommends the following:

➤ Feel your arms, shoulders, stomach, buttocks and legs. Are your muscles well-toned or are you soft and flabby?

➤ Give yourself the pinch test. Take hold of the skin just above your belt. Are your fingers separated by more than one-half inch?

This publication describes cardiovascular, balance, flexibility, agility, strength and power tests to assess your physical fitness. Their descriptions follow.

Cardiovascular Tests

Cureton's Breath-Holding Test. One simple way to test your respiratory capacity is to step onto and off a chair, bench or stool (approximately 17 inches high) for a period of one minute and then see how long you can hold your breath. You should be able to hold it for at least 30 seconds. If you can't, it indicates your cardiovascular function has deteriorated below a desirable level.

Kasch Pulse Recovery Test (3 min.). This test can be performed at almost any age. Only the infirm or the extremely unfit would find it too strenuous. You should not smoke for one hour or eat for two hours before taking the test. Also, rest for five minutes before taking the test.

EQUIPMENT
12-inch bench or stool
Clock or watch with a sweep second hand

PROCEDURE

a. Start stepping onto and off the bench when sweep second hand is at 11.
b. Step 24 times per minute, total 72.
c. Duration is three minutes.
d. Stop stepping when sweep second hand is again at 11, after three revolutions, and sit down.
e. Start counting the pulse rate when sweep second hand reaches 12 on the clock, using either the artery located inside the wrist or the carotid artery in the throat. Count every 10 seconds and record for one minute.
f. Total the six pulse counts for one minute and compare with the following scale:

Classification	0–1 Minute Pulse Rate after Exercise
Excellent	71–78
Very Good	79–83
Average	84–99
Below Average	100–107
Poor	108–118

Cooper's 12-Minute Walk/Run Test. Find a place where you can run/walk a measured distance of up to two miles. A quarter-mile track at a local school would be ideal; however, a nearby park, field or quiet stretch of road can be used. The test is quite simple—see how much of the two miles you can comfortably cover in 12 minutes. Try to run the entire time at a pace you can maintain without excessive strain. If your breath becomes short, walk until it returns to normal, then run again. Keep going for a full 12 minutes; then check your performance on the following scale:

Fitness Category (under age 30)	Distance Covered in 12 Minutes (in miles)
Very Poor	less than 1.0
Poor	1.00–1.24
Fair	1.25–1.49
Good	1.50–1.74
Excellent	1.75 +

(*NOTE:* People over age 30 should not take this test until they have had a complete medical examination and have completed approximately six weeks in a "starter physical fitness program.")

Balance Test

Stand on your toes, heels together, eyes closed, and your arms stretched forward at shoulder level. Maintain this position for 20 seconds without shifting your feet or opening your eyes.

Flexibility Tests

Trunk Flexion. Keep your legs together, your knees locked, bend at the waist and touch the floor with your fingers.

Trunk Extension. Lie flat on your stomach, face down, fingers laced behind your neck and your feet anchored to the floor. Now raise your chin until it is 18 inches off the floor. (Note: Average for male students at the University of Illinois is 12.5 inches.)

Agility Test

Squat Thrusts. Standing, drop down to squatting position, palms flat against floor, arms straight. Next, with weight supported on the hands, kick backward so that your legs are extended fully. Immediately kick forward to the squatting position and stand up. You should be able to perform four in eight seconds.

Strength Tests

Pull-ups. Hang from a bar, hands slightly wider than shoulders, palms turned away, arms fully extended. Pull up until your chin is over the bar. Lower yourself until your arms are fully extended and repeat. You should be able to perform four pull-ups.

Push-ups. From the front leaning rest position, hands slightly wider than the shoulders with fingers pointed straight ahead, lower your body until your chest barely touches the floor. Push up to the front leaning rest position, keeping your body straight. Standards from the Institute for Aerobics Research for push-ups done in one minute are:

> 60 and up, superior;
> 50–59, excellent;
> 35–49, good;
> 25–34, average;
> 18–24, below average; and
> 17 or less, poor.

Sit-ups. Lie on your back with your hands behind your neck, with your legs straight and free. Flex the trunk and sit up, and then return to the starting position. Standards from the Institute for Aerobics Research for sit-ups done in one minute are:

> 49 and up, superior;
> 46–48, excellent;
> 42–45, good;
> 40–41, average;
> 33–39, below average; and
> 32 or less, poor.

Power Tests

Standing Broad Jump. From a standing position, jump as far forward as you can, landing on both feet. Do not take a running start. The length of your jump should equal your height.

Vertical Jump. Stand facing a wall, feet and chin touching the wall, arms extended over your head. Using chalk, mark the height of your hands on the wall. Now jump up and touch the wall as high as you can with one hand. (Again, use chalk.) Note the difference between the two marks on the wall. You should be able to perform a vertical jump of 18 inches or more.

Even if you successfully pass all these tests, be sure you remain in good physical shape. Your lifestyle may be such that you do not require a formal physical fitness program. Many people who are active in sports such as swimming, tennis, jogging or running do not need to do much more to keep in shape. If, however, you have a relatively sedentary lifestyle, you may want to start a basic physical fitness program.

A BASIC PHYSICAL FITNESS PROGRAM

An exercise program should start gradually and then build up. Oldham (p. 76) suggests: "Walking is one of the easiest and most beneficial of all cardiovascular exercises. Recent studies have found little difference between walking and running." You should exercise at least three times a week. As you progress into your fitness program, you can increase the number of weekly workouts. Numerous books and articles outline fitness programs. Find one that suits you.

Tips

The following tips on exercising might be considered:

➢   Exercise to music.

➢   Vary your exercises to give yourself some variety.

➢   Drink water during your breaks.

➢   Plan your program to easily fit your daily routine. Exercise at the same time each day.

➢   Start small and work up to a full regime gradually to reduce your chance of injury.

➢   Record your efforts.

➢   Do not expect immediate benefits. It takes regular, long-term effort.

➢   Wait 10 minutes after your cool-down to take a warm shower. *A hot or cold shower can dangerously affect your blood pressure.*

➢   If you stop exercising for a while—even a week or two—start at a lower level and gradually work your way up again.

(*NOTE:* Never pursue an exercise program without consulting with your physician.)

Sticking to Your Fitness Program

We are creatures of habit. And if your previous habit has been to skip the bike ride in favor of watching highlights of the Tour de France from the comfort of your sofa, you may find it difficult to stick to a fitness program. Creating a new habit, no matter how beneficial to you, takes a sustained effort. The key to long-term success with an exercise routine is to stay motivated. Rod Dishman, PhD, director of the exercise psychology laboratory at the University of Georgia, offers five strategies to keep your fitness program afloat (Kallen, 2001, p. 72):

1. Give yourself plenty of support. Work out with an encouraging partner, join an exercise group, or frequently remind yourself that putting time and effort into your exercise program is worthwhile.

2. Tell yourself you're getting benefits beyond a better-looking body. Keep in mind that regular workouts help you feel better about yourself, reduce stress, help you sleep and improve your overall health.

3. Set both idealistic long-term goals—so you'll have something to look forward to—and flexible short-term goals that will help you chart your progress without demanding too much from yourself.

4. Put your workouts into your weekly schedule, and stick to them just as you would any social engagement or business appointment.

5. Offer yourself extra rewards by arranging to do things you enjoy, but only after you've had your workout.

The Challenge of Maintaining Fitness

It is a "given" that you will be expected to be fit when you apply for certain criminal justice careers (any of the first-responder positions, to be sure), and you may have no problem ramping up your activity level for a short while to prepare for your fitness tests. The real challenge comes after you've graduated the academy and landed that job and settled into your cruiser (or desk). Krainik (p. 56) states: "While it is mandatory for recruits to pass fitness tests to be accepted into a department, once they are hired there are very few departments that make it mandatory for their employees to remain at an appropriate fitness level."

Dr. Paul Davis, an internationally recognized authority on the subject of fitness standards and employment opportunity issues, has developed job-related physical performance and medical standards for a number of law enforcement agencies. In addition to consulting for a number of criminal justice organizations, including the DEA, U.S. Secret Service, IACP and the FBI, Dr. Davis has also conducted in-depth studies of the physical performance requirements for SWAT, K-9 and industrial security positions. He (2002, p. 35) contends:

> Considerable effort is expended in the training academy environment enhancing the fitness level of cadets. I'm certain that the annual effort expended to provide a modicum of fitness costs taxpayers millions of dollars. The better model is to hire people who present for employment ready to perform the essential function of the job. Then, rather than having to rehabilitate people who should have been ready for employment in the first place, effort is better spent in training that is focused on other law enforcement topics. The current model creates, at best, only a temporary change in the fitness condition. Peer pressure is one of the cultural forces that retards organizations from implementing change. Hiring individuals who have no penchant for fitness perpetuates a practice of mediocrity. As we know, so much of what we attempt to accomplish in the academy is undermined once the officer leaves the sanctity of the training environment.

When you select a career in criminal justice, you must accept physical fitness as part of your cache of skills that, like firearms use and defensive tactics, will deteriorate if not actively maintained. Strandberg (p. 42) notes:

> Police academies are doing a good job of setting the table for lifelong fitness. In the past, the academies only tested the fitness of recruits, but now are trying to train them to look at fitness not as a short-term "help me pass the test" goal but rather a lifelong goal. Classes at the academy are now more about the benefits of a healthy lifestyle, sensible fitness programs, good nutrition and all the elements of being fit.

As Daniel Barnett, fitness instructor for the Louisville (Kentucky) Police Department, points out: "A lot of studies show that fitness decreases sick days, cardiovascular disease and more, so in the long run it will help with health care costs. Also, there is nothing better to relieve stress than working out" (Strandberg, p. 40).

FITNESS AND STRESS

Careers in criminal justice and security can be highly stressful—and so can seeking employment in these fields. Zhao et al. (2002, pp. 43–44) state: "[A] careful monitoring of stress is particularly important for the police profession, widely considered to be among the most stressful occupations due to the range of discretion allowed to officers in oftentimes critical circumstances." Atkinson-Tovar (2003, p. 119) adds: "Constantly, officers are asked to take on more and more responsibilities and become increasingly more efficient at the performance of their jobs. The increased complication comes with the factor of exposure to traumatic events during the course of a day." An important part of being physically and mentally fit is managing stress.

> Physically fit bodies are better able to cope with stress, and stress is abundant in the professions of criminal justice and private security. Keep fit to ward off stress.

Some personality types tend to be more susceptible to stress, particularly those identified as *Type A:*

> The concept of Type A behavior was formulated almost 40 years ago, when two cardiologists noted that the majority of their heart attack patients seemed to have the following behavioral traits: impatience, a sense of time urgency, an unrelenting urge for recognition and power, unusual preoccupation with work, and an unusually competitive and aggressive attitude. . . . Such individuals were subsequently shown to manufacture increased amounts of stress-related hormones known to damage heart muscle, and cause serious disturbances in cardiac rhythm (Rosch, 1998).

If you are a Type A personality, which many people drawn to criminal justice and security are, be aware of these risks. Exercise and relaxation techniques can help reduce them.

> People with Type A personalities are more susceptible to stress and are at increased risk for heart disease. It is vital for such people to learn and use exercise and relaxation techniques.

Reese (2001, p. 15) posits "six keys to stress-free living" that can help protect against the negative stress everyone experiences as part of living in our fast-moving, complex society: challenge, choice, change, courage, control and commitment. He (pp. 15–17) explains: "The first key to consider is that of challenge. Law enforcement officers are drawn to the occupation because of the challenges it presents to them daily." Some of the occupational challenges inherent in criminal justice professions include shift work, a paramilitary structure, court rulings perceived as too lenient on offenders or too restrictive on methods of criminal suppression and investigation, and anxiety over the responsibility to protect others (Reese, p. 16). *Challenge* also means accepting setbacks as something to be overcome.

The second key to controlling stress is *choice:* "While we may blame others for our current occupation, position, financial status, and more, we are actually the product of the choices we have made in life. Among the many choices we make every day, our attitudes are most important. . . . Among our many choices are: . . . the type of job we seek, the job we finally accept, how we see ourselves in that job, whether or not to seek a promotion, seeking a transfer, getting bitter or getting better" (Reese, p. 16).

The third key, *change,* is a paradox because of its constancy. Change can cause significant stress, but it is imperative that you treat change as something to be adapted to. As U.S. author and marketing executive Bruce Barton stated: "When you're through changing, you're through."

Courage, the fourth of Reese's keys to stress-free living, is doing that which you believe in, even if it means taking the unpopular or difficult path. For those in criminal justice, courage might mean reporting unethical behavior by a fellow officer or working with juvenile delinquents to get their lives back on track.

Control means taking charge of your life, being confident in your ability to direct your own life rather than letting it be directed by outside forces. And *commitment* means being actively involved and caring about your family, friends, job, hobbies and the like. It also includes being committed to personal fitness. As Harpold and Feemster (2002, p. 6) assert: "Choosing to be healthy is the best weapon against the negative influences of stress. Once a commitment is made to fight back against the negative factors of stress, life becomes healthier and more enjoyable."

The Upside of Stress

Not all stress is negative. Most people need a certain amount of stress to keep them sharp. Think of the last time you had a deadline to meet. It was the stress of the deadline that probably finally got you moving. The website for a stress and emotional intelligence consulting company (http://www.essisystems.com) states:

> Stress is a life energy force in the body and is the key ingredient in optimal performance. Positive stress is actually essential and beneficial, and can be our strongest ally for leading stimulating healthy lives, filled with vitality and resilience.
> Quick! Think of three positive stress words.
> Did you think creativity, zeal, passion, excitement or motivation? These are stress words as well. Positive stress words.

The key is to keep stress from becoming *distress*.

FITNESS AND NUTRITION

The U.S. Army's total fitness program emphasizes nutrition. Among the concepts it stresses are the following:

➢   Drink 6 to 8 glasses of water a day.

➢   Avoid too much sugar.

➢   Avoid too much sodium (salt).

➤   Include fiber in your daily diet.

➤   Cut down on protein and fats.

Scoville (2002, p. 52) suggests:

> Treat deep-fried foods and cheese eats with the same contempt you'd normally reserve for a
> violent third-strike offender: Lock 'em up and throw away the key.
> If you're starving and the only eating establishment in sight is a Stop 'n Rob, skip the beef jerky
> and grab a nutrition bar. . . .
> Try to eat like you do at home (unless you eat like a pig there, too). Skip the "glutton specials"
> and stop "super sizing." Eat normal-sized meals, as portions are an important consideration.

Obesity

Recall the heightened incidence of heart disease and diabetes among those in the law enforcement
profession. Obesity is an important risk factor in these diseases and contributes to the shortened life span
of affected individuals. High blood pressure, common among police officers, is also related to obesity.

Unfortunately, many police officers and those in related professions are obese. In fact, Krainik (p. 55)
reports the American Obesity Association estimates nearly 65% of Americans are obese. She further
notes: "Officers who are overweight will have more health problems, due to the strain the extra weight
will put on their bodies. Many health problems are directly related to diet and obesity, such as high
cholesterol, high blood pressure, coronary artery disease and diabetes."

Calculate your BMI using the equation: Weight $\div$ Height (in)^2 $\times$ 704.5 $=$ BMI. According to Krainik (p. 55):

> A BMI of 30 or more is considered obese, and a BMI of 25–29.9 is considered overweight. However, keep in
> mind that muscle is dense and heavy, and an officer who is very muscular may have a high BMI due to his
> muscular frame, not due to unhealthy habits.

The key to losing weight is a sensible diet and exercise. Physicians and health club consultants can
suggest what diet might be best for you if you have a weight problem.

> Proper nutrition is an important part of fitness and avoiding obesity, which is believed to increase the risk of
> certain diseases and to shorten the life span.

FITNESS AND LIFESTYLE

As discussed, fitness, to be truly effective and beneficial, must be incorporated into the way you live every
day—your lifestyle. Spain and Franks (2001, p. 3) put it simply: "On average, physically active people
outlive those who are inactive. Regular physical activity also helps to maintain the functional
independence of older adults and enhances the quality of life for people of all ages."

The Centers for Disease Control and Prevention (CDC) asserts: "Given the numerous health benefits of
physical activity, the hazards of being inactive are clear. Physical inactivity is a serious, nationwide
problem. Its scope poses a public health challenge for reducing the national burden of unnecessary illness

and premature death." According to the CDC: "Poor diet and physical inactivity lead to 300,000 deaths each year—second only to tobacco use." Furthermore:

> Chronic diseases—such as heart disease, cancer, and diabetes—are the leading causes of death and disability in the United States. These diseases account for 7 out of every 10 deaths and affect the quality of life of 90 million Americans. Although chronic diseases are among the most common and costly health problems, they are also among the most preventable. Adopting healthy behaviors such as eating nutritious foods, being physically active, and avoiding tobacco use can prevent or control the devastating effects of these diseases.

> In the United States, many deaths each year are attributed to chronic diseases brought about by unhealthy lifestyles.

Fitness also involves more than just exercising, eating right and maintaining a proper weight. Lifestyle habits such as getting seven to eight hours of sleep each night and avoiding cigarettes, drugs and alcohol can significantly enhance longevity.

Smoking, Alcohol and Other Drugs

These substances are harmful to your health and your career. Keep in mind that an increasing number of both public and private agencies are limiting candidates to those who are nonsmokers. So if you smoke, quit. If you use controlled substances, stop. And if you drink alcoholic beverages, do so in moderation. Other people's lives, not to mention your own, depend on you having a clear head and quick reflexes.

To understand how drug use could seriously affect your employment potential, consider this scenario:

> A few months ago, Grace was in the middle of looking for a security job. She had been on over a dozen interviews, but no job offers had been made and she was beginning to lose hope. One weekend, her friends suggested going to an outdoor concert to help lift her spirits, and she agreed it might help take her mind off her unemployment.

> Early into the concert, Grace noticed one of her friends take something from her jacket pocket, light it, take a hit off it and pass it to the friend next to her. When it got to Grace, she hesitated. Her best friend leaned over and whispered, "C'mon, Gracie. You need to lighten up a little. It won't kill you."

> A second later, Grace felt her lungs filling with smoke, and as she held it in she thought, "Yeah, I do need to relax." After a second hit, she passed the joint on to her friend. The rest of the evening was spent swaying to the music and getting high.

> On Monday, Grace got a phone call from one of the security firms, wanting her to come in for a second interview. At first she was thrilled . . . then panic set in when she realized there might be a drug test.

Increasingly, companies are conducting random drug tests on current and prospective employees.

BENEFITS OF BEING PHYSICALLY FIT

Some benefits of being physically fit, many of which would be advantageous to the job seeker, are:

➤ More personal energy
➤ Increased ability to handle job-related stress

➤ Slowing of the aging process
➤ A better self-image and more self-confidence

➤ Less depression, hypochondria and anxiety   ➤ A more attractive body

➤ Fewer aches, pains and other physical complaints   ➤ More restful sleep

➤ More efficient digestion   ➤ Better concentration at work

➤ Stronger bones

Schultz and Acevedo (2000, p. 34) state: "Individual officer fitness . . . can have a tremendous impact on how well a department functions. Studies have consistently demonstrated that healthy and fit officers improve work productivity, lower absenteeism rates, and reduce health risks." The benefits of fit officers extend well beyond the individual and department:

> "The significance is that law enforcement is here to protect the citizens of the community, and if their health is maximized, the community will benefit," says Marty Tuley, fitness author. . . . "Law enforcement suffers to the same degree as the general population from obesity issues and general health concerns. People perform better if they are physically healthier. There is no job that won't be enhanced by someone who is physically fit. It's just more obvious with jobs that are physically demanding" (Strandberg, p. 40).

CONCLUSION

Your future in criminal justice or security, your very life and the lives of the civilians you're sworn to protect depend on your physical fitness. Being "out of shape" can even become a legal issue. Fortunately, fitness is one area you *can* control. Once you get in shape, *stay there.* This may not be easy because the very nature of criminal justice and security jobs can contribute a great deal to being out of shape. However physically fit bodies are better able to cope with stress, and stress is abundant in the professions of criminal justice and private security.

Everyone has made decisions they later wish they had not. It is what we are doing now that makes a difference. Some decisions may be countermanded by what we have done with them. For example, paying off debt shows an ability to be accountable for oneself. Fitness is different, in that "what you see is what you get," at least at interview time. For the most part, preparing yourself by getting into shape for the job-seeking process gives you the opportunity to present yourself in the best possible light. This is a significant opportunity, particularly in professions that understandably demand fitness.

AN INSIDER'S VIEW

FITNESS: THE MOST IMPORTANT WEAPON YOU WILL EVER CARRY

Ron J. Nierenhausen

Sergeant, Patrol Division
Elk River (Minnesota) Police Department

The most overlooked and grossly neglected aspect of an officer's arsenal is their fitness. We concentrate on firearms, defensive tactics, procedure, policy and equipment yet fail to focus on the most important weapon you will ever carry—fitness. During my 16 years in law enforcement I have staunchly opined that without a proper fitness regimen an officer's performance will be greatly hampered. A sound mind and body equals sound and safe decisions. One cannot be successful without the other.

But fitness does not just pertain to people on the job; it's as important to those seeking employment in any area of criminal justice. How you present yourself and how you plan to maintain your fitness level are important attributes to any hiring authority.

Officers typically have two excuses for not adopting a personal fitness plan, the first being lack of time. Understanding the rigors of law enforcement—schedules, shifts, court appearances, etc., it is feasible to see why so many simply push a fitness plan to the bottom of the list. Although other commitments are important, so is the commitment to fitness. You may be able to keep up with the hectic schedule for awhile, but eventually it will wear you down to the point of serious risk. It has been well established in the medical community that fitness affects all aspects of life. The healthier you are, the better your ability to fight off disease, ailments and fatigue, along with enhanced injury recovery.

The second excuse used is lack of instruction or knowledge. I find this ironic since those who choose a life in law enforcement are inherently curious individuals. We spend countless hours searching for "bad guys" and investigating crimes yet refuse to do a small amount of research on fitness. A trip to the local bookstore will reveal volumes of "How To" books on fitness and exercise lining the shelves. You may even ask other officers in your department for help since they may be the best resource of all. They can be tremendous mentors if you are new or a support system if you have experience yet lack the continued desire.

Image is another aspect of fitness in law enforcement that must be addressed. The better you present yourself to the public, the more receptive they will be. It would be difficult to listen to a doctor's advice on health if they were unkempt, overweight and, most importantly, unprofessional. The same holds true for police officers. Your first impression may set the tone for the entire call. If a citizen feels you look the part, then they'll assume you fit it also. During hazardous situations an offender will size you up before making a move, and if you look unbeatable they will assume you are unbeatable. Either way you go home at the end of the shift in one piece.

Durability is key to the success of an officer's career. By incorporating a fitness plan into your daily life you will be more apt to sustain the rigors of the schedule. Working overnights and double-backs while wearing 40 pounds of gear can take its toll. Not to mention dealing with offenders. As we age our bodies tend not to recover as well or as quickly as when we were young. Being fit won't stop you from aging but will help your body maintain a higher level of durability and resilience.

Finally, self-esteem must be addressed. The more fit you are, the better you will feel about yourself. I have seen many officers who just don't care anymore. That's a terrible mindset to be in, since much of what we do is mindset itself. We need to adopt a warrior attitude from the aspect of "never lose, never back down." We are a symbol, and that symbol must be proud at all times.

The benefits of a well-planned, well-attended fitness program will help you during your job application efforts, carry you through the rough times and give you the added energy needed to handle the rigors of criminal justice employment. So much is discussed about the benefits that I cannot list them all in this short submission. I can only reaffirm what you already know. Criminal justice and fitness go hand-in-hand and should be viewed as "the most important weapon you will ever carry."

Ron J. Nierenhausen *is a patrol sergeant with the Elk River (Minnesota) Police Department, having worked there for 16 years. In addition to supervising patrol officers, he is also a SWAT team member, honor guard member, fitness instructor, firearms instructor and Field Training Coordinator. Sgt. Nierenhausen holds a BA in Criminal Justice from St. Cloud (Minnesota) State University and an MA in Human Services from Concordia (Minnesota) University. He is a graduate of Northwestern University (Illinois) School of Police Staff and Command and holds certificates in Police Fitness Instruction from both Northwestern University and Cooper Aerobic Institute (Dallas, TX). Sgt. Nierenhausen instructs both officers and city employees on fitness and helps coordinate the city wellness program. Ron is married to wife Kathy and has one stepdaughter, Ashley.*

INSIDERS' VIEWS ONLINE

Additional *Insiders' Views* for this chapter are "Pre-Employment Physical Fitness" by Capt. Richard W. Stanek and "What Physical Fitness Really Means: Everyone Talks about It, But Not Many Understand" by Dr. Sheldon T. Hess, found on the Wadsworth website: http://www.wadsworth.com/criminaljustice_d/.

 ## MIND STRETCHES

1.   How would you judge your current level of physical fitness?

2.   Are you currently working out? What is your fitness program?

3.   Why do you imagine the stereotype of the overweight, donut-eating cop exists?

4.   How do law enforcement and security careers tend to prevent fitness?

5.   Is being overweight and out of shape possibly part of the "macho" image of being a cop or security guard? If so, is this changing?

6.   What does an out-of-shape officer communicate to the public by appearance alone?

7.   Why do you think so few Americans exercise regularly?

8.   Recognizing that perhaps working the night shift would make keeping in shape difficult, in what creative ways could an officer working such a shift exercise?

9.   Are criminal justice and private security more stressful than other careers? Why or why not?

10.   How would you define *physically fit?*

REFERENCES

Atkinson-Tovar, Lynn. "The Impact of Repeated Exposure to Trauma." *Law and Order,* September 2003, pp. 118–123.

Blum, Jon. "Physical Training for Law Enforcement . . . A New Approach?" *The Law Enforcement Trainer,* July/August 2000, pp. 12–15, 48.

Centers for Disease Control and Prevention. Online: http://www.cdc.gov/nccdphp/sgr/ataglan.htm; http://www.cdc.gov/nccdphp/ bb_nutrition/index/htm

Colbridge, Thomas D. "The Americans with Disabilities Act: A Practical Guide for Police Departments." *FBI Law Enforcement Bulletin,* January 2001, pp. 23–32.

Collingwood, Thomas; Hoffman, Robert J.; and Smith, Jay. "The Need for Physical Fitness." *Law and Order,* June 2003, pp. 44–50.

Davis, Paul O. "A New Approach to an Age-Old Problem: Officer Fitness and Readiness." *The Law Enforcement Trainer,* July/August 2002, pp. 33–37.

Ebling, Patti. "Physical Fitness in Law Enforcement: Follow the Yellow Brick Road." *FBI Law Enforcement Bulletin,* October 2002, pp. 1–5.

Essi Systems. Online: http://www.essisystems.com

Harpold, Joseph A. and Feemster, Samuel L. "Negative Influences of Police Stress." *FBI Law Enforcement Bulletin,* September 2002, pp. 1–7.

Kallen, Ben. "How to Stick to Your Fitness Plan." *Men's Fitness,* August 2001, pp. 68–73.

Krainik, Peggy Wilkins. "Chicago's Fit Officers Count Their Benefits." *Law and Order,* February 2003, pp. 55–57.

Oldham, Scott. "Physical Fitness Training for Police Officers." *Law and Order,* June 2001, pp. 75–77.

Physical Fitness for Law Enforcement Officers. Washington, DC: Federal Bureau of Investigation, U.S. Department of Justice, no date.

Reese, James T. "6 Keys to Stress-Free Living." *The Associate,* publication of the FBI National Academy, January/February 2001, pp. 14–17.

Rosch, Paul J. "Type A Behavior: What You Should Know." MSNBC TV News, 1998. Online: http://www.msnbc.com/onair/nbc/nightlynews/stress/

Schultz, Ray and Acevedo, Art. "Ensuring the Physical Success of a Department." *Law and Order,* 2000, pp. 34–37.

Scoville, Dean. "Code 7." *Police,* July 2002, pp. 46–52.

Spain, Christine G. and Franks, B. Don. *Healthy People 2010: Physical Activity and Fitness.* Washington, DC: President's Council on Physical Fitness and Sports, Research Digest, March 2001. Online: http://www.presidentschallenge.org/misc/news_research/research_digests/60493.pdf

Strandberg, Keith W. "Fitness after the Academy." *Law Enforcement Technology,* November 2002, pp. 38–43.

U.S. Marshals Service. Online: http://www.usmarshals.gov/careers/basic_training.htm

Zhao, Jihong "Solomon"; He, Ni; and Lovrich, Nicholas. "Predicting Five Dimensions of Police Officer Stress: Looking More Deeply into Organizational Settings for Sources of Police Stress." *Police Quarterly,* March 2002, pp. 43–62.

CHAPTER 8

OTHER FORMS OF TESTING

Experience is not what happens to you; it is what you do with what happens to you.

—Aldous Huxley

Do You Know:

➤ What test anxiety is and how common it is?
➤ How you can improve your test-taking performance?
➤ What areas of general knowledge you might be tested on?
➤ What other kinds of knowledge you might be tested on?
➤ What the most common kinds of tests are and what you should know about each?
➤ What assessment centers are and what purpose they serve?
➤ What psychological tests measure and if you can prepare for such tests?
➤ What integrity tests try to determine?
➤ What polygraph tests try to determine, how accurate they are and what law governs their use in preemployment screening?

INTRODUCTION

The tests used in the hiring process are likely to include the following:

➤ Knowledge

➤ Psychological

➤ Polygraph

This chapter reviews areas commonly tested to help you understand what the tests are and what purpose they serve. You will not be given "suggested" answers. In fact, for some tests, preparing for or trying to "out-psych" them can be a mistake. It's important to know what to expect and what aspects of the testing you can prepare for. Before considering the specific areas, however, take a few minutes to look at a very common phenomenon: *test anxiety*.

TEST ANXIETY

Test anxiety is a general uneasiness or dread characterized by heightened self-awareness and perceived helplessness that frequently leads to diminished performance on tests. It includes the psychological, physiological and behavioral responses to stimuli associated with the experience of testing. Test anxiety is a reality for most people. Recognize its existence and take control of it. How? By being as prepared as possible. The fewer surprises a test-taker encounters, the less anxiety is felt.

> Test anxiety is the worry, concern and stress commonly associated with any circumstance in which individuals find themselves being evaluated. It is a reality for most people.

It is possible for applicants to prepare for entrance exams, and consequently improve their scores, by *practicing*. Many books are available that provide hundreds of practice questions typical of those found in written tests. For example, policetests.com is a website offering exam guides for a wide variety of criminal justice careers, including police, corrections, probation, 911 dispatchers, treasury enforcement agents and border patrols. Arco publishes several general intelligence study references to help you prepare for the written tests used by many criminal justice agencies and departments. Specific books are listed at the end of the chapter to help officer applicants prepare for such exams. Whichever aspect of criminal justice you are interested in, you can improve your testing success through practice and repetition. And as you gain confidence in your test-taking abilities, you will also likely notice a decrease in test anxiety.

> Test performance can be improved through practice and repetition. The more practice you have with such written tests, the better you are likely to do.

In addition to being as prepared as possible, the following will help reduce test anxiety:

➢ Get a good night's sleep before the test.

➢ Eat.

➢ Take at least two pens, two #2 pencils and a large eraser.

➢ Know exactly where the test is to be given and how to get there. (You might make a practice run to the site.)

➢ Arrive with time to spare so parking or other hassles do not make you anxious.

TESTING KNOWLEDGE

It is hard to imagine that only a few years ago a person could become a law enforcement officer by merely responding to an advertisement. In fact, many fine officers today applied for their jobs rather spontaneously one day and were handed a gun and badge the next. Even today, many security jobs, some involving immense responsibility, require little, if any, knowledge by the applicant.

As appealing as this may sound at this stage of your job search, it is easy to see the many problems associated with what is quickly becoming a practice of the past. As these fields strive to become recognized professions and respond to the increasing demands and potential liability created by our complex society, employing agencies must take their hiring practices much more seriously. Whether the job for which you are applying requires certification or licensure or just requires applicants to be responsible individuals, almost all employers will want to assess what the applicant knows.

General Knowledge

Some tests are designed to assess certain basic levels of ability in areas such as math, English, grammar and composition. Because communication skills are vitally important, employers want assurance that the people they are considering hiring (for *any* level job) can express themselves well. Many large departments, particularly those sensitive to minorities, focus more on general knowledge, such as reading comprehension, vocabulary, analogies and general math. Written exams in criminal justice also commonly test map skills. Computer literacy and keyboarding skills are also becoming more critical.

General knowledge that is commonly tested includes reading comprehension, vocabulary, analogies and general math—basic reading, writing and arithmetic. Computer literacy is also becoming more important.

While different tests can be used to examine these basic areas, they will all look at the same basic abilities. Ask yourself if you possess the necessary reading, writing and math skills required of any employee (usually a college freshman level). If you are not at this level, immediately start a plan to improve your skills. Many community colleges have a policy of open admission. As part of the process, the student is tested in reading, writing and math skills. The college offers remedial courses for the underprepared student.

Once on the job, lack of basic reading, writing and math skills can't be hidden long from an employer. To avoid wasting everyone's time, many job applications include some basic questions to let the hiring agency know if you have these basic academic abilities. An increasing number of application forms have a section that requires a brief essay to test your writing, spelling, grammar and organizational abilities.

For example, the Minnesota Police Corps requires applicants to submit a personal essay *and* be prepared to write three short essays during testing:

Part VI. Personal Statement and Essays

Attach a personal statement to this application. Word limit: 500–700 words.

Tell us something about yourself. Why do you think you would be a great candidate for the Police Corps? What do you consider your greatest strength and why? What do you consider your greatest weakness and why? If you feel that you have faced difficult circumstances in your life, please write about how you have overcome these obstacles.

Although you are not required to write about any specific topic, an essay that shows growth, maturity, leadership, courage and commitment could be particularly helpful to your application. We are looking for a demonstrated interest in law enforcement and dedication to public service. **(5 points)**

Be prepared to write several essays when you are called in for testing.

You will be required to write a short (200–300 word) essay on each of the following topics. Your written statements should be concise and should reflect your true feelings and beliefs. Please give some thought to each topic ahead of time. Your writing must be legible. Illegible answers will not be graded and you will lose those points.
- Why are you applying to the Police Corps? **(5 points)**
- What do you see as the primary challenges confronting children growing up today in the communities of Minnesota? What role do you see for the police in addressing those challenges? **(5 points)**
- List three books that have influenced your thinking or contributed to your development. Briefly explain how and why. **(5 points)**

The essays are evaluated by the following standards:

➢ A clear main idea that fulfills the assignment.

➢ Adequate, specific support.

➢ Organized into logical paragraphs with coherent transitions.

➢ A concise style.

➢ Appropriate word choice.

➢ Sentences that are complete, varied and effective.

➢ Standard grammar: correct use of pronouns, adjectives, adverbs, negation, articles, subject/verb agreement.

➢ Mechanically correct: spelling, abbreviations, numbers, capitalization and punctuation.

Because writing is a skill you will need for the rest of your life, regardless of your professional pursuits, do not overlook this all-important area now. Take advantage of classes during your education, and if you have already completed any degree-seeking program, do not hesitate to return to school to become an adequate writer. There is no getting around it—you must be able to write well. Even if you somehow obtain a job without having adequate writing skills, this is an area you will be evaluated on during your probationary period when you will write, literally, constantly.

If you need remedial help in any area, get it *now*. Many opportunities exist to improve yourself. Often the only thing stopping someone from improving themselves is that they feel too embarrassed to ask for help. The help you need may be in a review book available from a library or bookstore, or you may want to enroll in a class at a community college or in an adult learning program.

Specific Knowledge

Applicants may be required to know specific information for certain jobs. In states requiring certification or licensure, successful completion of requisite levels of training or education will be evidence of such knowledge. Certainly such required knowledge will indicate the areas of specific knowledge you will be expected to know. For example, in Minnesota, which requires a minimum of two years of college to be eligible to be licensed as a police officer, areas of required knowledge include:

➢ Administration of justice   ➢ Firearms   ➢ Report writing
➢ Criminal investigation   ➢ Human behavior   ➢ Statutes
➢ Criminal procedure   ➢ Juvenile justice   ➢ Testifying in court
➢ Cultural awareness   ➢ Patrol functions   ➢ Traffic law enforcement
➢ Defensive tactics   ➢ Police operations and procedures

Less specific knowledge is required to be a private investigator in Minnesota, but in addition to passing a strict background investigation, a minimum of three years' experience in security work is required.

Even if the areas of specific knowledge are not set forth clearly, you should be able to foresee what may be asked during an oral interview. Basic statutes that apply to public or private officers would be likely questions. Often, such questions are intertwined with the "What would you do if . . . ?" question. This allows employers to test not only specific knowledge, but the application of it using problem-solving techniques and communications skills.

> Applicants should expect to be tested on some specific knowledge in areas pertaining to the field, such as relevant statutes and procedures.

It's your responsibility to be prepared to the best of your ability. If you do not know what you might be tested on, it does no harm to call ahead to ask. The worst that could happen is that they won't say. But it is much more likely you will be told, putting you a giant step ahead of applicants who haven't a clue as to what will be asked.

It's also a good idea to learn as much as possible about the department or agency you are applying to. If it is a law enforcement position, try to arrange for a ride-along, thus providing an opportunity to ask questions about the department. If it is a corrections position, arrange to visit the institution if possible. If it is a private security position, visit the facility and talk with a security officer. With the Internet, the availability of information about a department and the community it serves has never been greater. Do some research on the neighborhood demographics, or the type of business or industry the private company you are applying to is involved in. Being able to speak intelligently about the setting the company, agency or institution operates in will set you apart from other candidates.

Do what you can to learn and review what you think will be asked. Remember, no one can know everything. Sometimes you will be able to immediately give the exact answer, maybe even amazing yourself. Sometimes you may give a wrong answer. Sometimes you may draw a complete mental blank. You are likely to experience all these reactions at one time or another during testing.

Keep in mind the purpose of the testing process. If the only thing employers wanted were accurate answers, they would replace their employees with computers. Employers want someone who can think and act human. Part of being human is to *not* know it all and yet to keep functioning. Even if totally stumped, to hang your head and mutter, "I have absolutely no idea," is never the best option. A man applying for an entry-level dispatcher position had no experience in the field, and so the various scenario questions asking him to prioritize calls and how calls would be handled proved quite challenging. There was no logical way answers could be "made up," but his answer of, "I don't know the answer to that yet, but I can't wait to learn how to handle that scenario as effectively as possible!" was good enough to get the job.

Some tests might even include an "off-the-wall" question just to see how you respond. In all probability, you will look a lot better admitting you are nervous and forgot, or don't know the answer (but know where to find it), than to fake it. In short:

➢   Be as prepared as you can be.

➢   Seek remedial help if necessary.

➢   Know as much as you can.

➤   Know how to find what you don't know.

➤   Don't make up answers or pretend to know more than you really do.

➤   Don't be afraid to admit what you don't know.

Memory and Observation Tests

Many police departments use tests to determine applicants' ability to recall information. For example, pictures of several "bad guys" may be flashed on a screen and personal information given about each of the individuals, such as names, ages, criminal activity, etc. The test then continues by flashing a picture on the screen and requiring the applicant to recall all the information about the subject, or recall a nickname, or match a crime with a face.

STRATEGIES FOR TAKING TESTS

No matter whether the tests cover general information, specific knowledge, memory and observation skills, or a combination of these, the successful candidate knows how to approach the specific type of test given.

> The most common tests are multiple-choice, true/false and essay, and each type of test has its own guidelines and strategies to follow.

Landsberger (2004) offers practical advice for approaching such tests.

Tips for Better Test Taking[1]

Successful test taking avoids carelessness. In general:

- **Read the directions carefully.**
  This may be obvious, but it will help you avoid careless errors.
  If there is time, quickly look through the test for an overview.

- **Answer questions in a strategic order:**
  1. **First easy questions**—to build confidence, score points, and mentally orient yourself to vocabulary, concepts, etc. It may help you make associations with more difficult questions.
  2. **Then difficult questions**—or those with the most point value.
     With objective tests, first eliminate those answers you know to be wrong, or are likely to be wrong, don't seem to fit, or where two options are so similar as to be both incorrect.

     With essay/subjective questions, broadly outline your answer and sequence the order of your points.

- **Review:**
  Resist the urge to leave as soon as you have completed all the items.
  Review your test to make sure that you have answered all questions, not mis-marked the answer sheet, or made some other simple mistake.

---

[1]Joseph Landsberger, author and developer of website *Study Guides and Strategies,* http://www.studygs.net/#tests, St. Paul, MN, USA, accessed July 30, 2004. Reprinted by permission.

Proofread your writing for spelling, grammar, punctuation, decimal points, etc.

Do not "second-guess" yourself and change your original answers. Research has indicated that your first hunch is more likely to be correct. You should only change answers to questions if you originally misread them or if you have encountered information elsewhere in the test that indicates with certainty that your first choice is incorrect.

Multiple-Choice Tests

Multiple-choice questions usually include a phrase or stem followed by three to five options:

Test Strategies:
- Read the directions carefully.
- Know if each question has one or more correct options.
- Know if you are penalized for guessing.
- Answer easy questions first.

Answering options
Improve your odds, think critically:

Cover the options, read the stem, and try to answer—Select the option that most closely matches your answer.

Read the stem with each option—Treat each option as a true/false question, and choose the "most true."

Strategies to answer difficult questions:
- **Eliminate options you know to be incorrect.**
- **Question options that grammatically don't fit with the stem.**
- **Question options that are totally unfamiliar to you.**
- **Question options that contain negative or absolute words**—Try substituting a qualified term for the absolute one, like *frequently* for *always* or *typical* for *every*, to see if you can eliminate it.
- **"All of the above"**—If you know two of three options seem correct, "all of the above" is a strong possibility.
- **Number answers**—Toss out the high and low and consider the middle range numbers.
- **"Look alike options"**—Probably one is correct; choose the best but eliminate choices that mean basically the same thing, and thus cancel each other out.
- **Echo options**—If two options are opposite each other, chances are one of them is correct.
- **Favor options that contain qualifiers**—The result is longer, more inclusive items that better fill the role of the answer.
- **If two alternatives seem correct**—Compare them for differences, then refer to the stem to find your best answer.

Guessing:
- **Always guess when there is no penalty** for guessing or you can eliminate options.
- **Don't guess if you are penalized** for guessing and if you have no basis for your choice.
- **Don't change your answers** unless you are sure of the correction.
- **Use hints from questions you know** to answer questions you do not.

True/False Tests

Every part of a true sentence must be true—If any one part of the sentence is false, the whole sentence is false despite many other true statements.

Pay close attention to negatives, qualifiers, absolutes and long strings of statements.

Negatives can be confusing.
If the question contains negatives, as "no, not, cannot," drop the negative and read what remains.
Decide whether that sentence is true or false.
If it is true, its opposite, or negative, is usually false.

Qualifiers are words that restrict or open up general statements.
Words like "sometimes, often, frequently, ordinarily, generally" open up the possibilities of making accurate statements. They make more modest claims, are more likely to reflect reality, and usually indicate "true" answers.

Absolute words restrict possibilities.
"No, never, none, always, every, entirely, only" imply the statement must be true 100% of the time and usually indicate "false" answers.

Long sentences often include groups of words set off by punctuation.
Pay attention to the "truth" of each of these phrases. If one is false, it usually indicates a "false" answer.

Guessing:

Often true/false tests contain more true answers than false answers. You have more than 50% chance of being right with "true." However, this is not always the case.

Essay Exams

Organization and neatness have merit.

Before writing out the exam:

Set up a time schedule to answer each question and to review/edit all questions

- If six questions are to be answered in sixty minutes, allow yourself only seven minutes for each.
- If questions are "weighted," prioritize that into your time allocation for each question.
- When the time is up for one question, stop writing, leave space, and begin the next question. The incomplete answers can be completed during the review time.
- Six incomplete answers will usually receive more credit than three complete ones.

Read through the questions once and note if you have any choice in answering questions

- Pay attention to how the question is phrased, or to the "directives," or words such as "compare," "contrast," "criticize," etc.
- Answers will come to mind immediately for some questions.
  Write down their key words, listings, etc., as they are fresh in your mind. Otherwise these ideas may be blocked (or be unavailable) when the times come to write the later questions. This will reduce "clutching" or panic (anxiety, actually fear which disrupts thoughts).

Before attempting to answer a question, put it in your own words

- Now compare your version with the original.
  Do they mean the same thing? If they don't, you've misread the question. You'll be surprised how often they don't agree.

Think before you write:
Make a brief outline for each question
Number the items in the order you will discuss them

- **Get right to the point.**
  State your main point in the first sentence.
  Use your first paragraph to provide an overview of your essay.
  Use the rest of your essay to discuss these points in more detail.
  Back up your points with specific information, examples or quotations from your readings.
  - Teachers are influenced by compactness, completeness and clarity of an organized answer.
  - Writing in the hope that the right answer will somehow turn up is time-consuming and usually futile.
  - To know a little and to present that little well is, by and large, superior to knowing much and presenting it poorly.

Writing and answering:
Begin with a strong first sentence that states the main idea of your essay.
Continue this first paragraph by presenting key points.

Develop your argument.
- **Begin each paragraph** with a key point from the introduction.
- **Develop each point** in a complete paragraph.
- **Use transitions,** or enumerate, to connect your points.

- **Hold to your time** allocation and organization.
- **Avoid very definite statements** when possible; a qualified statement connotes a philosophic attitude, the mark of an educated person.
- **Qualify the answer when in doubt.** It is better to say "toward the end of the 19th century" than to say "in 1894" when you can't remember whether it's 1884 or 1894. In many cases, the approximate time is all that is wanted; unfortunately 1894, though approximate, may be incorrect, and will usually be marked accordingly.

Summarize in your last paragraph
Restate your central idea and indicate why it is important.

Review:
   Complete questions left incomplete, but allow time to review all questions.
   Review, edit, correct misspellings, incomplete words and sentences, miswritten dates and numbers.

Not enough time?
   Outline your answers.

ASSESSMENT CENTERS

Garner (1998, p. 77) reports: "Assessment Center Testing has been around for [more than] 70 years. Both the Allies and the Axis used it during World War II to train their spies. The technique involved putting the candidates in a situation where they must role-play the position they are seeking." The International Association of Chiefs of Police (IACP) website (http://www.theiacp.org) states:

> The assessment center process is a powerful technique. . . . Observing candidates' behavior in simulations of on-the-job challenges offers in-depth information concerning candidate strengths and weaknesses. In an assessment center, each candidate participates in a series of exercises that simulate actual situations from the target job. The performance of candidates is evaluated by expert assessors, providing information unattainable from written tests, interviews or any other source. . . . Because of their accurate simulation of the job and its duties, assessment centers have proven highly defensible as a selection strategy. Our assessment centers are comprehensive, and a variety of assessment methods are available to meet every selection need from entry level to top executive.

Assessment centers are processes that identify a candidate's strengths and weaknesses to evaluate how well that candidate is likely to perform on the job. Situational tests are a common part of such assessment centers.

According to Hurley (2001, p. 176): "Currently, 35% of law enforcement agencies in the United States use some type of assessment center in their hiring or promotional process. This number is certain to increase in the future as agencies attempt to find a standardized format for the hiring and promotional process." Regarding their use in promotion decisions, Hurley (p. 175) notes: "Assessment centers offer police managers a 'snapshot' of any candidate's performance at a higher rank." He continues:

> Candidates for promotion are assessed by an independent organization that is detached from the police agency and local politics. This is key: it removes personality conflicts, friendship and influences from the promotional process, a frequent complaint of those who are passed over for promotions.

PSYCHOLOGICAL TESTING

Psychological testing is a cause of anxiety for applicants because so much of it is out of their control. What should I say? How should I answer? What are they looking for? Psychological testing is an immense and complex subject about which hundreds of texts have been written. So what do you need to know? First, such tests should not and probably could not be prepared for through such traditional means as memorization. It is better to understand what these tests are meant to do, how they are administered and what they can show.

Purposes of Psychological Testing

Although psychological testing is a relatively new practice, no doubt you have taken some form of psychological test, probably at some point in your school career. According to Ho (2001, p. 319): "Psychological testing has become a crucial element in the police officer recruiting process since the President's Commission on Law Enforcement and the Administration of Justice (1967) aggressively promoted the necessity of psychologically screening police applicants' emotional stability." Holzman and Kirschner (2003, p. 85) assert: "In the area of law enforcement psychological evaluations have proven invaluable as one of the necessary pre-employment activities for prospective officers. Due to the nature of law enforcement work, psychological evaluations serve a unique role by being able to identify potential officers who may not adjust successfully."

As Rostow and Davis (2002, p. 101) explain: "All police executives are aware that they are responsible for the misbehavior of officers, and may be brought to court under *42 USC 1983*. . . . In general, the failure to properly select an officer is a form of negligent hiring." Bercaw (2002, p. 134) adds:

> Departments want to make sure the applicant is not emotionally unbalanced—paranoid schizophrenics and psychopaths need not apply. Beyond that, the department needs to know something about the applicant's motivations for wanting to become an officer, what his personal strengths and weaknesses are, and what the likelihood the applicant will successfully complete the academy's training program or remain in law enforcement is.
>
> Additionally, how does the applicant manage stress, frustration, and anger? Is the applicant a team player? Does the applicant exhibit good judgment and have integrity? Would this individual actually be in harm's way as a weapons carrying officer? Can this person assert authority in such a manner that doesn't escalate situations, which are already potentially volatile? Does the applicant have a support system?

Ho (p. 334) states: "All else being equal, . . . applicants were almost 8.4 times more likely to be recruited by the police department if they had a positive recommendation by psychologists relative to those applicants who were not recommended by psychologists."

Most people would agree that law enforcement officers should be mentally and emotionally stable. But defining and assessing what this consists of is a complex, challenging task.

Most psychological tests measure differences between individuals or between the reactions of the same individual on different occasions. Preparing for such tests is very different from preparing for more traditional "knowledge-based" tests, but you *can* prepare for them.

Sgt. Dennis Conroy, St. Paul (Minnesota) Police Department, also a clinical psychologist, gives the following advice concerning psychological tests administered to police/security candidates:

> To prepare for a psychological evaluation, applicants must begin to get psychologically "fit" several months before the examination. Preparation for a psychological evaluation *cannot* be rushed. Applicants must begin preparation early enough so they can make changes to assure that they are as psychologically healthy as possible. This includes looking at relationships, mature behavior and ways to deal with tension.

Frequently applicants take psychological evaluations just after finishing school. Their lives have been hectic. They have not taken time to relax for months. They are wound tighter than a $2.00 watch. This stress affects their entire being. It determines how they see the world. It is crucial for applicants to take time to relax before a psychological examination. This requires more than a 15-minute process the day before the evaluation. Some practical suggestions after you have taken time for yourself are as follows:

- Don't fight with your wife or husband, boyfriend or girlfriend or parents the night before the evaluation.
- Get plenty of sleep the night before. Make sure you are at your best.
- Get up early the morning of the evaluation so you have time for yourself. Take a walk and relax.
- Leave early for the evaluation. Get there with about 15 minutes to spare. Take time to relax when you get there. Read the paper or something.
- During the exam, *be honest.* You have honestly worked toward entering this profession for a long time. Don't change now. Copy from the person next to you only if you are *absolutely sure* you want his or her personality and are willing to bet your career on it.

Testing Methods

Methods vary greatly from test to test. Personality tests are of two main types: objective and projective. Objective personality tests, such as the California Personality Inventory (CPI) and Inwald Personality Inventory (IPI), ask objective true/false or multiple-choice questions. These questions are then grouped into scales to measure different aspects of personality. Projective tests involve ambiguous stimuli that the subject must interpret by "projecting" into the interpretation aspects of his or her own personality. Common projective tests are the Rorschach Inkblot Test and the Thematic Apperception Test (TAT).

Specific Psychological Tests

In attempting to anticipate how an applicant might perform on the job, evaluators look at both the past (grades, job references, traffic and police records, etc.) and the present. Psychological tests are tools employers use to learn about the applicant's present state of mind, what is important to that person and how that person is likely to respond to certain stimuli. An applicant's answers form patterns that are evaluated by psychologists, who compare the patterns with past studies to determine a psychological profile of the applicant. Tests frequently given include:

- ➤ Minnesota Multiphasic Personality Inventory-2 (MMPI-2)
- ➤ Myers-Briggs Type Indicator™ (MBTI)
- ➤ Inwald Personality Inventory (IWI)
- ➤ Behavioral Personal Assessment Device (B-PAD)
- ➤ California Psychological Inventory (CPI)
- ➤ Watson-Glaser Critical Thinking Appraisal (WGCTA)

- ➤ Strong Interest Inventory (SII)
- ➤ Thematic Apperception Test (TAT)
- ➤ Rorschach Inkblot Test
- ➤ Wonderlic Basic Skills Test (WBST)
- ➤ Personality Assessment Inventory
- ➤ 16PF

The *Minnesota Multiphasic Personality Inventory-2* (MMPI-2) is used primarily for emotional stability screening and frequently for entry-level psychological screening. This self-report questionnaire is *the* most widely used paper-and-pencil personality test being used (in all fields). Respondents are asked to indicate "true," "false," or "cannot say" to 567 statements covering a variety of psychological characteristics such as health, social, political, sexual and religious values; attitudes about family, education and occupation; emotional moods; and typical neurotic or psychotic displays such as obsessive-compulsive behavior, phobias, hallucinations and delusions.

Conroy asserts the MMPI is virtually impossible to study for. Its validity scales have cross-indexed questions and, in most cases, applicants who try to "fool" the test "fool" themselves out of a job instead. The MMPI has numerous sufficiently similar items so that it is difficult to lie consistently. The best advice here, again, is to tell the truth. One candidate tried to beat the MMPI and was denied a federal job. When the same candidate took the test again a year later and told the truth, he got the job.

The *Myers-Briggs Type Indicator*™ (MBTI) is a widely used measure of people's disposition and preferences. Millions of people in a wide variety of occupations have taken the Myers-Briggs. The test describes 16 easily understood personality types based on individuals' stated preferences on four indexes:

- ➤ Extroversion-Introversion
- ➤ Sensing-Intuition
- ➤ Thinking-Feeling
- ➤ Judgment-Perception

The *Inwald Personality Inventory* (IPI) is a 310-question test in which an applicant has to respond to a statement as either "true" or "false," based on experience, attitude or feeling toward the content of the statement. Designed specifically for police departments, the IPI's purpose is to screen out psychologically unsuitable law enforcement candidates. As Ho (p. 325) notes: "The IPI is designed to measure 26 behavioral characteristics, such as job difficulties or hyperactivity, which are presumably relevant to police-related functioning. . . . [Researchers] have proclaimed that the practical values of the IPI psychological measurement are critical to predict applicants' job performances as police officers in the future."

The *Behavioral Personal Assessment Device* (B-PAD) is one of the most progressive testing instruments in police recruiting and is used to measure problem-solving ability, judgment under pressure, decisiveness, diplomacy and interpersonal skills. Presented in video format, the test has applicants view numerous video screens and respond as if he or she was the officer at the scene. B-PAD was designed to assess an applicant's ability to effectively evaluate a variety of situations typically encountered by police officers. Other B-PAD video formats are available to test applicants for fire, EMS, corrections and communications dispatcher positions.

The *California Psychological Inventory* (CPI) is a 434-item objective inventory including 20 scales that measure a broad array of individual difference variables and personality characteristics, including social expertise and interpersonal style; maturity, normative orientation and values; achievement orientation; and personal interest styles. Thirteen Special Purpose Scales are derived to report on Creative Temperament, Managerial Potential and Tough-Mindedness.

The *Watson-Glaser Critical Thinking Appraisal* (WGCTA) is an assessment tool designed to measure an individual's critical-thinking skills and has five subtests: (1) Inference, (2) Recognition of Assumptions, (3) Deduction, (4) Interpretation and (5) Evaluation of Arguments. The test has 80 items, including problems, statements, arguments and interpretations of data like those encountered daily at work and in the classroom, and is to be completed within 60 minutes. The short form is comprised of 40 items to be completed in 45 minutes.

The *Strong Interest Inventory* (SII) is based on the idea that individuals are more satisfied and productive when they work in jobs or at tasks that they find interesting and when they work with people whose interests are similar to their own. The SII contains 317 items that measure individual interests in a wide range of occupations, occupational activities, hobbies, leisure activities and types of people. It compares a person's interests with the interests of people happily employed in a wide variety of occupations. It measures *interests,* not aptitude or intelligence.

The *Thematic Apperception Test* (TAT) is a projective instrument similar in context to the Rorschach Test but with no quantitative scoring technique. The test includes 31 picture cards with specific subsets for men and women. The purpose of the TAT is to provide insight into an applicant's self-image, perception of interpersonal relationships, relative strengths and various needs by inducing thoughts, attitudes and feelings about a subject depicted on the picture cards. The picture cards are used to stimulate stories or descriptions about relationships or social situations and can help identify dominant drives, emotions, sentiments, conflicts and complexes.

The *Rorschach Inkblot Test* consists of 10 inkblot patterns of various shades and colors. The applicant is shown a pattern and asked what it might be. This test helps evaluate basic personality structure and detect possible psychopathology. Because reading is not required for administration, this test can overcome language barriers.

The *Wonderlic Basic Skills Test* (WBST) is a 95-item paper-and-pencil test that can be taken individually or in groups. This test predicts success in learning situations and is a very accurate estimate of intelligence that serves as a quick assessment of cognitive skills or as a screening device to determine the need for more detailed evaluations. It can be used to benchmark prospective employees' basic skills as defined by the U.S. Department of Labor in the *Dictionary of Occupational Titles.*

The *Personality Assessment Inventory* (PAI) is a 344-item instrument that takes 50–60 minutes to administer. Each item is rated on a 4-point scale ranging from false, somewhat true, to very true. The PAI consists of 22 nonoverlapping full scales covering the constructs most relevant to a broad-based assessment of mental disorders: 4 validity scales, 11 clinical scales, 5 treatment scales and 2 interpersonal scales. To facilitate interpretation and cover the full range of complex clinical constructs, 10 full scales contain conceptually derived subscales.

The *16 Personality Factors* (16PF) questionnaire is used by organizations and human resource professionals to assesses the 16 personality factors of warmth, reasoning, emotional stability, dominance, liveliness, rule-consciousness, social boldness, sensitivity, vigilance, abstractedness, privateness, apprehension, openness to change, self-reliance, perfectionism and tension. Five additional global factors are also measured: extraversion, anxiety, tough-mindedness, independence and self-control.

Integrity Tests

One type of psychological test commonly used by employers is the paper-and-pencil honesty questionnaire. The first test of this type was developed in 1951 by John E. Reid and was called the Reid Report. Since then, various other ways have been devised to test applicants' integrity, which is defined as "steadfast adherence to a strict moral or ethical code; the state of being unimpaired" (*American Heritage Dictionary,* 2000). Barrett (2001, p. 3), commenting on preemployment integrity testing, notes:

> Two other terms have come into usage more recently, "employee reliability" . . . and "counter-productive behaviour." . . . These two terms reflect the broadening of the meaning of honesty and integrity from the relatively narrow conceptualization of theft, lying, and cheating that first defined the overt integrity tests of the early 1980s, through to a range of behaviours, attitudes, and dispositions that were considered "not conducive to efficient and effective work practices" or counter-productive to organizational "health."

Barrett (p. 6) asserts: "The most obvious way to assess the integrity and honesty of an individual is to interview them and ask questions that seem relevant to the evaluation of the job applicant's character and integrity." He adds:

> If considering using an interview to assess an applicant's honesty and counter-productive attitudes, it is prudent to use a formal structured technique such as the Reid Integrity Interview from Reid Associates Inc. This is a highly structured interview procedure for job applicants. The purpose of the interview is to develop factual information about the applicant's past behavioural patterns and outlook. The following areas are assessed during the interview: employment history, theft and related activities, work-related alcohol use, violations of company policy, use of illicit drugs, and past criminal behaviour. In a recent study reported by Reid Associates, although not yet published, the information developed from Integrity Interviews conducted on police candidates was compared to the information acquired from more traditional background "checking." According to Reid Associates, the congruence between the information acquired from the Integrity Interview and that from traditional checks was 100%, with over one third of the interviews exceeding the information content of the background checks.

Integrity tests are psychological tests commonly used by employers to determine trustworthiness. The test asks questions about the candidate's ethics, criminal record, recent drug use and work history.

POLYGRAPH TESTING

In 1892 Dr. James MacKensie invented the "Ink Polygraph," which recorded heartbeat, venous pulse and arterial pulse. A clock spring mechanism drove a paper ribbon with time markers every fifth of a second. Three decades later the Larson Polygraph, credited as the original "lie detector," was built for Berkeley Police Chief August Vollmer. Bulky and complicated, the device took half an hour to set up.

Modern polygraphy involves devices that are much more compact. Conventional instruments, sometimes referred to as analog instruments, are about the size of a briefcase and record data on streaming graph paper using mechanical pens or wet ink. Computerized polygraph systems (CPS) use specialized software run on either a laptop or desktop computer and display data on the monitor, which can then be printed to hardcopy and/or saved to a disk.

Whichever type of instrument is used, the polygraph will collect physiological data from at least three systems in the human body and measure changes in:

➤ Relative blood pressure and pulse rate (cardiovascular activity)

➤ Galvanic skin resistance (GSR), or perspiration (sweat gland activity)

➤ Stomach and chest breathing patterns (respiratory activity)

Use of the polygraph in preemployment is so controversial that it has become strictly regulated through the Employee Polygraph Protection Act (EPPA), signed into law by President Reagan in 1988. The American Polygraph Association (APA) notes that the EPPA "prohibits most private employers from using polygraph testing to screen applicants for employment." However:

> It does not affect public employers such as police agencies or other governmental institutions. In the testimony regarding EPPA it became clear that there were no current and reliable data on a variety of important issues about police applicant screening, although polygraph testing had reportedly been used for

that purpose since at least the early 1950's. In recognition of this gap, the APA Research Center at Michigan State University embarked on a survey of police executives in the U.S. to determine the extent of, and conditions in which, polygraph testing is being used for pre-employment screening. The survey population included 699 of the largest police agencies in the United States, excluding federal agencies, and produced usable returns from 626 agencies, a response rate of 90%. The major results of the survey showed the following:

> Among the respondents, 62% had an active polygraph screening program, 31% did not and 7% had discontinued polygraph screening, usually because of prohibitive legislation. These results make it clear that a great majority of our largest police agencies do have a polygraph screening program in effect. These agencies employ, on average, 447 officers and service a population averaging 522,000 citizens. They primarily use the polygraph to screen applicants for sworn positions, although 54% also screen persons interested in non-sworn positions. Approximately 25% of the persons tested are disqualified from police employment based on the information developed during polygraph testing which, by the way, is used both to verify information provided in an application form and to develop information that cannot be gotten by other means. Only a very small proportion (2%) of agencies use polygraph testing as a substitute for a background investigation. A rank ordered listing of topics covered during polygraph testing revealed that investigation of illegal drug usage, employment related dishonesty, and involvement in felonies are the most important. . . .

> Over 90% of these agencies expressed either moderate or high confidence in their polygraph screening program, and 80% of them reported that in their experience the accuracy of the testing ranged between 86%–100%. The only procedure that was considered to be as useful as polygraph screening was a background investigation.

Thus, although using the polygraph during preemployment is prohibited in most fields and some states have extended this prohibition to police agencies, it is not prohibited in most law enforcement agencies or for many private security jobs. Therefore, make no objections if you are asked to take such an exam. The employer probably has the right to request this. Just be yourself. Relax, and tell the truth.

> Polygraph tests are used to determine a candidate's honesty and, according to most field practitioners, are generally very accurate. Use of the polygraph during preemployment screening is *not* prohibited in government jobs, including law enforcement.

The primary use of the polygraph is to substantiate the information gathered during the background investigation.

BACKGROUND CHECKS

Another type of test candidates must pass is the background check, also referred to as preemployment screening. The background check typically includes contacting past employers and references listed on the candidate's application form. It may also include a check on credit history, driving record, academic background, criminal record and the possession of any and all required professional licenses. An area generally scrutinized closely is the applicant's work history, for as Nelson (2000, p. 87) states: "The greatest predictor of future behavior is past behavior. If the applicant has an established pattern of poor work history, it is unlikely to improve."

Considering the impact of globalization and the increasing diversity among our nation's population and workforce, verifying background information has become more challenging. Background checks on applicants who have lived, worked or gone to school in another country are likely to involve a number of hurdles. Lashier (2003, p. 108) notes:

> [A] critical security concern is privacy laws that protect criminal histories in some countries. Japan, for instance, will not provide any criminal history information to a third party. . . .

> The process of verifying education deserves special attention. Some countries, such as Australia, consider education records off limits to investigators, even if a person is to be employed in the United States, where college transcripts are regularly used in the hiring process.

Verifying military service claims is another challenge for hiring authorities, yet as Dallas (2003, p. 112) asserts: "Military service is an important part of a person's background, well worth a prospective employer's attention." The plethora of official forms, filled with military jargon, acronyms and codes, can complicate the investigation, but Dallas (p. 108) stresses:

> The federal government prohibits civilian employers from interpreting and using these [military] codes in making hiring decisions; they are considered to be for informational purposes only. It is legal, however, to ask to see an applicant's DD-214 [discharge papers], and the information is part of the public record.

Candidates already employed in law enforcement but looking for a job with a different agency (known as lateral hires) also face background checks. According to Slowik (2003, p. 101):

> Laterals differ from other types of police applicants in that their skills, knowledge, experience and abilities as they directly relate to the police job being considered need to be checked out and verified. . . .

> In addition, there clearly are differences based upon the type of law enforcement agency the candidate comes from: many federal law enforcement agencies do not deal with either the kinds of people or crimes that are required to be mastered at any city police department. Obviously Railroad Police is not the equivalent of Campus Police is not the same as Military Police.

ON BEING DISHONEST

Candidates for all jobs in criminal justice and security should anticipate a rigorous background check conducted by investigators trained in this specialty area. As odd as it may seem to even include, it is worth repeating: *Do not lie.* For reasons that should be obvious to anyone considering a career in criminal justice, honesty and integrity are required attributes. And don't try to hide anything. Today's background investigators will find it. They know who to ask, what to ask and how to look for any indications of problem behavior that might later cause someone to allege the hiring agency "should have known" the potential risks posed by an employee. Furthermore, in addition to whatever it was you were hiding, you will now be viewed as dishonest, a trait no agency wishes to deal with. Also bear in mind that most background investigators will want to know where else you have applied. If you have been dishonest during the application process in the past, it will follow you.

While you may be able to change your level of physical fitness, you cannot change your background. In addition to certain actions that will statutorily prohibit people from entering professions, some past acts will at least be of concern to potential employers. You will have the opportunity to address these issues, and maybe even turn some indiscretions around to your advantage (proving how you addressed a problem and have learned and improved as a result), but be assured lying in any manner about your background will be a legitimate reason for disqualification.

CONCLUSION

The testing process is another opportunity to prove to a prospective employer that *you* are the one to hire. Present yourself as you are. If you do not feel you would test well now, improve yourself by developing a rigorous plan to increase your fitness level, your knowledge and your writing skills. Take some practice tests. Be *realistic* about who you are and what you can be. Be honest with yourself. Because work greatly influences *all* aspects of your life, you do not want to pursue any career that will be a dead end. View the testing phase of the application process as a positive experience for both the employer and you in determining if there is a match. If not, it is best for everyone to learn this while there is time for you to find a different niche in the world of work.

AN INSIDER'S VIEW

PREPARING TO DO YOUR BEST

Dennis L. Conroy, PhD

Former Director of the Employee Assistance Program
St. Paul (Minnesota) Police Department

In preparing for tests to become a police or security officer, it is crucial that you properly prepare for the various tests. There are likely to be tests in the areas of knowledge, physical fitness, psychological preparedness and perhaps even a polygraph.

You *can* study for knowledge tests. You must be able to not only understand the police/security function, but to articulate that function, specify ways in which that function can be fulfilled and how you will fit into the system to fulfill the function. In other words, expect more than just a multiple-choice or true/false test of knowledge. You must be able to state what police/security officers do (protect and serve), how that can best be accomplished (specific methods of protecting and serving) and what role you see for yourself in that system (how you see yourself functioning as a police or security officer).

Tests of physical fitness require significant preparation. There will often be tests of stamina (cardiovascular fitness), strength (muscle tone) and agility (mobility). Almost any fitness center has programs to help prepare for such tests. It is best to find the specifics of the department you are applying for and train to meet those standards.

Studying for a psychological test is much like studying for a urine test. There *is* important preparation, but it cannot be done the night before the exam, or even a week before.

You must begin to prepare for the psychological exam *at least* several months before the actual test itself. You must present yourself as psychologically fit to do police or security work, and such preparation takes time. It should be more a reaffirmation process than change. You should not be afraid of psychological examinations. Just be honest. If the assessment indicates that you may not be suitable for police work or security work, it is just as often indicating that police or security work will not be good for you.

Dr. Dennis Conroy, *licensed psychologist, has recently retired after 30+ years of service with the St. Paul (Minnesota) Police Department. During his career, he had such diverse assignments as patrol officer, juvenile officer, patrol supervisor, vice/narcotics investigator, director of the Professional Development Institute, director of the Field Training Program and* *director of the Employee Assistance Program. His clinical experience spans more than 20 years and includes working with children, adolescents and adults. Dr. Conroy has also taught upper-level college courses blending the fields of psychology and law enforcement, including Adolescent Psychology, Human Behavior in Law Enforcement, Police Stress, Peer Counseling in Law Enforcement and The Psychology of Victims.*

INSIDER'S VIEW ONLINE

An additional *Insider's View* for this chapter is "Learning Should Never Stop" by Russell M. Anderson, found on the Wadsworth website: http://www.wadsworth.com/criminaljustice_d/.

 MIND STRETCHES

1.   Does your field require proof of certain levels of knowledge? How will you prepare for this?

2.   What do you anticipate a battery of psychological tests will say about you? Are there factors in your life that need to be attended to before you pursue your chosen career?

3.   How do you feel about taking a polygraph examination? Are there skeletons in your closet that you need to honestly confront?

4.   As part of your job-search strategy, have you taken into account what you can and cannot prepare yourself for?

5.   What areas of the hiring process do you have such limited control over that you can't prepare for them? Is there any area of the hiring process that you have absolutely *no* control over, or is there always something you can do to give yourself an edge over the competition?

6.   Is what you have done in the past a realistic indicator of how you will perform in the future?

7.   Have you ever taken a psychological test? If so, how did you feel: positive, neutral or negative? If negative, what can you do to reduce these feelings?

8.   If you suffer from test anxiety, what can you do to reduce it?

9.   How well do you write? How can you know for sure?

REFERENCES

American Heritage Dictionary of the English Language, 4th ed. Houghton Mifflin Company, 2000. Online: http://www. bartleby.com

American Polygraph Association (APA) website: http://www.polygraph.org

Barrett, Paul. *Pre-Employment Integrity Testing: Current Methods, Problems, and Solutions.* Paper presented at British Computer Society: Information Security Specialist Group, March 29–30, 2001, Milton Hill, Oxford. Online: http://www.pbarrett.net/integrity_doc.pdf

Bercaw, George H. "Psychological Assessment." *Law and Order,* July 2002, pp. 132–136.

Conroy, Dennis L. Former Director of the Employee Assistance Program, St. Paul (Minnesota) Police Department. Information provided specifically for this text, July 2004.

Dallas, James M. "Know the Code for Service." *Security Management,* December 2003, pp. 107–112.

Garner, Kenneth. "Assessment Center Testing." *Law and Order,* November 1998, pp. 77–82.

Ho, Taiping. "The Interrelationships of Psychological Testing, Psychologists' Recommendations, and Police Departments' Recruitment Decisions." *Police Quarterly,* September 2001, pp. 318–342.

Holzman, Arnold and Kirschner, Mark. "Pre-Employment Psychological Evaluations." *Law and Order,* September 2003, pp. 85–87.

Hurley, James J. "Assessment Centers: Judging Promotability without Conflict." *Law and Order,* October 2001, pp. 175–176.

International Association of Chiefs of Police. Online: http://www.theiacp.org

Landsberger, Joseph. Author and developer of *Study Guides and Strategies* website. St. Paul, MN, USA, accessed July 30, 2004. Online: http://www.studygs.net/#tests

Lashier, Ron. "Global Challenges of Background Checks." *Security Management,* March 2003, pp. 105–108.

Nelson, Kurt R. "A Tale of Two Cities: A Comparison of Background Investigations." *Law and Order,* May 2000, pp. 85–88.

Rostow, Cary and Davis, Robert. "Psychological Screening." *Law and Order,* May 2002, pp. 101–106.

Slowik, Stanley. "Background Checks on Lateral Hires." *Law and Order,* July 2003, pp. 98–102.

RECOMMENDED TEST PREPARATION BOOKS

ARCO Law Enforcement Exams, 4th ed.
by Eve P. Steinberg
ARCO, © 2000

ARCO 24 Hours to the Law Enforcement Exams
by John Gosney
Peterson's, © 2001

Guide to the Police Exams
by John E. Douglas
Kaplan, © 2000

How to Prepare for the Police Officer Examination, 6th ed.
by Donald J. Schroeder and Frank A. Lombardo
Barron's, © 2001

Police Exam Preparation Book, 2nd ed.
by Norman Hall
Adams Media Corporation, © 2003

Police Officer, 16th ed.
by Fred M. Rafilson
ARCO, © 2003

Police Officer Exam, 2nd ed.
by Michael Spano
LearningExpress, © 2003

Police Officer Examination Preparation Guide
by Larry F. Jetmore
Cliff's Notes, © 1994

CHAPTER 9

ATTRIBUTES OF SUCCESSFUL CANDIDATES

It's not your aptitude, it's your attitude that determines your altitude.

—*Anonymous*

Do You Know:

➤ If a lack of law-related experiences seriously hurts your chances of obtaining employment in the fields of criminal justice or private security?
➤ What your past is a good predictor of?
➤ What past employment says about you?
➤ What the benefits of volunteering are?
➤ Where you might look to gain some work-related experience in criminal justice or security?
➤ If military experience is beneficial or detrimental to one seeking a job as a police, corrections or security officer?
➤ What advanced education says about an applicant?
➤ How important communication skills are?
➤ What the benefits of internships are?
➤ How you should handle past mistakes when applying for a new job?
➤ What role ethics plays in law enforcement and security?

INTRODUCTION

 Imagine yourself as an employer responsible for selecting the best candidate from a number of applicants. What criteria would you use to make this decision, which is sure to have important consequences? What positive attributes or characteristics would you, as an employer, look for? List these in your journal.

 What negative attributes would influence you *not* to hire a candidate? Again, write them down.

Employers are not just selecting employees; they are selecting people who will often directly influence other people's lives and who will also be representing their department or agency.

Police officers routinely deal with the most private business of the public for whom they work. Officers bandage wounds, intervene in disputes, guard property, search homes and offices and educate children. Officers may bring victims back to life or have to watch them die. They uphold the law, which not only benefits the public, but also holds the guilty responsible by drawing them into the criminal justice system in a way that will alter those defendants' lives forever. Being a police officer is an *awesome* responsibility.

Correctional officers perform a vital function in guarding those sentenced to any of the variety of corrections facilities throughout our country. They deal with our nation's offenders daily and have the power to make positive changes in inmates' lives. Correctional officers are also tasked with protecting society from these offenders by making sure those they are guarding do not escape. Some correctional positions involve counseling inmates while others consist of an armed position in a watchtower.

Security officers also have great responsibility. Most security directors have complete access to every part of a company's assets—its secrets, its property, its cash—all are literally under the protection of the security manager and the security officers. Other professionals in criminal justice and public safety fields are equally entrusted with important issues. Whether social workers, psychologists or others in the helping professions, *all* employees in criminal justice are truly professionals.

What criteria are used when hiring criminal justice and security personnel? These criteria range from how you present yourself to who you really are.

HOW DO YOU APPEAR ON PAPER?

Impressions are important. Initial contacts, résumés and follow-ups are critical. Employers *will* look at both what you have done and how you have done it. If you are determined to get the job, take control of your future by establishing a solid background of knowledge and experience. Many opportunities are available to acquire those attributes employers seek in candidates.

PERSONAL ATTRIBUTES

What kind of background will help you get that entry-level job? Recognize that employers are often as interested in non–law-related experience and attributes as they are in law-related ones.

Most employers are more interested in the type of a person you are than in what you know about law enforcement, corrections or security work, especially for entry-level positions. A more general background helps anyone broaden the perspective of their world. Those doing the hiring want to know how you can relate your past experience to law enforcement, even if all you've done is flip burgers. Did you deal with customers? Did you have to solve problems? Did you do public relations? Did you have to communicate with people? These things will help the candidate get the job even if there has been no "police experience."

Many candidates have difficulty recognizing the positive traits implied by past jobs. For example, the student who has worked for the same grocery store for three years but is now managing it while the owner is away, making the bank deposits, handling stock and supply issues, opening and closing—these tasks demonstrate not only responsibility and the capacity to work independently without supervision but also the respect in which he or she is held by the employer. Similarly, some students are embarrassed by their experience as bartenders and are reluctant to mention this part of their work history to a prospective employer. However, such students are failing to recognize that these jobs require the ability to handle unruly customers and demonstrate the applicant's ability to handle aggression and respond well under pressure—some of the same traits required of law enforcement officers, correctional officers and security professionals.

A lack of law-related experience by no means disqualifies you as a candidate for work in criminal justice or security. In fact, most employers are more interested in the type of a person you are than in what you know about law enforcement, corrections or security work.

Perry et al. (2003, p. 31) contend: "The factors that can be responsible for an officer's ultimate success or failure at a department can be identified most helpfully at the pre-employment stage." Indeed, as Mahoney (2001, p. 194) observes:

> For recruitment to be successful, law enforcement agencies must parse out those critical characteristics that cannot be trained from those characteristics that can. Then they must focus employment-screening procedures on accurately and reliably measuring those "cannot train" features. Two attributes often linked to successful performance in rapidly changing high-risk situations [such as those found in police work] are fluid intelligence and the ability to stay task-focused under stress.

Law enforcement agencies also screen recruits for a variety of other characteristics linked to successful performance as an officer, including "general cognitive ability; the ability to reason in novel, unfamiliar situations; the ability to apply knowledge and skills acquired through formal training to current problems; the effects of distractibility on memory; the capacity to focus attention under stress; and the ability to read the emotions of others through voice tone and body language" (Mahoney, p. 194).

This final attribute, the ability to "read" a suspect, is what Pinizzotto et al. (2004, pp. 5–6) call *intuitive policing*:

> Since the first law enforcement officers accepted the responsibility of protecting their communities, accurately recognizing which individuals pose a threat to the safety and security of those jurisdictions has challenged all who belong to the profession. . . .
>
> Intuitive policing represents a decision-making process that officers use frequently . . . [whereby] officers observe actions and behaviors exhibited by criminals that send danger signals to them that they react to before becoming consciously aware of these warnings. Such "gut feelings" or "intuitions" have saved many lives, not only those of innocent citizens but officers as well.

Perry et al. (p. 31) state: "A number of research studies show that cognitive ability is the most powerful predictor of job success across a range of occupations. The ability to exercise sound judgment is particularly important in the field of law enforcement, as the problems faced by officers on the job are often challenging and ambiguous." They (p. 33) add: "Officers' success and their safety depend in large measure on their ability to assert themselves and to take action that is appropriate to the circumstances at hand." Furthermore (p. 37):

> Although many dimensions are important to consider in hiring law enforcement officers, it is most crucial, according to our research, that departments employ individuals who meet their standards in the areas of problem-solving, assertiveness, motivation level, and openness to feedback.

Other desirable officer applicant characteristics include maturity, openness, flexibility, cheerfulness, judgment, congeniality, the ability to handle social situations, the ability to deal with people at their worst and tolerance for other opinions.

These same characteristics are vital if you're considering a career in corrections or private security. These traits are not genetic; they're learned. The more general life experiences you have, the better your chance of acquiring these traits. Broad experience also helps you better understand human behavior, a valuable attribute.

Other important attributes are ego strength and anger control. Ego strength is essential and comes from having good self-esteem and a good self-valuing system. Anger control is especially important because of the nature of the work. An empathetic attitude toward those who come to your attention because they are violating the law or a company policy is highly desirable. True professionals do not take client behaviors personally. They keep emotion out of decisions that affect others' lives through *intellectualization*—that is, they think before they act.

In addition to having the preceding characteristics, successful candidates have also performed well in the past.

> A good predictor of how candidates will perform in the future is how they performed in the past.

Experiences that can reflect positively on a candidate include:

> ➢ Past general employment
> ➢ Volunteer community experience
> ➢ Work-related experience
> ➢ Military service

> ➢ Education
> ➢ Communication skills/experience
> ➢ Computer, typing and word processing skills
> ➢ Interning

Past General Employment

While some employers may be looking for specific experience, those hiring entry-level personnel are usually more interested in a person's general background. Past employment says a lot about a person. The simple fact that a person was successfully employed says that someone wanted to hire that person and that they were responsible enough to stay on the job. Keeping a job says that the person could operate on a schedule, complete assigned tasks, not take advantage of the basic trust placed in all employees and get along with others.

It might also be said that the more remote a person's past jobs were from the position being applied for, the more favorable the experience would be viewed. Many employers would rather hire entry-level personnel and train them "from scratch." Also, more general backgrounds provide a broader view of the world and opportunities to have developed varied experiences.

Don't worry if the only work experience you have is flipping burgers or stocking shelves. It says you chose to work. The more and varied experiences you have, the better you'll look—at least on paper. What previous jobs say about you is important enough that career counselors frequently advise students, particularly younger ones, that it will enhance their ability to be hired if they get a responsible job for a few years. Employers, especially those in such critical fields as criminal justice and security, would prefer not to be the first employer a person has.

> Past employment, regardless of the setting, says a lot about a person, such as the person was responsible enough to stay on the job, could operate on a schedule, complete assigned tasks, not take advantage of the basic trust placed in all employees and get along with others.

Volunteer Community Service

Volunteering speaks highly of the way we view our neighbors, reaching out to help when needed. Those who give of themselves make the statement, "I am willing to help." Because a fundamental role of criminal justice and security professionals is interacting with and helping people, any volunteer community service will reflect positively on you.

Many people looking for work, especially younger people, are frustrated that most employers want some experience. The dilemma: How do you get a job without experience? How do you get experience without a job? Volunteering in any way in your community is an exceptional opportunity to gain experience. Furthermore, the trend in modern professional law enforcement is to emphasize *community policing*. Many police agencies want to know you are able to work in the community in something other than an enforcement capacity and that you genuinely want to be a contributing community member. For example, an interviewer might ask prospective candidates, "What do you do for your community?"

> Volunteering is an exceptional opportunity to gain experience and reflects positively on you by telling a prospective employer you are willing to help your community.

Work-Related Experience

While experience not directly related to your career goals has many benefits associated with it, you may be eager to become involved in your chosen field. Opportunities for such experiences are abundant and provide a strong base from which to seek employment. Explorer posts, for example, provide opportunities to combine social and learning experiences. Similar to Boy Scouts and Girl Scouts, law enforcement explorer groups have a great deal of fun while learning about the profession. Generally sponsored by a community law enforcement agency, explorers learn such skills as shooting, first aid, defensive tactics and crime scene investigation. Good-hearted competition helps to hone these valuable skills.

Police reserve units also serve several valuable functions. Not only do such units provide backup to the paid officers in such situations as crowd control and crime scene searches, but it is yet another chance to gain experience in the field while serving the community. Participating in a reserve unit says you can work as part of a team and not abuse this association.

Volunteer and paid-on-call fire departments offer another opportunity to do more than "get your feet wet" (literally). Firefighting, recognized as an extraordinarily dangerous activity, demands the same attributes required of police, corrections and security officers: a cool head, the ability to work on a team and the ability to confront dangerous obstacles. Because police officers may answer fire calls, too, it helps to know how to respond.

Other agencies have opportunities that provide valuable experience. For example, some sheriffs' departments have special rescue squads, water patrol units and even mounted posses—all staffed by volunteers. Some departments have opportunities available for qualified individuals to provide patrol services to supplement their paid officers. In addition, some colleges have security departments staffed by students, another excellent opportunity to acquire experience in private "policing."

> Work-related experience may be gained by becoming involved in an explorer post, police reserve unit, volunteer fire department, special rescue squad, water patrol unit or mounted posse.

Note: Do not strive exclusively for work-related experience. If the only experiences you have include police reserves, police explorers, playing in the police band and volunteering with the police holiday food drive, you will be viewed as a candidate with a shallow experience from which to draw. Many employers will place greater emphasis on the *non*–police-related experiences candidates have made for themselves.

Military Service

Military service has many advantages for people considering work in security and criminal justice. First, military service provides an opportunity to enter an admirable field of work with absolutely no previous experience. It allows you to gain valuable experience while enhancing your reputation and developing maturity—not to mention drawing a paycheck. Military service is a great chance to spend some time serving your country, even if you aren't sure about what your final career goals will be. Rather than wasting the time after high school or college by drifting, you could demonstrate your ability to develop in a professional field by joining the service.

Employers recognize that law enforcement, corrections and security are paramilitary and that successful military service is a very good indication of potential success in such civilian service. If you know early enough that you seek involvement in security or criminal justice, getting into a military policing unit can give you valuable experience.

On the other hand, the trend is toward a more humanistic, less authoritarian style of policing in both the public and private sectors. Because the military trains its officers to follow military law rather than the U.S. Constitution, such training may be a detriment to civilian policing. According to one employer, those who had been in the military drew more citizen complaints than their nonveteran counterparts. Furthermore, military veterans tended to be less flexible and less problem-solving oriented than their nonmilitary comrades in police work. Veterans tended to look for "by-the-book" answers. Rigidity and by-the-book responses are out of sync with the current objectives of community policing and problem solving. Additionally, bear in mind that the military teaches interdependence and teamwork, and while both are important parts of policing, the majority of police work is done by the officer acting alone.

A significant benefit employers recognize from military experience is discipline because, right or wrong, some think today's young people lack discipline. Military training makes a strong statement to the hiring authority. Some employers assert that individuals having military experience combined with advanced education make excellent officers.

> Military experience can benefit those seeking employment in police, corrections or security work because it develops discipline and allows the individual to mature. However, military training may also be a detriment because civilian policing strives for a more humanistic, less authoritarian approach and reversing the military training may be difficult.

Education

Education is more important today than ever in many fields, including criminal justice and private security. If these fields are to be considered professions, which they are striving to do, then education plays an important role.

New focus has been placed on how well our schools are preparing young adults for life in the working world. To examine this issue, the U.S. Department of Labor formed, in 1990, a committee known as the Secretary's Commission on Achieving Necessary Skills, or SCANS, with the goal of encouraging a high-performance economy characterized by high-skill, high-wage employment. The Commission's first report, issued in 1991 and titled "What Work Requires of Schools," identified the need for schools to help students develop a foundation of basic academic skills, thinking skills and personal qualities necessary to achieve competency in the workplace, as shown in Figure 9–1. More than a decade later, these fundamental skills and competencies remain the focus of SCANS, as stated on their website. For more detailed definitions of these competencies and skills, or to learn more about school-to-work programs and education reform, visit the SCANS 2000 Workforce Skills website: http://wdr.doleta.gov/SCANS/whatwork/whatwork.pdf (p. iii; accessed January 12, 2005).

For the past three decades, every national commission on violence and crime in America has concluded that college education can improve police performance. Over 25 years ago the National Advisory

---

WORKPLACE KNOW-HOW

The know-how identified by SCANS is made up of five competencies and a three-part foundation of skills and personal qualities that are needed for solid job performance. These include:

COMPETENCIES—effective workers can productively use:

- ➤ **Resources**—allocating time, money, materials, space, and staff;
- ➤ **Interpersonal Skills**—working on teams, teaching others, serving customers, leading, negotiating, and working well with people from culturally diverse backgrounds;
- ➤ **Information**—acquiring and evaluating data, organizing and maintaining files, interpreting and communicating, and using computers to process information;
- ➤ **Systems**—understanding social, organizational, and technological systems, monitoring and correcting performance, and designing or improving systems;
- ➤ **Technology**—selecting equipment and tools, applying technology to specific tasks, and maintaining and troubleshooting technologies.

THE FOUNDATION—competence requires:

- ➤ **Basic Skills**—reading, writing, arithmetic and mathematics, speaking, and listening;
- ➤ **Thinking Skills**—thinking creatively, making decisions, solving problems, seeing things in the mind's eye, knowing how to learn, and reasoning;
- ➤ **Personal Qualities**—individual responsibility, self-esteem, sociability, self-management, and integrity.

FIGURE 9–1   SCANS Skills

SOURCE: The Secretary's Commission on Achieving Necessary Skills. *What Work Requires of Schools: A SCANS Report for America 2000.* Washington, DC: U.S. Department of Labor, June 1991, p. iii. Accessed online January 12, 2005: http://wdr.doleta.gov/SCANS/whatwork/whatwork.pdf

Committee on Criminal Justice Standards and Goals warned: "There are few professions today that do not require a college degree. Police, in their quest for greater professionalism, should take notice." In response to conflicting data regarding the value of higher education to officer performance, Polk and Armstrong (2001, p. 97) state:

> Although the literature review revealed that there are inconclusive findings in prior studies about whether or not increased education caused an increase in the ability of law enforcement officers to perform their duties, this study showed no ambiguity in finding agencies are responding as if there are benefits if employees are more educated. . . .
>
> The study demonstrated conclusively . . . that those persons who hold higher levels of education, regardless of what other traits or personality characteristics they may possess, are more likely to hold higher rank and progress more quickly through their career path.

Education says something about those who obtain it. It says the person can identify, pursue and accomplish important goals. It shows patience, drive and self-determination. It shows the ability to commit to both short- and long-range goals. It says those seeking education are interested in both themselves and the world in which they live. Education *does* make you view the world differently. Education expands horizons, helping you better understand the differences that make our diverse society not a threat, but a challenge.

These same arguments apply to other positions within criminal justice and security.

> Advanced education is valuable to anyone seeking employment in criminal justice or private security not only because of the actual knowledge gained but also because of what pursuing such education says about you to a prospective employer—that you can identify, pursue and accomplish important goals; that you have patience, drive and self-determination; that you possess the ability to commit to both short- and long-range goals and that you are interested in both yourself and the world in which you live.

In addition, many agencies now *require* some college. Hickman and Reaves (2003, p. iii) report: "In 2000, 15% of departments, employing 32% of all officers, required new recruits to have completed at least some college, up from 6% of departments, employing 10% of officers, in 1990." In some instances, completion of specific coursework can place an applicant at an advantage, as noted by Lambert et al. (2003), who studied law enforcement hiring practices and the value attached to job applicants' skills and knowledge. They ("Study Verifies Utility . . .," 2004, p. 39) found: "Overwhelmingly, law enforcement agencies reported that some forensic science background was deemed preferable. . . . Regarding specific skill areas of importance for new recruits, the areas of knowledge assigned the highest value were interviewing techniques, crime scene documentation, evidence collection, and fingerprint analysis."

No longer do legal barriers stand in the way of police departments requiring college education. In *Davis v. Dallas* (1986), a U.S. Court of Appeals upheld a requirement by the City of Dallas that entry-level police recruits have completed 45 college credits with a C average.

You should keep a personal training log or journal documenting any training or educational programs in which you participate. Such a journal may be useful in preparing your résumé or in answering any questions prospective employers may ask about your training and/or education.

Can You Be Overeducated?   In all honesty, the answer might be "yes," at least in some employers' eyes—particularly for employers who may have achieved their position in the more traditional way of coming "up through the ranks" and at a time when higher education was considered less important for officers' career development than it is today. They may not regard advanced education as a necessary or desirable attribute. Some might see it as an outright threat to them.

While it is not as much a problem as it might have been once, candidates with a master's degree, for example, will want to be prepared to answer any similar questions to "Why did you pursue your education at the graduate level?" Those holding law degrees, PhDs or other doctoral-level degrees will undoubtedly be asked about this, especially those applying for an entry-level position. You will have no difficulty pointing out the benefits the degree will have for the department if you are hired, but hiring authorities may have a legitimate concern whether you will be bored at the job you are applying for. Even if not asked directly, you will want to address this because they are probably, albeit silently, wondering about it.

Communication Skills

Communication skills are critical for public and private officers, for they communicate orally and in writing every day. Hennessy et al. (2001, p. 15) stress: "Communication is a critical part of policing. Research has shown that 93 percent of police work is one-on-one communication, and the ability to communicate with citizens from cultures different from one's own is critical to successful policing." Finnimore (2003, p. 23) adds: "In the business world, poor communication skills can cost companies revenue. In law enforcement, a lack of quality communication skills could prove deadly." How well you communicate will also, to a great extent, determine how far you advance.

Writing skills are especially important because once something is in writing, it is *permanent.* Moore (2004, p. 82) asserts: "Poor writing skills can damage a department's reputation. Worse, sloppy report writing can result in problems in the courtroom." Nelson (2002, p. 226) states: "Paperwork . . . is the drudgery of law enforcement. However, . . . what officers do not often recognize is that their reports are part of the arsenal with which they put criminals behind bars. A well-crafted report is as important as the investigation, for without the former the latter is meaningless." In addition:

➢ The police reports are often the first impression a judge or defense attorney has of an officer's competence, both generally and in regard to the specific elements of the offense charged.

➢ The decision to charge someone with a crime is based upon the police reports, usually alone.

➢ Complete and well-written police reports help to speed up the entire system. Delays in prosecution often occur because of incomplete reports.

➢ A well-written report alone can settle a case.

Moore (p. 82) recommends agencies emphasize literacy during the hiring process and continuously work to improve veteran officers' literacy skills. Unfortunately, most schools do not teach what the workplace requires. Any experiences you can have that enhance your ability to communicate, both orally and in writing, are extremely important.

> Communication skills—oral and written—are critically important for public and private officers and may determine how far you will advance in your career.

Computer, Keyboarding and Word Processing Skills

You may be thinking, "I'm not applying for a secretarial job. Why do I need to know how to keyboard?" But face it—we've become an increasingly technological society. With today's reliance on the computer to generate reports and manage casework, keyboarding and computer skills are essential for entering the fields of criminal justice and security. For example, it is estimated that probation and parole officers spend approximately 75 percent of their workday *typing* presentence investigation reports. Clearly, knowing your way around the keyboard is a must for this job.

Today's job applicants in many, if not most, fields are expected to have adequate computer skills. If you've been putting off learning these skills, you must stop procrastinating and get some training. The everyday duties of police officers have become inextricably dependent on computers. Many agencies (private and public) are going to computerized report writing and making an effort toward the "paperless office." Also, more and more police departments are giving their officers laptop computers or mobile data terminals (MDTs) in their squad cars, expecting them to write their reports, possibly at the scene, and send them wirelessly to headquarters. An example of such a system is the Advanced Law Enforcement Response Technology, or ALERT, an on-board computer that performs numerous vital functions, including controlling patrol car devices (lights, sirens, radar) and enabling officers to write and transmit reports.

A caution regarding the accuracy of spelling in reports and an overreliance on computer spell-check functions: Although spell-checkers are great, they do not guarantee error-free reports. Consider the following examples—all of which would get past a spell-check:

➢ He was arrested for a mister meaner.

➢ She was an admitted drug attic.

➢ The series of homicides is most likely the work of a cereal killer.

Computer skills are no longer something you can add to a résumé; they are something expected of a viable candidate. It's difficult to contemplate a job in criminal justice or security that doesn't involve the routine use of computers. If you aren't comfortable with or knowledgeable about computer basics, become so.

Interning

A great way to break into the real world of work while still learning is by interning. Internships were discussed in depth as the focus of Chapter 6 but are worth mentioning again, as many criminal justice programs across the nation are implementing internship programs and courses to help prepare their students for future careers. Ross and Elechi (2002, p. 297) note: "Traditionally, internships have provided a unique way for criminal justice students to gain work experience while earning academic credit." They (p. 297) studied student attitudes regarding internships and found tremendous support for such programs: "Moreover, (1) students felt their undergraduate curricula adequately reflected the practical realities of criminal justice operations, and (2) internships were regarded as invaluable in preparing students for criminal justice careers."

Interning is seldom a requirement for a job and typically serves less-experienced job seekers better than those already holding down a responsible position, even if not in a criminal justice–related field. However, more and more agencies use their interns as a pool from which to consider actual job applicants. If an agency solely draws from its entry-level agency pool of candidates, then you may want to consider an internship. Research into the agency will help you decide whether interning will benefit you.

Internships provide a unique opportunity to look into a field to determine if it's the right profession for you while allowing you to gain some valuable experience.

PAINTING A PICTURE

Consider your job application, in all respects, as a painting—a unique painting. It is not going to be like that of anyone else. Yours will be made up of the experiences you have developed for yourself and will have aspects others do not. You will have strengths where others have weaknesses, and there will be areas where you are building skills and improving. There may even be areas you have to clarify or explain to the person viewing it. Yet everything you have done and are doing will contribute to this picture that is uniquely you.

 What experiences do you have that make a statement, and what do they say about you? Write them in your journal.

MAKING THE BEST OF BAD SITUATIONS

How many people can honestly say they have absolutely no blemishes on their records? If you're like most people, you learn more by making mistakes than by doing it right the first time. Did you really believe your mother when she said the stove was hot? Honestly? Or did you have to see for yourself?

A popular poster reads: *When life gives you lemons, make lemonade.* However you say it, if you have made a mistake—which everyone has—it does not mean you have forfeited your future in security or criminal justice. Granted, *some* mistakes will bar you from certain positions in these fields. For example, no state will permit you to be a police officer if you have a felony on your record. They may, however, allow a misdemeanor or traffic offense.

Know in advance how you will deal with past mistakes, and accept that they do not automatically make you an outcast from society or from your chosen profession. Most professions accept mistakes, but they do *not* accept people who cannot change their ways, nor do they accept dishonesty. To lie on an application says nothing less than that you can't be trusted. It may even be a crime.

How do you deal with blemishes such as traffic citations or misdemeanor criminal charges? Approach them up front and honestly. Since the best defense is often a good offense, you will usually want to confront these issues head on. It looks better if you bring them up rather than having the employer learn about them during the background check. If they dredge up one questionable issue from your past, they may wonder what else might be hidden.

Once you have admitted you made a mistake (or two, or three), take it one step further. Share what you learned from the experience. If you have a less-than-perfect traffic record or a shoplifting charge from your youth, it would sound better to explain how that experience influenced you to want to become a police officer or a security officer. Consider how a hiring board would react to being told you were so influenced by the professionalism shown by the police officer who gave you that ticket that you wanted to become a police officer and positively influence others in the same way. What about a DWI conviction? Rather than eliminating you from the running, it could result in your taking subsequent steps to get your life together. To admit any shortcoming and prove you took advantage of an opportunity to grow and change does not make you an undesirable person. It makes you exceptional.

Imagine, for example, that you had a questionable driving record and were in competition with one other applicant. Other than the driving record, you have identical attributes. Would the hiring board use your driving record to decide against you? Or maybe even for you? They might if you accept that you are what you are. Present yourself in the best light—honestly. While you might have made some admittedly questionable decisions in the past, you want them to fully understand that that was then and you learned from it. To do otherwise makes you look, at best, on the defensive and, at worst, a liar.

Judge for yourself—which sounds best in response to an interviewer's question: "How is your driving record?"

> **Candidate #1.** Fine. (If this is true, great. But it will take about 10 seconds to verify this on the computer. If you lied, you're out.)

> **Candidate #2.** Well, I've had a few tickets. But I was only a kid, and the cops in my town had it in for me because of that. I think they just had to meet their quotas and it was easier to do by picking on us kids.

> **Candidate #3.** As a matter of fact, I got some traffic tickets when I was a teenager. I can't say I didn't deserve them because I did. I learned about obeying traffic regulations the hard way— having to work summer jobs to pay for the tickets and the increased car insurance premiums. But it taught me a valuable lesson. *I* was accountable for my actions. It wasn't the fault of the officers who gave me the tickets or my parents for not picking up the tab. It was my own fault. It worked for me. This is one reason I want to be a police officer—to help others learn.

You get the picture. Consider another situation, this time with candidates responding to an interviewer's question: "Have you ever used illegal substances?"

> **Candidate #1.** No. I would never do anything illegal. (Again, if this is true, great. But if the background investigation proves you to be a liar, you are out.)

> **Candidate #2.** To be honest, as a teenager I did experiment with marijuana. Most of my friends smoked pot, and I gave in to their pressure. It didn't do a thing for me, and I was forced to think about who was running my life—my friends or me. I knew it was time to stand up for myself, and it was a good learning experience. In fact, most of my friends quit too. We each thought the others expected it of us. What an eye-opener that was!

To take care of minor problems that would generally bar employment, consider interviewing with a mid-sized agency that has hired applicants with minor problems. And remember, you can't change the past, but you *can* present it so it looks positive rather than negative.

Although some mistakes will bar you from certain positions in these fields, most employers accept mistakes *if* you are open and up front about them during the preemployment interview, share what you learned from the experience and express honestly how you have changed your ways.

This is not to suggest you will be able to justify or "explain away" every indiscretion in your background. For example, a pattern of alcohol-related problems or financial difficulties are sure to concern those considering your application. Having chronic problems or an abundance of unresolved issues may well eliminate you from consideration. You must be realistic in this area, particularly if it continues happening as you apply for positions.

CRIMINAL JUSTICE, PRIVATE SECURITY AND ETHICS

Ethics has become a buzzword in almost every profession. Certainly criminal justice and private security demand the highest ethics. Fuller (2001, p. 6) contends: "The police service in this country is more closely scrutinized and subject to more uninformed, biased criticism than any other occupational group, with the possible exception of presidential candidates. The average street cop is expected to conduct his or her personal and professional life with more integrity and decorum than most other citizens, however unrealistic and difficult that may seem at times."

According to Josephson (2002, p. 37):

> Officers who think of police work as a calling tend to meet and overcome ethical challenges much better than those who view it simply as a job. Generally, missionaries do better than mercenaries.
>
> Getting new officers who have the proper missionary zeal is an issue of both recruiting and training. Law enforcement agencies must be more concerned than ever about the kind of people they bring into their departments. The simple strategy is to hire for character and train for skills. Without good character, an officer is just a scandal waiting to happen.

You can anticipate having to deal with this issue. In fact, ethics is a favorite topic of interview boards, so carefully consider your values and what you believe ethical behavior to be.

> The ethics of police, corrections and security officers play a large role in whether these fields are viewed as true professions. In fact, ethics is a favorite topic of interview boards, so you should thoughtfully consider your values and what you consider to be ethical behavior.

To develop and maintain a professional reputation, codes of ethics have been adopted in both law enforcement and private security. The Law Enforcement Code of Ethics is shown in Figure 9–2.

Grant (2002, p. 12) explains:

> The law enforcement code of ethics is used as an oath of office during the graduation ceremony for many law enforcement personnel. Prospective law enforcement officers offer the oath to the state in exchange for the employment they receive. This oath remains morally binding throughout the officer's entire length of service in law enforcement.

The International Association of Chiefs of Police (IACP) has also developed a Police Code of Conduct that covers primary responsibilities of a police officer, performance of the duties of a police officer, discretion, use of force, confidentiality, integrity, cooperation with other officers and agencies, personal/professional capabilities and private life. See Appendix A for the entire IACP Police Code of Conduct. The security profession has also developed a similar code of ethics, which is presented in Appendix B.

As a law enforcement officer, my fundamental duty is to serve the community; to safeguard lives and property; to protect the innocent against deception, the weak against oppression or intimidation, and the peaceful against violence or disorder; and to respect the constitutional rights of all to liberty, equality and justice.

I will keep my private life unsullied as an example to all and will behave in a manner that does not bring discredit to me or my agency. I will maintain courageous calm in the face of danger, scorn or ridicule; develop self-restraint; and be constantly mindful of the welfare of others. Honest in thought and deed both in my personal and official life, I will be exemplary in obeying the law and the regulations of my department. Whatever I see or hear of a confidential nature or that is confided to me in my official capacity will be kept ever secret unless revelation is necessary in the performance of my duty.

I will never act officiously or permit personal feelings, prejudices, political beliefs, aspirations, animosities or friendships to influence my decisions. With no compromise for crime and with relentless prosecution of criminals, I will enforce the law courteously and appropriately without fear or favor, malice or ill will, never employing unnecessary force or violence and never accepting gratuities.

I recognize the badge of my office as a symbol of public faith, and I accept it as a public trust to be held so long as I am true to the ethics of the police service. I will never engage in acts of corruption or bribery, nor will I condone such acts by other police officers. I will cooperate with all legally authorized agencies and their representatives in the pursuit of justice.

I know that I alone am responsible for my own standard of professional performance and will take every reasonable opportunity to enhance and improve my level of knowledge and competence.

I will constantly strive to achieve these objectives and ideals, dedicating myself before God to my chosen profession . . . law enforcement.

FIGURE 9–2   Law Enforcement Code of Ethics

SOURCE: Reprinted with permission from the International Association of Chiefs of Police, Alexandria, Virginia. Further reproduction without express written permission from IACP is strictly prohibited.

The IACP has recommended a Law Enforcement Oath of Honor as a symbolic statement to ethical behavior (http://www.theiacp.org):

On my honor,
I will never betray my profession,
my integrity, my character,
or the public trust.
I will always have
the courage to hold myself
and others accountable for our actions.
I will always uphold the laws of my country,
my community and the agency I serve.

Values

To a potential employer, a person's values say a great deal about who they are and what kind of employee they will prove to be. Values are more than just having ethics or a positive background. Values are what's important to an individual. In fact, many consider one's values the best overall statement of *who* they really are. For example, the core values of the Minnesota State Patrol, which their cadets learn, are the essence of this organization. They provide a strong basis for the group and for the individual.

The mission of the Minnesota State Patrol is
working together to ensure a safe environment
on Minnesota's roadways.

The Minnesota State Patrol has adopted
the following core values as part of its training curriculum:

Core Values

Pride
Preservation of Life
Pursuit of Excellence
Ethics
Loyalty
Professionalism
Trustworthiness

As an organization has basic values, written or unwritten, so does every individual. The picture you paint of yourself will reflect the values you hold to be important. Obviously, your values will make an impression on a prospective employer.

CONCLUSION

Your life is like a painting being continuously worked on. It will be developed, refined, altered and improved. It is never completed. Although the canvas may occasionally be briefly set aside, the paint is never completely dried—unless you allow it to be. At every phase of your life, you will appear to others as you have developed yourself. How will you appear to prospective employers? How can you add to your "life's painting" to be as appealing as possible? If you need more substance to your picture, get it. You have the control, the opportunity. Do you have the ambition and foresight?

AN INSIDER'S VIEW

GETTING YOUR FOOT IN THE DOOR

Michael P. Stein

Former Chief of Police
Escondido (California) Police Department

In California it is estimated that only one applicant out of 100 successfully competes for a police officer position, from the initial application to the final interview. As overwhelming as those odds are, some strategies can help you be that one in 100.

As departments go to community policing, the requirements for police officers are changing from the traditional enforcement role to one of community activism and facilitation. Police agencies are looking for candidates with experience in problem solving and working with various community elements. The successful candidate is one who has work experience with community agencies that aim to solve problems for the community good. Think about volunteering at your local Boys' and Girls' Clubs, your local school district or any other social agency in the community. This will give you hands-on experience in working with others and being a "team player."

It is never too early to begin planning to compete for that police officer position. When I was finishing high school, I knew that I wanted to join the police profession, but really didn't know how to go about it. After four years in the military, I was able to compete with just a high-school diploma. This is no longer the case. Now an applicant will be competing with many who are currently working toward a degree at the community college level and many others who may have a bachelor's degree.

Our department has recognized the need for better-educated applicants, even at the high-school level. In cooperation with the local high-school district, we have started a program called the "Code 3 Academy," where police officers present classes, lectures, field trips and physical training to students interested in preparing for a law enforcement career. Students learn based on what is being taught at local police academies. English classes include studies in report writing, computer keyboarding, powers of observation and exercises in written and verbal communication with their peer group and members of other cultures. The program gives students an opportunity to form a mentorship with police professionals who can assist them in their future law enforcement career goals. Another opportunity for high-school students is to join their local police department's Explorer Program. This gives the student the ability to see what police work is really about.

Any position that gets your foot in the door of a police agency is beneficial. Does your local department need volunteers? Does it have a police auxiliary or a reserve program? Establishing this type of personal relationship with a local department is one key thing you can do to increase the odds of being selected.

Once a year, our department holds a special recruitment for police officer trainee positions, when any of our active reserve officers can compete. The number then falls from one in 100 to something like one in 15 for a position. In the last 35 years, 49 of our reserve officers have been selected as police officer trainees with our department, and many others have been hired by other law enforcement agencies.

Does your local police academy allow you to attend without a department affiliation? In California a student can put himself/herself through any police academy in the state. Once you have your certificate of graduation from an academy, you then compete with only other academy graduates, not the at-large public. All departments are looking for experienced or previously trained candidates, and this is a real advantage as you compete for a position.

When applying for a police officer position, ask if any other positions are currently being recruited for in the department, such as community service officer, traffic control officer, dispatcher, etc. These are positions where the competition must not be as stringent as for police officer, but, if hired, this gives you an opportunity to show your work ethic to the department as you compete later for a police officer position. In our department, nine former community service officers now serve as police officers.

Does the agency that you aspire to join serve a large population of non-English speakers? In many southern border states, because of the influx of monolingual Spanish speakers, being bilingual in Spanish and English is an asset all police departments desire. Many departments do bilingual Spanish recruitments where applicants need to be proficient in both languages to apply. This lowers the overall number of applicants, but again increases the chances of those who have this skill to be successfully recruited. The other benefit of these recruitments is that they allow the departments to be more reflective of the newly diverse communities they serve.

The preceding recommendations used individually or collectively will enhance your ability to secure a law enforcement position. Best of luck!

Michael P. Stein *rose through the ranks of the Escondido (California) Police Department to become the chief of police. Now retired, he has 36 years' experience in law enforcement, holds a bachelor's degree in Public Administration and a master's degree in Human Behavior. Chief Stein is a graduate of the 129th Session of the FBI National Academy and is currently an adjunct professor at Palomar Community College in San Marcos, California.*

INSIDER'S VIEW ONLINE

An additional *Insider's View* for this chapter is "Out of the Ordinary" by Monte D. Zillinger, found on the Wadsworth website: http://www.wadsworth.com/criminaljustice_d/.

 ## MIND STRETCHES

1. Do you believe your past is an accurate assessment of your employment potential?

2. Who would be a better risk as an employee: candidates who tested the system as juveniles, occasionally having run-ins with the law, or candidates who walked the "straight and narrow," never doing anything "wrong," but also never testing their own limitations?

3. What are important benefits of attending college?

4. What volunteer opportunities exist in your community?

5. What do good writing skills say about you? How can you develop them?

6. Name five important attributes an employer might seek from applicants, regardless of the job. How can you develop these attributes?

7. Why is ethics of particular importance to criminal justice and private security?

8. As you look at your past, are there facts that could hurt you as a job applicant? How will you address them to put them in the most positive light?

9. What are your personal and professional strengths?

10. Is it possible to be "overqualified"? Why or why not?

REFERENCES

Finnimore, Ian J. "Learning and Applying Good Communication Skills." *The NAFTO News,* Spring 2003, pp. 23–24.

Fuller, John J. "Street Cop Ethics." *The Law Enforcement Trainer,* May/June 2001, pp. 6–8.

Grant, J. Kevin. "Ethics and Law Enforcement." *FBI Law Enforcement Bulletin,* December 2002, pp. 11–14.

Hennessy, Stephen M.; Hendricks, Cindy; and Hendricks, James. "Cultural Awareness and Communication Training: What Works and What Doesn't." *The Police Chief,* November 2001, pp. 15–19.

Hickman, Matthew J. and Reaves, Brian A. *Local Police Departments 2000*. Washington, DC: U.S. Department of Justice, Bureau of Justice Statistics, January 2003. (NCJ 196002)

International Association of Chiefs of Police. Online: http://www.theiacp.org/documents/index.cfm

Josephson, Michael. "Character Counts Now More than Ever." *The Police Chief,* September 2002, pp. 36–39.

Lambert, Eric; Nerbonne, Terry; Watson, Phillip L.; Buss, Jack; Clarke, Alan; Hogan, Nancy; Barton, Shannon; and Lambert, Janet. "Forensic Science Needs of Law Enforcement Applicants and Recruits: A Survey of Michigan Law Enforcement Agencies." *Journal of Criminal Justice Education,* Spring 2003.

Mahoney, Mark. "Law Enforcement Recruiting Software." *Law Enforcement Technology,* October 2001, pp. 194–199.

Moore, Carole. "Strong Report Writing Presents Positive Image." *Law Enforcement Technology,* January 2004, p. 82.

Nelson, Kurt R. "The Police Report in the Officer's Arsenal." *Law and Order,* September 2002, pp. 226–228.

Perry, Julia N.; Scullard, Mark; and DiLorenzo, Norma. "Are They Up to the Job?" *Minnesota Police Chief,* Spring 2003, pp. 31–37.

Pinizzotto, Anthony J.; Davis, Edward F.; and Miller, Charles E., III. "Intuitive Policing: Emotional/Rational Decision Making in Law Enforcement." *FBI Law Enforcement Bulletin,* February 2004, pp. 1–6.

Polk, O. Elmer and Armstrong, David A. "Higher Education and Law Enforcement Career Paths: Is the Road to Success Paved by Degree?" *Journal of Criminal Justice Education,* Spring 2001, pp. 77–99.

Ross, Lee E. and Elechi, Ogbonnaya Oko. "Student Attitudes towards Internship Experiences: From Theory to Practice." *Journal of Criminal Justice Education,* Fall 2002, pp. 297–312.

Secretary's Commission on Achieving Necessary Skills (SCANS), U.S. Department of Labor, 1991. Online: http://wdr.doleta.gov/SCANS/whatwork/whatwork.pdf (accessed January 12, 2005).

"Study Verifies Utility of Forensic Science Education for Law Enforcement Careers." *Criminal Justice Research Reports,* January/February 2004, pp. 39–40.

CHAPTER 10

THE RÉSUMÉ: SELLING YOURSELF ON PAPER

Writing a Résumé: Spend time on self-assessment first. Identify all the achievements of your past that illustrate skills. Describe them in active verbs and look for consistencies. That's the clue as to what you should emphasize. A résumé is scanned, not read. It's a sales tool that should give someone a sampling, not details in full.

—*Jean Clarkson*

Do You Know:

➢ What a résumé is?
➢ What purposes a résumé serves?
➢ What seven steps are involved in creating a résumé?
➢ What items to include in your résumé?
➢ What is best left off your résumé?
➢ What three basic types of résumés are commonly used and how they differ?
➢ What is important about the format of your résumé?
➢ What the key to writing an effective résumé is?
➢ How to make your résumé computer compatible?
➢ What to keep in mind when printing your résumé?
➢ When to send a cover letter and what elements are essential?
➢ The best way to deliver your résumé and what to do after the delivery?

INTRODUCTION

You've spent a lot of time thinking about your goals and yourself, your fitness, education and attributes. Now it's time to pull all this information together into one of your most important job-seeking tools—the résumé.

Résumé is a French word (pronounced *REZ-oo-may*) that means "summary." You probably know what a résumé is, but that's a little like saying you know what surgery is. A vast amount of territory exists between recognizing a concept and grasping its true meaning. To have a working understanding of such a concept is even more involved. This chapter provides you a working knowledge of the résumé.

WHAT IS A RÉSUMÉ?

Webster's defines *résumé* as: "A short account of one's career and qualifications prepared typically by an applicant for a position." Résumé guru Yana Parker (http://www.damngood.com) offers a more dynamic definition: "A résumé is a self-promotional document that presents you in the best possible light, for the purpose of getting invited to a job interview. It's *not* an official personnel document. It's not a job application. It's not a 'career obituary'! And it's not a confessional."

> A résumé is a brief, well-documented summary of your education, abilities, skills, experience and career achievements, which highlights *significant* aspects of your background and identifies your qualifications for a given job. It is a promotional tool designed to *sell* you to a prospective employer.

And the sales pitch must work quickly. The *Land That Job!* website (http://www.landjob.com) states: "Your resumes and resume cover letters can be reviewed and rejected in as little as 5 seconds! Both must communicate your qualifications at a glance." According to *Resume.com:* "The hiring manager will eliminate your resume in less than 10 seconds if it's not the very best in the stack." *Resume Logic* (http://www.resumelogic.com/index.htm) echoes: "Most staffing managers and recruiters (headhunters) scan and discard each resume in 10 to 15 seconds unless the resume provides them with a compelling reason to flag it for an in-depth review."

The competition to attract an employer's attention is keen, bitter and brutal. A well-prepared résumé can be the determining factor in whether an employer calls you for an interview, allowing you a "foot in the door." Your résumé may be your first contact with a potential employer. It may also be the last. The choice is yours.

In some cases, however, particularly in larger agencies and institutions, résumés are not used. Instead, the agency goes through a civil service commission. Applicants fill in only the commission's paperwork and can add nothing to it. A résumé can backfire if you include it and it is *not* asked for or wanted.

THE PURPOSES OF THE RÉSUMÉ

The résumé serves both the employer and prospective employee. The résumé is important to the *employer* because it helps weed out unqualified candidates. For most employers, this is the most important function of a résumé. Employers will use *any* flaw in a résumé to cut down the number of individuals to be interviewed. Résumés help employers cut through a lot of preliminary questioning about applicants' qualifications and help employers structure their interviews.

The résumé is important to *you* because it can help get you in the door for an interview. In fact, Barthel and Goldrick-Jones (http://www.rpi.edu/web/writingcenter/resume.html) assert: "A resume has one purpose: to get you a job interview." JobWeb (http://www.jobweb.com/resumes_interviews/resume_guide/res.htm) presents the résumé's purpose another way: "A resume does its job successfully if it *does not* exclude you from consideration."

The résumé serves other purposes as well. Preparing your résumé will force you to take a hard look at your skills, qualifications, past experiences and accomplishments. It will require you to recall (or look up) dates and addresses. It will compel you to organize your past clearly and concisely, which will help you present yourself in an organized manner during the interview as well. This will enable you to approach the interview confident that you have the qualities and background the employer is looking for, or why would you be called in?

Résumés serve a variety of purposes for both the employer and the applicant. A résumé helps an employer by weeding out unqualified candidates, answering preliminary questions about an applicant's qualifications and structuring an interview. A résumé helps applicants obtain interviews and organize their experiences, accomplishments, present skills and qualifications so they may be coherently discussed during an interview.

During the interview, the résumé will save time by providing a common ground to start from. It will also keep you honest. The temptation to exaggerate your experience or accomplishments will be removed when you know the employer has seen your résumé. Now that you know how important your résumé is, look at the specific steps in creating one.

STEPS IN CREATING A RÉSUMÉ

Creating a résumé is like painting a picture of yourself. From the conception of the idea to the completion of the masterpiece, you need to take seven specific steps.

The seven specific steps to creating a résumé are:

1. Compile all relevant information.
2. Select the most appropriate type of résumé.
3. Select a format.
4. Write the first draft.

5. Polish the first draft.
6. Evaluate the résumé and revise if necessary.
7. Print the résumé.

Creating an effective résumé is *hard work,* but the results will be well worth it. Without an effective résumé, you are wasting your time applying for most jobs. You won't get to first base. Even if an agency does not require a résumé, they will expect you to be a "living résumé" at the interview. Get yourself organized before that. Make up your mind to devote several hours to this important document.

COMPILE INFORMATION

Gather all the information that could possibly be included in your résumé. Some will be used; some won't. Painters gather all of their brushes and paints before they begin to work so they aren't interrupted during the creative process. Likewise, you will want to gather all the information you *might* decide to include. You don't want to interrupt the creative writing flow to look up a phone number or address.

 Use the worksheets in Appendix C to organize your résumé information. Flip to the back of the book and place a paper clip at the top of Appendix C to help you locate it quickly while working through this section. Don't cut corners during this first step. Your background makes a great deal of difference. As you compile information, you may be amazed at how much data an employer will need to even consider you.

You'll look at three kinds of information: (1) data you must include, (2) data you might include and (3) data you should probably not include but should be prepared to discuss. Don't guess at dates. Verify them. Don't guess at addresses. Check them out if it's been awhile since you worked or lived somewhere.

Look first at what *MUST* be included: personal identifying information, your educational background and your work experience.

Personal Identifying Information

Name. Obvious? Yes. But believe it or not, some people actually forget to include their name. In addition, think carefully about how you want your name to appear. Do you want to include your middle name? An initial? A nickname? A title? If you include a nickname, put it following your first name with quotation marks around it, like this: *Robert "Bob" T. Jones.* This lets the employer know what you prefer to be called. Avoid extreme or inappropriate nicknames such as "Killer." Parker advises: "Don't mystify the reader about your gender; they'll go nuts until they know whether you're male or female. So if your name is Lee or Robin or Pat or anything else not clearly male or female, use a Mr. or Ms. prefix."

 How do you want your name to appear in your résumé? Write it on the worksheet.

Address. It is usually best to give only your home address. Put the street address on one line. Do not abbreviate. Put a comma between a street address and an apartment number. Put the city and state on the next line and separate them with a comma. Use the two-letter state abbreviation—both letters capitalized and NO period. Include your zip code. Do *not* put a comma between the state and zip code.

>   Example: 123 Third Avenue South, #401
>   My Town, MN 55437

 How should your address appear? Write it on the worksheet.

 If you move frequently, you may want to include a permanent address in addition to your present address.

 E-mail address: E-mail is no longer a novelty or a luxury—it is how most businesses communicate today. If you don't currently have an e-mail address, we suggest you obtain one because (1) it makes it easier for prospective employers to contact you and (2) to not have one in today's online climate reflects negatively on your technological, specifically computer, skills. Remember to check your e-mail daily.

Phone Number. *Always* include a phone number. Busy employers often prefer to call rather than write. Make it easy for them. Give the area code, followed by a hyphen and then your phone number. Indicate if it is a home, work or cell number. Many people prefer to *not* include a work phone to avoid being called at work. Would getting job-search–related phone calls at work cause you any problems? If so, do *not* include your work number. Some people also include the hours they can be reached at a given number. Others put this information in their cover letter.

>   Example: Work Phone   612-555-9929 (9 am to 5 pm)
>   Home Phone   612-555-8818 (6 pm to 10 pm)
>   Cell Phone   612-555-2222 (9 am to 10 pm)

 Enter your phone number(s) on the appropriate line on the worksheet.

Did you know there was so much to think about in simply giving your name, address and phone number?

Education

Information about your education is crucial to your résumé.

 College. List each college attended, city and state, number of years completed, major/minor, unique areas of study and degree(s) earned. Start with the most recent and work backward. Include any honors, awards or leadership positions. Include grade point average *if* outstanding.

 Professional Schools. Include the same information as for colleges. Include academies here also.

 Internships. Include the place and length of the internship.

 Certificates. Relevant certificates would include first aid, CPR and the like. Give the year the certificates were awarded and expiration dates, if relevant.

 Other Educational Experiences. Include any relevant seminars, workshops, correspondence courses and the like.

 High School. Include name, city and state, year of graduation, and grade point average if it is outstanding. Include your high school *only* if you graduated within the last 10 years or if you have no other education to include.

Work Experience

Recall from Chapter 9 that past general employment of any type is valuable in the job search, even if not related to your field. Volunteer experience, work-related or not, should also be included on your résumé. Of special importance are the qualifications and skills you bring to the job. You may want to refer to Chapter 9 for attributes most employers are looking for. Your résumé should stress achievements more than education and experience.

 Begin with your present job, or your most recent job if you are not currently employed. Work back in time. Use the worksheet in Appendix C. Make a copy of this worksheet for each job you have had. Use the work experience section to describe your qualities and skills wherever and however you can. If applicable, you might demonstrate these qualities and skills in the education portion of your résumé as well.

Several other areas of information might also be included in your résumé, depending on your background. Even if you decide *not* to include much or most of the following information, it is important for you to think about it and have it clear in your mind because it could come up during the interview.

Position Desired or Employment Objective

What specific job do you have in mind? Are you open to *any* position in your chosen field? This information can be very helpful to busy employers as they skim through stacks of résumés. An attractive job candidate is one who knows what he wants to do. In fact, to the question: "What is the most common résumé mistake made by job hunters?" Parker replies: "Leaving out their Job Objective! If you don't show a sense of direction, employers won't be interested. Having a clearly stated goal doesn't have to confine you if it's stated well."

 In Appendix C, write down the position desired and, if relevant, your employment objective. An example might be: *Position desired: Entry-level officer with opportunity to provide _____.*

 Tell what you can do for the employer—not what the employer can do for you.

Other Information

Other information that may be put in your résumé includes the following:

 Willingness to travel or relocate, military experience, professional memberships, knowledge of foreign language(s), foreign travel, awards, publications, community service or involvement, interests and hobbies. Also, list your accomplishments and don't be modest.

 You might also want to include your availability—can you start immediately or do you need a certain amount of time to give notice to your present employer? Can your present employer be contacted?

References

If you get to the point in the hiring process where you are being considered, most employers will want to check your references.

 Choose references *now* and fill in that portion of the worksheet in Appendix C. Try to have business, professional and academic references as well as personal references.

Choose your references carefully. Recall from Chapter 8 the advice on selecting references for the background check. *Always* ask your references if they are willing to provide you with a *positive* reference. Most people do *not* include the references in their résumés. You can simply state: "References available on request," and prepare a separate sheet of references to make available to employers who request them. This also keeps your references confidential until a request is made for them.

Photograph

Some books on résumés suggest that a photograph should never be included with a résumé; other books highly recommend it. Those who are against it suggest that it violates antidiscrimination laws by providing information an employer cannot legally ask about. For example, race, sex and approximate age are revealed in a photograph. If you feel these factors may work in your favor, you may decide to include a photograph.

One advantage of including a photo is that it will probably make your résumé stand out from the rest, always a primary goal. However, unless it represents you in a way the employer will appreciate, the photo could detract from your résumé. If you do include a photo, be certain it is recent, professional and puts you in a favorable light. You should be neatly groomed, and the reproduction should be clear and crisp.

Items you *must* include in your résumé are personal identifying information (name, address and phone number), educational experience, work experience and your employment objectives. You might also include your willingness to travel or relocate, military experience, professional memberships, knowledge of foreign language(s), awards, publications, any community service or involvement and your availability. You should include a statement that references are available upon request. Whether to include a photograph is debatable. Include a photograph only if it is recent, professional and presents you in a favorable light.

What *Not* to Include

What not to include is a matter of opinion. While you will *never* lie on a résumé, you will want to present yourself so that even negative occurrences look good for you. If you have to explain them in depth during an interview, that's fine, as long as you *get* to the interview.

Including too much data is a major fault of many résumés. Not only does this create a document that is so long it won't get read, but you can harm yourself by saying too much. For example, do not state in a résumé why you left past jobs. Newfield (2004) warns: " 'Company sold,' 'Boss was an idiot,' and 'Left to make more money' have no place on your résumé." If the reason was somewhat spectacular, for example a series of promotions, put it in, but the presumption will be that you moved upward and onward to better positions. Also, the résumé is not the place to explain difficulties you've had. It is a chance to provide a *brief* overview of yourself, to be expanded on once it has gotten you an interview. Be certain everything you include is relevant and cannot in any way detract.

Exceptionally personal data can also detract from the emphasis that should be on your skills and qualifications. Newfield asserts: "Personal information does not belong on a résumé in the United States. Don't include information on your marital status, age, race, family or hobbies." Parker advises:

> Don't include hobbies on a résumé unless the activity is somehow relevant to your job objective, or clearly reveals a characteristic that supports your job objective. For example, a hobby of Sky Diving (adventure, courage) might seem relevant to some job objectives (Security Guard?) but not to others. . . .
>
> Don't include ethnic or religious affiliations (inviting pre-interview discrimination) UNLESS you can see that including them will support your job objective. Get an opinion from a respected friend or colleague about when to reveal, and when to conceal, your affiliations.

> Including too much data is a major fault on many résumés. Don't overdo it. *Avoid including:*
>
> ➤   Reasons for leaving your current or previous job
> ➤   Salary (previous or desired)
> ➤   Age, marital status and family details
> ➤   Religious or church affiliations
> ➤   Race, ethnic background, nationality
> ➤   Political affiliations/preferences
> ➤   Hobbies or special interests
> ➤   Anything that negatively dates your résumé

SELECT THE TYPE OF RÉSUMÉ

When you go fishing you select the bait that will best serve your purpose based on the specific conditions at that particular time and the fish you're after. Likewise, you should have all the "bait" you need to land an interview in the form of the data you have just put together. Now decide how to present it. Three basic types of résumés are commonly used:

➤   Historical or chronological

➤   Functional

➤   Analytical

Each type has a specific format, content and purpose.

Historical/Chronological Résumé

The historical/chronological résumé is the most traditional and is often considered the most effective. As implied by the name, this style presents information in reverse chronological order, starting with your most recent work experience and moving back in time to your past work experience. The educational and employment information worksheets in Appendix C are organized this way. Both education and employment lend themselves to this style. Always include dates and explain any gaps in the chronology.

The historical/chronological résumé is easy to read and gives busy employers a familiar form that can be quickly read. It is the best format to use when staying in the same field. It is not the best format if you have little related experience. Use a chronological résumé if:

➤   You have spent three or more years with previous employers and have not changed jobs frequently.

➤   You are seeking a position in the same field in which you have been employed.

➤   You have worked for well-known, prestigious companies.

➤   You can show steady growth in responsibilities.

See Appendix D for a sample chronological résumé.

Functional Résumé

The functional résumé stresses experiences and abilities as they relate to the job you are applying for rather than a chronological listing of past employment. Dates do not receive as much attention. Hofferber (2004) suggests:

> If you've held a number of different or unrelated jobs during a relatively short period of time and are worried about being labeled as a job-hopper, the functional résumé (also known as a "skills-based format") could be the answer for you. This format can also work well for those entering the workforce for the first time or after a long absence (such as recent grads with no formal work experience, stay-at-home moms or dads now seeking outside employment, or caregivers who have spent a year or more treating an ill or aging family member). It could also be a good choice if your prior work experience is more relevant to your current job target than what you're doing presently.

This style emphasizes a candidate's strengths in key skills categories and maximizes scant work experience while minimizing irrelevant jobs, employment gaps and reversals. Use a functional résumé if:

➢   You are seeking a job in a field new to you.

➢   You have been unemployed for more than three months.

➢   Your responsibilities are complicated and require explanation.

➢   You can point to specific accomplishments on your last job.

➢   You are competing with younger applicants.

See Appendix D for a sample functional résumé.

Analytical Résumé

The analytical résumé stresses your particular skills. It is especially helpful if you are changing career goals but you have obtained necessary skills and qualifications from your present and past jobs. It lets you stress those *skills* and *talents* instead of your work history. Dates are usually omitted, but past jobs and experiences are referred to at some point. Again, you must determine if this approach can best reflect your particular abilities.

See Appendix D for a sample analytical résumé.

The three basic types of résumés commonly used are the historical or chronological résumé, the functional résumé and the analytical résumé.

➢   The *historical/chronological* résumé, the most traditional and often considered the most effective, presents information by beginning with the most recent experience and going backward in time.
➢   The *functional* résumé emphasizes your qualifications and abilities; minimizes irrelevant jobs, employment gaps and reversals; and maximizes scant work experience.
➢   The *analytical* résumé is appropriate if you are changing career goals and stresses *skills* and *talents* instead of past jobs.

What about Creativity?

You may be wondering if these three styles are rather boring. You may want to be somewhat more creative. Think carefully about it. An imaginative or creative approach may be of great benefit, or it may burn you. The positive side of such an approach is that it may set your résumé apart from the dozens, hundreds, even thousands of others, thus receiving the attention it deserves. The negative side of a creative résumé is that it might be the reason the employer is looking for to jettison your résumé, along with any others that do not appear "normal." Remember, many employers feel a résumé is a business matter and should be presented in a businesslike manner.

If you decide to use an imaginative/creative résumé, be sure to include all the information any other style would present. If you can do so, you just might be on to something. For example, what could possibly catch a police department's eye quicker than a résumé that takes on the appearance of a "Wanted" poster? It might work, but give very serious consideration to such an idea at an entry-level position.

FORMAT THE RÉSUMÉ

The format is the layout of the information—what comes first, second and third. The format should be attractive, businesslike and professional. Actually *design* your format on a sheet of paper. *Block* your material and use *headings* to guide the reader.

Plan for margins at the top, bottom and sides. Use white space freely. Will you center your identifying information? Have it flush left? Will you use one or two columns for the bulk of the information? Try to fit all the information on *one* page. However, if you need two pages, use them. Reducing the font size just to fit everything on one page can become problematic for the employer. Newfield recommends: "If your career warrants a two-page résumé, then go ahead and create a document that reflects the full range of your experience and accomplishments. Don't reduce the type size to such a degree that your résumé becomes difficult to read."

Keep in mind: If your résumé is too long, you risk it not being read; too short, and you risk leaving out relevant information.

> The format of your résumé should be attractive, businesslike and professional. Not too long; not too short.

Note: Formatting considerations for e-mailed résumés and other computer compatibility issues are discussed later in this chapter.

WRITE THE RÉSUMÉ

If possible, use a word processor to write your résumé. This will make editing and updating it less painful and e-mailing it much easier.

The traditional advice for writing an effective résumé has been to use short, action-packed *phrases*.

Short. Omit all unnecessary words. This includes:

➤ Personal pronouns: *I, me* and *my*

➤ Articles: *a, an* and *the*

Action-Packed. Write with *verbs*, not with *nouns*. For example, don't say *conducted an investigation,* say *investigated.* Writing with verbs is also shorter than writing with nouns. Look at the following:

> I conducted an analysis of all the incoming calls to the dispatcher, and I compiled detailed analytical reports based on my analysis.

Twenty-two words. Eliminate the pronouns (*I, my*) and articles (*an, the*) and use verbs instead of nouns. What you'll get is something like the following:

> Analyzed all incoming calls and wrote detailed reports.

Which statement would you rather read? Which conveys an image of the writer as focused and authoritative?

Phrases. Phrase your writing. Watch where lines end. Avoid hyphenating words at the end of the line. For example, read the following:

> It was a difficult job because my boss was a rat-
> her rigid person.

One way to write an effective résumé is to use short, action-packed *phrases.*

Get the idea? Pay attention to effective ads on television and in print. Notice how the words are strung together for maximum effect. You can do the same in your résumé. Try using short "bullet" phrases that begin with active verbs. Strive for variety in your verbs. Here are some that might fit your experience:

achieved	consulted	guided	organized	scheduled
adapted	controlled	hired	planned	selected
administered	coordinated	identified	presented	served
analyzed	decided	improved	produced	set up
applied	delegated	increased	proved	solved
approved	designed	inspected	provided	spoke
arranged	developed	invented	published	supervised
assessed	edited	investigated	recorded	surveyed
assisted	educated	led	redesigned	taught
built	encouraged	managed	represented	trained
chaired	established	modified	researched	updated
completed	evaluated	monitored	reviewed	wrote
conducted	examined	operated	revised	

Parker suggests:

> Fill your resume with "PAR" statements. PAR stands for Problem-Action-Results; in other words, first you
> state the problem that existed in your workplace, then you describe what you did about it, and finally you
> point out the beneficial results.
>
> **Here's an example:** "Transformed a disorganized, inefficient warehouse into a smooth-running operation by
> totally redesigning the layout; this saved the company thousands of dollars in recovered stock."
>
> **Another example:** "Improved an engineering company's obsolete filing system by developing a simple but
> sophisticated functional-coding system. This saved time and money by recovering valuable, previously lost,
> project records."

Although the traditional recommendation of writing résumés using verbs is still sound, today's job
seekers must also be cognizant of a new résumé rule which Challenger (2000, p. 6) notes as: "Use as
many nouns as possible . . . and be as specific as possible." The simple reason for this new rule is the
growing use of e-résumés.

Preparing an E-Résumé

According to Challenger (p. 6): "Computers and the Internet have changed the way résumés are written,
distributed and read. . . . Today, employers use sophisticated computer programs to scan in-house and
independent databases that can contain tens of thousands of résumés. These programs search for selected
words and phrases that best apply to their ideal candidate." When creating an e-résumé, the rule about
sticking to one page becomes more flexible because the programs used to scan résumés for keywords
can comb through a two-page résumé just as easily as a single-page one. And as Challenger (p. 6) warns:
"E-resumes that are too short are less likely to contain the magic phrases."

To prepare an e-résumé to be most compatible with a variety of electronic databases, use a common typeface,
like Courier or Arial. Challenger (p. 6) cautions: "Exotic fonts may not be readable by the employer's
computer." Keep the font size between 10 and 14 points; and avoid italic and boldface type. Hayes (2000,
p. 15) adds: "Instead of avoiding jargon, *use it often*—computers target words specific to an industry and are
likely to select resumes containing those words multiple times." Challenger (p. 6) suggests including a
keyword section at the end of your résumé with as many variations of applicable words as possible.

As more companies go online, "Please e-mail your résumé in ASCII format" is becoming an increasingly
common statement in job listings. ASCII (pronounced "askee") files or text-only documents do not retain
special formatting commands, thus allowing different word processing applications to read and display
the same text information. Guidelines to follow when creating an ASCII-formatted résumé are:

➢ Do not use special characters such as mathematical symbols.

➢ Use your spacebar rather than tabs.

➢ To indent a character or center a heading, use the spacebar.

➢ Use hard carriage returns to insert line breaks, not the word-wrap feature.

➢ Font size and typeface will be whatever your computer uses as its default, so boldface, italics and
  various sizes will not appear in the ASCII version.

➤   Always run a spell-check on your document before you save it as a text-only file.

➤   Instead of bullets, use asterisks or plus signs at the beginning of lines.

➤   Instead of lines, use a series of dashes to separate sections. Don't try to underline text.

A basic rule of thumb is to keep it simple, as if you were using an ancient typewriter with no function keys or fancy formatting devices.

> Make your résumé computer compatible by using a common typeface, avoiding use of italic and boldface type and saving the document as a "text-only" file.

Preparing a Scannable Résumé

It is common practice in many companies to scan résumés received via regular mail so they may easily search for keywords and transmit the document to any and all interested parties. The scanning process uses Optical Character Recognition (OCR) software to convert hardcopy images into digital computer data. Fancy graphics, complicated formatting and general clutter typically do not scan readily, and the résumé that appears on the recruiter's monitor may simply look too messy and unappealing to even warrant a read-through. Isaacs (2004b) offers the following tips for creating a scannable résumé:

> Since companies use different scanning hardware and software, it is impossible to know for sure how to format a resume. The best way to ensure that the document is formatted properly is to call the company's HR department and find out if they have specific guidelines. If you don't have this information, there are steps you can take to optimize scannability:
>
> - One of the most important factors is whether or not letters touch each other. Scanning systems have difficulty interpreting characters that are melded into one, so make sure that no characters touch each other. Italics and bold are both fine, as long as the letters do not touch.
> - Choose a common, nondecorative sans serif font (such as Arial or Optima) and keep the font size between 10 and 14 points.
> - Underlining and horizontal/vertical lines are okay, as long as the lines do not touch any of the letters.
> - Avoid columns (the OCR reads the text from left to right).
> - Do not use round, hollow bullets (they may be interpreted as the letter o). Instead, choose round, solid bullets.
> - Do not use ampersands, percent signs or foreign characters (they may not translate properly).
> - Add a space in between slashes so that the slash doesn't touch the letters (e.g., IT / IS).
> - Use light-colored paper (white is best) and avoid paper that contains dark speckles.
> - Do not staple your resume.
> - Mail your resume in a flat envelope. If you fold your resume and the crease lands on a line of text, the laser toner may flake off and render the entire line unreadable.
> - Make sure you have keywords throughout your resume, so that you will be found in a database search.

Tailoring Your Résumé

A final suggestion: Tailor your résumé to fit the job. With all the preceding suggestions and choices, you may find it difficult to settle on one "perfect" format or word choice for your résumé, especially if you are applying to a variety of types of employers. So don't. To the common dilemma: "What if I have several different job objectives I'm working on at the same time? Or I haven't narrowed it down yet to just one job target?," Parker advises: "Then write a different resume for each different job target. A targeted resume is MUCH, much stronger than a generic resume."

Once you have written your first draft, let it sit overnight. You will then be ready to edit and polish it.

EDIT AND POLISH YOUR FIRST DRAFT

First drafts simply don't cut it. Continue to work with it until it has the punch you want. Because employers are busy, say as much as you can with as few words as possible. Spend time refining each phrase. Work at developing brief statements that explain clearly and strongly what your education and experience are, what opportunities you've taken advantage of and what qualifications and skills you would bring to the job.

You might consider hiring a professional editor or even a professional résumé writer at this point. Using such services will be less expensive if you have completed all the background research, designed a format and written the first draft. Razek (2001, p. 12) states: "For a fee, Vault.com's career experts evaluate your resume and provide career coaching by phone. Prices range from $39 to $319." The Web address is: Vault.com/careerservices

Proofread your draft. Check the spelling of every word. Check every capital letter and punctuation mark. Then check it again. Better yet, have a friend whose writing skills you respect check it for you. It is very hard to see your own writing errors. Some people find it helpful to proofread by going from right to left in each line, looking at each word. Morem (2001 p. D2) provides the following examples of real résumé gaffes:

➢   "Worked party-time as an office assistant"

➢   "Planned and held up meetings"

➢   "Computer illiterate"

She states: "You want your résumé to generate interest, not laughs: make sure it is error-free, and take the time to step away from it before you proofread and do your final editing."

EVALUATE AND REVISE

 Use the form in Appendix C to evaluate your résumé. Consider both appearance and content. Grade each category as Excellent, Average or Poor. If a category is poor, decide how to improve it.

PRINT YOUR RÉSUMÉ

You are at the final step. Don't blow it now. Have your résumé professionally printed or use a high-quality printer. Consider the following:

➢   Buy a quantity of blank 8½-by-11-inch white bond paper and matching 9 × 12 envelopes.

➢   Print only on one side and use black ink.

➢   Use a type that is easy to read, at least 10-point size, preferably 11- or 12-point.

➤ If necessary, slightly reduce the font size to assure adequate margins.

➤ Do NOT use all capital letters, script, bold or italic print. Use graphics sparingly or, better yet, not at all.

➤ Most people prefer a *serif* typestyle. Serifs are the little curves or feet added to the edges of letters to make them more readable. This book uses a serif typestyle. *Sans serif* typestyles do give a crisp, clean appearance, but are much harder to read. (Example: Arial Typeface—compare p and p, or A and A.)

Have your résumé professionally printed in black ink, on 8½ × 11 inch white bond paper. If necessary, reduce the type slightly to assure adequate margins, and use capital letters, script, bold and italic print and graphics sparingly, if at all.

MAKING IT A "10"

Your résumé is a direct reflection of you on paper. Be sure it depicts you as you want—a professional for a professional job. Everything about your résumé will say something about *you*. Because employers have to start cutting back the number of finalists, they look for reasons *not* to pursue you as a candidate. For example, typos on a résumé have served as a legitimate reason for disregarding an application for any number of positions. Sometimes, when there are a lot of very good applicants, reasons for getting rid of one résumé and keeping another become, at best, arbitrary.

Put your résumé in an attractive binder or enclose it in an attractive envelope with the name and address of the prospective employer typed. This may say that this particular applicant put that extra effort into the process and should, therefore, be given consideration—an interview. Do not, however, use anything slippery or difficult to file. You don't want your résumé to stand out because it is hard to handle.

THE COVER LETTER

Never send a résumé without a cover letter, even if the employer has asked you to send a résumé. Cover letters should be individually typed, addressed to a specific person and company or department and signed. Anything less will be ineffective.

Keep your cover letter short and to the point. It is a brief personal introduction of the "you" embodied in your résumé. Don't repeat résumé information. Entice the reader to want to find out more about you. Make clear in your opening paragraph the type of résumé submission:

➤ Unsolicited. If so, give a reason for selecting this particular employer.

➤ Written as a referral or from personal contact, for example, "My mechanic told me your department was looking for qualified security officers."

➤ Written in response to a job advertisement.

Avoid starting every sentence with "I." *Never* start with: "I am writing this letter to apply for the job I saw advertised in the paper." BORING! Focus on the reader. More effective would be something like this: "Your opening for a police officer advertised in the *Gazette* is of great interest to me." Isaacs (2004a) offers the following advice about cover letters:

> Your cover letter is the first thing employers see when they open your materials. Avoid these 10 mistakes, and make your first impression an impressive and lasting one.
>
> **Don't Overuse "I."** Your cover letter is not your autobiography. The focus should be on how you meet an employer's needs, not on your life story. Avoid the perception of being self-centered by minimizing your use of the word "I," especially at the beginning of your sentences.
>
> **Don't Use a Weak Opening.** Job seekers frequently struggle with the question of how to begin a cover letter. What results is often a feeble introduction lacking punch and failing to grab the reader's interest. Consider this example:
> - **Weak:** Please consider me for your sales representative opening.
> - **Better:** Your need for a top-performing sales representative is an excellent match to my three-year history as a #1-ranked multimillion-dollar producer.
>
> **Don't Omit Your Top Selling Points.** A cover letter is a sales letter that sells you as a candidate. Just like the resume, it should be compelling and give the main reasons why you should be called for an interview. Winning cover letter strategies include emphasizing your top accomplishments or creating subheadings culled from the position ad. For example: "Your ad specifies . . . and I offer . . ."
>
> **Don't Make It Too Long or Too Short.** If your cover letter is only one or two short paragraphs, it probably doesn't contain enough key information to sell you effectively. If it exceeds one page, you may be putting readers to sleep. Keep it concise but compelling, and be respectful of readers' time.
>
> **Don't Repeat Your Resume Word-for-Word.** Your cover letter shouldn't just regurgitate what's on your resume. Reword your cover letter statements to avoid dulling your resume's impact.
>
> **Don't Be Vague.** If you're replying to an advertised opening, reference the specific job title in your cover letter. The person reading your letter may be reviewing hundreds of letters for dozens of different jobs. Make sure all the content in your letter supports how you will meet the specific needs of the employer.
>
> **Don't Forget to Customize.** If you're applying to a number of similar positions, chances are you're tweaking one letter and using it for multiple openings. That's fine, as long as you are customizing each one. Don't forget to update the company/job/contact information—if Mr. Jones is addressed as Mrs. Smith, he won't be impressed.
>
> **Don't End on a Passive Note.** Put your future in your own hands with a promise to follow up. Instead of asking readers to call you, try a statement like this: I will follow up with you in a few days to answer any preliminary questions you may have. In the meantime, you may reach me at (555) 555-5555.
>
> **Don't Be Rude.** Your cover letter should thank the reader for his time and consideration.
>
> **Don't Forget to Sign the Letter.** It is proper business etiquette (and shows attention to detail) to sign your letter. However, if you are sending your cover letter and resume via e-mail or the Web, a signature isn't necessary.

Keep your letter short—one page. Be direct in requesting an interview. Send the letter to a specific person and use that individual's title. You can usually get this information by calling the agency or department, asking who is in charge of hiring and asking for the spelling of that person's name and official title. The little time this takes can pay big dividends.

As with your résumé, be sure to carefully proofread the cover letter. Morem (p. D2) reports: "A recent survey by the Society of Human Resource Management found that more than 80 percent of human resources professionals spend less than one minute reading a cover letter; 76 percent said a typo or grammatical error would remove an applicant from consideration."

Always send a resumé with a cover letter. Cover letters should be individually typed, short and to the point, addressed to a specific person (including his or her title) and a specific company or department and signed.

An effective format for a cover letter is the full-block style—everything begins at the left margin. The parts of the letter should be as follows:

> Your name
> Your address (street number, street name and apartment number, if applicable)
> Your city, state and zip code
> Your phone number(s) with area code
> Your e-mail address
>
> The date you are writing
>
> The name of the person you are writing to
> That person's title
> The name of the company/department
> The address of the employer
>
> Salutation (Dear . . .):
>
> Opening paragraph—why you are writing.
>
> Second paragraph—provide some intriguing fact about yourself as a lead into your résumé.
>
> Concluding paragraph—ask for an interview and state where you can be reached.
>
> Complimentary closing (Sincerely, or Yours truly),
>
> (Skip four lines—sign in this space)
>
> Typed name
>
> Encl: Résumé

Notice the spacing between the various sections. Notice the capitalization and the colon following the salutation and the comma following the complimentary closing. A sample cover letter is given in Appendix E.

SENDING YOUR RÉSUMÉ

Mail your cover letter and résumé unfolded in a 9 × 12 envelope. Everybody else's is going to be folded and crinkled. Résumés that travel flat are going to look better than all the others. As one employer commented: "When I looked for résumés, the easy ones to find are the flat ones. They stand out in the pile of folded résumés." Also, mail your letter and résumé to arrive in the employer's office on a Tuesday, Wednesday or Thursday.

One final suggestion—consider using certified mail, with a return receipt requested. Not only will you eliminate those nagging doubts about if it got delivered, but again, it says something to the employer about the kind of person you are. Here is a candidate concerned enough to make *sure* it arrived. That's the kind of attention to detail a lot of employers are looking for.

Electronic Submission and Faxing of Résumés

Sending material electronically is good—it makes a statement that you possess computer skills that today's employers desire—but keep the following in mind:

➤ Always keep a copy of anything you send, should you need it in the future.

➤ Make sure your electronic communiqués appear every bit as professional as those submitted in hardcopy. Begin with a proper salutation (Dear "recipient") and finish with a professional closing (Sincerely).

➤ Never use electronic communication simply because it is easier for you. Use it only because that is what is requested by the employer.

➤ Clearly state the purpose of your e-mail in the subject line (Application for job posting . . .). Never leave the subject line blank, as many antispam filters delete such "unannounced" e-mail. Furthermore, it may be considered rude or careless to not inform the recipient of the nature of your correspondence—they likely will not recognize your name and may simply delete the file without opening it.

➤ Do not assume electronic communications are always received. Glitches occur, servers go down, systems crash, antispam programs interfere—following up on all electronic correspondence is crucial in ensuring the intended recipient did, indeed, receive your material.

In the search for ways to get your résumé to prospective employers faster, it may be tempting to use a fax machine. And while fax and e-mail submissions are routine and acceptable for many employers, do not assume it is acceptable for all of them. You must ask first before you submit your résumé via fax machine. However, considering the relatively poor visual quality of most faxes as compared to e-mailed and printed documents and the increased likelihood of employers having e-mail capabilities, faxes now place a distant second to e-mail as a way to transmit documents instantaneously.

HAND DELIVERING YOUR RÉSUMÉ

It's always a good idea to hand deliver a résumé if possible because it allows the employer to associate your name with a face. Dress well and look professional when you deliver your résumé. Even if you don't get to the boss, you will make a good impression on the staff person accepting it. These people can have a great deal of influence on their bosses. Don't let your guard down because you aren't dealing directly with upper management. When you drop your material off, it is another opportunity for you to emphasize that you really want the job. Keep in mind many secretaries and receptionists are gatekeepers. Establishing a positive contact with the person taking your résumé (or answering the phone) may also help you get that interview.

FOLLOWING UP

Be sure to follow up. The follow-up is another opportunity to prove what kind of person you are—the kind they should hire! A day or two after you have mailed or hand delivered your résumé, write a brief letter to the employer. Recognize that the employer will be busy and only a short letter stands a chance of being read.

Confirm that you delivered your résumé and thank the employer for the opportunity to participate in the hiring process. Even if this merely gets stapled to your résumé without getting read initially by the employer, or gets forgotten by the employer who might read it, it is something that just might catch the attention of the interview committee when your résumé surfaces. If they are looking for reasons to keep some and get rid of others, this could be the reason yours stays in the running. See Appendix E for a sample follow-up letter.

> Hand deliver your résumé if possible to enable the employer to match your name with a face. Dress well and look professional when you deliver your résumé. A day or two after you have delivered your résumé, be sure to follow up by writing a brief letter to the employer confirming the delivery of your résumé and thanking the employer for the chance to participate in the hiring process.

But *don't* become a pest. Too many letters or calls can just as easily land you in the "no" pile, identified as overly eager or unable to exercise enough common sense to known when it's "too much."

FOR MORE HELP

Bookstores and libraries have dozens of texts on résumé writing, each with its own particular advice. Other sources of information and assistance may be found online—search under the keyword "résumé." The references and URLs at the end of this chapter provide a start if you want to go into this topic in more detail or from other perspectives. If you are in college, your computer career center can be of help.

CONCLUSION

One of your most important job-seeking tools is the résumé. A résumé is a brief, well-documented summary of your education, abilities, skills, experience and career achievements, which highlights *significant* aspects of your background and identifies your qualifications for a given job. Its main purpose is to *sell* you to a prospective employer. But don't overdo it. Including too much data is a major fault of many résumés. And remember, *always* include a cover letter with your résumé, even when delivering the résumé in person.

AN INSIDER'S VIEW

THE RÉSUMÉ: A BALANCE OF MODESTY AND SELF-CONFIDENCE

Gil Kerlikowske

Former Police Commissioner
Buffalo (New York) Police Department

The law enforcement field offers a wide variety of employment opportunities. Police agencies operate with a number of specialists in areas such as finance, computer technology, planning and education as well as enforcement officers. Having hired individuals for these positions has given me an opportunity to review thousands of résumés. I have also served on search committees for CEOs. Nothing can be of more importance than the quality of the application and résumé submitted.

The cover letter should be specific to the individual job you are interested in. Photocopies and generic cover letters are an automatic turn-off to reviewers. The letter should be addressed to an individual, not "Personnel Department" or another title. Match your qualifications to those requested in the advertisement and keep the letter to one page. A balance between modesty and self-confidence is what you are striving for. If the letter shouts out how outstanding you are, the reviewer might question your sincerity to be a team member. On the other hand, you want to stand out from the hundreds of other applicants.

There are several types of résumés and numerous books to guide you in developing your individual résumé. If you have experience in the criminal justice field and are interested in a more senior position, I would recommend a style that illustrates experience and accomplishments. An applicant who is new to the field and is looking for an entry-level position should opt for a style that emphasizes their interest, education and dedication.

The résumé should also *fit the specific qualifications* the job requires. *Length* depends upon your experience and age. One to two pages is sufficient for entry-level positions and no more than four to five pages for management and executive positions. Education and specialized training (dates, course titles and degrees, of course) in an easily read style are a must. Where they are included is another style question; however, large-type headings for Education, Experience, Training, etc. make it easy to scan the résumé and check off important qualifications.

If you do not meet minimum qualifications, it is *generally* not worth your effort to apply for the position. Individual jobs just have too many applicants who *do* meet the requirements. However, if you know other positions you may be qualified for are going to become open, I suggest you *meet with someone* in that division to discuss your interest. Having someone in the department know your name and interest may be the extra push that helps you land the job you want in the future.

One automatic disqualifier for me has always been information that is not completely accurate. Most employers are careful to make sure individuals have the degrees and experience they claim. Areas of experience are more subjective. The rule of thumb is to be cautious in stating your qualifications. For example, if you once filled in for a crime prevention officer at a community meeting, do not cite experience as a crime prevention specialist.

Finally, photographs, copies of diplomas and other material are not necessary in an initial application. After you make the cut, those items may be requested. My personal feeling is that newspaper and magazine articles about you are self-serving. In the second or third phase of the employment process these materials, if they are focused on a program or unit you worked in or managed, are acceptable.

The employment process is different in every locality and can be frustrating and time-consuming. Professionalism and perseverance will be your greatest allies in finding the job you desire. And remember, nothing can be of more importance than the quality of the application and résumé submitted.

Gil Kerlikowske *is the former police commissioner for the Buffalo (New York) Police Department and has 26 years' experience in criminal justice. Prior to working in New York, Commissioner Kerlikowske was the chief of police in Fort Pierce, Florida, for four years. He holds an MA in Criminal Justice.*

INSIDER'S VIEW ONLINE

An additional *Insider's View* for this chapter is "Three Key Opportunities" by Chief Jim Clark, found on the Wadsworth website: http://www.wadsworth.com/criminaljustice_d/.

MIND STRETCHES

1. Imagine you have been assigned the task of reducing an extremely large pile of résumés to a more workable number. Regardless of the position, what are five reasons you can think of to get rid of applications right away?

2. What are three things you might look for that would make a résumé stand out as being worth taking time to look at further?

3. Paint with words the picture you want your résumé to make. Use three words. Use six words.

4. How can you liven up your résumé?

5. What might be dangerous about preparing a résumé that is too creative? What benefits might result?

6. What attributes do you have that will impress an employer?

7. What concerns do you have about your qualifications that you will need to consider in preparing your résumé?

8. What are five power verbs you associate with yourself?

9. Which résumé style could work best for you? Why?

10. What unique ways can you present your résumé?

REFERENCES

Barthel, Brea and Goldrick-Jones, Amanda. The Writing Center, Rensselaer Polytechnic Institute. Online: http://www.rpi.edu/web/writingcenter/resume.html

Challenger, John A. "Surprise! Resume Rules Have Changed." *Bottom Line Personal,* March 15, 2000, p. 6.

Hayes, Kit Harrington. "Scannable Resumes." *Bottom Line Personal,* September 15, 2000, p. 15.

Hofferber, Karen. "Breaking Tradition with a Functional Resume." Monster Career Center, 2004. Online: http://resume.monster.com/articles/functionalresume

Isaacs, Kim. "Ten Cover Letter Don'ts." Monster Career Center, 2004a. Online: http://resume.monster.com/coverletter/donot/

Isaacs, Kim. "Tips for Creating a Scannable Resume." Monster Career Center, 2004b. Online: http://resume.monster.com/articles/scannableresume/

JobWeb. Online: http://www.jobweb.com/resumes_interviews/resume_guide/res.htm

Land That Job! Online: http://www.landjob.com

Morem, Sue. "Don't Make Mistake of Erring with Résumé." (Minneapolis/St. Paul) *Star Tribune,* November 13, 2001, p. D2.

Newfield, Peter. "Ten Resume 'Don'ts'." Monster Career Center, 2004. Online: http://resume.monster.com/dosanddonts/resumedonts

Parker, Yana. *Damn Good Resume Guide*. Online: http://www.damngood.com

Razek, Rula. "Setting Your Sites on Finding a New Job." *USA Weekend,* August 31–September 2, 2001, p. 12.

Resume.com. Online: http://www.resume.com

Resume Logic. Online: http://www.resumelogic.com/index.htm

HELPFUL WEBSITES

http://10minuteresume.com
http://eresumes.com
http://collegegrad.com

CHAPTER 11

PREPARING FOR NOT GETTING THE JOB

Accept that some days you're the pigeon and some days you're the statue.

—Roger C. Anderson

Do You Know:

➢   What you can do to prepare for and effectively handle rejection in your job search?
➢   Why a support system is beneficial?
➢   The importance of maintaining a positive attitude?
➢   What emotions are part of the sequential reaction to loss and change?
➢   What feelings follow the transition curve?

INTRODUCTION

It's hard to get a job in these fields! It is most unusual for a person to get the first job they apply for. And because the job market today is changing so rapidly and downsizing is more prevalent than ever, you will find an increasing number of people competing for work. You should gain comfort in knowing that the vast majority of successful applicants were eventually successful because they had a lot of experience in the application process. In a negative situation, many people fail to take advantage of a great opportunity to gain from it. Energy *is* present, albeit uncomfortable, and can be rechanneled in a positive direction.

While the bulk of this book deals with how to get a job, this brief but important chapter deals with *not* getting a job—a realistic part of any job search. As Bolles (2004, p. 37) states: "Many if not most people find at times in their lives that the job-hunt is nothing but a long dreary process where, at the end, you may indeed find acceptance (a job). But prior to that it's a series of seemingly endless rejections." You need to know how to deal with failure in order to continue on. You may want to reread this chapter when you get that first, almost inevitable, rejection, to assure yourself that your feelings are normal and that you must go forward.

HANDLING REJECTION

Many adages apply to not obtaining something . . . and with good reason. We all experience rejection. Think about it: For every individual hired, many more did not get hired for that job. Everyone in the job-search market will face rejection, and the adages reflect this reality:

> *Failure is not falling down; it is remaining there when you have fallen.*
> *He who dares nothing need hope for nothing.*
> *The only time you mustn't fall is the last time you try. —Charles F. Kettering*

You may hear similar sentiments following a less-than-successful interview:

> There must be something better around the corner.
> They didn't deserve you. Besides, they're probably all jerks anyway.
> You can do better than that place.

These statements may be true, and you will no doubt hear them from your friends and family. After all, they want to support you. You will agree, of course, but inside you may be thinking things like:

> I knew I could never get that job.
> I'm no good.
> Everyone else is better than me.
> I'll never get a job.
> I should never have gone into this profession.
> Etc., etc., etc. . . .

If you are not careful, this negative "self-talk" might overwhelm you and become a self-fulfilling prophecy. If you get to the point that *you* don't believe in yourself, why should a *potential employer* believe in you? Remember, success comes in "cans"—failure comes in "can'ts."

Tell yourself everyone must take their share of rejection. Sure, some take a little more, some take a little less, but everyone takes it. It's simply part of looking for a job. If you understand ahead of time the reality of rejection and are prepared for it, when the first one hits you, it's not likely to knock you down so hard. And if you're one of those fortunate few who hears "yes" on the first try, way to go! You beat the odds on this one. For the rest of us, each "no" we hear brings us one step closer to that "yes" . . . as long as we don't give up. Keep in mind: It takes an average of two years to land an entry-level job in law enforcement.

It has been said the average job seeker must send out ten résumés to get one interview, and that it takes an average of ten interviews to get one job offer. If you do the math, you'll see that it takes the average person 100 résumés to receive one job offer. That's 99 "nos" for every one "yes"! So don't get discouraged—the "yes" will come.

 Try this exercise: Take a deck of standard playing cards and shuffle them well. Pretend every face card is a job interview and that one of them, say the queen of hearts, is a job *offer* following a dynamite interview. The rest of the deck (aces through tens) are flat-out "nos." With the deck facedown and starting with the top card, flip over cards until you get an interview. How many flips did it take? Flip again until your next interview. Try this several times and you'll get the picture. Sometimes you get an interview on the first flip; sometimes it takes seventeen flips and then you get four interviews in a row—and the queen of hearts is one of them! Or she could be at the bottom of the deck, under 51 rejections. But she's there. If you stop flipping after the fourth, fourteenth or even forty-fourth "no," you'll never get to her.

No one ever said job hunting was easy. For all practical purposes, job hunting will have to be a full-time job itself, at least for awhile. If it isn't full-time timewise, it will be energywise. But, in the beginning, you'll probably believe rejection could never happen to you.

It's similar to the "It Can Never Happen to Me" syndrome frequently heard in discussions of officer safety. The idea is that an officer's daily existence would be too difficult if he or she thought that harm or perhaps death was lurking around every corner. Officers instinctively develop the "It Can Never Happen to Me" attitude in order to continue on with their day-to-day lives. To a certain degree it helps prevent them from becoming hopelessly paranoid. Problems arise, however, when all caution is thrown to the wind. Police, corrections and security officers must accept the natural risks associated with their jobs, but they must also be prepared. They must be realistic. Similarly, job applicants must balance the risks. If you know you're going to be rejected, why even try? This is what happens to some job seekers who start out feeling they will never be rejected. Two or three rejections turn them into defeatists who simply go through the motions.

Consider the applicant who had become so defeated after several "thanks but no thanks" letters that when he woke up on the morning of an interview and found that it was raining, the weather became the last straw. He decided to stay in bed. This would-be police officer made it easy for the employer to weed out one more applicant. Who does this applicant really have to blame for this failure?

Success is getting up one more time than you fall down. Make up your mind right now to accept the facts of job seeking.

➤   Fact #1: Criminal justice and security are *very* popular, sought-after, competitive jobs.

➤   Fact #2: You're up against many, many applicants.

➤   Fact #3: Eventually you will get hired IF you're right for the job.

The benefit of having to repeat the application process is that you will improve each time. The downside is that it can get you down. The choice is *yours*.

> To prepare for and effectively handle rejection in your job search, be aware that it does happen to just about everyone and that the only ones who fail are the ones who stop trying. Avoid negative self-talk and never lose faith in yourself. Each "no" brings you closer to a "yes."

Bolles (pp. 37–38) describes the "rejection shock" experienced by many job hunters searching for that elusive "yes":

> You thought this was going to be easy, you thought this was going to be fast, but you're *striking out* again and again. Consequently, you experience "rejection shock"—caught totally by surprise by the difference between the vision you had, and the way in which it's actually unfolding, and the feeling that there is something totally wrong with *you*.
>
> Typically, job-hunters fight "rejection shock" by lowering their expectations, sinking into depression, feeling a real desperation and despair. Rejection shock can assume all the proportions of a major crisis in your life, your personal relations and your family, leading to withdrawal (often), or estrangement (frequently)—where divorce is often a consequence and even suicide may be contemplated.
>
> And you learn—oh, how you learn!—that the worst outcome of a job-hunt is not what you thought it was. You thought that it was that you wouldn't find a job. Now you know differently: the worst possible outcome of a job-hunt is that you lose your self-esteem.

To avoid this damaging loss of self-esteem, it is crucial for you to be realistic, know the odds you are working against (an average of 99 "nos" for every "yes") and maintain a positive attitude.

REMAINING POSITIVE

You can and, in fact, must turn the negative energy from rejection into positive momentum. Rather than giving up, become determined to strive that much harder, knowing you are stronger and more polished. How does that saying go? *That which doesn't kill me makes me stronger.* It's what makes a boxer or any other professional athlete more determined—what's often referred to as "having the heart of a champion." No one likes to be turned down, especially for a desperately wanted job. But it is bound to happen, and it is going to sting. It does not get any easier the second, third or sixth time. In fact, the more you are turned down, the heavier it may weigh on you.

Maintain a positive attitude. To deal most effectively with that most common part of job hunting—the rejection—keep the following basics in mind:

➤   Go into the process understanding you probably will have to try for several jobs. With so many applicants, the odds are against you.

➤   Not getting this job does not mean you deserve to be banished from the planet. It simply means you did not get this one job.

➤   Another job is just around the corner (trite, but true). Avoid the temptation to believe that a particular job is your one-and-only dream job.

➤   If you need help, *ask for it!* No law says you must go it alone. If you are not confident about your job-seeking skills, seek help. If you get depressed, seek help. Just ask—not always easy for officer-types!

➤   Most important—keep trying. You've come this far. It is no time to give up. *Listen* when everyone tells you that you can get a job. You can. Just give yourself time.

Take advantage of everyone else's understanding of rejection and build a support system from the start. It really helps to talk, and you might be surprised by how many people have experienced similar rejection. Besides, there *is* strength in numbers.

> Support systems are valuable because they allow you to talk out your frustrations and realize you are not the only one who has ever felt rejection—everyone else has experienced it too. People in your support system may be able to share what worked for them in getting past their rejection.

Do not be afraid to get support and help if you need it—professional or otherwise. Frustration and disappointment is normal. Do not let it get the best of you. Negative feelings can become overwhelming, and they can also be self-perpetuating. Feeling depressed and gloomy often leads to deeper feelings of depression and gloominess. Besides not feeling good, they can sap so much of your energy that your interview skills become less than adequate, and you will not perform as you need to.

Employers are very aware of how much competition you have—they have to sit through all those interviews! What would happen if you went into your tenth interview all worn out and depressed and the next person after you was upbeat and positive because it was only their first interview? Presenting the same energy and freshness during your tenth interview that you possessed at your first one will not only leave a positive impression on the interviewer but will help fuel positive feelings in yourself. You have a choice: You can come out of the interview feeling even worse because you *knew* you were mopey and unenthusiastic, or you can come out feeling great because you gave it your best shot.

In short, if you do not deal with the uncomfortable feelings that go along with rejection, you will eventually come to believe that you do not deserve to be hired, and it will show. Pick up and press on.

> Remaining positive is crucial to a successful job search. A positive attitude leaves a favorable impression on an employer, and it helps fuel positive feelings in yourself.

To help handle the sense of failure you may feel when your job search seems to lead only to rejection, keep in mind the words of Bill Gates (2000): "Once you embrace unpleasant news not as negative but as evidence of a need for change, you aren't defeated by it. You're *learning* from it."

LEARNING FROM THE PROCESS

Ask prospective employers who turned you down what could have made a difference. If approached in a nonthreatening way, people will usually be honest and open. As one employer states: "I was impressed several times by young applicants who, after being turned down for a job, called and made an appointment to visit with me to discuss their job-hunting strategies. I even ended up hiring a couple of them."

Bolles (p. 13) states: "As job-expert Richard Lathrop observed long ago, the person who gets hired is not necessarily the best person for the job, but the one who knows the most about how to get hired." Recognize that, sometimes, the fact you didn't get a particular job may not have had anything to do with you. There may have been factors at play beyond your control, and even if you had done everything "right," that specific job was not meant to be yours.

NORMAL REACTION TO LOSS

The fear of the unknown is always the worst. Since it helps to know what to expect, here's a brief explanation of what many people experience when they lose something (such as a death in the family, a ruined relationship or a lost job opportunity). Called the *sequential reaction to loss and change,* it describes how many people *normally* act when they lose something important. If you get a rejection, you may feel the following, in roughly this order:

➢ Denial

➢ Anger

➢ Sadness

➢ Hopelessness

➢ Disorganization

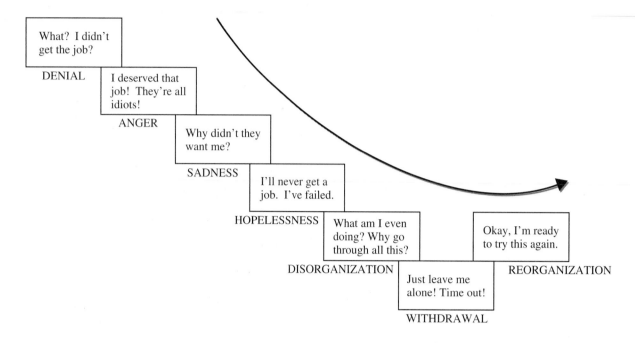

FIGURE 11–1   **Sequential Reaction to Loss and Change**

➤   Withdrawal

➤   Reorganization

This sequential reaction to loss and change is illustrated in Figure 11–1.

Denial. This is the "It can never happen to me" phase, and it's completely normal. It hasn't quite sunk in yet that you didn't get the job. Denial helps by keeping you from getting too hurt from rejection(s). It can be harmful, however, if you don't move on or get too hung up on that rejection (possibly thinking that this is the only job in the world for you). Accepting the loss is a necessary step on the journey to being able to continue on with life.

Anger. Once you have accepted the rejection, the understandable response is anger. "I wanted that job! I deserved that job! They won't get away with this! The process is unfair!" These things may be true, but the fact is you did not get the job. Staying angry too long will, at best, depress you and, at worst, drive you to do something you may later regret, like writing a nasty letter, making a nasty phone call or paying a hostile visit to the employer. It's in your best interest to not burn bridges, should another opportunity arise there in the future. The anger must be dealt with. The challenge is to find an appropriate outlet.

Sadness. After the anger subsides, you may feel sad. Sadness can run from a mild case of the blues to a bout with deep depression. It depends on many factors and reflects the absolute need of a strong support system as you seek work. Don't beat up on yourself too much if you feel down. Who doesn't after rejection? Many people tend to ignore it because being "sad" is not their style. However, rather than fight it, accept it, draw some energy from it, and move on. If it becomes overwhelming to the point of your being unable to continue the job search, or if it begins to seriously affect other areas of your life, get help. You need to work through the sadness, but not let it consume you and keep you from moving on.

Hopelessness. Hopelessness may occur as the feelings of anger and depression subside. The hopelessness may seem overwhelming, but it is a normal part of adapting to rejection. The natural assumption after one or more employers reject you is that you are unemployable. No one wants you. This is not true. It simply means those jobs did not work out. You have to keep going, which isn't always easy because of the natural progression of feelings.

Disorganization. At this point you may want to continue on, but nothing seems to fit anymore. You find it hard to organize your time or your thoughts. You spend time haphazardly reading help-wanted ads and making futile attempts to schedule a productive day. Frustration may set in, and you may simply give up.

Withdrawal. Wanting to give up or withdraw is also natural. It is understandable that you are frustrated, uncomfortable and wanting to simply quit. This is how your psyche lets you rest, regroup and get ready to jump into the battle again. Rather than fight the desire to withdraw, help it along. Get away from job hunting for awhile. Go to a movie, take a long walk or even go on a vacation. Retreat and regroup. Do not, however, withdraw by skipping scheduled interviews or by showing up and not putting forth your best effort. If you need a break, take it.

Reorganization. At last! You have worked through the normal feelings associated with being rejected. Here is where you are getting closer to the pot of gold at the end of the rainbow. Having worked through the previous emotional stages, you're now ready to get back out there and get that job.

The progression of feelings involved in the sequential reaction to loss and change are denial, anger, sadness, hopelessness, disorganization, withdrawal and, finally, reorganization.

According to Nathan and Hill (1992, p. 30), many other people go through a somewhat different set of feelings, a pattern they refer to as *the transition curve,* which is characterized by the following chain of reactions:

> *Shock, denial:* Unable to believe that it has happened. "You're joking!" A feeling of emptiness, perhaps numbness.
> *Euphoria:* Making the best of it, and minimizing the reality of the change. "Now I've got time to . . . paint the house, take a holiday . . .—I didn't like the job anyway."
> *Pining:* Hoping that the job will come back—an unrealistic expectation that the next job will be exactly the same.
> *Anger:* Blaming someone—"I never could work with him (my boss) anyway." "They should have . . ."
> *Guilt:* Self-blame—"They chose me because I wasn't up to it/did something wrong."
> *Apathy:* A sense of powerlessness and hopelessness as the reality sinks in.
> *Acceptance:* Letting go of the past, and the emergence of a new energy.

Nathan and Hill's transition curve is illustrated in Figure 11–2.

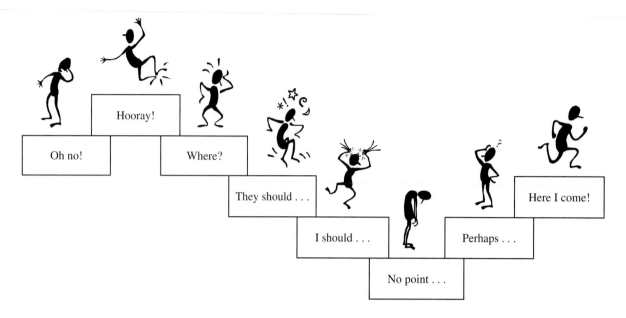

FIGURE 11–2   The Transition Curve

SOURCE: Robert Nathan and Linda Hill. *Career Counseling,* p. 30, © 1992 by Sage Publications, Inc. Reprinted by permission of Sage Publications, Inc.

> Another common progression of feelings following rejection are those of the transition curve, namely, shock or denial, euphoria, pining, anger, guilt, apathy and acceptance.

Regardless of the intensity of the feelings you experience following rejection, how long it takes you to work through the negative feelings depends on how serious the rejection is. The first rejection is not as bad as the second. The more rejections, or the more important a job is to you, the more extreme your reactions may be. Remember: Accept the inevitable and understand that this is how it is going to feel. There is strength in self-awareness. As George Bernard Shaw says: "Better keep yourself clean and bright; you are the window through which you must see the world."

CONCLUSION

The knowledgeable, prepared applicant understands and accepts that *everybody* experiences these negative feelings when they lose something they want. To prepare for and effectively handle rejection in your job search, be aware that it does happen to just about everyone and that the only ones who fail are the ones who stop trying. Avoid negative self-talk and never lose faith in yourself. Each "no" brings you closer to a "yes." But whatever setbacks you may experience, "nos" you may hear or rejection you may feel, DO NOT GIVE UP!

> *You may be disappointed if you fail, but you are doomed if you don't try.*
>
> *—Beverly Sills*

AN INSIDER'S VIEW

EACH FAILURE IS ONE STEP CLOSER TO SUCCESS

Timothy J. Thompson

Vice President
Verification, Inc.

Accomplishing your employment objective is often not in your control. Any decision to hire involves many factors. Since you're looking at the situation of *not* getting the job offer, let's analyze the hiring process to understand why you sometimes don't have control. As discussed in previous chapters, the hiring process involves three main areas:

➢   Education—what you've been taught
➢   Work history—what you've done
➢   The interview—how you appear

One other additional component of the hiring process is vital in employee selection: *who* is doing the hiring. If you know someone involved in the hiring process or are related to the president of the company, your chances of getting the job are obviously many times better than those without such connections.

How the hiring is done and by whom often differs greatly from agency to agency and firm to firm, making it hard for applicants. To be properly prepared, you must research the hiring process as well as the position. The process may involve a simple application to a company president or personnel manager or may be much more complex, involving panels and boards. Because the process is not uniform, the people doing the hiring are not always proficient at employee selection. Many do not have practical experience to adequately evaluate the ability and qualifications of applicants. Police commissions and selection boards are good examples of such lack of practical experience. All too often the hiring groups are made up largely of community laypeople, lacking professional credentials in the field for which applicants are applying. Even city managers and personnel directors sometimes lack experience in hiring to make good choices.

So where does this leave you? Well, when the candidates appear on paper to be equally qualified (i.e., their educational credentials and work history are very similar), the selection comes down to an interview and personalities. With so many variables operating, no one can pick a favorite. But if you have an outstanding résumé, you can make yourself appear more qualified than the rest. How? Consider these guidelines.

Your résumé should reflect information pertinent to the position for which you are applying. Entry-level positions should generally be a page or two, tops, but should contain information necessary to qualify for the position. Employers have neither the time nor the interest to read lengthy résumés for entry-level positions. In these cases, the cover letter will help sell your qualifications.

For nonentry-level positions where prior experience is desired or required, additional information can be added to the résumé and cover letter. This information should include specific experiences and accomplishments but, again, should be brief. If you are applying for a management position, your résumé can, and in some cases should, include as much information as possible regarding your background, education, experiences and achievements. However, this information should be compiled in an easy-to-read format with appropriate headings and short paragraphs. Employers seeking managers want to know as much about the applicant as possible before the interview. This is why telephone interviews are becoming more popular with personnel recruiters. It is better to have the information already prepared on your résumé than to have to think about it when someone calls. And your chance of getting that call improves the more the recruiter is impressed with your submitted credentials.

I have discovered that my ability to conduct interviews and effectively examine applicants' backgrounds to determine job suitability has dramatically increased with experience. Unfortunately, many management people, selection boards, firms and the like lack adequate experience to hire effectively. It is no wonder many people are performing jobs for which they are unsuited. It is also no wonder that perhaps you and your talent are being overlooked. Even when you have done all your homework, researched each position, individualized your application and résumé for the job, looked for inside people to help and prepared for each interview separately, you still may not get the position.

It is easy to become frustrated, bitter and resentful when you have worked so hard to prepare and you feel so confident in your ability to perform the job—given the chance. Remember, you are seeking employment in extremely popular fields, and you have plenty of competition. You do not have to give up, however. You *will* get a job that is right for you. And it may come when you least expect it. I know how frustrating it is to get rejection letters. I have a file full of them. I want to share from my experience some do's and don'ts related to the feelings of frustration and hopelessness involved in being rejected for a job.

DO

➢ Develop a support system. It is important to have an avenue to vent your feelings. Find an understanding friend who will listen while you express these feelings.

➢ Keep networking. The more people you know, the better your chances of learning about job openings. Often when you least expect it, a job will appear. Just ask some friends and acquaintances how they got their jobs.

➢ Look for alternatives. Often people get tunnel vision when looking for jobs, limiting themselves to one particular area when in fact they have abilities in many areas. You may want to be a police officer, but what about other possibilities such as being a U.S. Marshal, a state fraud enforcement officer, a postal inspector, an FAA enforcement officer, an FBI secret service agent and on and on.

➢ Consider relocating as an option if possible.

➢ Use the Internet for your job search.

DON'T

➢ Don't spend every minute worrying about your job situation. Take time for other things, especially recreation. Remember, a job often appears when you least expect it.

➢ Don't give up. Talk with friends. Acquaint yourself with other people in your chosen field. Join associations.

➢ Don't make compulsive decisions. This is no time to make major changes in either your employment situation or your lifestyle. Do not, for example, pack up and move to Florida because you believe more job opportunities exist there, unless you really want to live in Florida. Nor should you buy a house or new car because you think it will make you feel better.

Hang in there. Press on. You *can* and *will* land that job.

Timothy J. Thompson *is a vice president for Verifications, Inc., a private detective agency. Mr. Thompson holds private detective licenses in more than 20 states. He is also a security trainer and security consultant performing security audits and assessments.*

His background includes more than 20 years in public law enforcement, serving as police chief for 7 years, and 19 years in the private sector, holding top management positions with Canterbury Downs Racetrack, Shakopee, Minnesota (security director); the Thoroughbred Racing Protective Bureau, Fairhill, Maryland (special agent); Minnesota Timberwolves, Minneapolis, Minnesota (arena manager and human resources director); and the University of St. Thomas, St. Paul, Minnesota (director of public safety and parking services). His experience includes managing, investigating, assessing needs, designing and planning security departments and communications centers, and writing policy and procedure manuals. He also has extensive knowledge in electronic security equipment as well as access control and card systems, risk management and parking services.

INSIDER'S VIEW ONLINE

An additional *Insider's View* for this chapter is "Life's Greatest Rewards Can't Be Measured in Dollars and Cents" by Penny A. Parrish, found on the website: http://www.wadsworth.com/criminaljustice_d/.

 MIND STRETCHES

1.   What benefits can come from *not* getting a job?

2.   Why is it helpful to understand the sequential reaction to loss and change and the transition curve?

3.   Why is it harmful to ignore negative feelings arising from a rejection to an application?

4.   Why would someone ignore these feelings?

5.   Do you think applicants for criminal justice or security jobs are less likely to deal with their feelings? Why?

6.   Why do you think unsuccessful candidates might lash out at an employer who didn't hire them? Could this ever be successful?

7.   Is there ever one perfect job?

8.   Is there danger in believing there *is* one perfect job?

9.   Who is included in your support system? How can you best use them?

10. Can you think of "failures" or "losses" in your life that actually benefited you?

REFERENCES

Bolles, Richard Nelson. *What Color Is Your Parachute? A Practical Manual for Job-Hunters & Career-Changers.* Berkeley, CA: Ten Speed Press, 2004.

Gates, Bill. *Business @ the Speed of Thought: Succeeding in the Digital Economy.* New York: Warner Business Books, 2000.

Nathan, Robert and Hill, Linda. *Career Counseling.* Newbury Park, CA: Sage Publications, 1992.

SECTION THREE

JOB-SEEKING STRATEGIES

A wise man will make more opportunities than he finds.

—*Francis Bacon*

You've decided what you're looking for in a career. You've also closely examined your personal characteristics and have found a fit. You've created an impressive résumé to demonstrate that fit to potential employers. And you're prepared to handle rejections. You're ready. Where to find jobs and how to get them is the focus of this section. Chapter 12 looks at the application process. It takes you through various strategies for locating job openings and making your availability and interest known. It discusses the importance of the application form and the role of your résumé, and it reviews the testing process.

If all goes well to this point, you will be invited for a personal interview. The basics of presenting yourself for an interview are the focus of Chapter 13—how to dress, communicate and follow up. Chapter 14 takes a closer look at the all-important interview process and what to expect from it. Figure S3 illustrates the steps you've already completed and what lies ahead.

FIGURE S3   Job-Search Steps

SOURCE: Ronald L. Krannich. *Change Your Job, Change Your Life,* 5th ed. Manassas Park, VA: Impact Publications, 1995, p. 101. Reprinted by permission.

CHAPTER 12

THE APPLICATION PROCESS:
FINDING AND APPLYING FOR JOBS

(1) Regard job hunting as a real job—and expect that it, like any other job, demands time, persistence, and discipline. (2) Recognize that while you can get a good job through ads or employment agencies, competition for jobs that are advertised tends to be fierce. (3) Apply directly to an employer even without any hint there is a job opening. Positions constantly become available and it's wise to be on a good list. (4) Try to get as many job interviews as you can and concentrate on smaller firms. (5) If you can see a layoff coming, start looking for a job while you are still working. (6) Expect to be discouraged. Guard against anger, apathy, or feeling defeated.

—Sylvia Porter

Do You Know:

➤ What you must identify before beginning your job search and how many hours you should spend each week looking for work?
➤ Which ads to read in the classified section of the paper and which papers to look in?
➤ What specialized periodicals to review?
➤ How the Internet can help?
➤ The variety of other places to check for leads on job openings in your field?
➤ The importance of looking and acting your best during any contact with a potential employer?
➤ How to make contact with a prospective employer by mail?
➤ What networking is and how important it is to your job search? Who you should talk to?
➤ Why it is important to never "burn your bridges"?
➤ What the entire application process usually involves?
➤ What information the application form usually asks for and what impact the Equal Employment Opportunity (EEO) guidelines have had on these application forms?
➤ The importance of follow-up?

INTRODUCTION

Although waiting to hear about a job opening may work once in a great while, you usually must *look* for work. More accurately, you have to *work at finding work*. Serious job searchers find that pursuing employment requires as much, if not more, effort than a full-time job and that a well-thought-out strategy is essential. A well-developed search demands action. No one who creeps or shuffles along a career path can expect success in this competitive world. They will be trampled over by people who really want to work and to advance. Unmotivated, unenthusiastic, undirected individuals are easily identified and weeded out by employers. Employers are looking for that *special* applicant who exudes drive, energy and genuine enthusiasm. Develop your strategy so you not only maintain the energy necessary to pursue your career goals, but so your energy *shines brightly* to employers.

Don't just plan to look for work. Chase it! Hustle! Scramble! Be creative! Have fun! Turn what can be a frustrating experience into a personal challenge. Each disappointment, each new challenge, is part of the training that will let you succeed. *Get what you want!* Let the process feed you, not defeat you.

If this all sounds a bit too "rah! rah!"—the opposite of the stoic, macho attitude police officers, corrections officers, security personnel and those in related fields are "supposed" to exhibit—think again. Employers are looking for *real* people who truly want the job and will, in turn, do a great job for them. Job hunting is frustrating at times, so you *need* to keep yourself charged up for the process.

DEVELOPING YOUR JOB-SEARCH STRATEGY

To keep on track—physically, emotionally and intellectually—you have to develop a strategy. The first step is to determine *what* you are looking for. Even the smaller newspapers have an incredible number of employment want ads. The unemployed are frequently asked, "How can you not have a job? Hundreds (thousands) are advertised for!" True, but take a closer look. You are not going to apply for every job advertised. Somewhere between *actuarial* and *zookeeper* are the jobs you will consider.

Begin with the questions: "What do I want? How do I get it?" If nothing short of police officer will satisfy you, do not apply for private security positions. On the other hand, might a position as an armored-truck driver, for instance, be a good stepping-stone to lead to your end goal? Unless you are desperate for money, taking a full-time position of no interest or value to your career goals could result in several problems. For example, say you start applying randomly, get a job in an unrelated field and eventually quit for a job you probably should have waited for in the first place. This could make you look like a "job jumper," create hard feelings with that employer when you leave and maybe result in a negative reference.

This doesn't mean you should sit at home unemployed until you get your "dream" job. For a variety of reasons, including financial and emotional, it is frequently much easier to get a job when you have a job. What is important is to identify what you want before going after it. Then, if you are completely employment-free, you must dedicate yourself to finding work as if the search itself was a full-time, 40-hours-a-week job. Bolles (2004, p. xi) states bluntly:

> It has been a rough year. A lot of people are out of work. And job-hunting has been a bitch, as they say out on the street. . . . In times such as these, it is well to keep certain basic truths in mind:
>
> 1. There are always jobs out there. (People get injured, or sick, quit, retire, or die).
> 2. There are a number of ways to look for them.
> 3. If you can't find the jobs that are out there, it's because you're using the wrong method to look for them.
> 4. If you can't find the jobs that are out there, you need to change your job-hunting method.
> 5. If you can't find the kind of job you've done before, you need to consider a career change—based on the fact that your functional skills are transferable from one field to another.
> 6. The key to job-hunting success is hope, and perseverance.

According to Bolles (p. 42): "Experts say one out of every three job-hunters in the U.S. becomes an unsuccessful job-hunter, *because they abandon their job-hunt prematurely.* And if you ask them why they abandoned it, they say, 'I didn't think it was going to take this long. And I ran out of energy.'" Your job-search strategy must include perseverance and a willingness to approach job seeking as a full-time endeavor. Bolles (p. 72) suggests:

> To speed up your search for one of the jobs that *are* out there, *you must think of yourself as having already found a job.* Your job, in this case, is that of hunting for work. . . . Even when the *world* would think of you as "unemployed," *you* must think of yourself as having a full-time job (without pay) from 9 to 5 every weekday.

> I emphasize this nine-to-five business, because studies have revealed the depressing fact that two-thirds of all job-hunters spend 5 hours or less hunting for a job each week.

> *You* must spend 35 hours a week, at least, on your search. . . . That should cut down, dramatically, the number of weeks it takes you to find work—more so than any other factor.

It is important to identify what you want before going after it. Then you must make job hunting a full-time commitment, spending 35–40 hours a week actively searching for work if you are currently unemployed.

WHERE TO LOOK FOR JOB OPENINGS

There are many avenues to explore when searching for job openings. Some are more effective than others. The best results are typically achieved by looking in several directions instead of focusing all efforts down one, narrow path. Bolles (p. 48) advises:

> A . . . recent study uncovered the fact that the likelihood of your uncovering those jobs that are out there *increases* with each additional method that you use, but only *up to four*. If you use more than four methods, your likelihood of uncovering those jobs that are out there starts to *decrease*. . . .

> The explanation may lie in the fact that if you try to do more than four methods you will end up not doing any of them very well.

Your options include checking newspaper want ads, specialty periodicals and job postings on the Internet; visiting government employment service offices and college or university placement offices; networking with family, friends and acquaintances; making personal inquiries at potential employers' places of business; and picking up the phone and calling prospective employers.

Newspapers

Begin with the most obvious place to look for employment—newspaper want ads. After watching the local papers daily for several weeks, you will identify the generally accepted procedure employers in various fields use to advertise for employees. Ads for law enforcement positions, for instance, are usually placed in the Sunday paper, under the heading of "police." Private security positions generally appear under the heading of "security." Is this how it is always done? Of course not.

Think creatively. Ads for police officers could appear under such headings as "law enforcement," "public safety" or "officer." Corrections positions may appear under "prisons," "jails," "guards" and the like.

Security jobs may appear under the title of "risk management" or "loss control." Take time to familiarize yourself with all the possible headings your job could fall under and continue to scan the entire listing.

Perhaps a clerk or a secretary placed the ad without knowing anything about the actual job and thought "safety officer" or even "city employee" or "state employee" would be the best spot. Maybe the ad will appear, accidentally or purposely, on a Tuesday only. Do not let yourself get lazy just because such ads are usually in the Sunday paper under a specific section.

 Under what other headings might a police position appear? List them in your journal.

 Under what other headings might a private security position appear? List them in your journal.

 If considering a related field, under what headings might it appear? Note these in your journal.

Job openings are usually placed in the classified ads that appear in columns, row after row. Take time, however, to also check the display (box) ads used most frequently by corporations. These bigger ads are more expensive, but occasionally a city or private employer that wants to state specific needs or is particularly in need of people will use this approach. Scan ALL the newspaper want ads.

Also consider the possibility of ads appearing in papers other than those published in your particular city. A Minneapolis job seeker, for instance, should check the St. Paul newspaper. The Oakland job seeker should check a San Francisco paper. The Seattle job seeker should be looking in a Tacoma paper. Read the local and neighborhood papers as well as those of surrounding cities.

> Begin your job search with the most obvious place to look for employment—newspaper want ads. Think creatively and scan ALL the ads. In addition to your local and neighborhood papers, check the papers of surrounding cities.

Bolles (p. 44) cautions, however: "This search method has a 5–24% success rate. That is, out of every 100 job-hunters who use this search method, between 5 and 24 will find a job thereby. 76–95 job-hunters out of 100 will not find the jobs that are out there—if they use only this method to search for them."

Many Jobs Aren't Advertised. It is essential to know that many jobs are either not advertised or are actually filled before an ad is placed. How could that be? Probably because an aggressive job seeker with an effective strategy found a way in (long before you ever became aware of the job opening), either by having established a relationship with the employer (perhaps as an intern) or by making the employer aware of their interest before the job opening existed. Frequently, in such cases, an ad is run because of department policy or to meet a legal obligation. Your strategy, then, is to learn about these jobs before these probabilities occur. Just because an employer doesn't yet know a job will open up doesn't mean you should not be trying for it.

Specialty Periodicals and Other Publications

Every field has trade publications. Law enforcement, corrections and private security have many journals, often containing ads. Such periodicals as *The Police Chief, Law and Order, Corrections Today, The*

Prison Journal, Corrections Compendium and *Security Management* not only contain position openings at the higher levels, but also contain current information beneficial to individuals applying in these fields.

Other publications deal with more general topics and could contain an ad for your job. For example, magazines that deal with municipal government could contain such ads. Become familiar with a variety of specialty periodicals. Also become familiar with periodicals that list only jobs. One such publication of particular interest to those seeking employment in law enforcement and private security is the *National Employment Listing Service,* which contains only related employment opportunities.

Other specific publications address only city, county, state or federal jobs. If not contained in such specialized publications, they will usually be posted. If you are interested in a federal job, the *Federal Jobs Register* is a valuable resource. Another source for federal positions or for positions out of the country is the U.S. Civil Service Commission (the address is given at the end of the chapter). *Job Search Guide: Strategies for Professionals* is a U.S. Department of Labor publication that discusses specific steps job seekers should follow to identify employment opportunities.

> Every field has trade publications. Check the specialty periodicals associated with your chosen field, whether it's police work, corrections, private security or a related criminal justice field.

Again, bear in mind what Bolles (p. 44) found regarding answering ads in professional or trade journals: "This search method . . . has a 7% success rate. . . . 93 job-hunters out of 100 will not find the jobs that are out there if they use only this method to search for them." Despite this dismally low success rate, Bolles points out there is at least one other job-search avenue with a worse track record—the Internet.

The Internet

According to Bolles (p. 16): "No one agrees on the *number* of Internet sites currently devoted to job-hunting—some experts say 1,000; some say 5,000; some, 10,000; some 40,000; and some, 100,000 or more. But all agree on the *purpose* of Internet sites devoted to job hunting. And that is, to make it easier for job-hunters and employers to find each other. It is, indeed, far far easier than it was back in 1985." He (p. 19) provides the following statistics regarding online job hunters:

➢   Traffic to job-hunting websites increased 80% from 1999 to 2000.

➢   67% of all Web users expect to conduct their next job search online.

➢   40% of *new* Web users come online specifically to look for employment opportunities.

➢   These are not necessarily the young, as one might expect. In fact, the age group most represented among online job-seekers are people with 21 or more years' experience in the workplace.

Furthermore, Bolles (p. 34) notes: "There are, as it turns out, five ways in which the Internet can help you when you are job-hunting: 1. **Testing** and **counseling.** 2. **Research**—of fields, jobs, organizations, and salaries. 3. **Networking**—establishing contact with people, as sources of information, contacts, and referrals. 4. **Job-postings.** And of course 5. **Resume-postings.**"

Yet, despite its popularity among job seekers and its *potential* to connect job hunters and prospective employers, the Internet has yet to prove itself as a premier avenue in helping people land jobs. Bolles (p. 31) laments: "In fact—alas and alack!—it only works a depressingly small percentage of the time. For a host of reasons, most jobs are not filled through the Internet." Results of several studies reveal that only 4 percent of Internet-using job seekers actually landed their most recent job by going online, and a mere 8 percent of employers' "new hires" were culled from the Internet (Bolles, p. 32). He (pp. 32–35) offers some statistics to explain why online job hunting so often goes awry:

> According to one study, 74% of online job-hunters experienced some degree of failure in applying for a job online, and 40% ended in complete failure. . . . Poorly designed job-sites were often the problem: broken links, pages that won't open, navigation systems that just don't work. . . .
>
> And even if your job application does go through, it can take an organization *forever* to work its way through the follow-up hiring cycle. . . . In many cases . . . up to 81 days . . . *that job-hunters are kept waiting for an answer. . . .*
>
> Some online job-hunters don't start with employers' job postings. They start by posting their own resume online—optimistic, hopeful, and impatient. . . . Of those [job-hunters] who placed resumes online . . . forty-five percent received no responses at all.

Thus, of the five previously noted ways the Internet can help job hunters, two methods (job postings and résumé postings) are relatively ineffective and can leave job hunters disappointed. However: "Some of these—research, and counseling in particular—work so well, that the 74% dissatisfaction we saw earlier with respect to just job-postings, is cut in half overall" (Bolles, p. 34).

Newspapers from across the country can be accessed over the Internet, making it much easier to research job openings in a variety of locations. Furthermore, you may access the ever-increasing number of websites available on the Internet to learn more about a specific company, organization, agency or even community. Go online and search for the agencies, companies or general locations you might be interested in.

Computer bulletin boards are becoming popular for interacting (networking) with others having similar interests and for finding information on a particular topic. A computerized job network system—*America's Job Bank*—is run by the U.S. Department of Labor and lists approximately 50,000 job openings a week.

The Internet has become an increasingly valuable resource, not so much for actual job listings but for researching specific agencies and communities where career opportunities are available.

Government Employment and Educational Placement Offices

The serious job hunter routinely stops at the federal, state, county and municipal offices every week or two to check job postings and to ask what job openings are available or anticipated. For law enforcement employment, one of the best information sources at the local level is the city or county personnel office. You may be able to subscribe to job listings used by government agencies as well as the privately published services. These are often quite expensive, so become familiar with what your local libraries have. Regularly review these sources.

Placement offices at colleges and universities that offer programs in law enforcement, corrections, criminal justice or private security often post job notices and have excellent employment listing services. Contact the career services office on campus for a list of current openings. These offices also coordinate interviews with agencies looking to hire and have reference libraries or agencies throughout the world. Know where to look and what to look for, and regularly watch postings and other resources. A list of such resources is provided at the following website: http://www.wadsworth.com/criminaljustice_d/. Be sure to check out the "Student Lounge" section there.

Networking

How many times have you heard the expression: "It's not what you know but *who* you know"? Rarely will there come a time in life when this saying is more true than when you are searching for employment. Family members, friends, neighbors, people you know through church, people whose kids go to the same school as your kids, other soccer moms and hockey dads, the guy you sweat next to on the treadmill at the gym every other morning—these are all the "who" resources you can tap for leads in the job market. According to Bolles (p. 46): "You ask them one simple question: do you know of any jobs at the place where you work—or elsewhere? This search method has a 33% success rate. . . . This is one of the five best ways to look for a job, but it should be noted that no job-hunting method is 'bulletproof.' No method works all the time and for everybody." The importance of networking will be discussed again shortly.

Personal Inquiries

Another approach to inquiring about a position is to stop in. Bolles (p. 46) notes: "Knocking on the door of any employer, factory, or office that interests you, whether they are known to have a vacancy or not . . . has a 47% success rate." However, this method can be *risky*. First, most employers are extremely busy and usually do not have or take time to visit with someone who has no appointment. This could result in closed doors or in aggravating a potential employer. On the other hand, it shows real interest on your part, as well as a willingness to take risks.

If you use this approach, don't take up too much of their time. Get in, deliver your message, and get out in a few minutes. In addition, never go empty-handed. Have a résumé to leave even if you are not able to see anyone. Follow up with a letter, especially if someone took time to talk with you.

Telephone Inquiries

Active job seekers put considerably more effort into their pursuit than just browsing through newspaper ads. You've got to get out there and investigate. An easy, quick, relatively nonthreatening way is to telephone and ask if a certain department, agency or company has, or expects, any openings. This is known as *cold calling*.

Of all the job-search methods presented thus far, this one demonstrates the highest success rates. According to Bolles (pp. 46–47), you can make such inquiries on your own or as part of a group of other job seekers:

> By yourself, using the phone book's Yellow Pages to identify subjects or fields of interest to you in the town or city where you are, . . . [call] up the employers listed in that field [and] ask if they are hiring for the type of position you can do, and do well. This method has a 69% success rate. . . .

In a group with other job-hunters, using the phone book's Yellow Pages to identify subjects or fields of
interest to you in the town or city where you are, and then calling up the employers listed in that field, to ask
if they are hiring for the type of position you can do, and do well . . . has an 84% success rate.

When making such calls, begin by asking whoever answers who you should talk with about possible job
openings. Ask if they send out a mailer for job openings or if you could get on a specific list to be notified
for a particular job. With a little polite interaction, you may be able to get an individual notice from the
contact person you impressed while inquiring. Even if the contact you made proves fruitless, never hang
up without asking if they know of anyone *else* who is hiring. Your goal is to develop an ever-expanding
list of resources and contacts.

Other places to check during your job search include the federal, state, county and municipal personnel offices;
your local library for job listing mailers used by government agencies and privately published services;
placement offices and employment information resources at local educational institutions and universities; your
local telephone directory; employment services and organizations; computer bulletin boards; and government
pamphlets and publications. You might also consider making personal or telephone inquiries at companies or
agencies that interest you, requesting information about current or anticipated job openings.

ON BEING YOUR BEST

An absolutely essential part of your strategy is to be your best at *every* phase of the job-search process.
Because of the natural frustrations of the process, this is sometimes difficult. Yet it is vital that you relate
positively, courteously and respectfully to everyone with whom you come in contact. You may not think
the receptionist, secretary or person who casually strolls up and asks if they can help you is important.
They are. You never know who you are talking with.

If you are making phone inquiries, be away from crying babies, barking dogs and other noises that
could be distracting for both you and the person you're calling. Consider dressing as you would for a
personal interview. If you look sharp, you will feel sharp and, in turn, will act sharp, making a better
impression than if you were calling while lounging in your bathrobe at 2 o'clock in the afternoon.
Besides, you never know if the prospective employer might say something like, "Can you come down
right now?" It happens. Also, don't assume your call will be answered by "just a secretary." The boss
may answer the phone when the receptionist is away from the desk. Furthermore, many employers
come in early and stay later than their administrative staff—phone calls at these times may reap
unexpected benefits.

When making personal contacts, coming across well is especially important. Applicants who drop off
résumés while wearing extremely casual attire or something bizarre take a possibly fatal risk. There is
always a chance you could meet with someone, even if you meant to only leave your résumé and ask
about possible openings. Perhaps the person responsible for hiring will walk by or has told the person at
the front desk to send any applicants to see him/her. Maybe a new receptionist or a temporary employee
will mistakenly send you into the employer's office. If you are wearing cut-up jeans and lizard-skin
cowboy boots, you have damaged what should have been a spectacular opportunity. The prepared job
seeker is always ready for the unexpected.

In addition, the first contact person may deliver your message or résumé to the boss *with* an editorial comment. It had better be something like:

➢   This applicant sure was polite.

➢   This person dressed well.

➢   This one seemed like she would fit in.

➢   This is the one who called and was so courteous.

You don't want something like:

➢   Wait till you see this slob.

➢   This guy was really rude just now.

➢   This is the gal who hung up on me last week.

You will likely be talked about after you leave, so make sure the talk is positive. You may also get something more from being polite—the person taking your call or greeting you at the front desk may be willing to give you advice or a tip on future openings. It is also possible they may go tell the boss, "There is someone here you should meet," or even call you with information about a new opening. Because you never know, always be prepared. Even if you feel frustrated, frazzled and tired, look like this is *the* most important contact you are making.

> An essential part of your strategy is to be your best at *every* phase of the job-search process. During phone contacts and especially during personal contacts, dress and act professionally. Expect the unexpected. You may be talking to the boss and not know it.

CONTACTS BY MAIL

The importance of appearance in making a good impression also applies to written material because it is a direct reflection of you. While you may not actually see the person doing the hiring, if you supply a résumé, chances are it will at least get looked at. Provide that person with something that interests them, not something that gives them a reason to throw it away. Résumé submission by mail (or e-mail or fax) was discussed in depth in Chapter 10.

Contacting prospective employers by mail is perfectly acceptable. Like telephoning, it is quick, easy and even more nonthreatening. It may, however, be less effective. While it may be hard to say "no" to someone in person, it is easier over the phone, and easiest with a letter (usually by dumping it in the circular file). Bolles (p. 43) notes:

> Mailing out resumes to employers at random . . . is claimed to have about a 7% success rate. . . . I'm being generous here with my percentage. One study showed that outside the Internet only 1 out of 1470 resumes actually resulted in a job. In other words, here resumes had a 99.94% failure rate. Another study put the figure even higher: one job offer for every 1700 resumes floating around out there.

In acknowledging this discouraging statistic, Bolles (p. 43) suggests: "Before you use any job-hunting method, know the odds. That way, if you know ahead of time that the odds are really bad (as here, with resumes), and subsequently you find out the method doesn't work for you, you won't take it so personally."

Nonetheless, letter writing is a viable strategy. Note here the recommendation is *not* "résumé mailing," but "letter writing." It makes little sense to send an agency or company only a résumé. The receiver will have little idea why it was sent, and even if a position is open, a bare résumé shows lack of common sense by the applicant. A cover letter makes the process more personal and sincere by introducing you and telling why you are writing. Whether responding to an ad or merely inquiring about what might be available, include both a cover letter *and* a résumé.

Writing skills are exceptionally important, and here is a chance to shine. To make a favorable impression when you write, consider the following:

➢   Don't provide a letter without a résumé or a résumé without a letter.

➢   Don't submit anything in pencil (and write neatly in ink only if you are absolutely unable to locate anyone within the free world who can type it for you).

➢   Don't use sheets torn out of a spiral notebook or lined, three-hole notebook paper.

➢   Don't use the back of a used piece of paper or an old invoice or receipt.

➢   Don't send form letters, especially when they were designed for another job area.

➢   Don't send copies of letters or résumés that have been copied so many times they are faded and hard to read.

➢   Don't fold your material into strange shapes. Enclose it unfolded in a 9 × 12 white envelope.

As difficult as it may be to believe, all of the preceding have been submitted, and all have been thrown away without ever allowing the applicant to recover from the negative impression he or she made.

Employers are busy, especially if they are shorthanded and need to hire more personnel. They will not have time to go through all the applications, so they will look for reasons to throw out most of them. Foolish applicants provide plenty of justifiable reasons to jettison their letters and résumés. When providing a prospective employer with *anything* in writing:

➢   Make sure it is neat.

➢   Make sure it is typed.

➢   Make sure it is personalized for *that* contact. Call to find out who to address it to and the proper spelling and title.

➢   Proofread it; proofread it again; and proofread it some more. Have another person proofread it. Then proofread it one last time. Improper grammar and typos provide excellent reasons to pitch a résumé.

> When providing a prospective employer with *anything* in writing, make sure it is neatly typed on good-quality paper, personalized and free of errors. Never send a résumé without a cover letter or a letter without a résumé.

NETWORKING BASICS

Because the vast majority of job seekers make several applications, you will want to constantly seek new contacts and new possibilities. After being hired, you may eventually change jobs (maybe several times), so you will need to continue to expand your contacts. This process, called *networking*, is THE most important component of the job search.

Salespeople have effectively used this networking concept for years, only they call it "developing leads." You are a salesperson, selling yourself. The process involves setting up a network of resources you will not forget and who will not forget you. It begins with making whatever contacts you already have and taking every opportunity to add to this list. You then use each contact to make more contacts, and more contacts, and so on. For instance, you make a contact at a particular company or city. You then ask if you should check with anyone or anywhere else. Imagine if each contact gave you two or three other employers' names. You could quickly develop literally hundreds of possible contacts.

What becomes difficult and complex is *how* you develop your networking strategy and to what extreme you should take it. Because networking can, and in fact should, mushroom into many contacts, proceed in an orderly way. This is best done in writing, with a plan in mind. Here's how:

1.   Make an initial contact.

2.   Document that step.

3.   Acquire additional contacts.

4.   Document them.

5.   Take action.

6.   Follow up.

It's easy until you start to develop more than about five contacts. Then you will want to record your efforts on something more workable than scraps of paper. You can buy networking workbooks, but it may benefit you to make up your own networking book. You can design it for your own particular needs, making the entire process more personal, not to mention more gratifying by accomplishing something concrete.

 In your journal, or in a separate networking notebook, list the important information you need to keep track of and organize it so it is workable. Data to be maintained should include:

- ➤   Company, agency, department name, address, phone, e-mail
- ➤   Names and titles of contacts (spelled correctly)
- ➤   What you did
- ➤   What you will do

Also have a separate calendar to set up dates you will contact or recontact sources. The first recontact should be a week or two after the initial contact. Follow up every month thereafter, but be sure to recognize the fine line between an assertive applicant sure to be remembered and a pest they want to forget. Strive for a balance.

Pursue your job search positively and energetically. Develop every opportunity to show yourself in your best light. Be creative and learn from each experience. Even the contacts that appear to be unproductive give you a chance to learn more about the market and yourself. If nothing else, you come away from the experience knowing you are tough enough to accept a setback and survive. Bolles (p. 88) advises: "Don't be wearied by rejection. . . . The typical job-hunt is NO NO NO NO NO NO NO . . . YES. Even if you get rejected at a lot of places, the more NOs you get out of the way, the closer you are to that YES."

> Networking—the process of connecting and interacting with people who can be helpful to you in your job search—is a crucial element in an effective job search. Place no limits on your network—talk to anyone and everyone.

ON BURNING BRIDGES

No matter what approach to contacting prospective employers you take, be it responding to an ad, phoning, sending a letter with a résumé, sending a fax, e-mailing or stopping in, *never* leave a door permanently closed behind you. Don't burn any bridges that may eventually lead to a great job.

Some people can be insensitive, unfeeling and downright rude. You are bound to get tense yourself because job seeking is difficult. But never show any negative feelings to anyone who may affect your future professional life. Don't be rude or vent your frustrations on anyone where you are applying for work, no matter how they treat you. If they treat you badly, it's probably not *you* they are upset with. They are likely just having a bad day. You may well return, *if* you have kept the door open. If you have sworn at someone, had a temper tantrum or otherwise behaved unprofessionally, you might as well cross that resource out of your networking notebook.

> Never burn any bridges. Doing so only removes any opportunities the future may have held for you.

YOU'VE FOUND AN OPENING AND THEY'VE ASKED YOU TO APPLY

Once you've found an opening and have been asked to apply for the position, you can expect to go through several steps, illustrated in Figure 12–1. The order in which these steps occur may vary, but in almost all instances, the first step will be to complete an application form.

> The application process usually involves completing an application form, taking a series of written tests, having a preliminary interview, undergoing a background check, having a final interview and taking a medical exam.

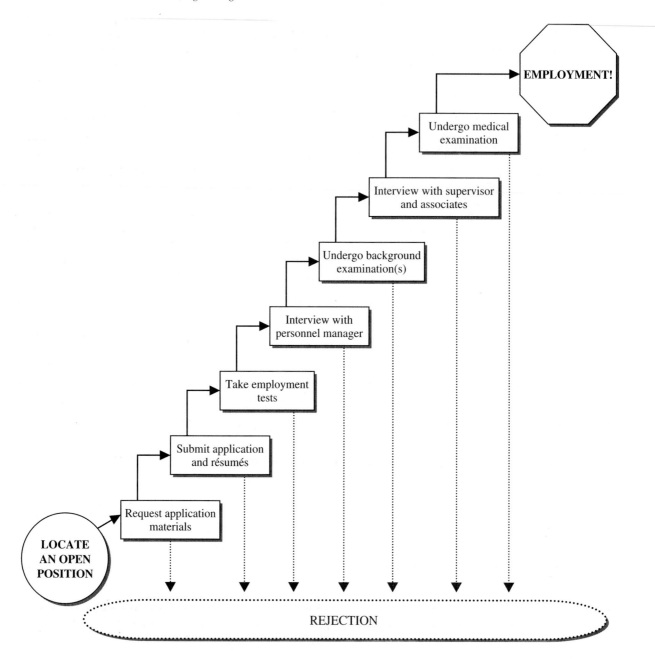

FIGURE 12–1   Typical Employment Process

The Application

Some application forms are very simple. Others are extremely complex. If you have done a thorough job on your résumé and have a copy along, you should have all the information you need at your fingertips.

If you are asked to complete the form on the spot, do so neatly using *black ink*—it copies better. Write legibly using your best *printing*. Write on the correct lines on a form. Sloppiness and inaccuracy on a job application may lead the employer to question your attention to detail and ability to follow instructions. Think before you write so you do not have to erase or cross out information. A high-quality erasable pen is a good investment. Be complete. If you do not understand something on the form, ask.

If they will allow you to take the application home, do so. We suggest you type your responses on the form. However, many applicants do not have access to typewriters these days. And trying to format your responses using a computer and running the application form through the printer, hoping everything falls in the right spaces, can be an exercise in futility. Consequently, many forms must be filled out by hand. It is wise to make several copies of the form to practice on, saving the original for your final draft.

> Application forms vary greatly in their complexity and depth, but they usually ask for the same information you gathered in preparing your résumé, so always have a copy of it with you. Although the Equal Employment Opportunity (EEO) guidelines make mandatory responses to questions about ethnic background, religious preference and marital status illegal, it is usually in your best interest to complete these optional sections.

The website (http://www.wadsworth.com/criminaljustice_d/) contains a sample application form as well as Equal Employment Opportunity guidelines.

Many departments and agencies are including a written essay as part of the application process, requesting candidates to write two or three pages on a specific topic, such as "Why are you interested in this field?" or "Why are you interested in being hired by this particular agency?"

 Take time *before* you apply for a job to write two- to three-page answers to the following questions:

1. Why have you selected this particular field?
2. Why have you selected this particular agency?
3. Who are YOU? (Write a brief autobiography.)

REMEMBER THE MAGIC WORDS—THANK-YOU

Your parents were right. One absolute: *Never* leave a contact without following up with a thank-you. Not only is this good manners in a world sorely lacking them, but it is also another chance to present yourself positively. The more you can get your name in front of employers, the more they will remember you at hiring time.

You can phone or write your thank-you for the opportunity to interview or to submit your résumé. If you can't decide which way is better, do both. Don't express your thanks to *only* the chief of police or the president of the security company who took time to see you. Also thank the secretary who took time to set up the meeting or greeted you for your appointment. Show them you are thoughtful and courteous, the kind of person they would like working with them.

> Always follow up a contact with a thank-you. It demonstrates your good manners and gets your name in front of the employer one more time.

WARNING

If you think job hunting sounds like a lot of work, you are absolutely correct. Every aspect of the process is emotionally and physically taxing and time-consuming. You will be approaching other people trying to sell yourself, knowing the chances of immediate success are slim.

None of us likes to hear the word *no*. It becomes increasingly difficult to dial the phone, knock on the door or send the next letter. It is risk taking at the most critical level. You are setting yourself up for a certain number of rejections. It is difficult, if not impossible, to keep from taking the entire process too personally. A rejection does not have to be a failure. Indeed, it can merely be the elimination of another job on your quest to find the job you are looking for.

Rejection can come for a number of reasons. Primarily, there needs to be a match between the candidate and the department. What may be inappropriate for one agency will be a gold mine for another. Rejection may simply mean it wasn't the best match for the department or for *you*.

Take care of yourself. If the whole thing starts to get the best of you, treat it like you would any other job. Set hours, including breaks. Plan your days. Take an occasional vacation. Finally, recognize the very real need for a support system. Plan time with people who accept you. You can do this informally with family or friends, or more formally by organizing a support group with others in the same position. Such groups work extremely well for sharing support, ideas and helpful hints. Most important, be sure your strategy allows you to keep at it. The next contact could have your job for you.

TESTING YOUR CAREERING COMPETENCIES[*]

INSTRUCTIONS: Respond to each statement by circling the number at the right that best represents your situation.

SCALE: 1 = strongly agree
          2 = agree
          3 = maybe, not certain
          4 = disagree
          5 = strongly disagree

1. I know what motivates me to excel at work.   1 2 3 4 5

2. I can identify my strongest abilities and skills.   1 2 3 4 5

3. I have seven major achievements that clarify a pattern of interests and
   abilities that are relevant to my job and career.   1 2 3 4 5

4. I know what I both like and dislike in work.   1 2 3 4 5

---

[*]SOURCE: Ronald L. Krannich. *Re-Careering in Turbulent Times: Skills and Strategies for Success in Today's Job Market.* Manassas, VA: Impact Publications, 1995, pp. 103–105. Reprinted by permission.

5. I know what I want to do during the next 10 years.   1   2   3   4   5

6. I have a well-defined career objective that focuses my job search on
    particular organizations and employers.   1   2   3   4   5

7. I know what skills I can offer employers in different occupations.   1   2   3   4   5

8. I know what skills employers most seek in candidates.   1   2   3   4   5

9. I can clearly explain to employers what I do well and enjoy doing.   1   2   3   4   5

10. I can specify why employers should hire me.   1   2   3   4   5

11. I can gain the support of family and friends for making a job or career change.   1   2   3   4   5

12. I can find 10 to 20 hours a week to conduct a part-time job search.   1   2   3   4   5

13. I have financial ability to sustain a three-month job search.   1   2   3   4   5

14. I can conduct library and interview research on different occupations,
    employers, organizations and communities.   1   2   3   4   5

15. I can write different types of effective résumés and job-search/thank-you letters.   1   2   3   4   5

16. I can produce and distribute résumés and letters to the right people.   1   2   3   4   5

17. I can list my major accomplishments in action terms.   1   2   3   4   5

18. I can identify and target employers I want to interview.   1   2   3   4   5

19. I can develop a job referral network.   1   2   3   4   5

20. I can persuade others to join in forming a job-search support group.   1   2   3   4   5

21. I can prospect for job leads.   1   2   3   4   5

22. I can use the telephone to develop prospects and get referrals and interviews.   1   2   3   4   5

23. I can plan and implement an effective direct-mail job-search campaign.   1   2   3   4   5

24. I can generate one job interview for every 10 job-search contacts I make.   1   2   3   4   5

25. I can follow up on job interviews.   1   2   3   4   5

26. I can negotiate a salary 10–20% above what an employer initially offers.   1   2   3   4   5

27. I can persuade an employer to renegotiate my salary after six months on the job.   1   2   3   4   5

28. I can create a position for myself in an organization.   1   2   3   4   5

You can calculate your overall careering competencies by adding the numbers you circled for a composite score. If your score is more than 75 points, you need to work on developing your careering skills. How you scored each item will indicate to what degree you need to work on improving specific job-search skills. If your score is under 50 points, you are well on your way toward job-search success.

CONCLUSION

Although waiting to hear about a job opening may work once in a great while, you usually must *work at finding work*. It is important to identify what you want before going after it. Then you must make job hunting a full-time commitment, spending a minimum of 35–40 hours a week actively searching for work if you are currently unemployed. An essential part of your strategy is to be your best at *every* phase of the job-search process. *Always* follow up a contact with a thank-you. And never burn any bridges. Doing so only removes any opportunities the future may have held for you.

AN INSIDER'S VIEW

LAW ENFORCEMENT JOBS: LEARNING HOW TO GET THEM TAKES THE SAME SKILLS REQUIRED TO DO THEM

John Lombardi

Professor of Criminal Justice and Criminology
Albany State College

Students want to pursue law enforcement positions for a number of reasons. There are also a number of different things a person can do in his or her travels from a student "wannabe" to a real cop, and getting the job is but one of these "rights of passage." This is not a personality contest. It is serious business. I do not believe all students are cut out to be police officers, nor are all police officers meant to be students. However, a student does not have to study law enforcement, but a police officer who aspires to be a professional must become a student of multi-methods of gathering different kinds of information. Dealing with the public, particularly with "street people," is an "art form" more than a science. It is more a pursuit of professionalism through continual training and education than an initial profession after graduating from an academy.

Serving the public is a truly honorable way to make a living, but always place your individual standards higher than those of the public you serve while still regarding them as equals. This is a lot to comprehend. However, if you cannot, it is likely you will be unable to muster the patience to make it through the "gatekeepers" who separate the "wannabe" from the "is." Consider the educational transformation you will experience during the job quest going from student "wannabe" to the world of law enforcement.

TALKING TO POLICE OFFICERS

For me and my POST [Peace Officers Standards and Training] undergraduate students in Minnesota, the search for a job starts early, during their sophomore year. Approximately one of three or four students applies for academy training in Minnesota. Most of my students apply outside the state because it takes less time to find a law enforcement job. Part of their training in their employment search is to speak with various police officers. This offers many benefits.

Scott Harr spent an hour with my criminal procedure class explaining procedures and answering questions from students, since we use his criminal procedures textbook. How does this work? I set up a call to the criminal justice professional, announce to the class who the speakerphone guest is and ask each student to make up at least one good question. The day of class I give the students several more minutes to look over their questions and collaborate with other students. The students are picked at random, come up to the speakerphone, ask their own questions and interact with the speaker. I have found that this opens up quiet students, gives them some confidence in speaking with authority figures and makes sense out of questions they have created from their own perspectives. It takes them away from books and the familiarity of the professor while, at the same time, shows them the overlap and consistency between the professor and what is learned in class and is supported by other criminal justice professionals with whom they speak and gather new information.

STATE APPLICATIONS

Students universally complain about filling out long applications. A simple solution to this for some positions is to request several state employment applications. Fill out one application, perfectly typed. The only spaces left open should be the date and job applied for. Copy this completed application, possibly 100 times. Also, ask that your name be placed on the state job mailing list or visit a state employment office weekly and file as many job applications as you wish. Most people who do this get a positive response relatively quickly. Remember, you will probably switch jobs a few times, according to research data. Consider "positioning" yourself for your second job as you contemplate your first. The first job *is* important but will likely be a stepping-stone along your career path.

TRAINING IN ORAL INTERVIEWS

I have taught a senior seminar in criminal justice that considers oral interviews, what types of questions to consider, possible responses and why, and the impact of what students have studied in college. The students are told to anticipate obvious questions:

➤ "Why do you want to be a police officer?" (Give three reasons including that you want to help people.)
➤ "Why do you want to be a police officer in this department?" (I have heard that your mandatory training opportunities are excellent; your department pays for graduate courses in management; your field training officer program is well known; etc.)
➤ "What are your strong points?" (I have been trained to be a problem solver, not a problem creator.)
➤ And "stock" hypothetical questions such as "What would you do in a situation that is either impossible or is one in which you surely have not been, as yet, trained?" (Call your supervisor, follow policy and chain of command, etc.)

As you gather information, cast it into question form. This will get you in the mind-set to think on your feet. You must learn to control situations and yourself. You should become sensitive, but sitting and crying for someone does not help that person and does not make you a problem solver. Finding solutions for the person in need is the beginning of helping that person gain control.

If asked, "How has your education prepared you for a police officer position?" the hiring board does not want an academic, laborious listing of your criminal law or abnormal psychology courses. It is more practical and useful to respond with answers concerning an understanding of (1) mandatory training, (2) the difference between formal education and academy training, (3) factors involved in what being a "professional" means, (4) understanding the chain of command, (5) knowing what "1983 actions" are and not being afraid to ask the hiring board what type of 1983 actions their department has and is experiencing and how their academy is responding to the litigation, (6) officer turnover and promotional list rates for similarly situated individuals in positions for which you are applying and (7) opportunities existing in areas for which you aspire (e.g., tactical teams, violent crimes units, task forces, etc.). Taking "a broader stroke" to responses shows you understand the "bigger picture" and are sensitive to the organization and the environmental impacts on the agency and its budgetary position.

Don't ask questions about salary. That can be found in job descriptions. And it is permissible to walk into an interview with a legal pad listing "solid" questions (e.g., education, mandatory retraining opportunities, outside "inner-city" voluntary opportunities for off-duty officers through various service agencies, etc.). If the hiring board asks you if you have any questions, you will be prepared. You can raise your oral board scores by asking several penetrating questions that allow board members to respond. This shows that you have thought ahead, that you have researched the agency beyond color coordination of uniform and squad car and that you are career-oriented.

SUBSCRIBING TO MONTHLY JOB OPENING LISTS

Local and national job openings can be purchased for a nominal fee. Ask at your local police department for such listings. In addition, investigate the possibilities in states that have high crime rates, as well as police academies that train for particular police jurisdictions (e.g., Florida). In other words, the state will not only train you, but will also help place you once you graduate. It is possible to qualify for 20 police departments or more with one application and then have an agency pay your salary when going through the academy. Check on hiring versus training rates—that is, how many people qualify each year in a particular state versus the number of persons actually hired.

BOOK LISTINGS OF LAW ENFORCEMENT AGENCIES

You can find annual listings of police agencies in the library or through local law enforcement agencies. You might pick agencies geographically and send a brief one-page request for an application, deadline dates and so on. Keep information on each mail-out, whether the agency is accepting applications or not. Call the agency to see if the application was accepted or when applications might be accepted. Write down the name of the officer spoken with and, when calling back, make sure to ask for the same officer.

WORKING OUTSTATE

In Minnesota, people like to stay instate. However, students who really want to be police officers will travel to states that have jobs. As Dr. Darrell Krueger, President of Winona State University, says, "Prepare for your second job." It is prophetic, since many of my students who have not found law enforcement jobs in Minnesota have gone to other states having reciprocity with Minnesota, that is, the student can work in another state as a fully sworn police officer for several years, then return to Minnesota and become a licensed police officer by counting the prior out-of-state police training accepted by POST. These officers simply need to pass a test to avoid the long waiting period of unemployment. This is good, smart business because it reduces loss and increases credentials.

THE MILITARY

The military can be a tremendous opportunity for immediate and future employment. If this is of interest, cultivate the recruiters starting in your junior year. The more a recruiter interacts with you, the more opportunity exists for that recruiter to see traits that would benefit the military occupational specialty for which you wish to contract.

NON–LAW ENFORCEMENT MAJORS

At a law enforcement training workshop, Dr. Jim O'Connor, at the time second in command of the FBI Academy in Quantico, Virginia, stated that within a few years many police departments will forgo the traditional street patrol requirement prior to becoming a detective and do direct hiring of business students into the detective ranks. Why? Because, according to Dr. O'Connor, traditional police training has failed to produce investigators capable of combating complex white-collar crimes that directly affect drug and violent crimes. You should know this as preparation for becoming a law enforcement professional.

EMPHASIS ON CRIME PREVENTION AND SECURITY

A major trend in law enforcement education and training is to include crime prevention and security functions. This is emphasized in many states, such as Minnesota, which has supported the Minnesota Crime Prevention Practitioners Association. This major movement blends the private sector with the public sector. The School of Criminal Justice at Michigan State has blended programs with their business school. The Florida State University School of Criminology has a long tradition of multidimensional methodological interdisciplinary training.

Be prepared to confront more complex issues in the future as an interested "problem solver," not simply a standard criminal justice major or veteran of many police ride-alongs. Even Forrest Gump understood the private sector. You cannot major in criminal justice and not understand the private sector.

TIMING AND SALESMANSHIP

In an employment search, timing is important. So is salesmanship. Do what you love, not just what you like. If all else fails, take second best or whatever is available. This is where "positioning for future jobs" becomes important. Patience is important when you realize that the first job is not what you want, but is doable until the "right one" comes along.

It is easy to seek comfort when the rejection form letters come in. Good people get rejection letters, the same as all others. The difference is that those meant to be police officers are persistent. You have to sell yourself. You buy from salespeople who believe or want to believe in their product. For the same reason you want to help people, the public wants to believe in the concepts you have to sell . . . "serve and protect." These are intangibles until you make them concrete. Each department can function well only if the majority of their officers practice what they preach. And this can happen only if each officer has faith in their ability to sell themselves, to let the public "buy into" that particular offer.

THE PERFECT TRAINING PROGRAM

I am often asked what I would include in the "perfect training program." I would include philosophy, English literature, verbal and written communication, business management, salesmanship and marketing, problem definition, resource allocation, policy development and an evaluation of what you think you'd accomplished after all that. Why? For *awareness.* For prevention of loss and reduction of faulty risk taking. For increasing accurate anticipation. *The same skills used to interpret a poem are used to write an accurate police report. And preventing loss is the same as increasing sales.*

In conclusion, do what you love and getting the job will be the easy part when you look back years later. And if you love what you do, the hard part will rarely surface unless you lose your sense of awareness, presence and problem definition. Love being a problem solver for a simple reason: it takes less effort to sell an idea you love. You are about to go places where most of the public would not go, but do you have what it takes? Would you hire yourself?

John Lombardi, *PhD, CST, CPO, NAPS, IAPSC, is a professor of criminal justice and criminology at Albany State College in Albany, Georgia, where he teaches graduate and undergraduate courses in methodology, crime prevention and organizations. He earned his PhD from the School of Criminology at Florida State University, has numerous national board certifications and is the former training director of the criminal justice training academy in Panama City, Florida, and POST coordinator/professor at Minnesota State University in Winona, Minnesota.*

INSIDER'S VIEW ONLINE

An additional *Insider's View* for this chapter is "From Both Sides of the Process" by Brian Beniek, found on the Wadsworth website: http://www.wadsworth.com/criminaljustice_d/.

 MIND STRETCHES

1.   List as many sources as you can in which employment ads might appear.

2.   Why are many jobs filled without being advertised or filled before the ad appears?

3.   List 10 contacts you have available right now through which you could begin networking.

4.   If you were an employer deluged with applications, how would you eliminate 50 percent of them right away?

5.   What errors could applicants make when contacting a prospective employer by mail?

6.   Whether you contact an employer by phone, mail or in person, what three things would you want that person to remember about you?

7.   What creative things can you do to get the attention of an employer? What possible benefits and detriments can you think of for each?

8.   What strategies will you use to locate employment opportunities?

REFERENCES

Bolles, Richard Nelson. *What Color Is Your Parachute? A Practical Manual for Job-Hunters & Career-Changers.* Berkeley, CA: Ten Speed Press, 2004.

Krannich, Ronald L. and Krannich, Caryl Rae. *Find a Federal Job Fast! How to Cut the Red Tape and Get Hired,* 3rd ed. Manassas Park, VA: Impact Publications, 1995.

ADDITIONAL CONTACTS AND SOURCES OF INFORMATION

Career Paths: A Guide to Jobs in Federal Law Enforcement
  by Gordon M. Armstrong and Frank Schmalleger,
  Regents/Prentice-Hall Publishers, 1994.
    Lists all major federal agencies, criminal justice positions
    available, addresses and phone numbers

U.S. Civil Service Commission
1900 East Street, NW
Washington, DC 20006

Career Path—a leading site on the Web for job seekers. After selecting a geographical location, the applicant can peruse the major newspapers' classified ads for current openings in that area. http://www.careerpath.com

The Police Officer's Internet Directory—over 1,500 individual home pages of information on law enforcement agencies across the country. Included is a state-by-state breakdown of agencies with current openings. http://www.officer.com

On Patrol—includes free postings of law enforcement opportunities on a state-by-state basis. http://www.onpatrol.com

*Many other links are included on these three websites.

CHAPTER 13

YOUR JOB-SEEKING UNIFORM:
PRESENTING YOURSELF AS *THE* ONE TO HIRE

You never get a second chance to make a good first impression.

—Will Rogers

Do You Know:

➤ What the employer's investment is in the hiring process?
➤ What the job-seeking uniform is and what elements it consists of?
➤ What the five-minute barrier and primacy effect are?
➤ How you can find out how you come across to others and why this information may be useful?
➤ How what you are wearing influences people's perception of you?
➤ Why it is important to begin your job search in good physical condition?
➤ What the purpose of the interview is and how important knowledge is to this purpose?
➤ The importance of follow-up?
➤ What your strategy will be for presenting yourself?

INTRODUCTION

One critical aspect of how you present yourself is in the written material you submit. The importance of written materials was discussed in Chapters 10 and 12. It is emphasized again here because it is a vital part of how you are viewed. Whatever you do, do it well. Don't submit insufficient, incomplete material or anything that doesn't look perfect. Just as "you are what you wear," so *you are what you write.*

Typos, misspellings, poor grammar, erasures and messy cross-outs tell an employer a lot. You cannot afford to look inept, uneducated, careless or sloppy. The weeding-out process becomes arbitrary at times, particularly with a number of equally qualified applicants. You may find yourself out of the running for something as simple as a misspelled word in your résumé. This is not necessarily fair, but it is a fact. How you present yourself begins with your written materials. If you do an effective job, you are likely to get an interview. How should you appear at such an interview? What makes up your job-seeking uniform?

In a sense, we *all* wear uniforms, whether they have badges, patches and whistles, and whether we are actually on the job. A uniform is apparel that makes a statement. The police, corrections or security officer's duty uniform is designed to make a specific statement: *I am in charge!* Clothing worn by undercover officers also makes a statement, although quieter: I fit in (hopefully unobserved). Similarly, nurses have uniforms that meet their professional needs, as do bus drivers, waitresses, letter carriers, custodians, delivery people, orderlies, flight attendants, pilots and military personnel.

When matching clothing to a day's work, consider: What image do I want to project? What encounters will I have today? What does this sport coat say about me? This dress? This tie? This scarf? These shoes?

THE EMPLOYER'S INVESTMENT

Before getting into specifics of *how* to present yourself, look first at the situation from the employer's perspective. When hiring, employers are making a significant financial commitment. The typical medium-sized police agency will spend a few thousand dollars just on the hiring process alone. After an applicant is hired, it is expected they won't be truly productive for at least the first year of employment, so the agency is expending a year's salary just to cover training and administrative costs. Furthermore, that does not include the salaries of those who will be doing the training, guiding and so on to bring the recruit "up to speed" so that he or she will become a productive team member.

During hiring, employers are also making an extremely important organizational decision. Employers are hiring someone to represent them to the public. In all areas of criminal justice and private security, public perception is critical. Employers can find themselves in serious trouble if they hire the wrong people for these jobs. In fact, employers may face civil lawsuits for "negligent hiring" (holding the employer responsible for hiring unsuitable employees who cause some sort of harm). Combine this with the fact that it is increasingly difficult to fire people, particularly in the public sector, and you can see the importance employers must place on the entire process.

> The employer has a significant investment in hiring the "right" people. In addition to the financial investment, those they hire represent the employer to the public. Also, hiring the wrong people can land an employer in legal trouble via "negligent hiring" lawsuits.

ELEMENTS OF YOUR JOB-SEEKING UNIFORM

Because employers have so much at stake when they hire personnel, and because their decisions are often based on a few pieces of paper and 30 minutes of personal time with you, you *must* make the most of those pieces of paper and 30 minutes. How you present yourself during an interview is an important aspect of the overall getting-a-job process. Your strategy for presenting yourself must encompass the entire spectrum of how the prospective employer views you. Many factors come into play here. Employers will tell you that while someone may appear spectacular on paper, the interview provides an opportunity to eliminate many candidates.

Appearance consists of the "whole person." The physical self, the emotional self and the spiritual/ethical self combine to create the balance that makes up "you." If one aspect outweighs the rest or is significantly lacking, you are out of balance. Something appears wrong. For instance, police officers may work odd schedules and perhaps compound things by attending school on the side. They may not have sufficient time to exercise regularly. Weight gain or a poor nutritional program could affect their health, making them feel run-down, irritable and out of sorts. Officers in this situation should reexamine their lifestyles to restore balance.

Employers will try to view the "whole" applicant during the hiring process. Employers will look for high self-esteem, alertness, intelligence, critical-thinking abilities and humanistic traits. They will also consciously watch for indications of sadistic, brutal, obsessive-compulsive personalities as well as those who might become victims of "groupthink" and "deindividualization" in the face of peer pressure. The obvious difficulty is that what employers get to see represents a small portion of your overall identity. After all, how long does it take for you to get to know another person, even yourself, before acquiring an accurate perception? Certainly more than the 30 minutes spent during the average interview.

> Your job-seeking uniform is how you present yourself during an interview. It consists of more than just the clothes you put on—your uniform includes how you come off during the initial contact; your grooming; physical condition; grammar and speech; body language, composure and personality; manners; and enthusiasm, knowledge and follow-up. It's your total package.

This is a lot of data to present to an employer, particularly in the short time you have. You must develop a strategy to maximize the opportunities to sell yourself in each area. Properly pursued, you will have more than enough time to provide employers with an accurate picture of you. To best understand this, consider the dynamics of the interview process, that is, the mechanics of the system and the importance of the first few minutes.

THE PRIMACY EFFECT AND THE FIVE-MINUTE BARRIER

The first moments of any interpersonal interaction are critical, for as the quote by Will Rogers at the beginning of this chapter states: "You never get a second chance to make a good first impression." Busenitz (2001) stresses:

> It is extremely important that people have a good first impression of you. Either you make a good impression or you will suffer for it! It is going to affect how your contact views you for the rest of that conversation. It can affect how fast a friendship starts, or how fast business relationships get going. . . .

> What is a "first impression"? Simply it is the first thoughts a person has toward you after seeing you or listening to what you have to say. These are made during the first five seconds and then the first few minutes of a conversation. It has been said that a speaker has 5 minutes to convince the audience that he/she has something good to say. How you act, dress, and talk are all going to affect "the first impression."

Underwood (2003) explains: "The common adage that first impressions count is known technically as the primacy effect. Weighted averaging would explain this effect by saying that the information we get first is weighted more heavily because it is assumed to be more important." And according to Anderson (2004): "Career-management experts estimate that more than 80% of job interviews are won or lost during the first five minutes of conversation."

> The five-minute barrier refers to the length of time it typically takes for the primacy effect to occur. According to this concept, the first five minutes of a social interaction are crucial to the continuance of the interaction.

You can test the primacy effect theory by asking yourself some questions:

➤   Have you ever sat next to someone on a bus, train or plane and almost immediately wanted to talk with them? Or—decided to quickly get your nose into your book or magazine? Why?

➤   Have you ever had someone come to your door seeking contributions for some worthy cause and known almost immediately that you'd probably contribute? Or cut them short? Why?

➤   Have you ever had a teacher you just knew wasn't approachable to discuss a grade you received? Why?

➤   Have you ever gone into a job interview and known within minutes that you were a strong candidate? Why?

    In your journal, list what turns you off when you meet someone. What turns you on to a person?

It is natural to like some people and not others. How do you get to feel that way? How long does it usually take? How do you come across to others? Have you ever considered asking someone how you came across to them when you first met?

DIFFICULT INQUIRIES

It is important to understand *how* you come across to others because you can seldom judge this for yourself. How could you know how others perceive you? Do you dare ask? Most people seldom think of this. It's just too risky. But it may be necessary, particularly if you are experiencing repeated rejections. We can all take constructive criticism. If that is what is needed to identify your weak points, take that risk.

For example, one officer left her initial law enforcement career path to go to law school and then returned to seek employment in the police field. Armed with experience, training and extensive education, she finished number two on almost every interview in which she participated. Why? She had to know. So she called several individuals she had applied to and explained her motives for inquiring—not to criticize, not to take another try at that job, but to understand how she could improve. She was stunned to learn she had not convinced them she did not want to practice law. They were all sure she would stay with them only until a "real" lawyer job was offered to her. Was this *their* fault? Of course not. It was hers for failing to anticipate this reaction and making false assumptions. Her only regret was not taking this step earlier. In this case it worked. She got the next job she applied for.

> Find out how you come across to others by asking. Although it may seem risky, the constructive criticism may help you identify and strengthen some of your weak points, particularly if you've been experiencing repeated rejections.

GETTING TO KNOW EACH OTHER

The goal of the preliminary process is really the same for both the prospective employer and for you: *getting to know each other.* It would be considerably more fair and accurate if time was unlimited. But it is not. For better or worse, you must deal with the brevity of the process and acknowledge the reality of the five-minute barrier. This is not all bad, however. If you recognize the elements of the interview, this is actually an ideal amount of time. Now take a more detailed look at each element of the job-seeking uniform, including what comes before and after the interview.

BEFORE THE INTERVIEW

One critical event before the interview might be a *phone call* to arrange the interview—or even a preliminary telephone interview. Vogt (2004) acknowledges: "Phone interviews can be tricky, especially since you aren't able to read your interviewers' nonverbal cues like facial expressions and body language during the session—a big difference from the typical interview." He further notes:

Many companies use phone interviews as an initial employment screening technique for a variety of reasons. Because they're generally brief, phone interviews save companies time. They also serve as a more realistic screening alternative for cases in which companies are considering out-of-town (or out-of-state and foreign) candidates.

So the chances are pretty good that, at some point in your job hunt, you'll be asked to participate in a 20- to 30-minute phone interview with either one person or several people on the other end of the line. In many ways, the way you prepare for a phone interview isn't all that different from the way you'd get ready for a face-to-face interview—save for a few slight additions to and modifications of your list of preparation tasks.

Here's what to do:

1. **Treat the phone interview seriously, just as you would a face-to-face interview.**
2. **Have your résumé and cover letter in front of you.** You'll almost certainly be asked about some of the information that appears on these documents.
3. **Make a cheat sheet.** Jot down a few notes about the most critical points you want to make with your interview(s).
4. **Get a high-quality phone.** This isn't the time to use a cell phone that cuts in and out.
5. **Shower, groom and dress up (at least a little).** Odd advice? Perhaps. But focusing on your appearance, just as you would for a normal interview, will put you in the right frame of mind.
6. **Stand up, or at least sit up straight at a table or desk.** Again, there's a psychological, frame-of-mind aspect to consider here. But on a more tangible level, research has shown that you project yourself better when you're standing up, and you'll feel more knowledgeable and confident.

Whitten (no date) suggests:

If your phone has a call-waiting feature, consider disabling it the day of the interview. . . .

Remember to speak clearly and listen attentively, just as you would if you were meeting with the interviewer in person. Even though no one can see you, your voice betrays attitudes and confidence. . . .

At the end of the interview, express your willingness to speak with the employer in person.

Ledgard (2004), a senior technical recruiter for Microsoft, offers additional advice:

Lose the distractions! Find a nice, comfortable, and quiet place for your phone interview.

Define your talking points! Think of creative stories that highlight your competencies and innovative ideas you have for the job that you want to make sure the interviewer hears. You should still let the interviewer drive the discussion and direction of topics, but these talking points will help you sneak in some of your own flavor, when it's applicable.

FAQs rule! No matter the company or job, some questions are frequently asked. Anticipate these questions and answer them in advance. Print out the list and have it handy for reference. Topics you might be asked to cover include: your passions, your strengths, your areas for improvement, a difficult challenge or situation you've encountered on the job and how you handled it, your most proud accomplishment, interest in this job and/or company, and your 5 year plan. Chances are, you'll be asked to expand upon at least one of these subjects during the interview.

Do you have any questions? Almost every interview ends with the interviewer asking, "Do you have any questions for me?" Since you know the question is coming, write down two or three questions you'd like to ask ahead of time. . . .

Self-motivation works! Okay, this is really silly, but I find this helps me. Type up something that says, "<Your name here>—you are the coolest. You are so smart. This company would be lucky to hire you. You have ALL the power, and YOU ROCK!" Print out this mantra and read it just before the interview begins. Glance back at the words during the interview. I guarantee this will help you maintain your poise and confidence.

Many of these recommendations, such as anticipating questions you'll be asked and preparing questions to ask the employer, will also help you prepare for a face-to-face interview, whether or not a phone interview actually occurs.

INITIAL CONTACT

The interview itself is the brass ring you strive to get. When you get it, you *must* be on time. Before your interview date, it's important to know exactly where you're going so you can get there on time. Making excuses for a late arrival as an opener for your interview gets you off to a rocky start. So, when you are called for an interview, get clear directions on how to get to the interview. Make a trial run of the actual trip so you know how to get there and how long it takes. Plan to arrive 10 minutes early to allow for traffic delays or parking problems.

CLOTHING AND GROOMING

Clothes make the person—and get (or lose) the job. Maher (2004) observes with amusement: "So far, no reality show follows the hapless job seeker who mixes plaid and pinstripes and flunks a luncheon job interview by drinking from the finger bowl. Such blunders may be extreme, but no one can deny the importance of making a solid impression on a hiring manager or boss." Like so many other things, the "experts" have made a science of dressing for success. John T. Malloy, who coined the term *wardrobe engineering,* was among the first to stress publicly the link between professional accomplishments and wardrobe in his well-known book *Dress for Success.* His research indicates that your credibility and likeability are immediately established by what you are wearing.

> Research indicates that your credibility and likeability are immediately established by what you are wearing.

Few would argue with the research that tells us that people's appearance has a direct impact on how they come across to others and how they will be treated. Since clothing is extremely important, how should you dress for a job interview to make a favorable impression? You have dressed effectively if your interviewers do not even remember what you were wearing. You want them paying attention to you, not your clothing.

It cannot be overemphasized that those doing the hiring for criminal justice and security jobs are likely to be older, conservative *men.* When a male applicant comes in with long hair, an earring and a tattoo, those doing the hiring will have already made up their minds before the first question has been asked. It isn't fair, and it probably isn't right, but employers are looking for people who will not cause problems by deviating from the norm all the time.

In planning an "appearance strategy," begin by identifying exactly what job is being interviewed for. An applicant for an executive position would dress differently than an applicant for a manual labor position. An interview for an officer position falls somewhere in between. Start with several givens:

    The jobs themselves are conservative.

    Extremists are generally not well received.

The fields are regarded as important and seek to be viewed as professions.

You've got to look the part.

Begin by deciding on clothes that fall between the extremes, that is, *conservative*. A spangled three-piece suit and lots of gold jewelry is obviously inappropriate. So is a hopsack loincloth or a low-cut dress. Most agree that a smart-looking, fresh, low-key appearance is called for.

Comfort is a factor. You will not perform up to your potential if you are dressed uncomfortably. If you do not feel good, it will show. Therefore, pick clothing you feel comfortable wearing. You can build on your interview outfit from this point.

A suit is traditional for an interview—for men and women. A suit conveys a statement: The person wearing it is businesslike, is capable of creating a positive image and is taking the interview and the interviewers seriously. The same can be said for a sharp sport coat with a nice pair of slacks, or a good-looking skirt with a neat blouse or sweater. The final decision is yours, but consider the following:

➤   Is your outfit conservative? Is it comfortable?

➤   Could a suit work to your advantage or disadvantage? (Might a rural jurisdiction view a suit as "too much"? Might another jurisdiction view a tweed sport coat as "too little"?)

➤   What do you own now? Chances are you feel comfortable in clothing you own.

➤   Can you afford to buy new clothes for your interviews? Can you afford *not* to?

➤   How do you think you look?

A frequently overlooked area is that of accessories: socks, belt, tie, jewelry, shoes and so on. In addition to being conservative, you should use *common sense*. To review a few basics you probably already know:

➤   No hats worn indoors.

➤   White socks? Absolutely NOT.

➤   Socks that are too short, or droop, or have runs or holes in them? Ridiculous.

➤   Hosiery that's more appropriate for evening or holidays? Hold off for the office party.

➤   An old, cracked, mismatched leather belt? Absurd.

➤   Too much jewelry? Leave it at home.

➤   Still using your father's old clip-on tie? Spend a few dollars for a new one.

➤   Worn-out heels or scuffs on the back of the heels from driving? Replace them.

➤   And don't forget to shine your shoes.

Avoid wearing pins or other jewelry identified with a particular fraternal, religious, athletic or other group or club, as you risk offending someone participating in the interview and give them something other than your face to focus on. Do not give them excuses to avoid eye contact. Also avoid loud colors, wild patterns or any unusual apparel. Seek help from clothing store clerks, who are generally fashion-conscious and can offer advice regarding your clothing needs. Consider other resources when setting up your dressing strategy, such as books and magazines. Such an approach may give you a slight advantage. Finally, since your perception of yourself is too subjective, solicit feedback from someone you trust. Ask them how you look. Hear the answer—good or bad—and make any necessary improvements.

Another consideration is personal grooming. Although these things may seem obvious, before an interview evaluate such things as hair and nail care, makeup, antiperspirants, fragrance and breath freshness. Some things can be fixed relatively quickly; others may take more time.

Make sure your fingernails are clean and trimmed. Women should use discretion in how long they allow their nails to grow. You don't want a prospective employer wondering if you can type a report or even pick a pen up without difficulty. If you choose to wear nail polish, select something subtle.

Women who wear makeup should choose a natural or professional look, not a dramatic look. Avoid heavy applications of eye shadow or cheek color, and select a lipstick that is flattering but doesn't scream "Read my lips!" Before the interview, make sure there is no lipstick on your teeth. If you're uncertain about how to achieve a professional look with makeup, consult a local department store cosmetics clerk.

Know if your antiperspirant works well in anxiety-producing situations. If it doesn't, find a new one! You'll be nervous enough without the added worry of body odor. However, don't overdo it on the fragrance. Go easy on the strong aftershave or perfume. While most people find body odor offensive, many people are just as offended by strong fragrances. Some people suffer allergic reactions to such smells, and it will do you no good if your interviewer has a sneezing fit throughout your entire interview.

Pay particular attention to your breath and oral hygiene. There is no bigger turn off than *bad breath,* and many people don't even know when they have it. But your interviewer will know. Be sure to brush and floss your teeth before an interview, and avoid drinking liquor or eating exotic foods. These things can stay on your breath long after you've ingested them. Furthermore, never smoke or chew gum during an interview. Put out the cigarette or spit out the gum before you even enter the building. Check yourself in a mirror one final time before entering the interview room. And *smile.* A friendly smile can be key to the impression you make during those critical first five minutes. Make them feel good when they look at you.

The bottom line is: You are selling something—*you!* You need the tools to make that sale. If you do not have the proper clothing to make a good impression, buy some, even if it means borrowing money. You can pay back the loan once you get the job. You *must* appear like someone the interviewers would want representing their city, county, department, agency, institution or company.

PHYSICAL CONDITION

Closely related to clothing and grooming is your physical condition. Chapter 7 was devoted entirely to physical fitness and its importance. The fact is simple: Few other professions require you to be more physically fit than those of criminal justice and private security. You are not expected to be at your peak for only a few seasons or to compete in a once-in-a-lifetime event like the Olympics. You need to be in top physical condition every day you report for duty. The public depends on it. Your partners depend on it. *Your* life may depend on it. The very nature of the job is stressful. Many officers die not at the hands of criminals but as victims of their own clogged arteries and unhealthy hearts.

Employers in these fields *will* notice your physical condition. Every police, corrections and security administrator knows it's hard to keep their officers in peak shape as the years go by. They certainly don't want to start out with out-of-shape officers. It's not good for the employee, and it's not good for the department. Every organization is concerned about its public image. So much of criminal justice and security work is accomplished by easily identified officers. They are often uniformed and drive marked cars. No department wants overweight, unfit officers representing them.

Your job-search strategy should include being in good physical shape, not only because employers expect it, but because you will feel more confident about yourself. And confidence shows.

Finally, don't smoke. If you do—quit. An increasing number of police departments and private employers are including "nonsmoker" in their initial requirements. Public buildings are also quickly becoming totally smoke-free. Besides the obvious health-related problems, smokers today look out of place, and many feel smokers present a bad image. Further, most smokers don't realize just how obvious the odor they have clinging to them is. An interview panel of nonsmokers will almost certainly be overwhelmed by the offensive odor of an applicant who smokes. It sends a message you don't want to send.

GRAMMAR AND SPEECH

Individuals employed in criminal justice and security are expected to present themselves like any other professional. As educational requirements for applicants increase, so do standards about communication skills. Use of slang, obviously mispronounced words or limited vocabulary can embarrass an applicant. Furthermore, people who speak nonstandard English rarely recognize the handicap they carry. Ask someone who speaks "good" (standard) English to listen to you and see if your speech needs improving. Zakar (2001) asserts:

> A positive physical appearance can be undercut quickly by poor speaking ability. Speaking ability isn't necessarily a matter of tone or inflection. You don't have to have a voice like James Earl Jones to be a good speaker. Nor does it depend on a professorial vocabulary. Rather, it's the ability to process information and arrange it in a coherent and insightful manner. The organization and selection of detail are what count. A good candidate understands the point of a question and addresses it with clarity and brevity.

Like physical fitness, communication skills take time to develop. Some people are better communicators than others, and some simply need to brush up in this area. If you need to improve how you speak, take speech classes. Join Toastmasters. Volunteer in ways that require you to interact with the public. Feeling confident in how you sound will make you feel better because you will know you will be perceived better.

Be yourself. Trying to come off too intellectually or too much like a seasoned professional will be perceived as phony. Don't address your interview panel as though you were giving a grand performance at Radio City Music Hall. Present yourself as you are.

BODY LANGUAGE, COMPOSURE AND PERSONALITY

The stress associated with the job-search process makes it hard to appear as well as you need to. Stress and anxiety can intimidate you to the point that you sit rigidly upright during the interview, responding with short, one-word responses—the only goal being to live through the interview. Relax. Be real. Let them see *you*. You wouldn't buy a car or house based solely on how it looked from the outside. The same goes for hiring someone.

As important as the words you say is the nonverbal communication you exhibit through your body language. As noted by the Life Coaching Studio (2003): "When meeting anyone for the first time 93% of the communication and impression that they make of you will be down to the way that you look, your body language and the sound of your voice. Only 7% will be down to the words that you use." According to Borrello (2001, pp. 23–24):

> As an officer walks through the door and greets the interview panel, interviewers see how he or she walks, moves, shakes their hands and gets seated. Does the officer's posture reflect confidence? Is he or she stiff and nervous? Is his or her handshake solid or like a wet fish? Is the officer's face lacking emotion, with shoulders slumped downward? . . . As the officer speaks, is there any eye contact? Does he or she seem to have physical energy, representing confidence and a willingness to perform?
>
> Does the officer ever smile or display facial expressions showing him or her to have a personality? Are the officer's hands unnaturally trapped in his or her lap, or can he or she comfortably and effectively use gestures to support and add emphasis to words and ideas? This is physical communication at work, and it is very powerful in making or breaking impressions.

Regarding a sense of humor, Zakar advises:

> Clearly, there are sound evolutionary reasons why humans developed a sense of humor. It's a survival mechanism that allows us to cope with stress and to interact more efficiently with other members of the tribe, or, as we call it today, the company. Humorless candidates will find themselves isolated in the workplace and, in some cases, feared. Winning candidates don't tell jokes, but they do make observations that show they have the ability to laugh.

MANNERS

Good manners make a great impression. They start with being on time for your appointment. Lateness shows a lack of respect for others' time and might lead the employer to wonder: *If you can't be on time for an interview, how can you be on time for work?* If circumstances beyond your control are making you run late, call to explain your delay.

Shake hands with and greet the interviewer(s) at the beginning of the interview contact. Make your handshake an extension of yourself. It can communicate warmth, strength and confidence. Use a firm, full, deep grip and maintain eye contact. (You might want to ask some friends how they feel about your handshake and, if need be, work to improve it.) Don't forget to smile.

Listen attentively throughout the interview, and *do not* interrupt the other person in your eagerness to answer their question. Finally, never let any contact with a prospective employer end without another handshake and a sincere "thank you."

ENTHUSIASM

Do you want the job, or do you *WANT* the job? Employers aren't interested in hiring someone who will pursue their work halfheartedly. They want people who greet each day as a unique challenge, make the most of every opportunity and do a *great job*. If you meander into the interview and respond casually to questions, why should they hire you? You must show them that you don't just want *a* job, you want *this job* with *this organization*. Let them know why. If you don't, someone else will. It is amazing how so few applicants, when asked *why* they want the job, exclaim it is because they really want to work here, for *this* organization. When the interviewer asks if you have anything else you'd like to ask or say, you should make it absolutely clear that you really *do* want this particular job and that you will do a great job for them . . . and be enthusiastic about it! But know the difference between sounding enthusiastic and sounding desperate, as Rurak (2004) cautions: "If you've been job hunting for a while and feel pressure financially, you may leap to accept the first position you're offered. But desperation is the kiss of death during interviews. . . . When meeting employers, strive to appear calm, self-confident and in control. Say that you're challenged most by the career opportunity and make money a secondary concern."

KNOWLEDGE

The biggest error applicants make when presenting themselves to prospective employers is misunderstanding what the employer is looking for. In the hiring process, this can be fatal. The purpose of the hiring process is for applicants to present themselves—the only thing the employer is interested in learning about is *you*. But most applicants go into the process thinking the employer wants to learn how much the applicant knows. If you were applying for a position as a brain surgeon or scientist, *what* you knew might be of primary importance. But for criminal justice and security jobs, particularly at an entry-level position or at the initial promotional stages, employers recognize that the right kind of person will be able to learn and grow with the job. If you get "hung up" thinking knowledge is all-important and concentrate entirely on memorizing facts, data, laws, rules and procedures, you have missed the point. Interviewers want to get to know *you*, not your capacity for memorizing. In fact, this is why the application process is so frightening for most applicants. They worry that they do not know enough. This is *not* what employers are looking for.

The purpose of the interview is for the employer to have a chance to get to know *you*, not your capacity for memorizing or how much you know.

In reviewing the elements of your job-seeking uniform, you can see where an overemphasis on what you *know* could effectively prevent you from concentrating on the important factors—showing good manners, being enthusiastic about the job you're applying for and letting your true personality shine through. The incorrect assumption is that you will be hired for what you know instead of for who you are.

Nonetheless, knowledge *is* important. That is why it is included as part of your job-seeking uniform. Part of what the employer must know about you is what you know, but it is only one part, and a fairly small one. Depending on what field and position you are being interviewed for, you will need to know certain things. For example, in Minnesota, a person applying for any law enforcement position must know elementary law such as the use of deadly force applicable and some fundamental Fourth Amendment search and seizure concepts. Such an applicant should be ready to answer questions about basic procedures, for instance, situations dealing with Miranda, citizen safety or officer safety. You might want to take some criminal justice classes to help prepare. Ask people who have applied for similar jobs what questions they were asked.

You should be able to demonstrate how you would solve more complex legal issues. For example, if asked about fifth-degree assault, be able to tell the interviewer where you would go for that information. Or, given a hypothetical situation and asked how you would respond, be able to explain the process you would use to analyze the situation rather than just saying what you would do.

It is also important to know about the organization you're applying to. *Never* enter an interview without having first checked out the website of the hiring authority. Not only does this make a statement about your interest in the position and agency, but it also speaks to your computer ability. If the hiring agency has a Web presence, it is here you will likely find their mission statement and other valuable information. For example, you should research and learn details about the follow specifics of a community:

- Population
- Racial climate
- "High-profile" issues
- Unemployment rate
- Type of government system in place

- Size of the police force
- If community policing has been implemented
- Chief's name and how long he/she has held the position
- Recent increases or decreases in crime statistics

If no website exists, or you're unable to locate a computer with Internet access, the local chamber of commerce may be able to provide up-to-date data.

FOLLOW-UP

Follow-up refers to the extra steps taken after the interview, the time when most applicants sit and wait to hear from the employer. Just as you must never leave a contact with an employer without saying "thank-you," you must not walk out of an interview never to be heard from again. A single follow-up thank-you letter can give you another chance to show off how well you wear your job-seeking uniform by reviewing such elements as:

- Grammar
- Manners
- Personality

- Enthusiasm
- Ability to follow up
- Knowledge

Six of the nine elements in your job-seeking uniform can be reinforced *after the interview.* You can also demonstrate again your proficiency with written material, and you provide the employer with one more reason to remember your name positively. Imagine the employer sitting with half a dozen or fewer résumés that all look good, pondering a decision. Suddenly you call to say thank-you for the interview. This simple thank-you can tip the scales in your favor.

How you follow up is up to you. Some employers prefer not to be called while they are making a decision. While a phone call may not be a bad idea, it should not replace a letter. A letter is a necessity. Write to everyone who participated in your interview. Get their names, proper spellings and titles from the secretary on your way out or call the secretary later to get this information. Remember a thank-you for the secretary too.

Always follow up after the interview with a thank-you letter and possibly even a phone call. However, recognize the fine line between being remembered positively and becoming nothing more than a pest. Don't lay it on too thick.

PLANNING YOUR INTERVIEW STRATEGY

Erickson (2004) examines the similarities between a job interview and an athletic competition and asserts:

> In athletics as well as . . . careers, possessing sufficient talent, skills and training is sometimes only half the battle. Success often belongs to those who gain a psychological advantage. Over the years professional athletes and their coaches and trainers have developed several psychological techniques to hone this mental edge. . . . Job hunters can draw on some or all of these techniques in interviews to help score extra points that will win the job.

One particularly useful technique is *mental rehearsal,* which Erickson explains:

> More than half a century ago, Dr. Edmund Jeffrey discovered imagined exercise stimulated human muscles the same way as physical exercise. Research on mental rehearsal revealed other remarkable findings. In one renowned experiment, a group of basketball players spent a half hour shooting baskets. A second group spent the same time imagining shooting swish shots. The group that imagined the perfect shots showed more improvement. . . .

> You can apply the same technique to your job interview. Imagine how the interview will unfold with as much clarity and detail as you can muster. The preview will give an idea of what to expect. Imagine the likely scenarios. Whom will you meet? What are they apt to ask? Rehearse how you're going to conduct yourself.

> Prepare your game plan and decide what to stress and what to ask. Picture the perfect interview and the warm farewell that ensues. Imagine the hiring manager's compliment as you part.

Take advantage of what you now know about what to expect during the interview and *plan your strategy* as to how you will present yourself.

 In your journal, write down your interview game plan. Then when you are done writing, read and reread your interview story until you are able to mentally rehearse it without looking at the words.

What things will you do when you first enter the interview room? Who will you meet? What will you say to them? What will they say to you? Remember, this opening scenario is driven by the primacy effect and the five-minute barrier—what impression are you going to make and how?

After initial introductions, the formal interview gets underway. This is your sales pitch scene—you must sell the interviewer on *you*. What questions are you likely to be asked? How will you reply? How will you present your skills, competencies, experience and career ambitions? How will you communicate to the employer that you are *the one* to hire? What can you do for their agency that sets you apart from the other applicants?

As the interview winds down, you will need to deliver a close. Make it positive and upbeat, one the employer will remember favorably. Write in your journal a closing comment or a positive question that might be asked at the end of an interview. A comment regarding the time frame of your job search sends the message that you are enthusiastic about getting going. Make your statement something you'd feel comfortable saying. Practice saying it. When the interview comes to a close, don't be caught off guard. You want your comment ready to roll off your tongue for the strongest possible conclusion to your interview story.

CONCLUSION

Your job-seeking uniform is just that—how you present yourself during an interview. It consists of more than the clothes you put on, however. Your uniform includes how you come off during the initial contact, your grooming, physical condition, grammar and speech, manners, personality, enthusiasm, knowledge and follow-up. Take advantage of what you now know about what to expect during the interview and *plan your strategy* as to how you will present yourself. Pick out your job-seeking uniform and put it on *before* your interview, just to make sure it fits and that you're comfortable in it. The more you wear it, the more natural it will feel. But you must practice putting it on and wearing it for it to be most effective. Plan how you will present yourself as *THE* one to hire.

AN INSIDER'S VIEW

PRESENTING YOURSELF AS *THE* ONE TO HIRE

Brenda P. Maples

Former Lieutenant
Memphis (Tennessee) Police Department

Whether you are applying for a position with a large law enforcement department or a small department, you will be required to complete a series of testing procedures. This allows the department to glean the best qualified from all the applicants. This battery of tests will probably consist of written, oral and physical agility tests. The testing procedure may vary from department to department; however, at some time during the hiring process you will be asked to come for an oral interview. This is your chance to sell yourself, to make a lasting and favorable impression.

First impressions do persist. Your initial appearance can go a long way toward impressing the interviewer, either positively or negatively. Take a long look in a full-length mirror. If you were running a business, would you hire someone who hadn't put on clean clothes or gotten a haircut in several weeks? Wear your "Sunday go to meetin'" clothes and get a fresh haircut or style so you appear neat. You will feel more poised when you know you look your best.

Don't go into the interview cold turkey. Prepare!! The purpose of the oral interview is to gather information and judge face-to-face interaction. This is an important element of law enforcement work because of the time spent dealing with the public, either as complainants, victims or suspects. You will be continually seeking information from others to make decisions.

An interviewee must be confident but not overly aggressive. An intelligent interviewee should anticipate the questions asked in a typical employment interview and rehearse the answers. To prepare, record yourself on video. This is a helpful way to practice your responses and gain confidence. When you review the video, be aware of any weaknesses or areas in which you might improve. Are you able to communicate effectively in clear and logical sentences? Do you use correct and accurate diction? Many judgments are made about other people's intellectual achievements by the way they talk.

While viewing your video, also be mindful of nonverbal communication. This can include facial expressions, fidgeting, hand and arm movements and lack of eye contact. Try to keep nervous mannerisms under control. Sometimes you say more with nonverbal communication than you realize. After all, how does a good investigator get that "gut feeling" when talking to a potential suspect?

You will be asked questions relating to your experience and any special skills or abilities you may possess. You probably have much more going for you than you think. Try to think of experiences where you demonstrated your abilities and skills.

With all these tips on how to sell yourself during an interview, you're still trying to present your unique self. A phony personality will be spotted by any seasoned interviewer. Sincerity and enthusiasm can go a long way in selling yourself as THE right person for the job.

Brenda P. Maples (retired) *is a former lieutenant with the Memphis (Tennessee) Police Department and has 26 years' experience in the criminal justice field. She holds a BS from Middle Tennessee State University and was national president of the Law Enforcement Alliance of America and the vice chair of the Tennessee Peace Officers and Standards Commission.*

INSIDER'S VIEW ONLINE

An additional *Insider's View* for this chapter is "Be Prepared" by Trooper Robert P. Meyerson, found on the Wadsworth website: http://www.wadsworth.com/criminaljustice_d/.

 ## MIND STRETCHES

1. What three things have made you feel accepted by another person while you attempted to break the five-minute barrier? What three things have made you feel unaccepted by another person while you attempted to break the five-minute barrier?

2. How would you work your responses to Question #1 into the job application process?

3. List opportunities you could create to sell yourself besides the traditional résumé and interview.

4. Why is it important to approach the elements of the interview as a whole rather than looking at the pieces separately?

5. Why is it important to develop a *strategy* rather than just jumping into the interview process?

6. Who could you ask for constructive feedback on how you come across to others by your clothing? Your handshake? Your cover letter and résumé? Their initial reaction to you?

7. Which elements of the interview do you think you need to work on? How will you do so for each?

8. How might videotaping yourself be beneficial in preparing for an interview?

REFERENCES

Anderson, Hugh. "Phone-Interview Tips for Savvy Candidates." *The Wall Street Journal Online,* 2004. Online: http://www.careerjournal.com/jobhunting/interviewing/19990310-anderson.html

Borrello, Andrew. "Preparing for the Oral Interview: It's More Than Just Talk." *Police,* January 2001, pp. 22–25.

Busenitz, Arlen. "Make a Superb First Impression." 2001. Online: http://www.theallineed.com/ad-self-help-3/self-help-042.htm

Erickson, Don. "Use Sports Psychology to Prep for Interviews." *The Wall Street Journal Online,* 2004. Online: http://www.careerjournal.com/jobhunting/interview/index3.html

Ledgard, Gretchen. "Ace That Phone Interview." 2004. Online: http://blogs.msdn.com/jobsblog/archive/2004/08/04/208403.aspx

Life Coaching Studio, 2003. Online: http://www.lifecoachingstudio.com/sit3.htm

Maher, Kris. "Image Makeovers Can Give Candidates an Added Edge." *The Wall Street Journal Online,* July 14, 2004. Online: http://www.careerjournal.com/jobhunting/jungle/20040714-jungle.html

Rurak, Maura. "These Interview Bloopers Could Cost You the Job." *The Wall Street Journal Online,* 2004. Online: http://www.careerjournal.com/jobhunting/interview/index4.html

Underwood, Mick. "Perception of Others." 2003. Online: http://www.cultsock.ndirect.co.uk/MUHome/cshtml/index.html

Vogt, Peter. "Mastering the Phone Interview." Monster Career Center, 2004. Online: http://interview.monster.com/articles/phone

Whitten, Chris. "Phone Interview." No date. Online: http://www.jobsfaq.com/interview/phone-interview.html

Zakar, Peter. "Impress Hiring Managers with Executive 'Presence.'" *The Wall Street Journal Online,* October 8, 2001. Online: http://www.careerjournal.com/columnists/perspective/20011008-fmp.html

CHAPTER 14

THE INTERVIEW: A CLOSER LOOK

Whenever you are asked if you can do a job, tell 'em, "Certainly I can"—and get busy and find out how to do it.

—*Theodore Roosevelt*

Do You Know:

➤ What the definition of *interview* is?
➤ What purposes the interview serves?
➤ What five types of interviews you may encounter and how they differ?
➤ How likely you'll be able to negotiate your salary?
➤ How you should close an interview?
➤ What the importance of follow-up is?

INTRODUCTION

The interview. It even sounds ominous. Fear of the unknown can be paralyzing. So take a good look at what you might expect because the interview *is* what it's all about in the job-hunting game.

Webster's defines *interview* as: "A formal consultation usually to evaluate qualifications (of a prospective student or employee). A meeting at which information is obtained." Here are some facts about job interviews:

➤ Interviews are anxiety-provoking.
➤ Interviews are necessary.
➤ Everyone has to have them.
➤ Everyone working has had them.

An interview is a meeting between someone who has a job opening and someone who needs a job, at which information is obtained and exchanged.

According to Hart (2002):

> By the time that law enforcement applicants have reached the oral interview stage of the hiring process, they have generally passed a written exam, a physical agility test, and a gross background investigation. The field of applicants has been reduced by 75% or more and it is time to recommend those survivors to the Selection Board. . . . Your oral interview with the Police Selection Board will be one of the most challenging aspects of the application process.

255

You must keep your wits about you. You need to present yourself in a professional, respectful, intelligent, mature, stable, sincere, and well-organized fashion to win the Board's approval. If you don't you are wasting your time.

PURPOSES OF THE JOB INTERVIEW

As discussed in Chapter 13, the purposes of the interview are for you to find out who the "real" employer is and for the employer to get to know the "real" you. Ask any employer, and they will have stories of applicants who looked nothing short of spectacular on their résumés but were absolutely unacceptable in person. A good résumé, in addition to the other preparatory material and contacts, is just your ticket *into* the interview. An advantage of the preliminary phases of the job-seeking process is that you can get outside help, for example, proofreading your résumé. But once you are led into the interview room, you are on your own. It is completely up to you—as it should be. Simple? Your entire future based on a brief interview?

Bolles (2004, p. 248) likens the interview to the "dating game": "Both of you have to like the other, before you can even discuss the question of 'going steady,' i.e., a job. So you're sitting there, sizing each other up." According to Bolles, employers have five key questions:

➤   Why are you here? (Why did you pick us?)

➤   What can you do for us?

➤   What kind of person are you?

➤   What distinguishes you from nineteen other people who can do the same tasks that you can?

➤   Can I afford you?

The main thrust of any interview is to see how you interact on a personal level. This is extremely important. The process of getting a job and developing a strategy to meet this challenge boils down to two critical aspects:

➤   Having a résumé that can withstand the "weeding out" process.

➤   Developing a strategy to not only withstand the interview process, but to emerge victoriously.

The Purposes—Up Close

The personal interview can fulfill several purposes.

The primary purposes of the personal interview are for the employer to:	
▪ Get a look at you.	▪ Observe how you analyze problems.
▪ Listen to you.	▪ Test your people skills.
▪ See how you perform under stress.	▪ Test your knowledge.

Looking at You. Employers would no more hire an unknown person than they would purchase a home or a car they had never seen. They want to see what they are getting. Particularly for a job in criminal justice or private security, you do not want to make a negative impression by presenting yourself in an extreme manner. If hired, you will represent the agency. To most future clients you will *be* the agency. Think about it! Rest assured the interviewers will be thinking about it.

The trend in recent years for law enforcement, as well as other "first-responder" positions, has been toward a professionalization of the career. To this end, the PoliceEmployment.com website states:

> It is a given that most interviewers will expect a man to wear a suit and tie, and a woman to wear a dress or a business suit to the interview. Most of the time, an interviewing panel is prohibited from disqualifying an applicant based on what he or she is wearing. However, if you walk into an interview wearing a pair of blue jeans and a tee shirt, they will find some other reason to write you out. You may look good wearing nice casual slacks, but you will look even better to the panel if you wear business attire. You want to project a professional image.

Remember the importance of grooming. Find the restrooms on your way into the building to make that final check: Comb your hair, straighten your tie, adjust your slip, zip up your zipper. Anything caught in your teeth? *Look sharp. Be sharp.* Also get a drink of water.

Listening to You. No matter how great your résumé looks or how sharp you look, employers want to know that you also speak English well. There will probably never be a better test of this than during the job interview. In addition to testing your general grammatical skills, employers want to hear how you sound. PoliceEmployment.com stresses:

> As you answer the questions, speak clearly and loudly. Oral communication is very important in law enforcement. One moment you may be chatting with the public, and the next moment you may be giving forceful verbal commands to a suspect. The panel is assessing your ability to communicate by what you say and how you say it. Speaking in a low tone of voice is not what they want to hear. Meek and mild are not the traits of a good police officer.

This advice holds true for applicants in other areas of criminal justice or related fields, such as corrections, probation and private security.

If you get uptight during an interview (and understand that everyone does), just be yourself. Do not try to cover up your anxiety by being cute, funny, smart-alecky or a host of other façades you've probably seen people try when uptight.

What if you *sound* nervous? Your voice may crack, you may say something you did not intend to, or you may just plain forget where you were or what the question was. Don't panic. It is reassuring to employers to see you as capable of recognizing a mistake and being able to reorganize and continue. Do not fake it. If a major goof occurs, simply proceed as follows:

1.   Take a deep breath.

2.   Admit to the interviewer(s): "This job is really important to me, and I guess I'm more nervous than I thought."

3.   Continue with your answer.

There is nothing wrong with being honest. If you're really nervous, admit it; 99.99% of the time interviewers are sympathetic. Your honesty will make a positive impression. Also, take a moment before you answer a question, especially if the question is *not* one you "practiced." What may seem like an eternity to you will likely be only a few seconds. Never answer without thinking through your response.

Seeing How You Perform under Stress. It's no secret; interviews are stressful. Employers know the stakes, and they've all been in your position before. If a candidate doesn't feel *some* degree of stress, it might indicate a complete lack of interest in the job they are interviewing for.

Although nearly every career involves periods of stress from time to time, criminal justice can be a particularly stressful profession. In today's post-9/11 climate, even once fairly passive security positions have taken on a heightened sense of importance and, consequently, an increased level of stress. Thus, it is important that you show an ability to remain cool under pressure.

Some employers use a specific interview technique called a "stress interview," the rationale being that the job you are seeking is stressful, so they want to see what you do under stress. Stress interviews are discussed later in the chapter.

Observing How You Analyze Problems. You may be asked to solve problems but, particularly at an entry-level position, you are not expected to know every answer. For example, an interview for a police dispatcher might include such questions as, "What would you do if 25 747s crashed in various parts of the city at once?" A potential corrections officer might be asked, "What would you do if you were the only guard in your pod and, during a power outage, 21 inmates became embroiled in a massive knife fight?" Or a potential security officer might be asked, "What if you were accosted by 17 chapters of Hell's Angels demanding a solution to world hunger?" Remember that even if there is an answer, in all probability you are not expected to know it.

Prospective employers want to know if and how you think. A good strategy is to begin your answers with your own variation of the "policy/will learn" statement. That is, you understand that every company or department is likely to have its own policy on how to handle most situations and that you are also eager to learn. For example, if asked, "How would you handle a situation in which you find an open door to an office after hours, and the boss is inside with his partner's wife?" A reasonable answer could be: "Because I have had no previous security experience, that situation is certainly a difficult one. Based on the information you have given me, I would follow the applicable company policy; for instance, filling out an incident report if required, as well as immediately advising my supervisor. In addition, I would anticipate learning how the company would want me to handle such sensitive situations during my training period. If it is not brought up, I will bring it up now that you've asked me about it." During such analytical interviews, rather than looking for a right answer, the interviewers are interested in the *process* you use in coming to some conclusions.

Testing Your People Skills. Your résumé may look spectacular, but if you don't come across as friendly, sincere and respectful, you will not get the job. No matter how nervous you get, no matter how frustrating the interview is, do not forget your manners. Let the interview board know you appreciate their time and the challenging questions raised. Shake hands with each interviewer, smile, say "yes" not "yeah," and *use common sense.* PoliceEmployment.com suggests:

> As you enter the interview room, greet everyone with a firm handshake. Look them in the eyes and smile as you greet them. Remember, you are applying for a law enforcement position. This is a field in which you

have to deal with people. You want to show the panel that you are a confident person. Giving someone a weak handshake while looking away is a signal that this occupation is not for you.

Whether or not the interview is specifically designed to create stress, it will! The "little things" are so easily forgotten. Before the interview, make a list of what you want to do. For example:

➢   Shake hands with everyone when introduced.

➢   Look at everyone personally during your responses.

➢   Thank the group at the end of the interview and again shake each interviewer's hand.

Thinking about it all ahead of time will put it in your head, making it easier to remember during the pressure of the interview.

Testing Your Knowledge.   As discussed in Chapter 13, the purpose of the oral interview is generally *not* to test your technical knowledge, as this is better assessed through a written exam. However, you may be asked questions during an interview to check your knowledge in specific areas, depending on the state in which you are applying. For police officers, you could be asked about very basic statutes, for example, the deadly force law. You should be prepared to answer as many of these questions as possible, but do not panic if you cannot. In such a situation admit that you do not know, but that you would look it up in the state statute book, or the traffic code or wherever it is likely to be found. *Do NOT guess.* If you draw a blank, admit it. In such a case, you may want to follow up with a letter providing the answer to show you can find needed information.

Most of the important purposes of an interview can be addressed during one question posed by the panel. A common question for police officer applicants is: "What would you do if you stopped an off-duty officer for drunk driving?" Try the "policy/will learn" approach to come up with an answer. For example, "If the department had a policy, I would follow it. I would certainly advise my supervisor. Recognizing that DWI is a serious offense and that police officers are not above the law, I would. . . ." You get the idea. Such a question gives you a great chance to appear at your best—or worst.

 Imagine you are an employer seeking to fill the position of either police, corrections or security officer. An applicant has just walked into the room. List in your journal five things that would turn you off immediately.

 Next, list five things that would strike you positively.

A temporary staffing service in Northern California asked 150 executives at some of the nation's 1,000 largest companies what the strangest thing they'd ever heard of happening in an interview was. Among the responses were the following ("Behavioral Blunders," 2003, p. 18):

➢   After answering the first few questions, the candidate picked up his cell phone and called his parents to let them know the interview was going well.

➢   The candidate asked for an early morning interview. He showed up with a box of doughnuts and ate them during the meetings, saying this was the only time he'd have to eat breakfast before going to work.

➤ When asked by the hiring manager why she was leaving her current job, the applicant said, "My manager is a jerk. All managers are jerks."

➤ After being complimented on his choice of college and the GPA he had achieved, the candidate replied, "I'm glad that got your attention. I didn't really go there."

Unbelievable, but true. What should you do during the interview? Bolles suggests paying attention to not only *what* you say but also *how* you say it. He (p. 243) notes various studies have shown that the people who get hired are typically those who speak half the time in the interview and let the employer speak the other half of the time. Bolles (p. 243) also advises that when it is your turn to speak in the interview, you should talk no shorter than twenty seconds and no longer than two minutes at any one time.

TYPES OF INTERVIEWS

Interviews provide employers with a chance to observe you from a variety of perspectives.

The majority of interviews can be classified as:

- Informational
- Mass
- Stress
- "Unnecessary"
- Courtesy

Informational Interviews

This is the "classical" interview, where you are asked to come in so employers have a chance to check you out in the areas previously outlined. These interviews are straightforward. Presumably you enter this interview in a relatively equal position with the other applicants. You have no say about what format your interview will take, so "go with the flow." The interview may be formal, relaxed or somewhere in between. You may have only one interviewer, or there may be several.

The formal interview is rather rigid, with questions being asked one after another and the interviewers giving little or no response to tip you off as to how you are doing. They purposely do not respond so that you will not have any advantage over other applicants. This can be rather disconcerting, since everyone likes feedback, but just continue on. On the other extreme, you may find yourself caught off guard by the informality of your interview. Your interviewers may be so laid-back, it may seem they don't even care. While possible, don't let a group that likes to have fun throw you off. In either case, provide your interviewer with as accurate a picture of yourself as you can. Just because you find yourself in a formal setting doesn't mean you must perform as rigidly as a stick, nor should informality lull you into a false sense of security and make you lose your edge.

The informational interview is the classical interview. These interviews are straightforward and are typically one-on-one, although there may be more than one interviewer present.

Mass Interviews

The number of individuals that employers like to interview varies. One or two applicants may be invited to be interviewed if they are exceptionally strong candidates, or several people may be asked in. Many applicants present themselves so poorly that a general informational meeting can serve to weed out a number of them. "Assembly-line" interviews are hard on everyone, including those conducting the interviews. Applicants seem to melt together, making it difficult to remember who was who. This is when it is critical to not only provide a very strong interview, but to also pay particular attention to follow-up.

> Mass interviews involve several candidates being interviewed in rapid succession, or in "assembly-line" fashion. In these situations, candidates may blur together in the interviewers' minds, and you must pay particular attention to your follow-up to stand out from the crowd.

Stress Interviews

Here you have good news and bad news. The good news first: "Stress interviews" are not too common in the world of job hunting. The bad news is that criminal justice and private security do lend themselves to this type of interview. These jobs involve a great deal of stress, so the approach is justified to see how applicants respond under stress. Don't expect these to be comfortable. They are designed not to be. You cannot do anything about it. Go into the interview with the commitment that, regardless of the type of interview you are confronted with, you will do your best.

During stress interviews rapid-fire questions give you little time to think about your answers or to regroup before the next question. The interviewer may seem harsh, if not downright mean. Furniture may be placed in unusual configurations; for instance, your chair may be put in a corner—or maybe you won't even have a chair.

Recognize what the game is here—to get you uptight. You *should* feel tension. In fact, you have much more reason to be concerned if you *don't* respond nervously to this setup. Draw energy from a stress interview and maintain your cool. Use the strength that brought you this far. When you get the job, you'll find yourself confronted with similar stress. The interviewers want to be sure you won't become overly defensive, hostile or panicky. While many interviewees would tell you that *every* interview is a stress interview, in fact, few are set up to purposely get you uptight.

> The stress interview's purpose is to get you uptight so the interviewers can evaluate how you handle stress. Rapid-fire questioning, interviewer hostility and unusual furniture configurations may all be parts of the stress interview.

When hiring law enforcement officers or security guards, employers may be concerned (and rightfully so) about how the applicant will handle a defiant, belligerent or otherwise "difficult" citizen, and may "test" the interviewee in various ways. Consider the scenario posed by Marcus (2000) and his recommendation for handling it:

> The interviewer is determined to make things difficult for you.
>
> Tricks they might try include frequently pointing out your weaknesses, constantly interrupting, trying to intimidate you with their knowledge of the field or continually disagreeing with your comments. These tactics are especially unnerving if you're being interviewed by two or more people simultaneously. In these settings, candidates often become so flustered or angry that they say things they later regret or forget to mention important information.

Your best defense is to play along with the interviewer. Your secret weapon is knowing that the interviewer's antagonism is a game. He or she simply wants to see if you can maintain your composure. By acting politely, calmly and evenly, no matter how rudely the interviewer behaves, you'll demonstrate confidence and maturity, qualities all employers seek.

Of course, the situation can get difficult. Some interviewers act badly to learn how aggressive or assertive you can be. They hope that you'll take offense at their demeaning behavior and object to it.

"Unnecessary" Interviews

Many jobs are filled before they are even advertised, but do not let this fact influence you too greatly. What if the job is offered to someone else? Who's to say that person will accept it? If they do, who's to say it will work out? What if the job isn't what the new hire expected? What if someone even higher up at that agency doesn't like that person? Most important, what if they like *you* better?

No interview is unnecessary. It's just that some seem more necessary than others. Yes, it is frustrating to be called to an interview merely so the employer can prove he or she has done a search before hiring the predetermined first choice. However, employers are also uncomfortable with this process. If you do well in the interview, the employer may keep you in mind for the next opening. At the very least, it is a chance to practice your interview skills and find out you can survive rejection. Both opportunities are valuable.

Because you are unique, you may be the perfect candidate. Never let an opportunity pass by. You have no way of knowing if this job will be *the one*. A lot can be said for the person who tries, even in the face of adversity.

> "Unnecessary" interviews may be conducted when the position is already filled but policy demands the position still be advertised or that a certain number of people be interviewed. Make the most of this opportunity—no interview is truly needless.

Courtesy Interviews

Never dismiss an opportunity by saying, "Ah, I only got this interview because the chief knows my dad. He did it as a favor to him." So what? It doesn't matter *how* you got into an interview, just that you did. Once you're there, it's all up to you. Some opportunities to interview do result because the applicant knew someone or was related to someone in the agency. And that's just fine. You've heard the saying, "It's not *what* you know but *who* you know." All that matters is that *now* you have the chance to impress the interview panel. Worrying about how you got there consumes valuable energy. Go for it!

> Courtesy interviews are done as favors or because of "connections," but they are still legitimate interviewing opportunities. Again, make the most of them.

TELECONFERENCING AND VIDEO INTERVIEWS —A NEW TWIST

Technology is changing the way jobs are pursued and found. While face-to-face meetings between job seekers and prospective employers are still most common, videoconference interviews are growing in popularity. Two primary reasons for the increasing use of this method are that others beyond the formal process can view the interview and that applicants a long distance away from a potential employer can effectively compete for a position without having to travel extensively.

Such "interviews" may consist simply of a candidate's videotaped responses to questions or it may be a "live" interview via video hookups, such as is done routinely on the national evening news. Internet technology makes it equally convenient for prospective employees or employers to communicate, interview and negotiate long-distance.

Rosemarin (2001) advises job seekers to be prepared to perform in more video interviews and offers the following suggestions:

> Relax. The rules for interviewing on camera resemble those of traditional face-to-face interviews: Let the interviewer lead, listen carefully so you can connect your value to the employer's needs, ask pertinent questions, keep your answers succinct and to the point and show enthusiasm for the job.

> Use the following tips to come across effectively during an upcoming video interview:

> **Prepare and Relax.** Most people freeze in front of cameras. . . . To avoid this problem, try practicing at home. Take out the camcorder that you use only on holidays and do some role-playing before going in front of the recruiter's camera. . . . Before any interview, you should prepare for the questions that you'll be asked. . . . Be ready to discuss examples of accomplishments that illustrate what you can bring to the company. Prior to the interview, find out how much time is scheduled and ask your recruiter or contact at the employer for advice on how to make the best impression.

> **Consider Production Values.** Arrive early to check out the setting and get used to the new medium. Work with the technician and try different viewing angles. . . . Try not to look down at the camera, since it's the least flattering angle. Put the camera at eye level to give yourself "a news-anchor look." . . . If your video interview is at home, select a room with an appropriate atmosphere. Examine the room from the camera's point of view. If there's anything inappropriate or unprofessional within the camera's range, hide it.

> **Personal Appearance.** While some may worry about not being telegenic and looking five pounds heavier on camera, what influences your appearance most is whether you feel alert and comfortable. Don't put on a new suit you haven't previously worn. If you aren't used to it, it might surprise you when you least expect it. Wear clothes that move with your body. During the interview, glance at the monitor occasionally to check your posture. If you're slouching, sit up. . . . You'll also need to add more oomph to your presentation. Cameras and television monitors have a way of sapping what would be considered normal enthusiasm in a traditional setting. Be sure to smile and use gestures, but not excessively. Gestures should underscore important information.

> **The Time Factor.** Time management is critical in video interviews. Most are scheduled to take about an hour. Be sure to address the interviewer's concerns as well as your own and leave time at the end for an unhurried, friendly close. . . . Another consideration is the time delay. Video interviewing can be like talking to someone overseas on the phone. A few seconds elapse between when the interviewer speaks and when you hear him or her. When the interviewer finishes speaking, stay quiet and listen to make sure he or she is truly finished. To be certain, let two seconds elapse before you reply.

Some additional strategies to optimize this opportunity include applicants presenting themselves in different modes to set off their personality. For example, some questions could be answered in a dress uniform, others in a suit and yet others more casually in a sweater. A fire service applicant might answer questions with a fireplace or fire truck behind him. This is a chance to plan how to present yourself in your best light and to be far more in control of the situation than in most conventional interviews.

TYPICAL QUESTIONS

Countless lists have been compiled of questions you should anticipate and be prepared for during job interviews. Some of these questions are construed as quite "self-incriminating," as explained by Raudsepp (2002):

> Expect to be asked several probing, hardball questions during your next job interview. In fact, if you aren't asked a few "stress" questions, your interview probably isn't going as well as you might think. . . . The following are . . . typical stress questions . . .:
>
> - Could you tell me a little about yourself?
> - Why did you leave your previous employer, or why are you leaving your present job?
> - What are your weaknesses?
> - What type of salary do you have in mind?
> - What do you like most and least about your present job?
> - Are you applying for any other jobs?
> - Why should we hire you?

To tackle the common interview question of "What are your weaknesses?" Raudsepp states:

> Most career advisers recommend turning this question around and presenting a personal weakness as a professional strength. . . .
>
> Assume that you're detail-oriented, a workaholic and that you neglect friends and family when working on important projects. You can turn these weaknesses around by saying that you're very meticulous and remain involved in projects until you've ironed out all the problems, even if it means working overtime. This way you've cast your weaknesses into positives most bosses would find irresistible.

Some other "tricky" interview questions that merit advance consideration include:

➤ *Why should I hire you?* Marcus notes: "Many job seekers become tongue-tied and make a poor impression when asked this question. Yet there's no better opportunity to establish your qualifications." Raudsepp adds: "It's a mistake to say what you hope to gain from a job. Instead, . . . ask [yourself] what you can do for the company. . . . The interviewer who asks you this is really probing your readiness for the job. . . . Show your readiness by describing how your experience, career progression, qualities and achievements make you an asset. Highlight your ability by discussing your specific skills and accomplishments. . . . To show fitness, say you're reliable, have integrity and will accommodate yourself to any difficulties the job entails."

➤ *Why have you been unemployed for so long?* To handle this heart-stopping question, Nemko (2004) suggests: "Give a brief answer and then move on to explain that you're a good fit for the position. For example, 'I wanted to be a full-time mom, but I've stayed current in the field. Now that my child is older, I'm eager to get back to work. When I saw your ad, I got excited, because I could be of help to you.'"

➤ *Why did you leave (or why are you seeking to leave) your company?* Martin (2004b) recommends: "If you're unemployed, state your reason for leaving in a positive context: 'I managed to survive two rounds of corporate downsizing, but the third round was a 20 percent reduction in the workforce, which included me.' If you are employed, focus on what you want in your next job: 'After two years, I made the decision to look for a company [department] that is team-focused [community-policing oriented], where I can add my experience.'"

➢ *Why were you fired from your previous position?* A sticky question indeed. Instead of getting defensive and blaming it all on the fact that your old boss "had it in" for you, Martin (2004a) advises: "Badmouthing former employers during the interview is a bad idea. . . . People get fired everyday. They move on and get new jobs, and you will too. No matter what the circumstances, put it behind you. Deal with your feelings about the firing, and prepare to talk about the experience in interviews." Admit to any shortcomings you may have had before that played a part in your being fired, and make it clear to the interviewer that you have learned and grown from the experience and are confident.

While the previous questions can be anticipated by nearly every job seeker in every profession, Hart (2004a) identifies some specific questions law enforcement applicants must be prepared to answer:

1. Why are you seeking a career as a police officer/deputy sheriff?

2. What education and experience do you possess that has prepared you for this career?

3. Describe the worst work situation you have encountered. How did you deal with the problem?

4. How do you feel about carrying a gun and possibly having to take someone's life in the line of duty?

5. What are the sources of stress in your personal and work life? How do you manage this stress?

6. What is your pattern of alcohol use?

7. What types of interpersonal conflict have you experienced in your work life?

8. What steps did you take to resolve the issues?

9. In what area are you looking for a change or self-improvement?

10. What personal qualities and traits do you possess that would make you well-suited for a law enforcement career?

11. What types of situations cause you to feel discouraged? Anxious? Irritated?

12. When have you had to take charge of a situation to quickly resolve a problem or crisis?

13. As a police officer, you pull over a speeding car. It's a friend of yours, and you think he may have been drinking. How would you handle the situation?

Following are some typical questions applicants may be asked during the law enforcement oral interview (Taken from www.policeemployment.com/interview/probing. Used with permission.). As you read through them, be mindful that, in many cases, there is no single "right" answer, but there *is* generally a right approach.

 You'll notice most of the questions call for more than a mere "yes" or "no" answer. Concentrate on *your* approach to each question. What would make a good response to each? Write them in your journal.

What do you know about their agency or department?

If you go into the interview not knowing anything about this particular job, it makes you look bad. . . . Lacking this knowledge makes it look like you are applying with any agency just to get your foot in the door. Even if this is true, you do not want to give the appearance that you will use this agency as a stepping-stone to a career with another agency.

Why do you want a career in law enforcement?

If you have always wanted to be a police officer since you were a little kid, then tell them that. Of course, what they really want to know is specifically why you want to go into law enforcement. If you tell them you want to kick butt and arrest people, you will not pass the interview. Tell them what it is about law enforcement you find attractive. Maybe you like investigative work and would enjoy the challenge of trying to figure out what happened or who did it. Emphasize the high moral standards you have. Protecting your community is something you would like to do.

The panel may also ask why you want a job with their specific agency or department. Do not tell them you always wanted a job with them. . . . They will not view your answer as sincere. To them, it looks like you are saying whatever you need to say to get the job. . . . You should tell them what you like about their agency. If you have heard good things about their department, then tell them that. If you know someone who works for them, you can probably mention their name. Tell them that this person had good things to say about them. Be honest but do not try to snowball them. After all, these are police officers who are interviewing you.

Have you applied to any other law enforcement agencies?

The reality is you should apply with every agency you are interested in. Putting all of your eggs in one basket greatly limits your chances of getting into law enforcement. Do not be afraid to answer this question. Tell them every agency you have applied with. They may even ask you what your hiring status is with these other agencies. This does not make you look bad. It shows you are determined to get into law enforcement.

What are your goals?

Usually this refers to your goals in law enforcement. However, they may ask you about your goals in life. The key is to give them some specific goals that are obtainable. Saying that your goal is to be the best police officer or agent that you can be is too vague. Is your goal to be the Director or Chief? This may be your goal and one day you may achieve that status. However, at this point in time, you should start with smaller goals. Tell them your first goal is to get into law enforcement. Your second goal may be to join a specialized field within the department. Perhaps you want to be on the SWAT team or serve as a canine officer or become a supervisor. If you are able to articulate your goals, this makes you a more desirable candidate.

What qualities do you possess?

This question may also be asked in other ways such as, "What are your strong points?" or "What assets will you bring to this agency?" This is your chance to brag about yourself. Everyone has good qualities. Tell them what characteristics you possess that will help you in your job performance. There is a big difference between articulating your strengths and boasting. State things matter-of-factly and avoid embellishing. If you were in a supervisory position, make clear your ability to manage people. Avoid statements such as: "Everyone likes me" or "Everyone knew how well I did this." State your strengths as measurable or documented things. Such statements would be: "There was a low turnover during the time I was a supervisor" or "My boss gave me additional responsibilities." Being liked is an admirable trait but showing your ability to perform is more important.

What traits do you need to improve upon?

After asking you about your qualities, expect them to ask you about the areas you feel you need to improve. You are not telling them that you are weak or terrible, but you are admitting there are things you could strengthen. This is not the time to air your personal laundry. Choose one or two items, state them and state how you are working to improve them. If you don't mention anything, then you are portraying yourself as being perfect, and the panel will feel that you are not being truthful.

What is your employment history?

The panel will probe into your work history. They will look at the duties you performed in your previous jobs. Share with them any supervisory responsibilities you held. You should mention any accomplishments you had or recognitions you received. Don't fret if your work history consists of minimum-wage jobs. You can still show them you are a dependable worker who will get the job done.

If you have worked several jobs, they will ask you why you left one job for another job. Be truthful in your answer. If you left because the new job paid more money or because you did not like what you were doing, then tell them that. If you were fired from a job, they will inquire as to why you were terminated.

If you have just graduated from college and have not yet joined the workforce, you probably still have a work history. You should talk about any summer jobs you had, or part-time jobs you had while in school. The panel is looking for reliability. Someone who arrives to work on time and gets the job done. Someone who does not abuse sick leave and has no problems taking orders from a superior.

Tell us about your military service.

If you were in the military, the panel will ask you about your time in the service—which branch you served in, what was your highest rank and what were your duties and responsibilities. If you saw combat, you should mention it to the panel. They will also want to know what type of discharge you received. They may ask you why you left the military.

If you received a medical discharge, the panel will explore this. They will want to know what percentage is your disability. They will also inquire as to the specific nature of your disability. You will need to show that you can perform the full range of duties required of a law enforcement officer.

Are you currently participating in any type of personal fitness program?

Physical fitness is one of the key attributes of a good police officer. The job may require you to chase a suspect, forcefully apprehend a subject or defend yourself from an attacker. These occurrences do not happen every day, but you must be physically prepared for them. The job of a police officer can be very stressful. Stress can lead to several ailments including heart disease. Studies have shown that a body that is in good physical condition is better prepared to handle stress. Therefore, law enforcement agencies are looking for individuals who have developed a healthy and fit lifestyle.

From your general appearance, the panel will be able to assess to a certain degree your physical condition. You will want to provide them with more detailed information on your current level of fitness. You do not have to be a person who works out every day performing all kinds of cross-training exercises. Even if your exercise program has been limited, tell them what you have been doing. It shows them that you care about yourself, and you are doing something to stay in shape. If you have not been exercising, then it would be wise to begin a doctor-approved program. Not only will this help you at the interview, but it will also help you in other stages of the hiring process.

Have you ever been involved in a motor vehicle crash or received a speeding ticket?

You can be sure they will run a computer check to see if you have had any motor vehicle violations. This is one example of where your ability to tell the truth will be verified. Just because you were ticketed for speeding, illegal parking or for a crash does not mean you are immediately disqualified from obtaining a position with them. Every agency will accept a person who has minor infractions. Nobody is perfect. The agency may have a certain number of violations they will accept. If you exceed the set number, then you are disqualified. For example, four or more speeding tickets in the past two years may be unacceptable. Each agency usually sets the standards they deem appropriate.

What they are looking for is a pattern of deviant behavior. You are applying for a job which enforces the law. If you have demonstrated that you continually break the law, no matter how minor the violations, they are not going to hire you. The other concern is that a police officer spends a great deal of time in a motor vehicle. They want to make sure you can properly handle a vehicle, and that you are not going to get into a crash.

Have you ever been arrested?

As with your driving record, they will run a criminal history through the National Crime Information Center to see if you have a criminal record. Nearly every police agency will not hire you if you have been convicted of a felony charge. A misdemeanor conviction does not necessarily disqualify you for the job. They will inquire as to what type of sentence you received. They will ask you about the details of the case. If this was something you did as a juvenile, then share that with the panel. Their concerns are whether or not this is the only time you were caught. If you were arrested but the charges were later dropped or you were found not guilty, they will question you concerning the charges. Were you truly innocent or did you get off on a technicality? Be prepared for them to inquire about any contacts you had with the police. For example, maybe you have not been arrested but you have been detained for questioning.

Do you drink alcohol?

Moderate drinking is acceptable. What they are looking for are those people who drink excessively. Too much drinking can lead to absence from work, poor work performance, bad health and financial troubles.

Have you ever used an illegal drug?

If you are currently using any illegal drugs, then you will not pass the interview. You cannot break the law while at the same time seeking a position that enforces the law. You should openly admit to any previous drug usage. Each agency has certain parameters as to the types of drugs and the amount of usage they will accept. If you fall outside of these parameters, there is nothing you can do but apply with another agency.

If you smoked a joint a few times in high school or college, admit to it. This does not necessarily disqualify you. As long as the panel believes this was an infrequent occurrence in your past, and that you are now a responsible adult, you should pass this portion of the interview.

Have you ever sold illegal drugs?
If you have ever sold drugs, don't count on getting hired.

Are you currently in any financial debt?
Just because you have an outstanding balance on your credit cards, a car loan, a student loan and/or mortgage payment does not mean you won't be hired. Most people have borrowed money to pay for the more expensive things in life. What they want to know is if you are credit-worthy. A person who is not capable of paying bills may not be a dependable employee. If you have accumulated a large amount of debt on your credit cards, this too may disqualify you. Accumulating large amounts of unsecured debt shows that you have exercised poor judgment and may be a risk.

Do you have any medical restrictions that would prevent you from performing a full range of duties?
The panel will probably question you about your overall health. They will ask if you are currently taking any medications. They may inquire as to what your vision is. They want to make sure you are physically fit for the job.

Are you willing to take a (drug, medical, psychological, fitness) test?
All they are looking for is a "yes" answer. If you add anything to your "yes" response or you respond with a "no," then you open yourself up for additional questioning.

PRACTICE, PRACTICE, PRACTICE

As with so many things in life, the more one goes through the interview process, the better one becomes at being interviewed. Herein lies the "upside" of interviews that do not result in a job offer. Practice helps. When you aren't interviewing, practice interviewing. With friends. With family. With anyone who will ask you questions or listen to yours. Also, take advantage of opportunities to ask others what questions they were asked, and how they responded. It might be wise to keep a list of these in your journal. The crazier the question, the better—it gets you prepared to think on your feet. For example, one interviewer likes to ask applicants what their favorite color is, not because it really matters but to see how the applicant reacts to an unexpected question. Practice will make you more agile when it's game time.

NEGOTIATING

Negotiating is sometimes not possible. The majority of criminal justice jobs are union jobs, or at least are positions that bargain collectively. Therefore, you will have little room to negotiate, particularly at entry-level positions.

Likewise, security positions generally permit little room for you to make demands. As you work your way upward in either the public or private sector, you may find room to negotiate. At almost all entry-level, and even mid-level lateral movements, you could easily appear too demanding if you want too much. Be realistic. Recognize the limitations of these careers. If you have specific needs, however, pursue them as far as you can.

> The opportunity to negotiate a salary in these fields, particularly in entry-level jobs, is very limited.

CLOSING THE INTERVIEW

The final impression you make on your way out is also important. Here is an opportunity to shine as the ideal, enthusiastic candidate. The interview is likely to close with the interviewer asking, "Is there anything you would like to ask?" Every other candidate will say something like, "Well, no, not really." Boring. Unmemorable. Your strategy should include having several closing questions, not about how many vacation days you'll get but rather questions about the starting date or a likely assignment.

Always leave on an assertive, upbeat, energetic note. Regardless of the words you choose, make sure the message comes across loud and clear: *I want this job, and I'll be spectacular at it!* One of the strongest conclusions an applicant ever gave me was to simply say, "You'll never regret hiring me!" Don't be too brash or boastful. Make your closing statement brief and to the point. Any last-minute chance you have will be ruined if you drag it out with question after question or statement after statement. As is true throughout your overall strategy, seek a balance.

In summary, let the interviewer know that you *want* the job. You would be astonished by how few applicants ever communicate that they've applied for the job because they *want* the job!

> Close the interview on an upbeat note by asking about a starting date or what a typical assignment might be. Never close by asking about salary or benefits. Finally, let the interviewer know that you really *want* the job.

FOLLOW-UP

Punctuate your interest with a follow-up. Follow-up is an easy way to score points during the hiring process because few applicants have developed a strategy that includes plain old courtesy. At the least, send a letter telling the interviewer(s) you appreciate the time and opportunity to meet. Such a letter not only demonstrates politeness but also offers one more chance to impress the employer with your strong points. Anything in addition, within reason, will probably benefit you.

Enelow (2004) asserts: "Writing powerful thank-you letters is not just a formality. Thank-you letters are marketing tools that can have tremendous value in moving your candidacy forward and positioning you above the competition." Droste (2004) adds:

> The thank-you note can be a critical piece of your job-hunting strategy. But should you send it by email or snail mail, handwritten or typed? In this fast-paced computer age, the question baffles even the most sophisticated job hunters. Follow these guidelines to help you through the maze.
>
> **Email Thank-You Notes.** How did the company initially contact you? If you have corresponded with people there via email for setting up the interview and answering questions, then by all means send an email thank-you note as soon as you return from an interview. However, make sure to follow it up with a typed note to show that you are not Mr. or Ms. Casual. Email thank-you notes have one clear advantage over their snail mail counterpart: They can put your name in front of the interviewer on the same day—sometimes within hours—of your interview.
>
> **Snail Mail.** If the company you interviewed with is formal and traditional, use snail mail to send your thank-you note. Should it be handwritten or typed? Typed is standard . . . [but] handwritten notes are appropriate if you'd like to extend your thanks to others in the [department] who helped you out.

She concludes:

> More important is what you say and how you say it. A standard thank-you note should accomplish several things:
>
> - Thank the person for the opportunity to interview with the company.
> - Recap some of the conversational highlights.
> - Clarify any information you needed to check on for the interviewer.
> - And most importantly, plug your skills. Use the last paragraph as the chance to state, "The job is a good fit for me because of XYZ, and my past experience in XYZ."
>
> Interviewers have short memories. A thank-you note is your final chance to stand apart from all of the others who want the same position.

> *Do not* forget to follow up. As stressed in previous chapters, following up helps you score points in the hiring process by demonstrating your courtesy and getting your name in front of the interviewer one more time.

MAKING A DECISION

Making a decision is something you probably can't imagine would be a problem. Selecting from several jobs would be a great problem, right? If this does become your "problem," take your time before deciding. Usually employers are happy to give you a reasonable amount of time to make a decision. The *Occupational Outlook Handbook* (*OOH*) (2004) notes: "Once you receive a job offer, you are faced with a difficult decision and must evaluate the offer carefully. Fortunately, most organizations will not expect you to accept or reject an offer immediately. There are many issues to consider when assessing a job offer. Will the organization be a good place to work? Will the job be interesting? Are there opportunities for advancement? Is the salary fair? Does the employer offer good benefits?"

If you are a final contender in another agency, you now have a card to play. There is nothing wrong with contacting these other employers to let them know you would like to work for them, but you have been offered another job elsewhere. Suddenly you have increased your desirability, since someone else wants you too.

As one large university's career placement website states:

> There are several issues that make every job offer you receive unique. While salary is important, you will be making a very limited decision if you focus only on money. The following factors introduce some important considerations involved with accepting or declining a job offer, including salary-related issues:
>
> **Issues with the position itself**—responsibility, authority, independence, working environment (coworkers and supervisors), growth and learning potential, variety and challenges, available training program
>
> **Issues with the [department/agency]**—reputation, future goals and vision, company size and culture, job security
>
> **Fringe benefits**—health insurance, life insurance, vacation and holidays, pension/retirement fund/ profit-sharing
>
> **Relocation**—moving expenses, dual-career relationship, new city's opportunities
>
> **Earnings**—salary, including potential earnings

It is recommended to look closely at each offer's positive and negative aspects in these categories when deciding about a job offer, whether you're considering multiple offers or not. Remember, just as the [department] needs to find an employee who will fit into their job opening, you need to make sure that the [department] and job fit into your situation (Cass Recruitment Media, 2002).

Weigh as many factors as you are aware of. Seek input from others, as recommended by the *OOH*: "If possible, speak to current or former employees of the organization." This will provide invaluable insight into the workplace culture and help you determine if it's a good fit for you. If you are the kind of person who prefers a more relaxed environment, accepting a position in a very formal agency where socializing is frowned upon and little after-hours camaraderie exists can feel very unfulfilling. If, on the other hand, you prefer a very "buttoned-down," more impersonal type of work climate, where little mixing of professional and private life exists, taking a job in an agency where coworkers openly share and discuss their families and like to hang out together after hours can leave you feeling alienated when you choose not to participate.

Even if you are not going to accept a position with an agency, let them know you appreciate them. Who knows, maybe you'll join them in the future.

A QUICK REVIEW

Review these job interview tips provided by Hart (2004b), and review them again when you have an interview lined up:

➤ Call the agency for directions to the interview site, if you are at all uncertain about the location.

➤ Review your application and background statement. Be familiar with key aspects of your education, job history and driving record.

➤ Research the department—Do your homework! Talk with some law enforcement officers.

➤ "Ride-alongs" and facility tours can be most informative.

➤ Get a good night's sleep. You will need it.

➤ Look sharp. Dress professionally. Select a conservative suit of clothing.

➤ Minimize jewelry.

➤ Be able to clearly and convincingly state your interest in law enforcement.

➤ Prepare a few relevant questions to ask the Oral Interview Board. This conveys your genuine interest and preparation.

➤ Arrive at least one-half hour early.

➤ Anticipate key interview questions and practice answering them with family members or friends.

➤ Be willing to ask that questions be repeated or clarified if you don't understand them.

➤ Relate to interviewers in a confident, courteous and respectful fashion.

CONCLUSION

The interview is what the job-hunting game is all about. Prepare by anticipating commonly asked questions and practicing your responses to these questions. Also prepare a few questions of your own to ask the interviewers. Close the interview on an upbeat note by asking about a starting date or what a typical assignment might be. Never close by asking about salary or benefits, and realize that the opportunity to negotiate a salary in these fields, particularly in entry-level jobs, is very limited. Finally, let the interviewer know that you really *want* the job. And do not forget to follow up.

AN INSIDER'S VIEW

YOUR TURN TO STAR

Jim Chaffee

Security Director
Fox Entertainment, California

BEFORE THE INTERVIEW

I would suggest you type all correspondence, including your application. One of my greatest "turnoffs" is to receive an application that is not typed. This is not to say I won't look at it, but when you are in competition with a hundred other candidates, every little edge will help.

I don't mean to suggest that if you type all correspondence that's all you need to worry about. Correspondence should be neat and organized and *should not* contain spelling errors or noticeably improper grammar. Some people have their résumés professionally done, which looks very nice and can be impressive. A résumé does not have to be done professionally, however. With today's computers, a professional-looking résumé can be done with little effort.

Do not include a poorly typed cover letter to go with a professional résumé. This only points out in a glaring fashion that the résumé was done professionally and for obvious reasons. When responding to a job announcement, try to include in the cover letter all your attributes that mesh with what was indicated in the ad. For instance, if the ad listed "map reading" as a desirable trait, be sure to highlight your qualifications and/or experience in map reading. As a general rule, the cover letter should not be more than one page long and should cover what the announcement asked for.

THE ORAL INTERVIEW

There is not a lot you can do to prepare for an oral interview. Unless you know the type of interview and the questions being asked, you are going in blind, so to speak. *Don't* worry about being nervous. Everyone is. Try not to be overly nervous, though, where your voice cracks and breaks and you perspire profusely.

On the other hand, *don't* be too relaxed and nonchalant. It does not look good in the interview process to sit back with your legs crossed and your arm draped over the back of the chair. *Remember* that the interviewers are not only listening to what you have to say, but they are surveying your mannerisms, posture, dress, grooming and the like. The interviewers may not have ever seen you before, and first impressions are lasting impressions.

Absolutely be on time. If you are late for an interview, it is almost like a kiss of death for that particular job. There may always be a reasonable excuse that caused your tardiness, but the burden will be squarely on you to show why you were late. Some examples of reasonable excuses are: "I was robbed, beaten up and sent to the hospital on my way over here," or "I was caught in a flood where several people were swept away, and I ended up saving all of them." If you *do* have a reasonable excuse for your tardiness, if at all possible telephone and try to let someone know. If you flat out miss the interview and don't call and explain why, you have just indicated your desire not to continue in the selection process.

Do dress appropriately. That does not always mean a suit or sport coat and tie, but it almost always does. Wear conservative clothing without loud colors or patterns. A white shirt, neutral tie and dark suit (gray, black or dark blue) is most appropriate. *Do not* forget about shoes and socks—you are being evaluated in totality, which includes your shoes and socks. Make sure your shoes are shined and your socks match whatever you are wearing. Try to make sure your entire outfit is color-coordinated and pleasing to the eye. *Do* make sure you are neatly groomed, for example, that your hair is combed and not too long. Also, women should not wear an overabundance of makeup or perfume.

ANSWERING QUESTIONS

Do *not* attempt to answer a question when you clearly do not know the answer. It is okay to ask to have the question repeated or to ask for clarification. Look the interviewer in the eyes, but not aggressively. If there are several interviewers, look at them also while answering the question. Try not to fidget.

TRICKS OF THE TRADE

When being introduced to the panel, repeat each interviewer's name. For example, "Good morning (or afternoon), Lt. Adams. Pleased to meet you." Doing this should help you remember each interviewer's name as you go through the process. It is impressive when you can repeat the interviewer's name at some time during the interview. For example, you may need the second part of a question reread, and you could say, "I'm sorry, Lt. Adams, but I did not understand the second part of the question." Try to work in each interviewer's name some time during the process, but don't do it unless it sounds natural.

Be prepared for trick questions that may or may not have anything to do with the job. Sometimes a question may be thrown in just to see what your reaction is. Sometimes it will be a humorous type of question, but be sure that it *is* before you laugh.

Also, be prepared for the unexpected. During one interview session we placed a lone chair way out in the middle of the room for the applicant to sit in. This very definitely causes stress to the interviewee. We were trying to see how the person coped with the situation. Some sat in the chair very appropriately, and others were obviously very nervous. We even had several drag the chair up to the interview table before sitting down. One candidate just stood and would not, or could not, sit in the chair. Some candidates appeared really perplexed when trying to decide the appropriate action to take regarding the chair.

Always follow up your interview with thank-you letters to the interview panel.

Jim Chaffee *is the security director for Fox Entertainment in California, and the former director of international security for the Walt Disney Company. He has over 28 years' experience in the field of criminal justice, including four years with the United States Air Force Security Police, eleven years as a police officer in Minnetonka, Minnesota, and three years as the public safety director in Chanhassen, Minnesota. Mr. Chaffee holds an MBA and is a certified fraud examiner.*

INSIDER'S VIEW ONLINE

An additional *Insider's View* for this chapter is "Promotion Interviews" by Capt. Albert J. Sweeney, found on the Wadsworth website: http://www.wadsworth.com/criminaljustice_d/.

 ## MIND STRETCHES

1.   Why would a mass interview put you at a disadvantage? An advantage?

2.   How could you make the interview process more enjoyable and memorable for an employer?

3.   At what point during any phase of the hiring process can you become a pest rather than an impressive, aggressive candidate? How can you maintain an awareness of this and prevent it?

4.   What could you do to remain cool during a "stress" interview?

5.   What could you do if you really blew an interview?

6.   What techniques could you use to deal with the understandable stress and anxiety everyone experiences during interviews?

7.   Why should you follow up with an employer you've applied to, even if you take a different job?

8.   List your three greatest concerns about being interviewed. How can you reduce these concerns?

REFERENCES

"Behavioral Blunders." *Training,* January 2003, p. 18.

Bolles, Richard Nelson. *What Color Is Your Parachute? A Practical Manual for Job-Hunters & Career-Changers.* Berkeley, CA: Ten Speed Press, 2004.

Cass Recruitment Media/Cass Communications, Inc. "Decision Making and Job Offers." 1999–2002. Online: http://umn. placementmanual.com/jobsearch/jobsearch-03.html

Droste, Therese. "Notable Thank-You Notes." Monster Career Center, 2004. Online: http://interview.monster.com/articles/ followingup/

Enelow, Wendy S. "Write Winning Thank-You Letters." Monster Career Center, 2004. Online: http://interview.monster.com/ articles/thankyou/

Hart, Mac. "Police Oral Board Blunders." *Police Interview Newsletter,* Vol. 1, Issue 4, April 2002. Online: http://www. policeinterview.com/news1-4.html

Hart, Mac. "The Firing Line." 2004a. Online: http://www.policeinterview.com/firingline.html

Hart, Mac. "Preparing Yourself for Your Police Interview." 2004b. Online: http://www.policeinterview.com/prep.html

Marcus, John. "Advice on Surviving Tricky Interviewers." *The Wall Street Journal Online,* February 11, 2000. Online: http://www.careerjournal.com/jobhunting/interviewing/20000211-marcus.html

Martin, Carole. "The Firing Squad." Monster Career Center, 2004a. Online: http://interview.monster.com/articles/fired

Martin, Carole. "Prep for the Top 10 Interview Questions." Monster Career Center, 2004b. Online: http://interview.monster.com/articles/iq

Nemko, Marty. "The World's Toughest Job Interview Question." Monster Career Center, 2004. Online: http://interview.monster.com/articles/toughest/

Occupational Outlook Handbook (OOH), 2004–05 Edition. Bureau of Labor Statistics, U.S. Department of Labor. Washington, DC: U.S. Government Printing Office, 2004.

PoliceEmployment.com Website. Online: http://www.policeemployment.com/interview/

Raudsepp, Eugene. "Don't Let Tough Questions Sabotage Your Interview." *The Wall Street Journal Online,* November 6, 2002. Online: http://www.careerjournal.com/jobhunting/interviewing/20021106-raudsepp.html

Rosemarin, Judy. "Be Prepared to Perform in More Video Interviews." *The Wall Street Journal Online,* October 11, 2001. Online: http://www.careerjournal.com/jobhunting/interviewing/20011011-rosemarin.html

ADDITIONAL CONTACTS AND SOURCES OF INFORMATION

Brush up on your interview skills at http://www.careerbuilder.com/gh_int_htg.html. You'll find tips on "making a good impression," what not to do during an interview and more.

SECTION FOUR

YOUR FUTURE IN YOUR CHOSEN PROFESSION

The future comes one day at a time.

—*Dean Acheson*

Destiny is not a matter of chance, it is a matter of choice; it is not a thing to be waited for, it is a thing to be achieved.

—*William Jennings Bryan*

What is the recipe for successful achievement? To my mind there are just four essential ingredients: Choose a career you love. . . . Give it the best there is in you. . . . Seize your opportunities. . . . And be a member of the team.

—*Benjamin F. Fairless*

The road to happiness lies in two simple principles: find what it is that interests you and that you can do well, and when you find it, put your whole soul into it—every bit of energy and ambition and natural ability you have.

—*John D. Rockefeller, III*

There are no secrets to success. It is the result of preparation, hard work, and learning from failure.

—*General Colin L. Powell*

Once you've landed your "dream job," another challenge begins. How do you not only make certain you keep the job, but also make certain you excel? Chapter 15 addresses this major challenge. Chapter 16 discusses how you can enhance your chances for promotion, and Chapter 17 looks at job loss and starting the job-seeking process all over.

Preparation for the future is critical because that's where you'll be spending the rest of your life!

CHAPTER 15

AT LAST! YOU'VE GOT THE JOB! CONGRATULATIONS!!!

When you are making a success of something, it's not work. It's a way of life. You enjoy yourself because you are making your contribution to the world.

—Andy Granatelli

Do You Know:

➢ What needs to be done once you get the job?
➢ As you keep trying to do well, what is important?
➢ How to be "appropriate" on the job?
➢ What the likely effects of "knowing it all" will be?
➢ How to approach politics on the job?
➢ How to respond to criticism?
➢ Why being yourself is critically important?
➢ How to maintain yourself?

INTRODUCTION

By the time you get to this chapter, you will have covered an exceptional amount of material that should give you a genuine edge during your job search. You have taken a look at where to find jobs, how to write a résumé, how to best present yourself, how to interview, how to follow up and even how to deal with those inevitable rejections. Hopefully you were able to assimilate all this information and emerge victorious.

Hold everything! The race is not over yet. In a sense, it is just beginning. The only thing expected of the unsuccessful candidate is to be a good loser. But for the successful candidate, the ultimate challenge is just ahead. Getting a job brings a whole new set of challenges, especially in fields where you usually face a six-month to one-year probationary period. Kaminsky (2001, p. 32) states: "The avowed purpose of the probationary period is to provide some protection to an organization while it determines whether or not the new employee is all that the organization hoped they would be when hired."

Entry-level employees, in particular, are subject to a multitude of unwritten rules. Because criminal justice and private security are fields traditionally closed to outsiders, you have no basis to understand the expectations. You'll learn all too soon that the expectations are extremely high.

Starting a new job is like going to court. It doesn't happen all that often, but when it does, officers are expected to know what to do without having to be told ahead of time. To make an error could be very serious. The same with getting the job. Do you act like the old-timers? Do you act like the rookies? It is imperative that you have at least some idea of what to expect. Call it learning from others' mistakes.

What a bitter disappointment it must be to be successful in the pursuit of your dream job—only to lose it because you don't know what these circumstances demand. While many job applicants who could probably do the job just fine never get the chance because they cannot interview adequately, the opposite is true as well. Many people who cannot perform adequately get the job because they came across very well during the interview. Being successful in an interview does not guarantee success on the job. You must have some idea of what to expect and what the circumstances demand if you want to hold on to the job.

Here's what needs to be done once you get the job:

- Keep trying.
- Be appropriate.
- Know nothing.

- Wait until you are asked.
- Understand politics.
- Accept criticism maturely.

- Be yourself.
- Maintain yourself.

KEEP TRYING

Do not stop putting forth your best effort just because you have the job. If anything, make even greater attempts to fit into the new job than you did to get it. As Abraham Lincoln was fond of saying: "Things may come to those who wait, but only the things left by those who hustle." This is particularly true for those who have not had a professional-type job before. Criminal justice and security jobs are demanding, both in expectations and workload. You will be expected to perform as a professional, even at an entry-level position. Most employers expect you to know the basics. They seldom take time to ask if you do.

It is far better to ask a "dumb" question than to make a dumb mistake. No one likes to appear unintelligent, but employers know that no one knows it all. Employers want to have employees who are intelligent enough to direct themselves while knowing enough to stop and ask for help when needed. In effect, there are no dumb questions.

Keeping a job takes constant effort. You must not be afraid to ask questions, for not doing so may lead to mistakes that may cost you your job.

BE APPROPRIATE

This aspect of easing into your new job may seem terribly simplistic, but it's not. The job you have landed is a far cry from most other entry-level jobs such as working at a fast-food restaurant, washing cars or bagging groceries. The usual horseplay and immature attitudes frequently found at such jobs are simply not tolerated in any criminal justice or security job. Anything short of professional behavior is not good enough. These fields are constantly seeking to prove their professional image and demand employees who will help in this mission.

It is hard for new employees to know just what *is* appropriate behavior, unless they have been police explorers, reserve officers, interns or have had some other association with the criminal justice or security fields. Few outsiders know what goes on "inside." For a newly hired individual, a conservative, low-key, quiet approach is not only appropriate, but it's key to survival.

The best way to discover what behavior is appropriate is to simply assume a wait-and-see approach and take the necessary time to observe what is happening around you. You will see what behavior is approved of and disapproved of. A quiet approach for a new employee is always appreciated, while giving you a chance to ease into an admittedly uncomfortable new role.

Particularly younger people who have had little experience in the job world are susceptible to starting out with some rather "extreme" behavior. An overconfident, "cocky" attitude is often a cover-up for some very natural feelings of discomfort, self-doubt and personal reservations. Coming on too strong, however, can be very abrasive to fellow workers. Such an attitude tends to keep people at a distance when you really need them to reassuringly welcome you to your new job.

> Learn appropriate behavior by assuming a conservative, low-key, wait-and-see approach, taking the necessary time to observe what is happening around you and observing what behavior is approved of and disapproved of.

KNOW NOTHING

It is frequently easy to tell who the new kids on the block are. They are often overbearing and brash, seeming to go out of their way to show the world they know it all—or at least *think* they know it all. Actually, the more experienced officers become, the more those officers acknowledge that there is always more to learn.

Fact: A hierarchy exists in every police department, correctional facility and security corporation. Entry-level employees, especially *new* entry-level employees, are at the bottom of the ladder. You may never recover from the damage unintentionally done by telling anyone above you how *they* should be doing something. Many rookies destroy relationships with senior officers (maybe senior by only a year) by advising them on a better holster to carry, or a safer way to make a traffic stop, or which lights to use on the squad car during a motorist assist.

Maybe the rookie is correct, as rookies have usually received up-to-date training that reflects better ways of doing things and have not had time to develop bad habits. *This is not the point.* You will have plenty of time to do it your own way. Irritate anyone early on and word will spread that you are a "know-it-all."

This is not advice to "play stupid." If you are asked for an opinion, give it. If you have to make a decision, make it. Show interest and a desire to learn. It may be difficult to admit to yourself and others that you *are* new and really do *not* know it all. But if you pretend that you do, you will have shot yourself in the foot. Not only will others not think you are dumb if you ask questions, but they will appreciate the fact that you really want to learn.

> Being a "know-it-all" will likely earn you a negative reputation and delay your being accepted by others in the department, institution or agency.

WAIT UNTIL YOU ARE ASKED

This is a continuation of "know nothing." Officers in law enforcement, corrections or private security are in positions of respect. They tend to expect it and generally receive it. Particularly as a new employee, you will get more respect from other employees if you show respect for them. They deserve it. They have passed those difficult early stages of the job. They are now "regulars" and have a great deal to offer you as a newcomer. Give them the opportunity to share their wisdom with you.

Make it clear you know you have much to learn, and take advantage of this opportunity to ask questions. Do not, however, ask questions that are personally or professionally challenging to the individual (e.g., "Why would you wear a holster everyone *knows* is dangerous *and* ugly?"). A better way might be to ask what equipment the officer suggests you consider when you purchase your gear.

It will not make a positive impression to say to an officer you are riding with, "My instructor told us to tag such a violator for speeding. Why didn't you?" Rather, you might ask what other violations could have been written or how the officer decided what to write on that particular stop. Many officers feel their own department or agency does not adequately recognize them for their knowledge and ability. To have someone new ride with them and ask well-thought-out, inquisitive questions is flattering to that officer. Your presence can be a positive experience for both of you *if* you take full advantage of it.

Keep in mind that people working in criminal justice and security make their living getting lied to by the best. Do not pretend to be interested or ask questions to "set up" the officer to tell you something for an alternative purpose. You will be spotted before you get the question completed, and you will be off to a terrible start.

Is it possible to ask *too many* questions? This is difficult to answer. Determine this on your own. Teachers *want* students to ask appropriate questions, but also come to cringe at those always-present students who chronically ask questions for the sake of hearing themselves talk.

UNDERSTAND POLITICS

Every organization has its own politics. *Webster's* defines *politics* as: "competition between interest groups or individuals for power and leadership in a government or other group." That is a fitting definition, but the complexities are so deep you can be caught in the political web before ever being aware of its existence.

To understand politics, recognize that politics are impossible to understand. This is an area to be particularly careful of. Even seasoned veterans can easily fall prey to internal politics. Politics can be a deadly game and should be avoided.

Although many officers are fond of asserting they are not politicians and so are not going to play politics, in reality, we are all politicians to an extent. Whether or not we're a "player" in the politics of our agency, we may become entangled in it. This is particularly true for newcomers, who do not know where the political lines are drawn. And it can happen more easily than you think: issuing a ticket to a city council member, taking a different position during a public meeting, having to take enforcement action against a family member or friend of a politician or just being involved in personality differences.

While certain people tend to be more than willing to give advice, such advice may not turn out to be at all sound. Eventually you will learn who you can talk to openly. Some people are willing to share helpful insights; others may well set you up for a fall. Some things you might innocently say may offend someone. *You just do not know,* so don't take a chance.

For example, if someone talks negatively about another employee, don't get involved. You may want to nod or grunt appropriately, but if you also start making comments about others, you will quickly expose yourself as a gossip.

Experienced officers learn that it is best to never write anything they do not want to show up because it inevitably will surface. Similarly, it is a good practice to never say things you don't want heard because statements always seem to get repeated. People will tell you things in confidence. An eight-hour shift in a squad car, working a cell block or on security duty lends itself to sharing a lot of thoughts and ideas. Should you make the mistake of telling others what was told to you, you may cause some serious relationship problems for yourself and others. Never say anything you do not want repeated, and never repeat what is told to you in confidence.

Do not play politics. Do not try to understand politics. Do not get yourself drawn into politics. This is important advice for anyone on the job, but absolutely crucial for a newly hired individual.

ACCEPT CRITICISM MATURELY

A natural aspect of getting into any new job is learning. Considering that most people learn from their mistakes, you, too, should want to learn from *your* mistakes—they present great opportunities. Everyone (yes, *everyone*) makes mistakes at work. Naturally, the newer you are, the more mistakes are likely to occur. Employers expect this and would probably feel you weren't trying if mistakes weren't made.

So what's the big deal about making mistakes? The problem is that many people can't deal with thinking they are capable of making mistakes. Whether because of ego or just plain embarrassment, many individuals react inappropriately to being told they did something wrong. Failure to respond appropriately to criticism received at work can negatively affect a critical phase of the new job.

Frequently, part of field training or the probationary period is seeing how recruits or new employees handle constructive criticism. Assuming you learn from your mistakes and are able to prevent them from recurring too often, what is really essential is that you can maturely accept critical comments and process them, hopefully improving as a result. To argue with a trainer or superior is a poor choice for those who have been at the job for a only a short while. It could prove fatal for someone on probation. Take advantage of the occasional times someone offers criticism to not only improve the particular skill at issue, but also to make sure the person leaves thinking about how professionally you handled the situation.

One aspect of this process that people often fail to recognize is that offering criticism is frequently as difficult to do, or more so, as receiving it. If you accept the comments in a positive way, even thanking the person for offering the comments, you may well end up scoring far more points than you will ever realize. It would be a serious mistake to get angry, challenge the superior, have a temper tantrum or go shooting your mouth off to others. In the unlikely event that you genuinely are being harassed or ill-treated, discuss this with the person first, and only then proceed up the proper chain of command to deal with it. In some situations, new employees have, for whatever reason, not hit it off with a trainer. Personality conflicts do occur, as do outright illegal discrimination and harassment. But the real issue will be how you choose to handle it.

For example, a newly hired individual had extremely offensive body odor. When the supervisor suggested that perhaps a change in deodorant might be in order, the new employee became incensed and stormed out of the building. When she returned to work the next day, she was told that she no longer had a job there. It was *not* the body odor that caused her to lose the job—that was correctable. It was her immature, hostile reaction to the suggestion that cost her the job.

> Accept criticism maturely, for such instances provide great opportunities for you to learn from your mistakes. Recognize also that offering criticism is frequently as difficult as receiving it, and if you accept the comments in a positive way, you may score far more points than you will ever realize.

BE YOURSELF

You managed to get the job by being yourself, and you will succeed by being yourself. Don't get down on yourself because you're nervous, afraid or feel inadequate—we all feel this way when we start new jobs. The first few weeks *are* going to be rough. Draw energy from it rather than allowing it to exhaust you.

> It is important for you to be yourself. Starting a new job, particularly in a field you are not used to, is uncomfortable and requires an adjustment. You will become exhausted if you spend energy putting on an act. Save your energy for learning the job.

Police, corrections and security officers make their livings dealing with people who are trying to run scams on them. Many of these individuals are very good and may be able to fool the professionals at first. You will not be able to. Trying to do so will only result in your being labeled as someone trying to be someone you are not. Officers must be honest!

Peer pressure is always hard to cope with. As a rookie, you will be expected to do as you are told. If you are unfortunate enough to get drawn into a bad group of fellow employees, you will face some tough decisions. Do not engage in brutality. Use the minimum force necessary under the circumstances to accomplish the objective. Do not let peer pressure lead you to violate this important principle. Recognize that to stand by and watch unethical, possibly illegal, behavior is only slightly less devious than actually participating. If you don't think you can resist the temptations from within or without, get out now.

If you are not happy, do something about it. These jobs are *not* for everyone. If you are unhappy, or if you can foresee problems, admit this to yourself as soon as you become aware of it. Miller (2003) helps put this into perspective: "Since September 11, people everywhere have been re-assessing their priorities and realizing life is too short to waste doing something you don't love. Many will undergo a total re-focus in life because of this. No explanation or repackaging required."

It is sad to see people suffer for years at jobs they dislike—especially those in jobs that provide the individual with a great deal of power and authority. Perhaps some officers "go bad" by becoming terribly abusive or sarcastic because the job is just no longer right for them . . . and it shows. Further, consider that professionals who dislike their work do not have the necessary concentration to be safe. Many horrible things can result from remaining in an unfulfilling job for too long.

MAINTAIN YOURSELF

Burnout. We've all heard about it. Maybe you've been there. Most of us have at one time or another. When starting a new job, consider ways of balancing it to keep it as attractive as it was when you first heard about it. Don't overdo it. Keep up your other friendships, activities and interests. Take care of your physical self: eat right, exercise and get enough sleep.

It is also important to keep your guard up, to stay on your toes and be mentally sharp. As noted in the *Occupational Outlook Handbook* (2004):

> Police work can be very dangerous and stressful. In addition to the obvious dangers of confrontations with criminals, officers need to be constantly alert and ready to deal appropriately with a number of other threatening situations. Many law enforcement officers witness death and suffering resulting from accidents and criminal behavior. A career in law enforcement may take a toll on officers' private lives.
>
> Uniformed officers, detectives, agents, and inspectors are usually scheduled to work 40-hour weeks, but paid overtime is common. Shift work is necessary because protection must be provided around the clock. Junior officers frequently work weekends, holidays, and nights. . . .
>
> The jobs of some Federal agents such as U.S. Secret Service and DEA special agents require extensive travel, often on very short notice. They may relocate a number of times over the course of their careers. Some special agents in agencies such as the U.S. Border Patrol work outdoors in rugged terrain for long periods and in all kinds of weather.

Maintain yourself physically and mentally. Stay current not only with things related to the job but also with things that interest you outside of work. This helps prevent burnout.

Sheehan and Van Hasselt (2003, p. 12), in referring to the terrorist attacks of 9/11, observe:

> These horrific acts harmed all Americans, including thousands of law enforcement officers. Clearly, large-scale critical incidents are stressful, but so are the numerous smaller scale events that so many law enforcement officers encounter on the job. Who can accurately measure the stress caused by being wounded in the line of duty, having a partner killed or injured, shooting another person, seeing abused or deceased children, and witnessing severe motor vehicle accidents? Who can calculate the effects of continued exposure to murders, suicides, kidnappings, hijackings, rapes, and other violent acts that assault the sensibilities of law enforcement officers? Too often, assistance is delayed until officers display maladaptive behaviors, such as excessive drinking, domestic violence, or even suicide.

Careers in law enforcement, fire protection and security carry a heavy burden of responsibility when compared to most other jobs. It is often easy for new recruits to feel overwhelmed by this and to overcompensate by placing a higher priority on the performance of their professional duties, to the detriment of all other areas in their lives. Solan and Casey (2003, p. 17) have identified this as "police work addiction" and note: "Certainly, expectations run high in the law enforcement profession. Establishing and maintaining [professional] relationships creates tremendous demands on time, resources, and energy; life balance easily becomes lost." They (p. 17) caution: "While law enforcement professionals should possess a strong sense of duty and responsibility for the public's welfare, they must not forget the well-being of their families, friends, and, most important, themselves."

In examining the phenomenon of police officer burnout, Hawkins (2001, p. 343) reports: "An important aspect of the burnout syndrome is increased feelings of emotional exhaustion. . . . Another aspect of the burnout syndrome is the development of depersonalization, that is, negative, cynical attitudes and feelings about one's clients. This callous or even dehumanized perception of others can lead the individual to view their clients as somehow deserving of their troubles." Do not become cynical because of the nature of the work, the clientele or opinions expressed by fellow officers. Watch for "burnout," and use R&R time effectively to relieve stress. Do not become a "mooch," sponging off cooperative retailers, which usually begins with free coffee. Remember the concept of *quid pro quo,* that is, *those who give usually expect something in return.*

The longer you remain in a job, any job, the harder it is to let go of the benefits. You will be much further ahead if you are honest with yourself and leave if the work does not suit you. Similarly, the work may suit you just fine, but the job may not. For a variety of reasons, not every employment opportunity will fit everyone. If you know you want to be a police, corrections or security officer, but personalities or any other factors make this particular job less than satisfying, do *not* stay around. It is unlikely that things will improve. There *is* a job out there for you. Your job is to find it.

CONCLUSION

Congratulations! You've got the job! These words will, and should, be a deserved conclusion to a significant amount of work. Relish them. You are well on your way to professional career fulfillment. Don't let your guard down, and don't give up pursuing excellence. Set exceptional goals for yourself, and you will be exceptional.

Bear in mind, your success during the interviews will not guarantee you success on the job. You must have at least some idea of what to expect and what the circumstances demand if you want to hold on to the job. Remember, keeping a job takes constant effort. You must not be afraid to ask questions, for not doing so may lead to mistakes that may cost you your job. Work in criminal justice, security and related fields is important. It is satisfying. It says something about you that people working in other fields cannot boast. Congratulations on choosing these fields to pursue employment in and for making the effort to do it well.

YOUR GAME PLAN FOR EXCELLING ON THE JOB

 Take time *now* to write out, on a *separate* piece of paper, three goals to help you excel in your new position. Put the paper someplace you will see it often. Let these goals guide you as you embark on your exciting new career. And again, congratulations!

AN INSIDER'S VIEW

SURVIVING PROBATION

Linda S. Miller

Former Executive Director
Upper Midwest Community Policing Institute

Now that you have landed that job, you probably think you can relax. Think again. You are about to undergo a period of the most intense scrutiny you've ever experienced. It's called *probation*. Usually a period of six months to a year, it gives the department a chance to see you in action and to evaluate your work, your judgment and your style of relating to others. You don't have that job wrapped until you "make probation." Think of this period as a time to apply what you've learned in school and what you will learn on the job. Advice from veteran officers as you begin your probationary period would surely include the following:

➤ Don't be a know-it-all. You may have been the star of the academy, but keep it to yourself or you may alienate your colleagues.
➤ Learn the basics well. Fancy shooting or exotic defensive tactics moves won't be of much help to you unless you can also write a good report and make a proper car stop.

➤ Concentrate on report writing. Carry a pocket dictionary if you are not a good speller.
➤ Don't be a "gadget" person. One can often tell a rookie by the surprising number of pieces of equipment hanging from the gunbelt.
➤ Watch respected veteran officers do their job and learn from them. Don't, however, adopt their "bad" work habits.
➤ Don't take short cuts. These are for veterans willing to live with the consequences. You can't afford it.
➤ Don't get a reputation for being too aggressive. You want to be a willing worker, very interested in doing your job, but not a crusader chosen to rid the world of criminals.
➤ Treat the public and your coworkers with respect. Displaying your personal prejudices can be detrimental to your continued employment. Don't make derogatory racial or sexual remarks, even if you hear others doing so.
➤ Try to develop a reputation of being cooperative and nonargumentative. Be a team player.
➤ You may be in social situations with coworkers where alcohol is served. Drink conservatively. You can be sure that what you say and do under the influence of alcohol will be the talk of the department by the next day at the latest. Alcohol abuse is a serious problem in this society and in law enforcement. Most departments will not be impressed with a rookie who displays even a hint of alcohol abuse.
➤ The same goes for sexual behavior. Keep your personal life personal. Above all, don't sleep around with fellow employees.

Remember, your training officer and the department's supervisors have your future in their hands. In many departments, probationary employees can be let go for *any* reason. With a little forethought, you can avoid providing a reason. You have what it takes for the job or you wouldn't have been hired. And the department wants you to "make it" too. They have invested time and money in your hiring and training. They need you to assure them they've made the right choice.

Linda S. Miller *is the former executive director for the Upper Midwest Community Policing Institute as well as a former sergeant with the Bloomington (Minnesota) Police Department. She was with the department 23 years, and was a police dispatcher, patrol officer, crime prevention officer, patrol supervisor and head of the planning, research and crime prevention division. Sergeant Miller had been a member of the Minnesota Peace and Police Officers Association, the International Police Association, the Midwest Gang Investigator's Association, the International Association of Women Police and the Minnesota Association of Women Police. She was a member of the People-to-People's Women in Law Enforcement delegation to the Soviet Union in 1990. Sgt. Miller is a frequent presenter to community groups and is also an instructor.*

INSIDER'S VIEW ONLINE

An additional *Insider's View* for this chapter is "Let's Be Honest" by Sgt. Lawrence J. Fennelly, found on the Wadsworth website: http://www.wadsworth.com/criminaljustice_d/.

 ## MIND STRETCHES

1.   Have you ever been "too enthusiastic" at a new job? Why do you think you were? Did it hurt you?

2.   What behaviors have you observed in people in uncomfortable situations (like in a new job)?

3.   Why do you think important people often seem so "down-to-earth"? Conversely, why do you think many "not-so-important" people act so brashly?

4.   How long does it take to fit in at a new job? What helps you fit in?

5. Have you ever felt pressured at a job to behave in a way you did not feel comfortable? How did you handle this situation?

6. Why do you think people, particularly officers, seem to like to complain or be negative? What traps can this create for new employees?

7. What dangers are there in "taking sides" in an office dispute? How can you avoid becoming involved?

8. Can people who work together get along "too well"? Are "office romances" good or bad? Can they be avoided, or do they "just happen"?

9. How would you handle a situation in which you knew a coworker was doing something illegal, immoral or unethical? Would you respond differently if the person was a peer or your supervisor?

10. At what point do you think people stop growing and developing professionally? What opportunities exist to help you maintain your own personal and professional vitality?

REFERENCES

Hawkins, Homer C. "Police Officer Burnout: A Partial Replication of Maslach's Burnout Inventory." *Police Quarterly,* September 2001, pp. 343–360.

Kaminsky, Glenn F. "Effective Utilization of the Probationary Period." *The Law Enforcement Trainer,* March/April 2001, pp. 32–33.

Miller, Jo. "Life Is Too Short to Waste Doing Something You Don't Love." CareerBuilder.com, 2003. Online: http://msn. careerbuilder.com/Custom/MSN/CareerAdvice/WPI_LifeIsTooShort.htm?sc_extcmp=JS_wi12_dec03_advice

Occupational Outlook Handbook, 2004–05 Edition. Bureau of Labor Statistics, U.S. Department of Labor. Washington, DC: U.S. Government Printing Office, 2004.

Sheehan, Donald C. and Van Hasselt, Vincent B. "Identifying Law Enforcement Stress Reactions Early." *FBI Law Enforcement Bulletin,* September 2003, pp. 12–17.

Solan, Gerard J. and Casey, Jean M. "Police Work Addiction: A Cautionary Tale." *FBI Law Enforcement Bulletin,* June 2003, pp. 13–17.

CHAPTER 16

THE CAREER LADDER:
INSIGHTS INTO PROMOTIONS AND JOB CHANGE

If you can dream it, you can do it.

—*Walt Disney*

Do You Know:

➢ Whether the promotional process differs from initial job seeking?
➢ What changes, besides promotions, may lead to personal and professional growth?
➢ What factors motivate people to seek change in their professional lives?
➢ Which basic job-seeking skills apply?
➢ How important "off-duty" activities are?
➢ Whether changing jobs can help or hurt future job-seeking efforts?
➢ If you can ever have "too much" education or education in the wrong area?
➢ When networking is important (other than during the job search)?
➢ How important the oral interview is to the promotional process?

INTRODUCTION

While this book began as a guide to help individuals find employment in criminal justice or security, it has also introduced you to information regarding the employment process as well. This chapter provides suggestions on how to prepare for the promotional process and what to expect. For the new job seeker, just *getting* that first job is the dream. But eventually everyone seeks change. For some it is seeking promotions on the way to "the top." For others it is changing within their present agency or looking for opportunities with others. And some want to change professions altogether.

Make no mistake about it—the world of work has changed dramatically over the decades. It is no longer the norm to remain in one career with one employer until retirement. While there is nothing wrong with that—if a person finds a niche and enjoys doing the same thing daily—the fact is that more and more people are changing jobs, either because they want to—or because they have to.

The final chapter discusses the impact of job loss and change. But what about the *desire* to change? This hasn't been considered the "norm" in a field of work that has traditionally involved staying with one agency, possibly seeking internal transfers or promotions. This chapter examines both. It also addresses the seemingly increasing desire people have to switch to entirely different careers. Whether seeking a promotion or other job change, developing a strategy will make the transition more successful.

You must keep in mind several important aspects of the promotional process. First and foremost, the basic job-seeking skills and strategies you are developing will also serve you well throughout your promotional ventures. Promotional interviews are similar to initial job interviews. Regardless of the level of employment you aspire to, you will still need to provide information about yourself that presents you as *THE* one to promote.

Second, it is important to create a plan for yourself. Life itself presents numerous opportunities, as does work. By thinking ahead, you develop not only some ideas of where you want to go in life (and work), but also the ability to recognize the many opportunities that present themselves. Recall how many careers people normally have during their lives. When you consider all the promotions or job changes people experience, it is easy to see how important it is to know how to prepare for opportunities. Indeed, as the saying goes, "Most people don't plan to fail. They fail to plan." Arnold (2000, p. 63) states:

> Few police officers plan their careers. Most do not focus on promotion possibilities early enough, and have not prepared enough—either through formal education or assignment selection—to equip themselves for leadership roles. Strategic career planning can be a kind of road map to professional success.

Third, recognize that in criminal justice and security positions, seniority and "paying your dues" also play important roles in promotions.

> Promotion-seeking skills are very similar to the basic job-seeking skills and strategies you are developing. Both scenarios demand you present yourself as *THE* one to hire/promote.

PROMOTIONS: WHAT THEY ARE AND WHERE THEY ARE

Traditionally, promotions are considered to be upward moves, usually within the same organization where one is presently employed. This is a valid concept for many promotions, but try thinking of promotions in a much broader way. Any promotion is a change, but is every change a promotion? Take it one step further. Obviously, every promotion provides new challenges, but so does every change—even those that don't initially appear to be upward. Consider *any* job change as an employment opportunity. This includes promotions, transfers and, yes, even demotions or dismissals.

Think about it for a moment. Many people who have confronted what appeared to be overwhelming adversity end up saying it was the best thing that ever happened to them. Why? Because they grew from the experience. The bigger the challenge, the greater the opportunity for personal and professional growth.

> Promotions are but one type of change that provides new professional challenges and allows for growth. Often the most adversarial changes, such as demotions or dismissals, lead to the greatest amount of personal and professional growth.

MOTIVATIONS FOR SEEKING CHANGE

The chapter on rejection addresses how you should strive to obtain energy from the process, and how you should control the process rather than let it control you. It *can*, *should* and (eventually) *will* result in growth for you. Richard Obershaw, founder of the Burnsville (Minnesota) Counseling Center of Grief, is fond of saying "a rut is a grave with the ends knocked out." And it is this feeling that frequently compels people to set their sights on bigger, better, or at least different, careers. While previous generations felt a stronger desire to remain at one job, it has become more common for people to follow their desire to find whatever feeds their souls.

Of course, considerations like better pay, more benefits or a desire to move to another community motivate people to change jobs. Other reasons may not present themselves as "positive" reasons for the change—downsizings, reorganizations, closings and even involuntary terminations force people to change. The work world is seeing upheaval the recent generations have not experienced. Layoffs are occurring by the tens of thousands. No job is guaranteed secure forever, even in government and union work, which previously had been considered untouchable.

> Motivations for seeking change include better pay, better benefits, the desire to live and work in another community, downsizing, reorganizations, closings and involuntary terminations. Some of these reasons originate in the individual, and some are forced upon the individual—but all lead the individual to change.

With regard to law enforcement promotions, Hamilton (2004, p. 25) notes the importance of being true to yourself, not just doing what you think others expect you to do: "While it is expected that people aspire to higher levels of job status, not everyone wants to leave patrol and join management." She tells the stories of several officers who faced promotion dilemmas:

> "I was a lieutenant in charge of Violent Crimes when I realized that I had promoted myself out of the job I really wanted to do. I signed on to be a street cop, not pay bills, do evaluations, handle grievances and the like. . . . It is a good thing to want to be a supervisor or commander and I applaud anyone who does. Just make sure it is what you really want to do. While administration is essential, 'real' police work is not done at headquarters." . . .

> Not everyone advances to higher positions, and it's not necessarily because they were passed over for a promotion. [Another officer] made a decision to remain a sergeant at the San Diego Police Department. He found that he liked working with people in the field instead of working behind a desk. He has no regrets.

Whether change results from unanticipated factors or your desire to better yourself professionally, seek a bigger paycheck with improved benefits or move to a different place, your job-seeking skills will serve you a lifetime.

SIMILAR SKILLS

Take time to reflect on the entry-level job search and the promotional process, and you can see the similarities. In fact, both are going to result in different jobs—new jobs, and the skills you will need are the same:

➤ Cover letters (sometimes called "letters of interest" in the promotional process)

➤ Résumés (now providing more specific training and experience records)

➤ Test-taking skills

➤ Interview skills

➤ An overall positive appearance as *THE* one to hire

> The job-seeking skills needed during the promotional process include writing effective cover letters and résumés, taking tests, interviewing and presenting yourself positively as *THE* one to hire or promote.

The changes you will notice as you work on your promotional strategies are simply a fine-tuning of the skills you developed earlier. It is through explaining how you have developed professionally and why you want the change that makes this job-seeking process different from an entry-level job search.

INCREASING YOUR CHANCES FOR PROMOTION—PREPARATION IS KEY

Booth (2002, p. 71) cautions: "Let me dispel the idea that there are tricks to help candidates succeed on promotional tests. Just as in any competition, success depends upon the knowledge, skills and abilities the contestant has developed and practiced over time." Fulton (2000, p. 118), echoing the general sentiment that "preparation is the key to getting promoted," suggests a 10-step plan:

1. Start early.

2. Learn from others (e.g., when fellow officers make a solid arrest, ask how they did it).

3. Avoid problems (e.g., when officers around you make mistakes, learn from their mistakes).

4. Be committed.

5. Prepare, prepare, prepare.

6. Make your intentions known. Let the "higher-ups" know you are willing to accept the responsibility of a promotion.

7. Get a mentor.

8. Learn the rules. Is the department's emphasis on academics, the written exam or the oral interview?

9. Get the resources you need.

10. Do your best.

With regard to step 1, "starting early," Lunney (2002, p. 5) observes: "There is a startling commonality found in the personal stories of many successful people. They describe the early phases of their working life, then strike to the heart of their experience, saying, '. . . and then I got serious.'" The sooner you "get serious" about preparing for promotion, the greater your chances of success.

As to steps 2 and 3, Hamilton (p. 26) suggests: "Look at those around you and learn from them." She notes how one sergeant looked to others for professional guidance: "I relied on what I saw from a wide range of experienced (and inexperienced) officers, friends, and citizens. I took what seemed to work for them and used it, eventually blending a wide cross-section of ideas into a way of policing that seemed to work well for me."

Being committed (step 4) means getting involved in the profession after hours. Commitment means joining and participating in professional organizations and associations. It may also include volunteering in the community, as Carter (2002, p. 35) explains:

> Police agencies are always looking for volunteers to help with United Way campaigns, annual picnics, Christmas or holiday festivities, special projects, charity events, neighborhood celebrations, and the like. If your agency is not doing these things, maybe you need to take on a leadership role and get something started. Community organizations such as Big Brothers and the YMCA offer other opportunities.

Such involvement demonstrates your desire to invest in the community you serve and underscores your commitment to your profession.

Being actively involved in such "off-duty" activities as professional organizations/associations and volunteering demonstrates a commitment to your profession, which is looked upon favorably by promoters.

Step 5—prepare, prepare, prepare—is a theme that runs through this entire discussion and, as has been emphasized throughout this text, is vital in every aspect of your career, from finding your first job through achieving your "ultimate" career objectives.

Step 6 can be accomplished very quickly and straightforwardly by simply saying to your supervisor, "I really want to move up to the rank of . . .," but, as the saying goes, actions speak louder than words. The more effective strategy, albeit more gradual and subtle, is to increase your visibility and show, through your actions, your desire to take on new challenges and expanded professional responsibilities. According to Carter (pp. 34–35):

> Exposure or visibility is absolutely critical to career advancement. Often underestimated by career aspirants, exposure accounts for much of your chance for advancement. If you are the greatest thing to come down the pike since café mocha but are stuck on a night shift in the most boring part of town then you likely will not be noticed. . . .
>
> By taking an active role in voluntary and other high-profile activities, you gain not only the personal satisfaction of serving others but also positive exposure that helps in networking and bumping into those who are in a position to help advance your career. . . .
>
> Taking on tough assignments, volunteering to teach and coach new programs or processes, becoming a mentor to others, and creating innovative improvements in the organization are just a few ways that you can increase your visibility and display your talents.

These actions clearly demonstrate to those with the power to promote that you are ready, willing and able to assume greater professional responsibility.

Step 7—seeking a mentor—has become an increasingly valuable strategy as the trend toward the professionalization of law enforcement continues. It is helpful to develop a relationship with someone you respect who can provide support and advice and lend an ear during the frequently stressful, sometimes discouraging, process of seeking employment goals. Support is considerably more important than many think, and the friendships that develop as a result of these mentoring relationships are a great benefit as well. Hamilton (p. 25) recommends:

> Cultivate relationships that will be beneficial to you. It may sound like a calculated plan, and it is, but it is one that can benefit both you and the officer who mentors you.

> [One sergeant] says he's found that mentorship is a worthwhile endeavor, although it's sometimes difficult to begin and maintain. "Making contacts is easy, but keeping up with them is the hard part," he says. "If you want to become a homicide detective, for example, seek out one who is open to helping you over the long term. What schools did she attend? What was her career track? What does she feel you must do in order to achieve your goals? What would she do differently?"

Learning the rules (step 8) may seem obvious, but many promotion-oriented officers have their sights so fixed on the "ends" they fail to examine the best, most effective "means" of getting there. It can, indeed, be of benefit to know the emphasis your department or agency places on higher education and specific promotional testing methods. For example, Booth (p. 75) states:

> Candidates frequently ask me how to prepare for an assessment center or other promotional testing process. I have consistently argued that candidates should not be preparing for the test. Rather, they should be preparing for the position. It has been my experience that those candidates who attempt to focus on the specific exercises they may encounter, or who take preparatory courses to learn tricks and tips for succeeding in an assessment center, do themselves a disservice.

However, some departments may place an inordinate amount of stock in how well an applicant performs on the written exam. Others may place a higher emphasis on academics. According to Armstrong and Polk (2002, p. 25): "Higher education leads to more rapid advancement and movement within [an] officer's career path, particularly at the earlier stages."

Bowman (2002, p. 11) advocates the mantra "Educate to Elevate," noting that academics "have pushed our department to a new level of professionalism and innovation." He contends: "If we expect to meet the growing demands of community policing, we must increase the education of our officers. . . . We require a four-year degree, not just for new recruits but for officers who want to advance in the department." Certainly not every department, agency or company in the country will have such stringent educational standards for those seeking promotion, but this "rule" is definitely worth investigating.

Step 9—get the resources you need—is an extension of steps 7 and 8. Mentors can be an invaluable resource, through their own knowledge and wisdom and in their capacity to point you in the direction of other valuable resources. If you know your department emphasizes higher education, enroll in the courses you will need to meet their standards. If you learn the organization is struggling with certain diversity issues within the community, seek appropriate sensitivity training or other resources that will provide you the skills and other qualities that will set you apart from other candidates. According to Booth (p. 74): "The more successful employee understands the philosophy, direction and expectations of the organization."

Fulton's final word of advice—step 10—is: "Your best chance for getting promoted is to be a professional at every rank you hold, prepare for the next rank, and always do the best you can."

Lunney (pp. 4–5), in examining professional development, has identified several elements that lead to top performance:

> **Show Up:** Showing up is the first law of policing, whether a rookie reporting on time for a shift or a superintendent scheduled for a meeting with a community group. . . .

> **Pay Attention:** Pay attention to the job at hand and pay attention to others. . . . It is amazing how seldom people today make an effort to truly listen to what another person is saying and meaning, listening without interruption and with full concentration. . . . When you pay attention, you impress people with your integrity and you honor them.

Have Courage: A display of courage in a critical situation is much admired in the police world. . . . But relatively few people have the opportunity to display uncommon physical courage. The more common and everyday challenges are moral and ethical, such as whether or not you are willing to speak out if confronted by wrongdoing or unethical behavior. . . . The ultimate test is a willingness to put your career interests on the line to preserve your integrity—that's having courage.

Keep Going: Perseverance, industry and endurance are essential to success in any field. In the face of criticism, occasional failure or disappointment, success favors the individual who unswervingly maintains a sense of mission and purpose.

Set Goals: Write a personal mission statement. Document your purpose in life and your long-term objectives. Set goals, including career goals and goals for your personal life. Be realistic, record your goals in a personal diary and keep them private. Refer to your list at regular intervals and update as your insights and circumstances change. This habit is the key to achieving personal goals.

Work Smart and Work Hard: The principles of management are not fully appreciated or practiced in policing. Becoming a student and practitioner of effective ways and means of getting things done provides an edge in a crowded field.

Keep Learning: Continuous learning is essential for leaders in this fast-paced society. Exercise your curiosity, read widely, undertake formal studies when you can; put yourself in the way of experts, seek out people who can provide the guidance or knowledge you need and emulate the leadership qualities you admire in others.

Keep Promises: Avoid getting overcommitted but once you make a promise, do everything possible to make good on it. If you can't always deliver because of circumstances beyond your control, explain why.

Be Generous: The best leaders are generous with their time, attention and understanding in their dealings with others. . . . A generous spirit earns the loyalty of others.

Be Positive and Enthusiastic: An indomitable spirit in the face of any condition, from boredom to adversity, is essential to maintaining one's own spirit and sustaining that of others.

Tempt Good Fortune: There is an element of chance in all things. Never discount factors such as being in the right place at the right time or developing a faculty for serendipity—making happy and unexpected discoveries by accident. Good fortune favors the prepared mind.

Again, the importance of being *prepared,* for what you seek as well as the unexpected, is an essential element in achieving your career goals.

A Final Note on Broadening Your Experience and Education

To move up, it commonly becomes necessary to step outside your comfort zone. Take advantage of new opportunities as they present themselves, and avoid spending your entire career in one area. One sergeant (Hamilton, p. 26) recommends: "Don't stagnate in a position for too long if you want to move ahead. Get experiences in as many areas as possible and if you particularly like one, become a subject matter expert in that field. Whether it is gangs, drugs, firearms, accident investigation, or some other field, your expertise will make you valuable to your department, unit, or section."

While broadening your experience may not be a big problem for people employed in larger agencies, as federal, state and large municipal agencies permit many opportunities for change, new challenges and promotional advancement, smaller agencies may demand that the motivated employee take new jobs outside their agency. These changes should be pursued as a part of your plan for achieving your employment goals, just like all other areas of developing your strategy. Change merely for the sake of change may become self-defeating. If you don't stay at a new job or a new assignment long enough to really benefit from it (or be of benefit to your employer), this may cause understandable concern to those doing the hiring. It's a tough call, and an individual one, to pursue another opportunity "too soon." Take the time necessary to think through frequent changes.

> Take opportunities that further your planned career path, but do not get carried away, jumping from one job to another. Be selective in your moves, or such job jumping may damage your future options in your profession.

Hamilton (p. 26) suggests: "Also think about furthering your education as part of your training and preparation for higher-level jobs. You can often get grants and scholarships or reimbursements from your agency. There's usually some kind of financial help available if the degree you're pursuing can be applied to your job."

> Education is akin to experience—you cannot acquire "too much" education or education in the wrong area.

It is difficult to understand how anyone's education could be viewed negatively, but it may. The two reasons that surface most frequently are a fear the applicant will soon move on to a "bigger and better" job and the fear of intimidating those "above." It is difficult to view this as anything more than jealousy, but some supervisors don't want their subordinates to have more education than they have. Do not fail to acquire advanced education because of what others might think, but be prepared to defend the choice, as well as to assure others that such education will benefit the department. Never stop learning.

NETWORKING AND OTHER VALUABLE PROMOTION-SEEKING TOOLS

As with the job search, *networking* for a promotion is very important. The more people you know, and the more people who know you, the better off you'll be. Again, becoming involved in professional organizations and associations is a great way to learn more and to get your name out there.

> Networking is as essential to promotion efforts as it is to job-seeking efforts.

Letters of commendation are another tool with high promotion-seeking value. They reflect positive actions in which a candidate was involved and highlight the leadership abilities or management skills sought when evaluating an employee for promotion. Don't be shy about asking for letters. Many people will tell you they appreciate your work but may need some encouragement to document it. You have a responsibility to yourself to do everything you can do to best convey your excellence. A good supply of such personal recommendations will put you in a great position to include the best and most applicable for your next effort.

Feedback is always beneficial, particularly for those who have not gotten the promotions they sought. Face it, most people are either too polite or too intimidated to tell an applicant why they didn't succeed. It takes guts to ask for honest feedback, but once you ask for it, you must be willing to accept it.

ADVANCEMENT IN THE OTHER PROTECTIVE SERVICES

While the bulk of this chapter tends to focus on the promotion process as it applies to law enforcement, keep in mind that many of the skills and suggestions are relevant to promotion in the other protective services as well. The following information is taken from the *Occupational Outlook Handbook* (2004) to supplement the previous discussion, for those looking to advance in areas other than law enforcement.

Correctional Officers

With education, experience, and training, qualified officers may advance to correctional sergeant. Correctional sergeants supervise correctional officers and usually are responsible for maintaining security and directing the activities of other officers during an assigned shift or in an assigned area. Ambitious and qualified correctional officers can be promoted to supervisory or administrative positions all the way up to warden. Officers sometimes transfer to related areas, such as probation officer, parole officer, or correctional treatment specialist.

Firefighting Occupations

Most experienced firefighters continue studying to improve their job performance and prepare for promotion examinations. To progress to higher level positions, they acquire expertise in advanced firefighting equipment and techniques, building construction, emergency medical technology, writing, public speaking, management and budgeting procedures, and public relations.

Opportunities for promotion depend upon written examination results, job performance, interviews, and seniority. Increasingly, fire departments use assessment centers, which simulate a variety of actual job performance tasks, to screen for the best candidates for promotion. The line of promotion usually is to engineer, lieutenant, captain, battalion chief, assistant chief, deputy chief, and finally to chief. Many fire departments now require a bachelor's degree, preferably in fire science, public administration, or a related field, for promotion to positions higher than battalion chief. A master's degree is required for executive fire officer certification from the National Fire Academy and for State chief officer certification.

Private Detectives and Investigators

Most private detective agencies are small, with little room for advancement. Usually there are no defined ranks or steps, so advancement takes the form of increases in salary and assignment status. Many detectives and investigators work for detective agencies at the beginning of their careers and, after a few years, start their own firms. Corporate and legal investigators may rise to supervisor or manager of the security or investigations department.

Security Guards and Gaming Surveillance Officers

Although guards in small companies may receive periodic salary increases, advancement opportunities are limited. Most large organizations use a military type of ranking that offers the possibility of advancement in position and salary. Some guards may advance to supervisor or security manager positions. Guards with management skills may open their own contract security guard agencies.

IMPROVING PROMOTIONAL EXAM PERFORMANCE

Promotional exams are a fact of life in the protective services. Fire service and law enforcement routinely use such exams to help determine which candidates should advance to the next rank. DiVasto (1990, p. 24) notes: "There may be nothing in the work life of an experienced police officer that can generate as much anxiety as a promotional exam. Officers who face armed hoodlums without so much as a blink will lose sleep for weeks worrying about a promotional exam." DiVasto[1] suggests some strategies to help reduce text anxiety. These strategies are to be implemented before and during the exam as follows:

Part I—Before the Exam

1. Have a clear idea of what material the exam will cover. Some departments publish reading lists, some circulate written materials, others just rely on word of mouth. . . .
2. Commit yourself to buy, borrow or share the books you'll need. Many of these, such as state codes and S.O.P. manuals, you might already have. Other materials, such as textbooks, you might have to buy or borrow. . . .
3. Determine what the test format will be. Find out, for example, if you'll be required to answer essay questions, true-false questions, multiple-choice questions, or a combination of these. . . .
4. "Train" for the exam. . . . Set out . . . a training plan . . . [including these] elements . . .:
   a. Commit yourself to study a minimum of 100 hours for your exam . . . only eight hours a week for the three months prior to the exam. . . .
   b. Begin studying not less than three months before the exam date.
   c. Set out your study plan on a calendar. . . .
   d. Find the time that is best for you to study. . . .
   e. Don't take on any major responsibilities, projects, or other energy-consuming activities while you're studying. . . .
   f. Give yourself time to relax a few days prior to test day. . . .
5. Before the test day arrives, be sure you know the time, place and what you're expected to bring. . . .
6. On the day of the exam, allow for extra time to drive to the test site, and plan on being there early. . . .

Part II—Taking the Exam

The most common type of written promotional examination is multiple-choice. . . .

1. Divide the test into hour-long segments. If there are one hundred questions and two hours in which to do them, plan on spending an hour on each fifty questions. If there's no time limit, allow yourself about a minute and a half per question or forty questions an hour.
2. Read each question very carefully and restate it to yourself in its most basic terms. If there are "distracters" in the question, eliminate them as you read. . . .
3. Answer each question by supplying the correct answer before you look at the choices. Your answer should match up with one of the choices listed.
4. Answer every question in your one-hour block before you go on to the next block. . . .
5. If you can't come up with the correct answer, eliminate the obvious wrong answers. . . .
6. Once you've eliminated the wrong answers, your choices will generally be down to two. Reread the question, restate it to yourself and take your best guess.
7. If you're taking a test made up from standard textbooks, forget the "real world" answer . . . the test maker doesn't ride in your patrol car. He is going by what the text writer said is correct, not how you would do it on the street.
8. Beware of the right answer to the wrong question. . . .
9. Take a few minutes of break time between each of your one-hour segments.

An abundance of resources are available online (most for a fee) to help candidates better prepare for promotional exams. One such website, PoliceCareer.com (http://www.PoliceCareer.com/leptadquestions. html. Used by permission.), provides 20 sample questions typically found on promotional exams and instructs candidates to respond to each question on a scale of 1 (strongly disagree) to 10 (strongly agree):

1. There are some situations where violating a department policy or even a minor law is the right thing to do.

2. Police professionals should be independent of local politics.

---

[1]Adapted from Peter V. DiVasto. "Improving Promotional Exam Performance." *Law and Order,* May 1990, pp. 24, 29. Reprinted by permission.

3. I can defend the viewpoint of my subordinates to the Chief of Police, even if I personally feel the viewpoint is wrong.

4. My motivation in seeking promotion is the increase in prestige.

5. I want to be promoted to Chief of Police one day.

6. It is fair to hold supervisors to a higher standard of ethical conduct than the standards police officers are held to.

7. I will not support an officer who commits a serious policy violation.

8. Officers who use a lot of sick time should be warned, disciplined and eventually terminated.

9. It is fair to hold supervisors and managers accountable for crime reduction.

10. Individualism is an important strength of a law enforcement officer.

11. I feel comfortable having someone else set my priorities.

12. There are some items I would change about myself if I could.

13. Gaining the trust and respect of fellow officers is one of the most important aspects of being in law enforcement.

14. I have avoided conflicts with department supervisors and managers.

15. I compromise to avoid problems, even when I am right.

16. Civilian review boards are more likely to rule against police officers in complaint cases.

17. With enough time and effort, most police officer performance problems can be solved.

18. I like to argue my point of view and try to convince other officers that I am right.

19. I avoid conflict in the workplace at all cost.

20. Bad things that happen to good police officers are brought about by their own mistakes or ignorance.

This site also notes that such promotional exams generally contain opinion, scenario and judgment questions in the following categories:

➢ Dedication to the Law Enforcement Agency and Profession

➢ Desire for Responsibility and Leadership

➢ Law Enforcement Ethics and Accountability

➤ Supervisory Judgment Under Stress

➤ Ability to Accept Responsibility for the Actions of Self and Subordinates

➤ Knowledge of Current Professional Trends and Topics

➤ Responsibility to Society and Community

➤ "Defense" of Subordinates and the Department Management

IMPROVING PROMOTIONAL INTERVIEW PERFORMANCE

Borello (2004) asserts: "An officer's performance during the oral interview is paramount because the process is highly competitive. Officers must 'out-score' others also vying for promotion. This is difficult in that candidates may be competing against dozens or even hundreds of other police personnel, many of whom may have greater education or more experience." Furthermore:

> Police officers and front-line supervisors who have tested in promotional oral interviews or who have sat in on oral interview panels will tell you that the information basics—leadership, risk management, sexual harassment, discipline, etc.—are important, but that having a solid comprehension of this knowledge has little value if candidates cannot articulate that information with professional skill and confidence. Anyone can memorize a definition for leadership. Most can repeat that definition with a little practice and preparation. Very few can deliver a dynamic well-rounded response that hooks the panel's attention, builds the answer with connective issues and articulates the information both verbally and nonverbally while exemplifying poise, energy, confidence and presents a clear nexus to the position being tested for. Studying books, articles, policy, and promotional materials for information is a limited process that will only prepare officers with the internal knowledge they need—"the what"—but falls short in giving officers the communication skills needed to verbally deliver what they have learned—"the how."

Narramore[2] (1991, pp. 161–162) has devised a comprehensive review on how to prepare for a promotional interview:

> The people involved in an interview to evaluate your qualifications try to ascertain three basic facts about you. These are the most important traits you will need to convey to the panel:
>
> ➤ You can handle the job.
> ➤ You will do the job to the best of your ability.
> ➤ You are a manageable team player.
>
> Candidates who communicate to the evaluators "yes" to the above questions will score the highest. You must be able to demonstrate willingness and ability during the interview process.
>
> The first time I competed for the position of police sergeant was a disappointment I will always remember. I felt very comfortable after taking the written examination. I had scored high and was in an excellent position. Because I felt so confident, I did nothing to prepare for the oral interview. I felt showing up in all my glory and answering the questions to the best of my ability would be enough. That was a very big mistake. I finished in the top five overall, but I was not in the winner's circle. I looked back and learned from my mistake. That experience taught me to take that extra step of preparedness for every phase of the testing process.

---

[2]Adapted from Randy E. Narramore. "Preparing for a Promotional Interview." *Law and Order,* September 1991, pp. 161–162. Reprinted by permission.

The interview is the most important part of the promotional process. A successful candidate will make the "question and answer period" an exchange of ideas between law enforcement professionals. Accomplishing this means you are qualified and prepared. . . .

Law enforcement agencies look for specific traits in individual profiles to help determine the type of supervisor a candidate may become. Being more skilled and more qualified does not prove they will be a team player. Education and experience alone does not guarantee they will fit into the scheme of the organization. Several traits are reviewed during an interview: ambition, motivation, communication skills, devotion, conviction and confidence. . . .

Narramore also addresses the basic "traps" so many well-qualified candidates fall prey to, some of which are so damaging, recovery is next to impossible:

Failure to listen to the question. Every question asked by an interviewer demands a specific answer. Do not ramble on with superfluous responses. Be brief, yet concise. For example: if asked how many years you have been in law enforcement, provide a specific number. However, if you are asked to relate your feelings about illegal drugs, provide a more general answer.

Not taking enough time before answering questions. Do not answer a question immediately. Think about what you are going to say. This gives the impression you consider your responses and do not respond spontaneously.

Answering questions not asked. Answering a question not asked is annoying. When the board wants more information, they will ask for it.

Not being brief and to the point. The board does not want drawn out answers providing little information. If you do not know the answer, don't attempt to deceive the board with flowered responses. Be brief and to the point.

Not turning a negative into a positive. You may be asked a question regarding a negative area of your career, or be asked to discuss a major weakness. Try to turn the atmosphere into something positive. Admit you had a certain weakness, but were able to recognize it and took the steps necessary to correct it.

Being flippant or a joker. Oral boards do not like flippant responses. One improper response could ruin the entire interview.

It is not always the best person who receives the promotion. The ones who receive the promotions are usually those who have qualities of efficiency, hard work and reliability. If you follow the above suggestions, you will have a much better opportunity receiving that promotion you deserve.

Borello (2003, p. 131) concludes:

Taking the oral interview is an art. The dynamics of interview performance are vast, involving communication skills, understanding how to build rapport, confidence, poise under pressure, job knowledge, seeing the big picture, skilled decision making, advanced preparation, physical and mental energy, and the list goes on.

Promotion is significant, and is often considered the exemplification of a successful and progressive career. Preparing for a promotion should never be taken lightly; it should be treated like an Olympic event.

The oral interview is the most important part of the promotional process. Prepare for it as enthusiastically as you did for your initial job-seeking interview.

As you prepare for your promotion interview, you may also want to reread the *Insider's View* by Sweeney. This may help you organize your thoughts.

CONCLUSION

Because work is such a significant part of life, job satisfaction is vital. Not only do satisfactory jobs provide monetary and other employment-related benefits to enable you to live the lifestyle you desire, but they also help you feel good about yourself.

Promotion-seeking skills are very similar to the basic job-seeking skills and strategies you are developing. Both scenarios demand you present yourself as *THE* one to hire/promote. Job-seeking skills needed during the promotional process include writing effective cover letters and résumés, taking tests and interviewing. Networking and researching the interviewing department or agency are also important elements. Whatever your reasons for seeking a new job or a change in the job you have, your ability to develop successful job-seeking strategies will help you realize your goals. Promotions and professional advancement require a well-thought-out plan that you will implement over time.

AN INSIDER'S VIEW

MAKING THE MOST OF YOUR LAW ENFORCEMENT CAREER

Richard D. Beckman

Former Sergeant (Retired)
Cloverdale (California) Police Department

Let's assume that you have passed all your tests, been appointed to the position of a law enforcement officer, successfully completed the academy and are performing well in your FTO program. Sounds like a dream, sounds like a long ways off, hard to imagine. With a strong set of values, persistence and a good, well-thought-out set of goals, you can do it.

By now you have figured out that law enforcement is not all the glitter and glamour of television, and all your expectations of the job have been shattered or changed considerably. With the academy behind you and your newly gained knowledge as an experienced trainee, you now have a unique opportunity to assess your career, reevaluate your goals based on your newfound knowledge and plan your future.

Law enforcement is a noble profession. We all had different ideas the first time we climbed into the passenger seat of that police car next to a seasoned veteran. With our eyes wide open, we were about to go through a transformation that would affect us the rest of our life. The old standard oral-board answer of, "I want to be a police officer so I can help people," took on a new meaning when you encountered the *real* world. You will learn and see many new things. You will see the worst and the best in people. Remember, we are all part of the same human race. The old adage, "Don't judge a person until you've walked in their shoes," has a lot of hidden meaning to those of us in law enforcement. Don't take things at face value. Look inside things, find out why they happen. Dig deep and you will be surprised by what you find and how it will affect your attitude. As the guardian of the public peace, you will do what is expected of you and do it to the best of your abilities.

Having a strong set of personal values is essential for a successful career. Basic values come from your parents, siblings, life experiences, interactions with others and your inner self. Some of the personal values required of a successful law enforcement professional would fall into the following categories:

Integrity. The lack of integrity destroys the effectiveness of the individual and can affect the entire organization. Integrity is the backbone of what we do and who we are. There is no room for dishonesty in our profession, and any breach of the public trust must be dealt with immediately and severely.

Loyalty. Loyalty is the hinge that ties individuals to their environment and creates the flow of power between employees and management. It is important to understand the prioritization of loyalties and the nuances of loyalty conflicts to be able to make decisions consistent with existing values.

Humility. Humility is one of the strongest values an individual can possess. On occasion where you have erred, nothing demonstrates your positive values so powerfully as a simple, humble apology. You must recognize that errors or failures will occur in life. You must be willing to accept the failure or apology of others if you expect others to tolerate your own human nature. Humility includes the recognition of the need to learn.

Tenacity. Tenacity tempered with patience gives the individual the ability to focus on long-term goals and creates consistency of purpose and successful change.

Courage. Courage is demonstrated most often as the result of a strong personal value system that supports action in the face of adversity. It requires "strength of character" and a strong moral fiber, which denotes a strong sense of values and ethics. Courage is not something that can be taught but comes from combining skills with your entire value system.

Responsibility. To be an effective law enforcement professional, you must accept responsibility for all that occurs in your purview. Responsibility ties directly into integrity and courage and, if you are wrong, humility.

Confidence. Confidence is a state of mind that exists in particular situations when an individual's knowledge or experience dictates a high likelihood of success or acceptable consequences in the event of failure. Confidence cannot be taught, but can be gained through repeated experiences in specific areas of knowledge. Confidence is your tool of survival. Confidence is a key element of a successful career.

Setting Goals. You have obviously set some goals for yourself as you have been successful in your quest for a law enforcement career. Goals are not something you set, attain and forget. To grow in your life and career, you must constantly reassess your goals. You may want to set long-range and short-range goals, such as being an FTO by the time you have three years on the job, or making sergeant within five years. You must work for these goals; they will not come to you. When you reach a goal, set another one. Do not become complacent in your career. Get as much overall, broad-based experience as you can. Don't be afraid to try. Avoid being stereotyped or stuck in a rut. See what you want and go after it, keeping in mind the basic values you have set for yourself and your career.

Expectations. Know what is expected of you at all times. Constantly communicate with your fellow officers about what you expect of each other. Don't be afraid to go to your supervisor and ask what is expected of you. This is an integral part of building your confidence and maintaining your value system.

Survival. During my 30-year law enforcement career, I saw many changes, both good and bad, in our profession. Early on, while driving around solo on those long night shifts, I started playing a mind game with myself that later enabled me to survive encounters that could have been deadly. After each call, as I got back in my car and drove off, I would mentally go through the call and play a "what if" game with myself. What if the guy had a gun? What if the lady attacked me? I would change the scenario several times and play it over in my mind along with my reactions to the situations. What I was doing (unknown to me) was building up a computer program in my mind as to what I would do and how I would react in hundreds, if not thousands, of situations. When confronted with a real-life, deadly encounter, I was (during a 30-second period) able to save the life of a fellow officer, a 17-year-old hostage and take out an armed suspect by reacting to that mental computer program.

Never stop playing that "what if" game, have confidence in your ability and live by a good set of values, and I hope your career will be as successful as mine.

Sgt. Richard D. Beckman *is a 30-year veteran of California law enforcement, now retired from the Cloverdale (California) Police Department. In 1988 he received the "Police Officer of the Year" award from the International Association of Chiefs of Police for his actions in saving the lives of a fellow officer and a 17-year-old hostage. In 1990 he received the Medal of Valor from the Attorney General of the State of California. Sgt. Beckman was referred to as a "true American hero" by President Ronald Reagan. He is a founding board member and president of the Law Enforcement Alliance of America, and travels extensively throughout the country promoting officers', citizens' and victims' rights as well as other pro-constitutional issues.*

INSIDERS' VIEWS ONLINE

Additional *Insiders' Views* for this chapter are "What Are They Looking For? Tips on the Promotional Process in Law Enforcement Agencies" by Capt. Luis Velez and "Identifying Your Worst Job-Seeking Enemy . . . It Isn't Who You Think It Is!" by J. Scott Harr, JD, found on the Wadsworth website: http://www.wadsworth.com/criminaljustice_d/.

   ## MIND STRETCHES

1.   What promotions do you see as being of interest to you now? In one year? Five years? Ten years?

2.   If you were promoting someone, what characteristics would you look for?

3.   Why would "off-duty" actions influence employers?

4.   Name what you are doing now that employers would view favorably.

5.   Name anything they could view unfavorably.

6.   Do you think someone could be "overeducated"? Why or why not?

7.   What schooling do you think could help you in your job pursuits?

8.   Consider those around you who have been promoted. What have they done to benefit themselves?

REFERENCES

Armstrong, David and Polk, O. Elmer. "College for Cops: The Fast Track to Success." *The Law Enforcement Trainer,* September/October 2002, pp. 24–26.

Arnold, Jon. "Strategic Planning for Career Development." *The Police Chief,* April 2000, pp. 61–63, 196.

Booth, Walter S. "Three Common Factors of Successful Promotion Candidates." *The Police Chief,* July 2002, pp. 71–75.

Borello, Andrew. "Promotional Oral Interviews." *Law and Order,* September 2003, pp. 128–131.

Borello, Andrew. "Oral Interview Dynamics." 2004. Online: http://hometown.aol.com/taiseng/myhomepage/business.html

Bowman, Theron. "Educate to Elevate." *Community Links,* August 2002, pp. 11–13.

Carter, J. Patrick. "How to Achieve Your Career Goals in Law Enforcement." *The Police Chief,* December 2002, pp. 33–36.

DiVasto, Peter V. "Improving Promotional Exam Performance." *Law and Order,* May 1990, pp. 24, 29.

Fulton, Roger. "10 Steps to a Promotion." *Law Enforcement Technology,* May 2000, p. 118.

Hamilton, Melanie. "How to . . . Get Promoted." *Police,* April 2004, pp. 24–26.

Lunney, Robert. "Puzzling Through the Politics." *Subject to Debate,* January 2002, pp. 1, 4–5.

Narramore, Randy E. "Preparing for a Promotional Interview." *Law and Order,* September 1991, pp. 161–162.

Occupational Outlook Handbook, 2004–05 Edition. Bureau of Labor Statistics, U.S. Department of Labor. Washington, DC: U.S. Government Printing Office, 2004.

PoliceCareer.com. "Sample LEPTAD Questions." Online: http://www.paulpatti.com/leptadquestions.html

CHAPTER 17

JOB LOSS AND CHANGE: THE ROAD LESS TRAVELED

In the middle of difficulty lies opportunity.

—*Albert Einstein*

Success is how high you bounce when you hit bottom.

—*General George Patton*

Do You Know:

➤ What besides death and taxes is inevitable?
➤ How common job-loss grief is?
➤ Why an effective strategy to deal with job loss is needed?
➤ What myths about employment are common?
➤ What basic job-loss survival strategies are needed?
➤ What emotions are normally experienced following job loss?
➤ What depression is? What to do if it occurs?
➤ When you should begin your job search after losing your current job?

INTRODUCTION

The cold, hard reality is that *getting* a job cannot be fully and properly addressed without discussing loss of that job. A fact of life is that you will lose every job you get, eventually. It will happen to you. It happens to everyone. It's just one more example of how life is a series of changes accompanied by inevitable losses. The Professionals in Transition Support Group (2000) states:

> Like birth, death, and taxes, job loss is inevitable at some point in your career.

➤ It's estimated that today's typical 40-year-old white-collar worker will change employers two or three times in the remainder of his or her career, at least once involuntarily.

➤ Unemployment has become the great equalizer.

Sometimes leaving a job is unexpected and unwanted. Sometimes it's a desired change. Sometimes it's a promotion or a demotion. Eventually it will be retirement. Maybe it has just happened to you, which is why you are focusing on this chapter. However, this is not as grim as it may sound because, like anything else, a well-thought-out strategy will make this ebb-and-flow of life more manageable.

This chapter is titled *Job Loss **and** Change* because even desired, positive employment changes are challenging. People often are surprised at the sadness accompanying these changes. In fact, the stress and fear of change prevents some people from pursuing promotions or other job opportunities, or to turn them down when offered. This may not make sense now, but it will.

> Transition is inevitable. And job loss is inevitable. It happens to everyone.

THE IDENTITY CRISIS

> "Who are you?" said the caterpillar.
>
> "I—I hardly know, Sir, just at present," Alice replied rather shyly, "at least I know who I *was* when I got up this morning, but I think I must have been changed several times since then."
>
> —Lewis Carroll, *Alice's Adventures in Wonderland*

Richardson (2004) observes:

> Some call it the cocktail-party question: "So, what do you do for a living?"
>
> Those few words can paralyze usually confident and accomplished adults who have lost their jobs, reducing them to stammering idiots. "Uh, I'm between jobs." Or "Well, I used to be. . . ." Or "In my former life, I was. . . ."
>
> Regardless of how you became unemployed, your public label or persona has changed. Not being able to lean on a job or occupation for their identity can be frightening to professionals who have relied on a title, position or company name to define or shape their image.

In addressing the emotions that follow job loss, Knox and Butzel (2002) note:

> There are few things worse than feeling you have failed. You feel pummeled, destroyed, violated, betrayed, terrified, angry, guilty, depressed, vengeful, lethargic, impotent and occasionally relieved and resolute. Your defenses have been shattered.
>
> You have sustained a severe blow, a loss of your very sense of self. And the more closely you identified yourself with the job, the greater that loss. Career failure is unlike any other loss; it is a sudden, brutal destruction of self-esteem. Even the death of a loved one does not attack *our* ego. Mourning for another does not obliterate our sense of self. Career failure often does.

> Job-loss grief is a universal experience.

Analogies sometimes help explain areas of life we have limited experience with, like losing a job. One such analogy comes from observing skydivers. The shock of the loss of employment is like falling out of an airplane (and may be every bit as terrifying). Lacking experience, you tumble earthward with absolutely no control, fearing for your life. Skydivers, however, have learned to control themselves during a free fall by adjusting themselves so that they *are* in control. They have developed a strategy to manage the descent. They return safely to earth, exhilarated. The key is *control*.

If you are reeling from job loss, you will find—like the skydiver—that when you are ready, the chute will pop open, and you will make a gradual, controlled descent (if you are prepared). The previous weeks or months may be a blur, but it's all part of dealing with job-loss emotions. Once you've slowed down and are more in control, you can reset your sights on where you want to land and get yourself there. But, as with skydiving, you don't just jump out of the plane without thinking. It requires thought and planning. And if, or when, you get shoved out the door, it becomes even more important that you have a plan—quickly. This chapter is intended to help you develop a plan, a strategy. You may not need the strategy now, but you will eventually.

WHY IS HAVING A STRATEGY SO IMPORTANT?

It is as important to develop a strategy to deal with job loss as it was to get the job in the first place. Why? Because it *will* happen, and it can be significant and downright painful. In fact, according to Rolls (2004):

> In the hierarchy of the 20 top stressors in life, losing one's job is #8. It's accompanied in the Top Ten by death (of a loved one), divorce and going to jail! Career and income loss can have serious consequences on lifestyle and health.

Hodowanes (2004) states: "Since you can't eliminate the possibility of a job loss, you should always be prepared to deal with it."

An effective job-loss strategy will not only enable you to feel more in control of very difficult circumstances, but it will allow you to move on in a healthy manner to the next job.

And there *will be* another job.

THE MYTHS AND HARD TRUTHS ABOUT WORK

Employment has changed drastically in the past several decades. Yet, despite these changes, people continue to believe in several myths about employment when they should, instead, be acknowledging some hard truths about unemployment.

The Myths

Myth #1:   My employment is secure—after all, I got the job, didn't I?
Myth #2:   If I do a good job, I'll continue to be recognized for it and be assured of a secure future.
Myth #3:   Job loss can happen only to someone else—not me.
Myth #4:   Even if it does happen to me, I'll be able to handle it without a problem.

Myth #1: My Employment Is Secure—After All, I Got the Job, Didn't I?   What is meant by *secure?* If it means you will always have your current job, this is incorrect. At most you will retire. Or you could be fired. You could be promoted, transferred to another division or even find yourself on long-term disability after being injured on the job. You might move. But you will *not always* have a particular job just because you once got it. Of course, it is everyone's hope that any particular job will end when *we* want it to. After all, it's *our* job. It belongs to us. It's a part of us, and we're a part of it. But unless you are truly self-employed, you do *not* own your job. Even the self-employed do not necessarily have a job that will last a lifetime.

According to Leider and Shapiro (2002, p. 89):

> The idea of a permanent job is obsolete. Your job, today, is never safe! The work world is in constant turmoil. . . . Companies whose names used to be synonymous with security have laid people off in record numbers. . . . These days, nearly everyone will be "between jobs" at some time.

No one is immune from the possibility of losing their job. And those who think they are may well be most at risk. Job loss is becoming an increasingly familiar scenario and one that must at least be acknowledged. To do otherwise will lull you into a complacency that makes you even more susceptible to risk. Leider and Shapiro (p. 90) caution:

> You must be prepared to go job-hunting for the rest of your life. No one owes you a job—not your present employer, not your union, not even if you work for Mom and Dad. It's up to you to create your future. In the 21st century, almost everyone, up through the highest ranks of professionals, will feel increased pressure to package themselves as a marketable "portfolio" of talents.

You are forewarned: It doesn't matter if you are union, senior, government employed or just really, really good at your job. There *are* circumstances that could, and eventually will, cause you to lose your job. The question is: *How will you handle it?*

Myth #2: If I Do a Good Job, I'll Continue to Be Recognized for It and Be Assured of a Secure Future. As just pointed out, *not necessarily*. This is an old paradigm. It's the way things might have been for our parents or grandparents, but it's no longer what employees can expect. In fact, it's just the opposite. A frightening prediction made in 1970 by Alvin Toffler in *Future Shock* anticipated societal change: "In the three short decades between now and the twenty-first century, millions of ordinary, psychologically normal people, will face an abrupt collision with the future. Citizens of the world's richest and most technologically advanced nations will find it increasingly painful to keep up with the incessant demand for change that characterizes our time. For them the future will have arrived too soon."

The future is now. More and more people have had their employment collide with this future, and they *are* in shock. No doubt you know some of these people. And you may well find yourself among them. Cutbacks, downsizing and other synonyms for *job loss* are occurring not only in corporate America. With the national cry for "Lower taxes!," public sector programs, personnel and even entire departments, once the bastion of security, are increasingly finding themselves part of the tax-reduction "solution." No shield can fully protect employees from inevitable change—not unions, not job performance, not popularity.

Myth #3: Job Loss Can Happen Only to Someone Else—Not Me. Wrong. Remember, that "someone else" is a "me." And as stated at the beginning of the chapter, *unemployment has become the great equalizer*. It can hit you just as easily as your cousin, your neighbor or the person you used to sit next to on the train every day on your way to work.

Myth #4: Even If It Does Happen to Me, I'll Be Able to Handle It without a Problem. It is all too easy to judge those experiencing the natural range of emotions resulting from job loss as "weak," self-pitying or otherwise not up to the task. Anyone who has lost a job will tell you it takes considerable courage to address this change. Richardson notes:

> At the end of their searches, many job seekers don't feel the sense of victory, accomplishment and security they expected. Some . . . experience nagging anxiety and self-doubt and have trouble trusting their new employer or believing their triumph was earned fairly.

> On the surface, they may seem fine, but in reality, they're recovering from the shock and humiliation of sudden unemployment. . . . For many, particularly those who haven't made frequent job shifts, the jolt of a job loss produced a lasting scar that impairs their ability to assimilate into new roles and move on with their careers.

We do not want to paint too bleak of a picture. Loss and change are a part of life, and one that actually builds character for most who experience it. It is just an area all too often ignored until it is on our own front doorstep. Every one of us who has "been there" has a whole new appreciation for the intensity of emotions that surface and a willingness to extend an understanding hand to those who will need it.

The Hard Truths

Instead of buying into the myths about work and hoping the "inevitable" doesn't happen to you, Tischler (2001) offers some hard truths to help you "respond to the new era of downsizing without downsizing your dreams":

> *Truth #1:   There are worse things than being laid off—like staying in a bad job for "security."*
> *Truth #2:   In fact, losing your job may be the best career move you'll ever make.*
> *Truth #3:   But don't be surprised if you are unemployed longer than you expected at first . . .*
> *Truth #4:   . . . Even though it often pays off to move fast.*
> *Truth #5:   By the way, the Internet won't necessarily solve your job-search problem.*
> *Truth #6:   You might have to settle for less money too.*
> *Truth #7:   And you might find yourself at a more conservative company.*
> *Truth #8:   You may also have to consider a different city.*
> *Truth #9:   For all the turmoil, never forget that your professional life span is longer than that of most companies.*
> *Truth #10: So your real job is to find what you love and then find a way to do it. (Return to Truth #1.)*

Tischler cushions these harsh realities with some final, more optimistic, words of advice:

> Don't forget the most important lesson of all. Markets go up, and markets go down. Digital technologies catch fire and then burn out. But through it all, the defining truth of the business world is that people are still front and center. If you're a talented person with a real passion for your work, you are living in the right times—layoffs or not.

Recall from Chapter 1 that service industries, including social services, legal services and protective services, are currently among the most rapidly growing occupations in the United States, with this trend projected to continue through 2012. While this bodes well for those presently seeking employment in criminal justice, security and related fields, it does not guarantee this trend will last indefinitely, nor does it give you immunity from future job loss. Things change. Be prepared.

DEVELOPING A STRATEGY

It's always better to have a plan in place before the emergency strikes, so if you happen to be reading this chapter *before* you need it—good for you. But human nature being what it is, you'll probably give it a lot more consideration when you find yourself needing it. Even then you can get a plan in place quickly and benefit from it. You'll find yourself needing just a few basics, but they are very important.

Basic job-loss survival strategies include:

➤ Building a support network now—for fun, for closeness and for information.
➤ Building a "survival nest egg" of at least six months' living expenses, maybe longer.
➤ Balancing your life so your job isn't the only important thing to you.

As you build your network, consider volunteering for an organization you are interested in.

 List in your journal individuals you want to keep in contact with not only for future job networking, but also because you enjoy them. Can you help any of them now? Can they help you?

 What volunteer opportunities might interest you and might also benefit you in a job search?

Layne (2001) suggests you "learn how to transform a layoff into a savvy sabbatical—a time to recharge your batteries and learn new skills without sabotaging your resume." Once strictly the domain of rabbis and tenured professors, sabbaticals are now benefiting a variety of displaced, downsized professionals wondering "What do I do now?" Loosely defined, a sabbatical is "time off"—a break, a retreat, a rest. It does not mean you can sit in front of the TV all day, eating cold pizza and waiting for the phone to ring with your next job offer. Instead, according to career coach Hope Dlugozima: "'Sabbatical' holds a certain power and intrigue to it. It denotes a plan of action and a deliberate path" (Layne).

Dlugozima advises people to take advantage of the upheavals in life and use this downtime to "build up rather than keep up, thrive rather than survive, and seek rather than hide." Use this time to ask yourself, "If I could do anything, what would I do?" Travel, volunteer, do new things and grow: "The smartest career move that you can make after a layoff is . . . [to embark] on a sabbatical that will restore self-esteem, independence, and drive" (Layne). Specific strategies are discussed in Dlugozima's *Six Months Off: How to Plan, Negotiate, and Take the Break You Need without Burning Bridges or Going Broke* (Henry Holt Publishing, 1996).

 How much money would you need if you suddenly lost your job?

 What interests or hobbies have you put off due to lack of time or money?

Survival strategies set a foundation for you to proceed. While they may seem elementary, they can be overlooked in the midst of chaos. They address the areas that need to be worked with and worked through: awareness, acceptance, support, putting the past behind you and, finally, moving ahead. You need to progress through all these areas. And that's one of the most challenging parts of the process.

THE SEQUENTIAL REACTION TO JOB LOSS AND CHANGE

You can't go around the emotions of job loss and change; you must go through them. There is no shortcut. Chapter 11, which dealt with *not* getting a job, discussed the predictable process most people experience when they lose something important (see Chapter 11, Figure 11–1). Whatever begins the sequence of emotional, sometimes physical, responses to job loss, the emotions are so universal that we know they've got to be dealt with. Failure to do so will keep you stuck in that phase (e.g., becoming overly angry or sad), and will affect all other areas of your life.

The normal emotions experienced following job loss are denial, anger, sadness, searching, withdrawal and reorganization. The sequence in which these emotions occur may vary, and emotions may repeat themselves.

These emotions were explained more fully in Chapter 11, but we'll briefly recap them here:

➤ *Denial* is normally experienced as, "I can't believe this happened to me." The ability to *accept* the loss is a necessary step in being able to continue on with life.

➤ *Anger* is "Why me?" You lost your job—who wouldn't be upset? But don't lash out at those close to you or burn bridges with your former employer. Another opportunity may arise there in the future, or your former employer may be called for a reference. Deal with the anger by finding an appropriate, constructive outlet.

➤ *Sadness* is another emotion to expect along the way. Do not ignore it. You need to let yourself feel the sadness so you can work through it and move on.

➤ *Searching* may involve you going back to your place of employment, even if only to drive by. You might call. You may hold on to the hope that "they" will come to their senses and ask you, beg you, to come back. It's like survivors going back to the disaster scene—it provides a reality check. Give yourself time to check out the old as you prepare to move on to the new.

➤ *Withdrawal* may be hard for family and friends to understand and may create stress for everyone. Pulling away lets you do your emotional work inside while you step back and assess where you fit into the world now. This takes time, and only you can do it. So when your family and friends see you as more quiet and withdrawn, no one need worry. It's simply another part of the process.

➤ *Reorganization* is when you've worked through the previous emotional stages and are ready to rebuild. Going through this exhausting set of emotions makes it understandable why people resist change—good or not. Young police officers have difficulty understanding why they keep getting called back to the same address on domestic disturbance calls. "If it's so bad, why doesn't one of them just leave?" The answer is that even as difficult as the situation is, it's known. It's predictable. What's on the other side of that door is unknown. Only when the pain exceeds the risk will change occur.

> All changes, even the most longed for, have their melancholy; for what we leave behind is part of ourselves; we must die to one life before we can enter another.
>
> —Anatole France, writer

Change is hard. To expect anything less is unrealistic. The emotions experienced are normal, natural.

Managing the Responses

It is not enough to know and anticipate the feelings you will experience. You must effectively *manage* them as well. This is *not* easy because of the intensity of the emotions and (fortunately) the relative lack of experience most people have dealing with such significant loss. What you do not want to do is add to your difficulties by letting the emotions overtake you. You will feel anger, but don't make inappropriate, hostile phone calls to or confront a former employer you blame for your job loss. Does this happen? Yes, even to extremes. We've heard about former employees who act their anger out with violence, sometimes even killing former employers and coworkers. It's probably not coincidence that workplace violence is increasing at the same time job loss is increasing across the country.

Nor do you want to take the emotions out on people trying to support you. You're angry. You're sad. The denial factor may keep you from seeing that it's your lost job causing these feelings. But you think you've got problems now, having lost your job? You don't want to lose those close to you, too. It is possible to "grieve other people right out of your life." Here is where you will benefit from objective help, professional or otherwise. Get it!

Understanding, accepting and managing the emotions associated with job loss is a huge step in moving forward. However, you must guard against one emotion that can be devastating: depression.

DEALING WITH DEPRESSION

The number of people suffering from depression is far greater than people may realize. It can be a miserable state to be in and, left untreated, can become debilitating and lead to illness and even suicide.

> Depression is not about being sad. It's about being in a cloud that casts a dark shadow over everything. The hopelessness associated with it may become devastating.

Those who experience depression know you can't just "snap out of it" or "tell yourself it will all be okay." If it were this easy, no one would be depressed. Allow yourself to feel all of what you are going through. You don't have to like it, but you do need to accept it and to accept help if the feelings become overwhelming. Perhaps no other group as a whole is less willing to reach out for help than criminal justice professionals. After all, they are there to help others, those who can't help themselves. It's surely not the stereotypic macho cop who admits to someone else, much less to themselves, that they need help.

Depression to some degree *will* result from job loss. The associated negativity and hopelessness can cast a bleak shadow over everything. Following are some thoughts from Byron's study of people in transition and their advice to others (1995, pp. 171–177) that may help you as you walk a path that may seem unbearably long. It's helpful to know that others have been there and survived.

➤ Don't be too hard on yourself, or set too many demands; this, like everything, will be resolved one way or another, sooner or later.

➤ Expect rejection. Don't take it personally.

➤ Be positive and work hard at the search (a new job won't just happen).

➤ Let your pride push you rather than hold you back.

➤ You are not simply what you do, and you should realize that the job revolution has resulted in people being out who have done nothing wrong.

➤   You are not what you own or your title.

➤   Never, ever believe your job is secure.

➤   Only a positive attitude will propel you into a good job that is the right job for you.

➤   Have your network in place before you ever need it.

➤   Nothing is forever. Things change. People change.

➤   Hang in there.

Things can get away from you. Don't try to go it alone. If you were a police, corrections or security officer, you'd never respond to a call alone if you knew you'd need additional officer-power and firepower at the scene. You'd never hesitate to call for help on the street, so don't hesitate to call for help now if you need it.

If you are depressed and need help—get it. It could be a matter of life and death.

Talk to friends, see a counselor or psychologist, join a support group, see a psychiatrist and get on medication if need be. But whatever you do, GET HELP. It takes a strong, courageous person to reach out in the midst of despair. But you can do it. You can!

Another way to break out of depression is to tackle the job search for your next job.

GOTTA GET WORKING

You know how to get a job. After all, you got the job(s) you no longer have.

As you move through the emotional steps of job loss, keep working at finding new work. As your energy level permits, keep developing the job search.

As you move forward, you'll build momentum and develop increasing energy to be even more creative in this effort. Birkel and Miller (1998, pp. 144–147), members of Professionals in Transition (PIT), have set forth what they refer to as "PIT's Top Ten Guerrilla Job-Hunting Tactics":

1. Remind yourself to be a winner.

2. Conduct a multilevel campaign (work with job-hunting allies, market yourself, and conduct informational interviews).

3. Create a business card (front: name, address, phone and general area of expertise; back: career objective and bulleted list of key strengths/skills).

4. Meet employers' needs (cover letter with left column headed "Your Needs" taken from advertisement and right column headed "My Qualifications").

5. Use large mailing envelopes (to stand out from other mail received).

6. Volunteer (there's always someone worse off than you).

7. Get out and meet people (to find advocates in your job search).

8. Recruit a coach (find a personal advocate to encourage and support you).

9. Keep a journal (to spot trends and learn from them).

10. Stay proactive (control your job search; reemployment possibilities are everywhere).

 Write in your journal which of the preceding tactics you'd like to try.

One tactic some people who have lost their jobs seriously consider is a lawsuit against the former employer.

TO SUE OR NOT TO SUE

No one who has lost their job thinks it was fair. It may well have not been. But unless it was illegal, no judge will care. Even then, you need to think about whether a lawsuit is the way to proceed. Sagario (2004) states:

> Wrongful termination from a job encompasses a wide-range of possibilities. The key, experts say, is to determine whether the actions against you were illegal.
>
> Because every worker's situation is unique, there are not any easy formulas or guidelines to determine whether a boss unlawfully fired you. Figuring whether there is a case can be a confusing and time-consuming process.
>
> Seeking the advice of a lawyer, along with resources from state and federal agencies, can help determine whether pursuing the underlying reasons for your dismissal is worth it. While laws might vary from state to state, grounds for wrongful termination include discrimination based on age, race, creed, color, sex, national origin, religion, disability or pregnancy.

Employment law is very complex, and a discussion of when a dismissal is illegal is beyond the scope of this book. It depends on your particular circumstances. Do you have a contract? Are you a veteran? What does your employee handbook include? Are you union? And the list goes on. You need legal counsel for answers.

Even if you have a legal cause of action, consider the consequences of suing a previous employer: What is the likelihood of prevailing? What will future prospective employers think of this action? Will a lengthy lawsuit prolong your agony and prevent you from beginning the healing process? How much might it cost? All these questions need to be considered. A competent attorney will be able to help with this, which is why they are also called counselors at law. But know that suing solely out of anger is never a good idea.

CONCLUSION

Like death and taxes, maneuvering through job loss appears to be inevitable. Most people who have a job will, at some point, lose that job. Remember: All endings lead to new beginnings. It just might not seem like it at the time. But you must believe there will be another side—a brighter side, a new job, new opportunities, new friends, a whole new world.

AN INSIDER'S VIEW

JOB LOSS AND GRIEF

Richard J. Obershaw, LICSW, MSW, ACSW

Founder of the Grief Center
Burnsville, Minnesota

Our job is a lot about who we are. When we lose our job, we lose who we *were*—not who we *are*. When we lose our job, we often lose our identity, our security, our friends, our coworkers, our financial security, our sense of accomplishment, our lifestyle, our routine, our sense of productivity, and sometimes we lose the reason for getting out of bed in the morning.

We often select "our work" because of who we *were*. For example, perfectionists seldom take on jobs that can't be done perfectly. If they do, they soon learn to look for another job. Individuals who enjoy people usually select jobs that involve people. During those years at the job we all change. The changes come because of maturational issues in our life as well as situational occurrences. But because of financial factors we seldom elect to leave our first job of choice. We learn to "live with the way I am now in a job that was selected for the way I was then." We adapt by mixing the *new me* with the *old me*.

Then the day comes when someone says you are no longer wanted, needed or capable of performing this job, or your job is eliminated because of (1) a change in the workplace, (2) economic factors or (3) interpersonal differences. It is at this point in our life that we have to once again ask, "Who am I now as an individual and what do I need for a job that matches this 'now' individual?"

This is the process of grief—letting go of the *old me* and learning who the *new me* will be. It is the job of reidentifying the self. After many studies on the topic of change and grief, we have come to learn that the process is somewhat predictable. No one follows the process in exactly the same pattern as others, but the overall general idea may help you understand your "normally crazy" thoughts, ideas, feelings and behavior during this period of reidentifying yourself.

Initially we find it difficult to accept the reality of our loss. Our **denial** system starts to protect us from the stress created by change. It may seem like a bad dream, or we may wish, sometimes out loud, that the old familiar activities will once again return. This may look unhealthy to others around us, but it serves as a buffer for us as we go gently from the *old me* to the *new me*. We may even decide not to tell our family and friends about the job loss because they will want to discuss it. But we aren't ready to deal with a discussion about it because it makes it too real. This denial will fade gently as we become more aware that we can cope with this change in our lives.

As we become more aware of the reality of the loss, we become more aware of the effort it will take to reidentify ourselves. It is at this point we get **resentful** of the effort needed to change, and we find ourselves with a general "anger all over" feeling. We get angry that we have to change. We get angry at the people who get to keep their jobs. We get angry at those who told us our job was ending. We get angry at God, and we get angry at ourselves. Because we are punched in the gut over this loss, we want to punch others. We want others to suffer with us.

Soon we find ourselves feeling quite restless and pacing around the house. Where do we belong? We awaken at the time we normally would to go to work, but find ourselves with no place to go.

Then comes the **search**—we may drive by and around the workplace feeling the need to check out if it's still there for us. We may search our minds and others to come up with the "real reason" this loss has been placed in our lives. We may search to find new meaning in our life without our old job. The term *job search* may also explain why initially we search to find a job—sometimes any job. And, because we find a job we take it—just to end the search and get a job back. These jobs often do not meet our new needs, our changed selves.

Another part of the grief process with job loss is **withdrawal.** We withdraw from our families, friends, former coworkers and often from ourselves. We sleep to withdraw from life and ourselves. We withdraw into television and spend countless hours staring at brain-dead talk shows that help us escape from our own grief and reidentification process. In extreme cases we may withdraw into obsessive-compulsive behaviors, alcohol and other drugs, dangerous hobbies, sexual affairs, excessive spending and even suicide.

If we survive all of the preceding, we begin the process of realizing we are new. Our thinking, our needs and our goals are often new. We start to know the *new me* and become more comfortable being changed. It is at this point we should begin with a true job search that fits the *new us*. If everyone had the financial security to wait this long, life would be easier, but the reality is, jobs are needed to earn money to pay the bills. Perhaps what we need to do is reassess how we choose to live our lives. Is the job where we work about collecting money or is a job about meeting our needs to be who we are?

Richard Obershaw, *LICSW, MSW, ACSW, is an internationally renowned expert on loss and change, grief and bereavement. He travels extensively, lecturing and consulting on these subjects in addition to his clinical practice. He is also founder of the Grief Center in Burnsville, Minnesota.*

INSIDERS' VIEWS ONLINE

Additional *Insiders' Views* for this chapter are "Who's in Control: You or Your Work?" by John Driggs and "Removing the Arrow: The Scott Harr Story" by J. Scott Harr, found on the Wadsworth website: http://www.wadsworth.com/criminaljustice_d/.

 MIND STRETCHES

1. If you needed them today, who makes up your support network?

2. What losses have you experienced? How did you work through the steps?

3. Why does job loss affect more than just the individual?

4. Why do you think job loss is more common now than in years past?

5. Do you think job loss can be harder to deal with than death? Why or why not?

6.   Why do people think job loss can't happen to them?

7.   What would you do to help yourself if you lost your job today?

8.   Why do people feel bad even if they choose to leave their jobs?

9.   If you were to lose your job now, would you say, "That's what I was" or "That's what I did"?

10.   Why do you think some people put more emphasis on their jobs than on the rest of their lives?

REFERENCES

Birkel, J. Damian with Miller, Stacey J. *Career Bounce-Back! The Professionals in Transition™ Guide to Recovery & Reemployment.* New York: AMACOM: American Management Association, 1998.

Byron, William J. *Finding Work without Losing Heart: Bouncing Back from Mid-Career Job Loss.* Holbrook, MA: Adams Publishing, 1995.

Hodowanes, Joe. "Negotiating a Smooth Job Exit." Net-Temps, 2004. Online: http://www.net-temps.com/careerdev/index.htm?type=topics&topic=layoff&id=213

Knox, Deborah L. and Butzel, Sandra S. *Life Work Transition.com: Putting Your Spirit Online.* 2002. Online: http://www.lifeworktransitions.com/exercises/stgesloss.html

Layne, Anni. "How to Move Forward When You're Between Jobs." *Fast Company.* Boston: Gruner and Jahr USA Publishing, June 2001. Online at: http://www.fastcompany.com/articles/2001/06/sabbatical.html

Leider, Richard J. and Shapiro, David A. *Repacking Your Bags: Lighten Your Load for the Rest of Your Life,* 2nd ed. San Francisco: Berrett-Koehler Publishers, Inc. 2002.

Professionals in Transition Support Group. 2000. Online: http://www.jobsearching.org/socially.cfm

Richardson, Douglas B. "How to Heal Your Job-Loss Wounds." *The Wall Street Journal Online,* 2004. Online: http://www.careerjournal.com/jobhunting/jobloss

Rolls, Sonya. "Dealing with Your Loss of Employment." Net-Temps, 2004. Online: http://www.net-temps.com/careerdev/index.htm?type=topics&topic=layoff&id=101

Sagario, Dawn. "Here's What to Do If You Think You Were Fired Unfairly." CareerBuilder.com, 2004. Online: http://msn.careerbuilder.com/custom/MSN/CareerAdvice/141.htm

Tischler, Linda. "10 Hard Truths about Layoffs." *Fast Company.* Boston: Gruner and Jahr USA Publishing, June 2001. Online at: http://www.fastcompany.com/articles/2001/06/10truths.html

ADDITIONAL CONTACTS AND SOURCES OF INFORMATION

How to Plan, Negotiate, and Take the Break You Need without Burning Bridges or Going Broke, by Hope Dlugozima. Henry Holt, 1996.

CareerBuilder.com—Provides a Layoff Survival Kit including discussion boards where people can commiserate and share job-hunting tips.

FastCompany.com—Serves people's individual career needs with six custom-built Career Zones. Each Career Zone contains Web-only stories, interactive tools, expert opinions and valuable connections to help Fast Company readers get ahead in the new economy.

JobHuntersBible.com—Richard Bolles, author of *What Color Is Your Parachute?,* guides career changers and suggests what to do once they've exhausted Internet job sites.

JobSearching.org—Sponsored by the Professionals in Transition (PIT) support group, this site helps the unemployed cope and retool skills.

Monster.com—Has suggestions for stress management and repositioning yourself in a tough market.

EPILOGUE

In three words I can sum up everything I've learned about life. It goes on.

—*Robert Frost*

A beginning. An end. A new beginning. This describes life, including your working life.

Work. It's much more complex than most people realize. Work can feed our souls, but it can also destroy them. Striking a balance in life is what "success" may well be. Home, family, education, faith, health, recreation . . . and work. Unfortunately, many people allow, knowingly or otherwise, the work component to overshadow the others, causing an imbalance that can affect every aspect of life. The danger in letting your work define you was encapsulated well by E. L. Sopow, Vancouver, Canada, during a discussion about work, job loss, change and resilience:

> Most people have come to equate what they DO with who they ARE. This means when they lose their job they experience two out of the three forms of death—death of self-image and death of hope. And in some unfortunate cases, the third form of death—clinical—is also a consideration. We might learn from biology rather than business school when it comes to dealing with death. Nature has survived 3.8 billion years by facing a crisis with enhanced communications, increased connectivity, and cooperation leading to evolution. We are not cogs in a machine. We are a network of complex, adaptive systems.

From an evolutionary perspective, the ability to adapt to a changing environment is a prerequisite for survival. Presently, the world of work seems more than ever to be a world of change. Adaptation may be one of the best strategies for success or, at the very least, survival in the work environment. You can't afford to get caught up in "what was," assuming things will always remain the same. They won't. They can't. It's just not the nature of things. In fact, the definition of "security" as it relates to the workplace has changed to such a degree that some argue it's gone altogether. "Employment security" is now best defined as having a well-thought-out strategy to adapt to change, to be secure with change.

Dr. Susan Stanek, training and development consultant, endorses the plan of people developing a *dual* career path to better prepare themselves for job change. Whether people tire of a primary job or find themselves needing another job, having the education and training to fit into another position is a wonderful means by which to adapt. This approach has served many people well, whether they found themselves estranged from their original position, by their own decision, or taking advantage of early retirement, yet not ready to quit contributing to the world around them in some way.

Through reading this book and completing the exercises within, you have had the opportunity to do far more than merely learn to write a résumé. You have had the opportunity to develop ideas on where you would like your work life to take you. You've been encouraged to consider the necessity of balancing the many aspects of life, including work. And you've prepared yourself for the changes you will surely face. Some of them will be good. Some won't. All will contribute to make up the person you are . . . and that, unquestionably, is of great value.

Work. It is so much a part of our lives. It deserves careful consideration. *But in the end, remember . . . it's only a job!*

APPENDIX A

IACP POLICE CODE OF CONDUCT*

All law enforcement officers must be fully aware of the ethical responsibilities of their position and must strive constantly to live up to the highest possible standards of professional policing.

The International Association of Chiefs of Police believes it is important that police officers have clear advice and counsel available to assist them in performing their duties consistent with these standards, and has adopted the following ethical mandates as guidelines to meet these ends.**

Primary Responsibilities of a Police Officer

A police officer acts as an official representative of government who is required and trusted to work within the law. The officer's powers and duties are conferred by statute. The fundamental duties of a police officer include serving the community; safeguarding lives and property; protecting the innocent; keeping the peace; and ensuring the rights of all to liberty, equality and justice.

Performance of the Duties of a Police Officer

A police officer shall perform all duties impartially, without favor or affection or ill will and without regard to status, sex, race, religion, political belief or aspiration. All citizens will be treated equally with courtesy, consideration and dignity.

Officers will never allow personal feelings, animosities or friendships to influence official conduct. Laws will be enforced appropriately and courteously and, in carrying out their responsibilities, officers will strive to obtain maximum cooperation from the public. They will conduct themselves in appearance and deportment in such a manner as to inspire confidence and respect for the position of public trust they hold.

Discretion

A police officer will use responsibly the discretion vested in the position and exercise it within the law. The principle of reasonableness will guide the officer's determinations and the officer will consider all surrounding circumstances in determining whether any legal action shall be taken.

---

*Adopted by the Executive Committee of the International Association of Chiefs of Police on October 17, 1989, during its 96th Annual Conference in Louisville, Kentucky, to replace the 1957 code of ethics adopted at the 64th Annual IACP Conference.

**The IACP gratefully acknowledges the assistance of Sir John C. Hermon, former chief constable of the Royal Ulster Constabulary, who gave full license to the association to freely use the language and concepts presented in the RUC's "Professional Policing Ethics," Appendix 1 of the Chief Constable's Annual Report, 1988, presented to the Police Authority for Northern Ireland, for the preparation of this code.

SOURCE: Reprinted with permission from the International Association of Chiefs of Police, Alexandria, Virginia. Further reproduction without express written permission from IACP is strictly prohibited.

Consistent and wise use of discretion, based on professional policing competence, will do much to preserve good relationships and retain the confidence of the public. There can be difficulty in choosing between conflicting courses of action. It is important to remember that a timely word of advice rather than arrest—which may be correct in appropriate circumstances—can be a more effective means of achieving a desired end.

Use of Force

A police officer will never employ unnecessary force or violence and will use only such force in the discharge of duty as is reasonable in all circumstances. Force should be used only with the greatest restraint and only after discussion, negotiation and persuasion have been found to be inappropriate or ineffective. While the use of force is occasionally unavoidable, every police officer will refrain from applying the unnecessary infliction of pain or suffering and will never engage in cruel, degrading or inhuman treatment of any person.

Confidentiality

Whatever a police officer sees, hears or learns of, which is of a confidential nature, will be kept secret unless the performance of duty or legal provision requires otherwise. Members of the public have a right to security and privacy, and information obtained about them must not be improperly divulged.

Integrity

A police officer will not engage in acts of corruption or bribery, nor will an officer condone such acts by other police officers. The public demands that the integrity of police officers be above reproach. Police officers must, therefore, avoid any conduct that might compromise integrity and thus undercut the public confidence in a law enforcement agency. Officers will refuse to accept any gifts, presents, subscriptions, favors, gratuities or promises that could be interpreted as seeking to cause the officer to refrain from performing official responsibilities honestly and within the law. Police officers must not receive private or special advantage from their official status. Respect from the public cannot be bought; it can only be earned and cultivated.

Cooperation with Other Officers and Agencies

Police officers will cooperate with all legally authorized agencies and their representatives in the pursuit of justice. An officer or agency may be among many organizations that may provide law enforcement services to a jurisdiction. It is imperative that a police officer assist colleagues fully and completely with respect and consideration at all times.

Personal/Professional Capabilities

Police officers will be responsible for their own standard of professional performance and will take every reasonable opportunity to enhance and improve their level of knowledge and competence. Through study and experience, a police officer can acquire the high level of knowledge and competence that is essential for the efficient and effective performance of duty. The acquisition of knowledge is a never-ending process of personal and professional development that should be pursued constantly.

Private Life

Police officers will behave in a manner that does not bring discredit to their agencies or themselves. A police officer's character and conduct while off duty must always be exemplary, thus maintaining a position of respect in the community in which he or she lives and serves. The officer's personal behavior must be beyond reproach.

APPENDIX B

ASIS SECURITY CODE OF ETHICS*

PREAMBLE

Aware that the quality of professional security activity ultimately depends upon the willingness of practitioners to observe special standards of conduct and to manifest good faith in professional relationships, the American Society for Industrial Security adopts the following Code of Ethics and mandates its conscientious observance as a binding condition of membership in or affiliation with the Society:

ARTICLE I

A member shall perform professional duties in accordance with the law and the highest moral principles.

Ethical Considerations

I-1 A member shall abide by the law of the land in which the services are rendered and perform all duties in an honorable manner.

I-2 A member shall not knowingly become associated in responsibility for work with colleagues who do not conform to the law and these ethical standards.

I-3 A member shall be just and respect the rights of others in performing professional responsibilities.

ARTICLE II

A member shall observe the precepts of truthfulness, honesty and integrity.

Ethical Considerations

II-1 A member shall disclose all relevant information to those having a right to know.

II-2 A right to know is a legally enforceable claim or demand by a person for disclosure of information by a member. Such a right does not depend upon prior knowledge by the person of the existence of the information to be disclosed.

II-3 A member shall not knowingly release misleading information, nor encourage or otherwise participate in the release of such information.

ARTICLE III

A member shall be faithful and diligent in discharging professional responsibilities.

---

*Reprinted with permission from the American Society for Industrial Security.

Ethical Considerations

III-1   A member is faithful when fair and steadfast in adherence to promises and commitments.

III-2   A member is diligent when employing best efforts in an assignment.

III-3   A member shall not act in matters involving conflicts of interest without appropriate disclosure and approval.

III-4   A member shall represent services or products fairly and truthfully.

ARTICLE IV

A member shall be competent in discharging professional responsibilities.

Ethical Considerations

IV-1   A member is competent who possesses and applies the skills and knowledge required for the task.

IV-2   A member shall not accept a task beyond the member's competence nor shall competence be claimed when not possessed.

ARTICLE V

A member shall safeguard confidential information and exercise due care to prevent its improper disclosure.

Ethical Considerations

V-1   Confidential information is nonpublic information the disclosure of which is restricted.

V-2   Due care requires that the professional must not knowingly reveal confidential information or use a confidence to the disadvantage of the principal or to the advantage of the member or a third person unless the principal consents after full disclosure of all the facts. This confidentiality continues after the business relationship between the member and his principal has terminated.

V-3   A member who receives information and has not agreed to be bound by confidentiality is not bound from disclosing it. A member is not bound by confidential disclosures made of acts or omissions which constitute a violation of the law.

V-4   Confidential disclosures made by a principal to a member are not recognized by law as privileged in a legal proceeding. The member may be required to testify in a legal proceeding to information received in confidence from his principal over the objection of his principal's counsel.

V-5   A member shall not disclose confidential information for personal gain without appropriate authorization.

ARTICLE VI

A member shall not maliciously injure the professional reputation or practice of colleagues, clients or employers.

Ethical Considerations

VI-1   A member shall not comment falsely and with malice concerning a colleague's competence, performance or professional capabilities.

VI-2   A member who knows, or has reasonable grounds to believe, that another member has failed to conform to the Society's Code of Ethics shall present such information to the Ethical Standards Committee in accordance with Article XIV of the Society's Bylaws.

APPENDIX C

RÉSUMÉ WORKSHEETS

Name: _____

Current Address: _____

Permanent Address: _____

Phone Number(s): _____

E-mail: _____

Colleges: _____

_____

Professional Schools: _____

_____

Internships: _____

_____

Certificates Held: _____

_____

_____

Other Educational Experiences: _____

_____

_____

High School: _____

EMPLOYMENT HISTORY
(Note: Make as many copies of this page as you have had jobs so you can complete one page for each job you've had.)

Dates Employed: From _____ to _____

Employer: _____

      Address: _____

      Phone/E-mail: _____

      Supervisor: _____

Position/Title: _____

Responsibilities: _____

_____

_____

_____

_____

Skills Acquired: _____

_____

_____

_____

_____

Achievements/Awards: _____

_____

_____

_____

Salary (NOT included in résumé): _____

Reason for Change (NOT included in résumé): _____

_____

Position Desired/Employment Objective: _____

_____

_____

Other information that may be put in your résumé includes the following:

Birth Date: _____ Height: _____ Weight: _____

Health: _____

Travel (willing to travel?): _____

Location (willing to relocate?): _____

Military (service, dates, rank, honorable discharge): _____

_____

    Reserve status: _____

Professional Memberships (committees served on, awards): _____

_____

_____

_____

Foreign Languages (read, write, speak fluently): _____

_____

Foreign Travel: _____

_____

Awards: _____

_____

Publications: _____

_____

Community Service/Involvement (organizations, offices held, etc.): _____

_____

Interests/Hobbies (avocations, nonbusiness pursuits): _____

_____

Availability (immediate or extent of "notice" required): _____

Present Employer Contact: _____
(Is present employer aware of your prospective job change? May the employer be contacted?)

Salary Desired: _____
(NOT included in résumé, but know what you'd expect.)

BUSINESS/PROFESSIONAL/ACADEMIC REFERENCES:

Full Name: _____

    Position: _____

    Address: _____

    Phone/E-mail: _____

Full Name: _____

    Position: _____

    Address: _____

    Phone/E-mail: _____

Full Name: _____

    Position: _____

    Address: _____

    Phone/E-mail: _____

PERSONAL REFERENCE: _____

Full Name: _____

    Relationship (neighbor, teammate, etc.): _____

    Address: _____

    Phone/E-mail: _____

RÉSUMÉ EVALUATION CHECKLIST

CATEGORY	Excellent	Average	Poor	How to Improve
APPEARANCE:				
Is the format clean?				
Is it easy to follow?				
Are headings effective?				
Does it make the reader want to read it?				
CONTENT:				
Do my qualifications stand out?				
Is the language clear and understandable?				
Have I used short phrases?				
Have I used verbs (action words)?				
Is it brief and to the point?				
Are all important skills and qualifications included?				
Does it create a true picture of me?				
Is irrelevant personal information left out?				
PROOFREADING:				
Is it error-free?				
Spelling?				
Punctuation?				

APPENDIX D

SAMPLE RÉSUMÉS

Historical/Chronological Résumé

WILLIAM A. SMITH
10 South First Street
Minneapolis, MN 55404

Home Phone: (612) 555-5650 / Cell: (612) 555-3333
Work Phone: (612) 555-9123

PERSONAL   Date of Birth: 6/3/79, 6′ 0″, 175 lbs. Married, one child. Will relocate.

EDUCATION

1997–2001   NORMANDALE COMMUNITY COLLEGE
                     Bloomington, Minnesota
                     Associate Arts Degree and Law Enforcement Certificate.
                          Member of football team.
                          Photographer for school paper.

1997   BLOOMINGTON HIGH SCHOOL
                     Bloomington, Minnesota
                     High school diploma. Honor student.
                          Member of football team.

**WORK
EXPERIENCE**

1998–present   SECURITY OFFICER
                     Dayton's Department Store
                     Minneapolis, Minnesota
                     Hired as store detective. Duties include plainclothes observation of retail sales
                          area to observe and arrest shoplifters. Assist in loss prevention seminars
                          for store employees.

1995–1998   WAITER
                     Fancy Joe's Burger Joint
                     Bloomington, Minnesota
                     Hired as dishwasher. Promoted to busboy and then waiter. Duties as waiter
                          included taking customers' orders, delivering food and beverage items to
                          the table, and assisting other wait staff.

References available on request.

Functional Résumé

WILLIAM L. SMITH
10 South First Street
Minneapolis, MN 55404
Home Phone: (612) 555-5650

Personal Data: Date of Birth 6-3-75, 6′ 0″, 175 lbs., Single.

Objective:
Position as a law enforcement officer.

Work History

1997–present   Southdale Shopping Center
                            Edina, Minnesota

Security Officer:

- Hired as uniformed security officer. Duties include patron assistance, emergency first-aid response, enforcement of property rules and statutes. Assist in training new employees by providing presentations on company rules and state criminal statutes. Frequently appear as witness in court cases resulting from my position. Work with the area law enforcement officers hired to assist during holiday seasons. Act as company representative to Minnesota Loss Control Society.

1995–1997   Kenny's Market, Inc.
                            Bloomington, Minnesota

Office Worker:

- Hired as assistant to the vice president. Duties included typing, filing, and telephone reception. In charge of confidential employee records. Assisted in organizing the company's first loss prevention program.

Education

1995–1997   BA, University of Minnesota, Minneapolis, Minnesota.

1993–1995   AA, Law Enforcement Certification, Normandale Community College, Bloomington, Minnesota.

1996   Emergency Medical Technician Registration, Hennepin County Vo-Tech, Eden Prairie, Minnesota.

References available on request.

Analytical Résumé

WILLIAM L. SMITH
10 South First Street
Minneapolis, MN 55404
Home Phone: (612) 555-5650 / Cell: (612) 555-3333
Work Phone: (612) 555-9123

Job Objective: Apply my proven ability in loss prevention.

Qualifications:

- Retail Security: Have developed knowledge and skills in the profession while employed as loss prevention officer for several retail stores. In addition to providing undercover and plainclothes loss prevention services as a store detective, have provided extensive training on the subject to store employees. Excellent performance reviews at each position. Continued increases in apprehension statistics. Received "Employee of the Month" award six times for excellent work as a security officer.

- Supervisory Skills: Promoted to supervisor of 17 loss prevention officers at most recent position. Duties included training, delegating duties, and scheduling. Performance statistics for the crew increased significantly.

- Organizational Skills: All jobs have required detailed activity reports. Hands-on experience using computers to organize data. Often provided oral reports to supervisors.

Employers

1993–present	Donaldson's Department Store, Edina, Minnesota.
1992–1993	Tom Thumb Stores, Inc., St. Paul, Minnesota.
1990–1992	Automobile Club of America, St. Louis Park, Minnesota.

Education

1993	Associate of Arts and Private Security Certificate, Normandale Community College, Bloomington, Minnesota.

Other

1994	Participated in organization of 1994 American Industrial Security Association National Convention.

References available on request.

APPENDIX E

SAMPLE COVER LETTER AND FOLLOW-UP LETTER

Sample Cover Letter

Ms. Jane Smith
1234 Second Street
Los Angeles, CA 90017

September 15, 2004

Lt. Pat Jones
Mytown Police Department
1234 First Avenue
Denver, CO 80203

Dear Lt. Jones:

I am responding to your ad in the *Los Angeles Times* for the position of police officer. With an AA degree in law enforcement and three years' experience as a reserve officer with the Los Angeles Police Department, I am ready to enter the law enforcement profession and hope it will be with your department. A résumé highlighting my background, qualifications and experience is enclosed.

I will call you the week of September 27th to make sure my résumé was, indeed, received and to arrange for a personal interview. I will look forward to talking with you then.

Sincerely,

Jane Smith

Encl. Résumé

Sample Follow-Up Letter

Mr. Scott Anderson
1234 Second Street
Boulder, CO 23456

July 21, 2004

Protection Plus Security
1234 First Avenue
Denver, CO 12345

Attn: Mr. Ronald Smith,
        President

Dear Mr. Smith:

Thank you for the opportunity to participate in the hiring process for the position of security officer. I delivered my résumé to your office yesterday and am sorry to have missed you.

I remain extremely interested in the position and look forward to the possibility of being considered for the job. Please call if you need any further information.

Very sincerely,

Scott Anderson

AUTHOR INDEX

Acevedo, Art, 145
Alarcon, Francisco "Frank" J., 68
Anderson, Hugh, 253
Anderson, Russell M., 163
Anderson, Teresa, 87
Armstrong, David, 108, 182, 303
Armstrong, Gordon M., 238
Arnold, Jon, 303
Arvidson, Joe, 68
Atkinson-Tovar, Lynn, 144

Barnett, Daniel, 138
Barrett, Paul, 163
Barthel, Brea, 203
Barton, Shannon, 182
Bauer, Lynn M., 48
Bayer, Patrick, 87
Bayer, Richard, 15
Beckman, Richard D., 301, 303
Beniek, Brian, 238
Bercaw, George H., 164
Birkel, J. Damian, 317
Blum, Jon, 144
Boldt, Laurence G., 108
Bolles, Richard Nelson, 108, 215, 238, 275, 318
Booth, Walter S., 303
Borello, Andrew, 253, 304
Bowman, Theron, 304
Burke, Sean, 47
Busenitz, Arlen, 254
Buss, Jack, 182
Butzel, Sandra S., 317
Byron, William J., 317

Cahall, Jack R., 14
Campbell, George, 78
Capsambelis, Christopher B., 47
Carter, J. Patrick, 304
Casey, Jean M., 287
Chaffee, Jim, 274
Challenger, John A., 203
Chase, Raymond, 87
Clark, Jim, 202
Clarke, Alan, 182
Cockell, Larry L., 78
Colbridge, Thomas D., 144
Collingwood, Thomas, 144
Conroy, Dennis L., 45, 46, 155, 162

Dallas, James M., 164
Danga, Amy, 15
Davis, Edward F., 182

Davis, Paul, 137
Davis, Paul O., 144
Davis, Robert, 164
DiLorenzo, Norma, 182
DiVasto, Peter V., 304
Dlugozima, Hope, 317
Dohm, Arlene, 15, 108
Donovan, Craig P., 126
Douglas, John E., 164
Driggs, John, 316
Droste, Therese, 275
Drowns, Robert W., 48

Ebling, Patti, 145
Elechi, Ogbonnaya Oko, 182
Enelow, Wendy S., 275
Erickson, Don, 254
Erickson, Timothy E., 13, 14

Farr, Michael, 15, 68
Feemster, Samuel L., 145
Fennelly, Lawrence J., 286
Finnimore, Ian J., 181
Fleetwood, Chad, 15
Forsgren, Laurel, 15
Franks, B. Don, 145
Fuller, John J., 181
Fulton, Roger, 304

Garner, Kenneth, 164
Garnett, Jim, 126
Gates, Bill, 209, 215
Gips, Michael A., 87
Goldrick-Jones, Amanda, 203
Gondles, James A., Jr., 68
Gosney, John, 164
Grant, J. Kevin, 181
Green, Bill B., 105, 107

Hagberg, Janet, 108
Halberg, Marsh J., 66, 67
Hall, Norman, 164
Hamadeh, Samer, 126
Hamilton, Melanie, 304
Hanson, Marce, 47
Harowitz, Sherry L., 87
Harpold, Joseph A., 145
Harr, J. Scott, 234, 303, 316
Harrison, Paige M., 68
Harry, Jennifer L., 68
Hart, Mac, 275
Hawkins, Homer C., 287
Hawley, Chris, 48

Hayes, Kit Harrington, 203
He, Ni, 145
Hecker, Daniel E., 15
Hendricks, Carter, 124, 125, 126
Hendricks, Cindy, 181
Hendricks, James, 181
Hennessy, Stephen M., 181
Hertig, Christopher A., 87
Hess, Kären M., 48
Hess, Sheldon T., 144
Hickman, Matthew J., 48, 182
Hill, Linda, 108, 215
Ho, Taiping, 164
Hodowanes, Joe, 317
Hofferber, Karen, 203
Hoffman, Robert J., 144
Hogan, Nancy, 182
Holzman, Arnold, 164
Horrigan, Michael W., 48
Hurley, James J., 164

Iannone, Robert B., 85, 86
Isaacs, Kim, 203

Jetmore, Larry F., 164
Johnson, Spencer, 103
Josephson, Michael, 182

Kallen, Ben, 145
Kaminsky, Glenn F., 287
Karberg, Jennifer C., 68
Kasanof, Adam, 68
Kerlikowske, Gil, 201, 202
Kiekbusch, Richard G., 68
Kirschner, Mark, 164
Knox, Deborah L., 317
Koivamaki, Molly, 46
Krainik, Peggy Wilkins, 145
Krannich, Caryl Rae, 238
Krannich, Ronald L., 108, 238

Lambert, Eric, 182
Lambert, Janet, 182
Lande, Nathaniel, 108
Landsberger, Joseph, 164
Lashier, Ron, 164
Lathrop, Richard, 209
Layne, Anni, 317
Ledgard, Gretchen, 254
Leider, Richard, 108, 317
Levinson, Robert B., 87
Lombardi, John, 234, 237
Lombardo, Frank A., 164

Lovrich, Nicholas, 145
Lunney, Robert, 304

Maas, John J., 67
MacKensie, James, 159
Maher, Kris, 254
Mahoney, Mark, 182
Malloy, John T., 244
Maples, Brenda P., 252, 253
Marcus, John, 276
Martin, Carole, 276
Meyerson, Robert P., 253
Miller, Charles E., III, 182
Miller, Jo, 287
Miller, Linda S., 285, 286
Miller, Stacey J., 317
Moore, Carole, 182
Morem, Sue, 203

Narramore, Randy E., 304
Nathan, Robert, 108, 215
Nelson, Kurt R., 164, 182
Nemko, Marty, 276
Nerbonne, Terry, 182
Newfield, Peter, 204
Nierenhausen, Ron J., 142, 143

Obershaw, Richard, 289, 315, 316
O'Connor, Jim, 236
O'Connor, Thomas R., 126
Ohman, Marie, 86
Oldham, Scott, 145
Oldman, Mark, 126

Parker, Yana, 183, 204
Parrish, Penny A., 215
Parsons, F., 108

Perry, Julia N., 182
Pinizzotto, Anthony J., 182
Polk, O. Elmer, 108, 182, 303
Pozen, David E., 87
Pulley, Mary Lynn, 15

Rackleff, Jo Ellyn, 68
Rafilson, Fred M., 164
Raudsepp, Eugene, 276
Razek, Rula, 204
Reaves, Brian A., 48, 182
Reese, James T., 145
Richardson, Douglas B., 317
Riley, Frank E., III, 68
Rogers, Will, 241
Rolls, Sonya, 317
Rosch, Paul J., 145
Rosemarin, Judy, 276
Ross, Lee E., 182
Rostow, Cary, 164
Rubinstein, Ellen, 126
Rurak, Maura, 254

Sagario, Dawn, 317
Samuels, Joseph, Jr., 87
Schmalleger, Frank, 238
Schroeder, Donald J., 164
Schultz, Ray, 145
Scott, Gerges, 68
Scoville, Dean, 145
Scullard, Mark, 182
Segal, Geoffrey F., 87
Shapiro, David A., 108, 317
Shatkin, Laurence, 15, 68
Shaw, George Bernard, 212
Sheehan, Donald C., 287
Shelley, Kristina, 15

Slowik, Stanley, 164
Smith, Jay, 144
Snyder, Donald H., Jr., 68
Solan, Gerard J., 287
Sopow, E. L., 319
Spain, Christine G., 145
Spano, Michael, 164
Stanek, Richard W., 144
Stanek, Susan, 319
Stein, Michael P., 179, 181
Steinberg, Eve P., 164
Strandberg, Keith W., 145
Su, Betty W., 15
Sweeney, Albert J., 275

Thompson, Timothy J., 213, 214
Tischler, Linda, 317
Trump, Kenneth S., 107

Underwood, Mick, 254

Van Hasselt, Vincent B., 287
Velez, Luis, 303
Vogt, Peter, 254
Vollmer, August, 13, 159

Watson, Phillip L., 182
Weisberg, Michael W., 48
Whitten, Chris, 254
Wilder, Beverly A., 68
Wilson, Jeff M., 87
Wrobleski, Henry M., 48
Wyatt, Ian, 15, 108

Zakar, Peter, 254
Zhao, Jihong "Solomon," 145
Zillinger, Monte D., 181

SUBJECT INDEX

adult corrections, 59
adult offenders, 59
Advanced Law Enforcement Response
    Technology (ALERT), 174
agility test, 135
Agricultural Revolution, 5
Air Transportation Association, 37
alcohol use, 141
    interview questions about, 268
Alcoholics Anonymous, 96
American Board of Medicolegal Death
    Investigators, 36
American Obesity Association, 140
American Polygraph Association, 159
American Society for Industrial
    Security (ASIS), 70, 85, 106
    CPP program of, 81
American Society for the Prevention of
    Cruelty to Animals (ASPCA), 38
Americans with Disabilities Act
    (ADA), 132
America's Job Bank, 223
analog instruments, 159
animal control officers, 40
anxiety, *See* job interview; testing
AOL Time Warner, Inc., 78
appearance strategies, 257, 263, 274
application forms, 230, 235, 273
    dealing with past mistakes on, 175
    painting a picture with, 175
application process, 218–238
    being asked to apply, 229
    typical, 230
apprenticeships, 110
armed couriers, 77
Arms Export Control Act, 27
assessment centers, 154
attitudes, positive or self-defeating, 97
attorneys, *See* lawyers
automated fingerprint identification
    system (AFIS), 26

Babylonian Code of Hammurabi, 110
background checks, 160
bailiffs, 56
balance test, 134
Behavioral Personal Assessment
    Device (B-PAD), 157
Best Jobs for the 21st Century, 8
bilingualism, 180
body mass index (BMI), 131, 140
Border Patrol, 25
Boy Scouts, 169

Bureau of Alcohol, Tobacco, Firearms
    and Explosives (ATF), 27
Bureau of Customs and Border
    Protection (CBP), 25
Bureau of Diplomatic Security, 28
Bureau of Immigration and Customs
    Enforcement (ICE), 25
Bureau of Indian Affairs (BIA), 22
    Office of Law Enforcement
        Services (OLES), 29
    Office of Tribal Justice, 29
Bureau of Justice Assistance, 27
Bureau of Justice Statistics, 27, 31, 72
Bureau of Labor Statistics, 5, 6
Bureau of Prisons, 27, 97
burnout, 283, 284

California Personality Inventory (CPI),
    156, 157
cardiovascular tests, 133
career
    age requirements for, 94
    alternative, 102
    background information needed
        for, 96
    brainstorming about, 93
    charting future course of, 92
    choosing, 89–108
    determining facts of, 94
    educational requirements for, 95
    excursion map for, 98
    geography and, 100
    goals of, 101, 102
    interests and, 101
    knowing what you want from, 98
    ladder of, 288–304
    life experience in, 97
    making the most of, 301, 302, 303
    map of, 102
    ongoing exploration of, 104
    past experience in, 97
    people environment of, 101
    physical requirements for, 94
    research on, 102
    responsibilities involved in, 101
    risks of, 103
    salary of, 101
    selecting and developing, 90, 91
    values, purposes and goals of, 101
    work experience in, 97
    working conditions of, 101
career coaches, 91, 93
career counselors, 91, 93

career drivers, 98
Career Guide to Industries, 8, 12
careering competencies, 232
case managers, 57
Centers for Disease Control (CDC), 36
    on fitness, 140
central alarm respondents, 77
Central Intelligence Agency (CIA), 39
CERT Coordination Center, 81, 82
certification, testing for, 149
challenge, 138, 139
change, 139
chemical dependency counselors, 57
chief security officer (CSO), 78
children, committing crimes, 7
choice, 139
CIA, 39
Citizenship and Immigration
    Services, 25
Civil Aviation Security Specialists, 28
Civil Service Commission, 222
Clerk of Court, 57
Coast Guard, 25
code enforcement officer, 75
cold calling, 224, 225
commitment, 139
communication skills, 7, 173,
    247, 257
community corrections, 63
community crime prevention
    specialists, 40
community policing, 169, 180
computer
    ASCII files on, 194
    laptop, 174
    Optical Character Recognition
        (OCR) software for, 195
    preparing résumé on, 194
    skills with, 7, 84, 174
    text-only files on, 194
computer security, 81
console operators, salaries of, 83
constables, 21
contract security and investigation, 82
control, 139
Cooper's 12-minute walk/run test, 134
Coordinating Council on Juvenile
    Justice and Delinquency
    Prevention, 28
coroners, 22
correctional treatment specialists, 62
corrections
    adult, 59

careers in, 51–69
community, 63
juvenile, 59, 64, 74
occupations in, 59
private, 74
residential facilities of, 63, 64
skills needed for, 61
working conditions in, 60
Corrections Compendium, 222
corrections officers, 60
advancement of, 296
outlook for, 9
responsibility of, 166
Corrections Today, 221
counselors, 57, 58
county agencies, 21, 22, 32, 223
courage, 139
court clerks, 57
court reporters, 55
technology used by, 55
courtesy interview, 262
courts, careers in, 51–69
cover letter, 197, 199, 213, 227, 273
crackers, 79
crime
children committing, 7
prevention of, 237
crime scene investigator (CSI), 37
criminal justice
ethics in, 177
internship in, 118
specialization in, 34
criminal record, 96, 268
Cureton's breath-holding test, 133
cyber-crime, 79

Davis v. Dallas, 172
demographics, trends in, 6
Department of Energy, special deputies
of, 76
Department of Health and Human
Services, 26
Department of Homeland Security
(DHS), 24, 25
Department of Human Rights, 23
Department of Justice (DOJ), 24
Department of Labor, 5, 6, 11, 223
Secretary's Commission on
Achieving Necessary Skills
(SCANS), 171
Department of State, 28
Department of Treasury, 24, 78
depression, after job loss, 312
deputy, special, 75, 76
deputy sheriffs, 56
detectives, private, 77
detention officers, 60
diabetes, 140
disabilities, 132, 133
dishonesty, 161
dispatchers, 41

distress, 139
divorce, 6
downsizing, 309
Dress for Success, 244
driver's license division, 23
driving record, 176
interview questions about, 268
Drug Enforcement Administration
(DEA), 26, 39
drug testing, 80, 132, 269
drug use, 96, 141, 176
interview questions about, 268, 269

education, 10, 34, 35, 236, 237, 295
furthering of, 295
lifelong, 13
upgrading of, 11
educational placement services, 223,
224, 271
electronic monitoring, 64
emergency medical technicians
(EMTs), 44
Employee Polygraph Protection Act
(EPPA), 159
employees
accepting criticism, 282
appropriate behavior of, 279
being oneself, 283
competencies of, 171
entry-level, 278
knowledge of, 171, 280
learning from others, 281
perseverance of, 279
prospective, *See* prospective
employee
questions asked by, 279
respecting others, 280
skills of, 171
successful, 165–182
understanding politics, 281
employer
importance of résumé to, 184
investment of, 240
knowledge about, 250
employment
being asked to apply for, 229
book listings for, 236
challenges of, 1–126, 278–287
finding and applying for,
218–238
future planning for, 277–318
future trends in, 8
hard truths about, 309
maintaining oneself, 283
monthly listings for, 236
myths about, 307, 308, 309
number of jobs due to growth and
replacements needs by major
occupational group, 10
offer of, making decision about, 271
past, interview questions about, 267

preparing for, 127–215
projected changes by major
occupational group, 9
screening for, 160
security of, 307, 308, 319
success in, in 21st century, 13, 14
successful candidates for, 165–182
survival and, 319
top performance at, 293, 294
trends in, 2–15
typical process of, 230
unhappiness with, 283
employment law, 314
Equal Employment Opportunity
guidelines, 231
e-résumé, 194, 200, 226
ethics, in law enforcement, 177
exercise, *See* physical fitness
experience, broadening of, 294
Explorer program, 169, 180

families, changes in, 6, 7
federal agencies, salaries at, 32
Federal Air Marshals, 28, 37
Federal Aviation Administration (FAA),
28, 37
Federal Bureau of Investigation
(FBI), 26
educational requirements
for, 95
FBI Academy, 236
FBI Laboratory, 26
fitness standards of, 131, 133
identification division of, 26
specialization in, 34
Federal Computer Incident Response
Center (FedCIRC), 26
federal corrections, 61
federal employment offices, 223
Federal Jobs Register, 222
federal judicial systems, 54
federal law enforcement agencies, 24
Federal Law Enforcement Training
Center (FLETC), 30, 113, 130
Federal Protective Service, 25
feedback, 295
financial counselors, 57
financial issues, interview questions
about, 269
fire captains, 42
fire inspectors, 42
fire investigators, 42
fire lieutenants, 42
fire service, 41
firefighters, 42
advancement of, 296
education and training for, 43
personal qualities necessary
for, 43
volunteer or paid on-call, 169
first impressions, 241, 252

first responders, 16–50
  advanced jobs of, 34
  burnout of, 33
  fringe benefits for, 33
  jurisdictions of, comparison
    of, 30
  promotions of, 33
  salaries of, 31, 32
  specialization of, 34
  transfers of, 33
fitness, *See* physical fitness
five-minute barrier, 241
flexibility tests, 134
flower exercise, 100
foreign missions, 25
forensic investigator, 36
formal interview, 260
future planning, 277–318

gaming surveillance officer, 77, 296
gender, 6
General Schedule (GS), 32
Girl Scouts, 169
Global Positioning Satellite (GPS), 64
goals, interview questions about, 266
government agencies, jurisdictions
    of, 30
government employment
    offices, 223
grief, following job loss, 315, 316
groupthink, 241
Gun Control Act of 1968, 27

hackers, 79
heart disease, 140
high blood pressure, 140
hiring
  negligent, 240
  practices of, 213
Holland Code, 101
house arrest, 64
human equation, 100
humane law enforcement officer, 38
Humane Society of the United States
    (HSUS), 39

image, 239, 240
Immigration and Naturalization Service
    (INS), 25
incarceration, alternatives to, 63
Industrial Revolution, 5
information age, 5
information technology security, 81
information technology skills, 11
informational interview, 260
insiders' views, 12
integrity tests, 158
intellectualization, 168
Internal Revenue Code, 28
Internal Revenue Service (IRS), 24, 28
  criminal investigation special agents
    of, 28

International Association of Chiefs of
    Police (IACP), 19, 72, 154
  Code of Ethics of, 177
  Oath of Honor of, 178
  online, 113
international law enforcement, 39
International Security Conference, 85
International Security Management
    Association, 78
Internet
  bulletin boards on, 222
  job listings on, 222
  locating internships on, 113
  newspapers on, 222
  posting résumé on, 222
  research on, 222, 250
Internet security specialists, 79, 81
interns
  active, 110, 111
  employers' expectations of, 114
  evaluation of, 120
  listening by, 115
  passive, 110, 111
  positive and negative traits of, 116
Internship Bible, 109, 116
internships, 102, 106, 109–126, 174
  being terminated from, 120
  benefits of, 124, 125
  completion of, 123
  credit *versus* compensation
    for, 113
  do's and don'ts of, 121, 122, 123
  history of, 110
  incompatibility of intern
    with, 118
  locating, 112, 113
  making the most of, 116
  practical, 110, 112
  school-related, 112
  search for, 113, 114
  survey, 110, 112
  ten commandments of, 116, 117
  throughout career, 121
interview
  defined, 255
  job, *See* job interview
  promotions, 299–301
*Introduction to Law Enforcement and
    Criminal Justice,* 20
intuitive policing, 167
inventurers, 98, 99
investigators, salaries of, 83
Inwald Personality Inventory (IPI),
    156, 157
"it can never happen to me" syndrome,
    206, 207, 308

job change
  insights into, 288–304
  involving loss, 305–318
  motivations for, 289
  sequential reaction to, 310

job hopper, 103, 106
job interview, 185, 214, 240 241
  analyzing problems during, 258
  answering questions during, 274
  anxiety during, 257
  appearance during, 257, 274
  arranging, 242
  behavioral blunders during, 259
  being on time for, 274
  body language during, 248
  closer look at, 255–276
  closing, 270
  clothing for, 244, 245, 246
  common sense during, 258
  communication during, 257
  composure during, 248
  courtesy, 262
  difficult inquiries during, 242
  displaying knowledge
    during, 259
  employer and employee getting to
    know each other
    during, 242
  enthusiasm during, 249
  follow-up on, 250, 270, 274
  grammar and speech during, 247
  grooming for, 244, 245, 246
  informational, 260
  knowledge during, 249
  manners during, 248
  mass, 260
  mental rehearsal for, 251
  people skills during, 258
  personal qualities during, 274
  personality during, 248
  physical condition for, 246, 247
  practicing for, 269
  presenting yourself as *the* one to
    hire, 252, 253
  purposes of, 256–260
  questions during, 259
  rehearsal for, 252
  sense of humor during, 248
  steps prior to, 242, 243, 244
  strategy for, 251
  stress, 261
  stress during, 258, 259, 274
  teleconferencing, 262
  telephone, 242, 243
  thank yous following, 250, 270
  tips for, review of, 272
  trick questions during, 274
  types of, 260
  typical questions during, 264–269
  unnecessary, 262
  videoconferencing, 262
  videotaping rehearsal for, 252
  your turn to star, 273, 274
job loss, 305–318
  denial after, 315
  depression after, 312
  grief following, 315, 316

identity crisis following, 306
legal action after, 314
managing emotions after, 311
networking and, 310
resentment after, 315
searches after, 316
sequential reaction to, 310
strategy for, 307, 309
using job search skills after, 313
volunteering after, 310
withdrawal after, 316
wrongful termination in, 314
job search
   after job loss, 313
   application process in, 218–238
   being asked to apply for
     opening, 229
   being one's best during, 225
   book listings for, 236
   cold calling during, 224, 225
   contacts by mail, 226
   cover letter for, 197
   developing strategy for, 219
   difficult inquiries during, 242
   dishonesty in, 161
   getting your foot in the door,
     179, 180
   image presented during, 239, 240
   lying during, 96
   monthly listings for, 236
   most successful method of, 224
   motivation for, 104
   negotiating during, 269
   networking during, 224, 228
   newspaper ads in, 220, 221
   non–law enforcement
     majors, 236
   not burning bridges during, 229
   perfect training program for, 237
   personal inquiries during, 224,
     225, 226
   positive attitude during, 97
   presentation of self during, 239–254
   rejection during, 205–215
   remaining positive during, 208
   résumé in, 183–204
   sequential reaction to loss and
     change, 209, 210
   skills involved in, 234, 235,
     236, 237
   specialty periodicals in, 221, 222
   steps in, 217
   successful, 278–287
   successful candidates for, 165–182
   support system during, 208
   talking to police officers
     during, 234
   telephone inquiries during,
     224, 225
   testing your careering
     competencies, 232

thank yous during, 231
timing and salesmanship
   during, 237
transition curve during, 211, 212
typical process of, 230
warnings about, 232
where to look for openings, 220
*Job Search Guide: Strategies for
   Professionals,* 222
job-seeking strategies, 217–276
job-seeking uniform, 239–254, 240
   elements of, 240
journaling, 251
judges, 54
judicial system
   careers in, 52
   opportunities in, 59
   workers in, 54
juris doctorate (JD), 52
justice system
   helping professions in, 57
   privatization in, 73
juvenile corrections, 59, 64
   private sector involvement in, 74
juvenile offenders, 59
juvenile officer, 35
juvenile record, 96
juvenile specialists, 40

K-9 units, 34
Kasch pulse recovery test, 133
keyboarding skills, 174
King, Rodney, 90
knowledge
   about job, 89–108
   about oneself, 89–108
   discussing during interview,
     249, 259
   testing of, 147, 148, 149

lateral hires, 161
Law and Order, 221
law enforcement
   advantages and disadvantages of, 17
   dangers of, 17, 18
   durability in, 143
   employment outlook for, 19
   employment requirements of, 18
   first responders in, 16–50
   image in, 143
   international, 39
   interview questions about, 265, 266
   making the most of career in,
     301, 302, 303
   nonsworn career options related
     to, 40
   not like on TV, 45, 46
   opportunities in, 20
   personal values required in, 302
   physical and psychological risks
     of, 18

positions in, 19, 20
responsibility of, 284
specialized venues of, 39
supportive careers for, 40
survival skills in, 14
Law Enforcement Code of Ethics,
   177, 178
Law Enforcement Training Institute
   (LETI), 39
lawyers, 52
   in government practice, 53
   many hats worn by, 66, 67
   in private practice, 53
LEAA grants, 13
legal assistants, 54
Lehman Brothers, 78
letters of commendation, 295
licensure, testing for, 149
lie detector, 159
local employment offices, 223
local judicial systems, 54
local law enforcement agencies, 20,
   32, 61
loss prevention specialist, 78
Luddites, 5

magistrates, 54
marriage counselors, 57
marshals, 21, 27
   federal air, 28, 37
   fitness standards of, 130
   special deputy, 76
Maslow's hierarchy of needs, 2, 3
mass interview, 260
medical condition, interview questions
   about, 269
medical examination, 132
medical examiner, 22, 36
medical testing, 269
medicolegal investigator, 36
mental health issues, 96
mentors, 292
Military Intelligence, 105
Military Police (Army), 30
military service, 30, 236
   interview questions about, 267
   verifying, 161
Minnesota Multiphasic Personality
   Inventory-2 (MMPI-2), 156
Minnesota Police Corps, testing by, 148
Minnesota State Patrol, values of, 179
minorities, hiring of, 31
mint police, 38
Missing and Exploited Children's
   program, 28
mobile data terminals (MDTs), 174
motor vehicle division, 23
municipal employment offices, 223
municipal police, 21
Myers-Briggs Type Indicator
   (MBTI), 157

National Advisory Committee on
    Criminal Justice Standards and
    Goals, 172
National Classification Management
    Society, 85
National Court Reporters
    Association, 56
National Crime Information Center
    (NCIC), 26, 268
National Cruelty Investigations
    School, 39
*National Employment Listing
    Service,* 222
National Explosives Detection Canine
    Program, 25
National Institute of Justice, 27, 36
National Law Enforcement Officers
    Memorial Fund, 18
National Park Service, 29
National Special Security Events, 25
needs
    compatibility of, with job, 100
    hierarchy of, 2, 3
networking, 224
    after job loss, 310
    basics of, 228
    calendar for, 229
    Internet, 222
    promotions and, 295
    workbooks for, 228
newspapers
    Internet, 222
    job openings listed in, 220, 221
nutrition, 139

obesity, 140
Occupational Outlook Handbook, 6,
    11, 271, 284
*Occupational Projections and Training
    Data,* 12
Office for Victims of Crime
    (OVC), 28
Office of Inspector General, 26
Office of Investigations, 26
Office of Justice Programs, 27, 28
Office of Juvenile Justice and
    Delinquency Prevention
    (OJJDP), 27
organizations, brief history of, 5

paperless office, 174
paralegals, 54
paramedics, 44
park rangers, 29
Parker v. District of Columbia, 129
parole officers, 62, 97
peer pressure, 241, 283
people skills, 258
periodicals, job openings listed in,
    221, 222
personal qualities, interview questions
    about, 266, 267

Personality Assessment Inventory
    (PAI), 158
personality tests, objective and
    projective, 156
physical condition, 246, 247
physical fitness, 128–145
    basic program of, 136
    benefits of, 141
    Chicago Police Department
        standards of, 131
    defined, 128
    importance of, 129
    interview questions about, 267
    lack of, excuses for, 143
    lifestyle and, 140
    maintaining, 136, 137
    medical examination for, 132
    most important weapon one will
        ever carry, 142, 143
    nutrition and, 139
    self-assessment of, 133
    standards of, 130, 131
    stress and, 138
    testing, 130, 132, 269
Police Chief, The, 221
police officers, responsibility of, 165
police reserve units, 169
politics on the job, 281
polygraph
    computerized polygraph systems
        (CPSs), 159
    ink, 159
    Larson, 159
    testing, 159
POST (Peace Officers Standards and
    Training), 234
postal inspectors, 29
power tests, 135
President's Commission on Law
    Enforcement and Administration
    of Justice, 13, 155
pretrial services officers, 62
primacy effect theory, 241
Prison Journal, The, 222
prisons
    labor staff of, 65
    private, 74
private detectives, advancement
    of, 296
private investigators, 77
    advancement of, 296
private patrol officer, 76, 77
private prisons, 74
private security, 105–107
    careers in, 70–88
    close look at, 74
    ethics in, 177
    guard, 76
    job outlook in, 81
    requirements for, 79
    salaries in, 82
probation officers, 62

experience requirements
    of, 97
probationary period, 278, 282
    surviving, 285, 286
problem-solving skills, 258
Professional Careers Sourcebook, 12
Professionals in Transition
    (PIT), 305
    top ten guerrilla job-hunting
        tactics of, 313
promotions
    examinations for, 296–299
    feedback and, 295
    increasing chances for, 291
    insights into, 288–304
    interviews for, 299–301
    letters of commendation
        and, 295
    networking and, 295
    preparation for, 291
    skills needed for, 290, 291
    what and where, 289
prospective employee
    ability to achieve goals, 172
    appearance of, on paper, 166
    communication skills of, 173
    computer, keyboarding and word
        processing skills
        of, 174
    cover letter of, 197
    education of, 170, 172
    ethics of, 177
    experience of, 168
    importance of résumé to, 184
    internships of, 174
    intuition of, 167
    military service of, 170
    past general employment of, 168
    personal attributes of, 166
    résumé in, 183–204
    screening of, 167
    values of, 178
    volunteer community service
        of, 169
    work-related experience
        of, 169
protection officer, 73
protective services
    advancement in, 296
    future growth in, 8
psychological testing, 154, 269
    methods of, 156
    purposes of, 155
    specific, 156
psychologists, 57
public information officer
    (PIO), 65
public justice, privatization of, 73
public safety dispatchers, 41
public safety first responders, 16–50
pull-ups, 135
push-ups, 135

questions
    during interview, 264–269
    stress, 264, 274
    trick, 264, 274

Reid Report, 158
rejection, 232
    avoiding negative self-talk
        after, 206
    do's and don'ts during, 214
    each failure is one step closer to
        success, 213, 214
    handling, 205
    preparing for, 205–215
    sequential reaction to loss and
        change, 209, 210
    shock, 207
    transition curve during, 211, 212
Research Security Administrators, 85
résumé, 183–204, 213, 273
    analytical, 191
    balancing modesty and self-
        confidence in, 201, 202
    compiling information for,
        185, 188
    cover letter with, 197
    creativity in, 192
    defined, 183
    educational information on, 187
    electronic submission of, 200
    e-mailing, 192, 194, 226
    faxing, 200, 226
    first draft of, 196
    following up on, 200
    format of, 192
    functional, 191
    hand delivering of, 200
    historical/chronological, 190
    listing skills on, 191
    mailing, 226
    PAR (problem-action-results) state-
        ments in, 194
    perfect, 197
    personal identifying information for,
        186
    photograph with, 188
    posting on Internet, 222
    printing of, 196
    proofreading of, 196
    purposes of, 184
    references on, 188
    research sources for, 201
    revising of, 196
    scannable, 195
    sending, 199
    specifying employment objective
        on, 188
    specifying position desired
        on, 188
    steps in creating, 185
    tailoring to fit job, 195
    type of, 190

typestyle of, 197
what not to include in, 189
words and phrases used in, 192,
    193, 194
work experience on, 187
writing, 192
ride-alongs, 150, 237
risk manager, 78
Rogers, Will, 241
rookies, 280
Rorschach Inkblot Test, 156, 158

SCANS (Secretary's Commission
    on Achieving Necessary
    Skills), 171
school resource officer (SRO), 35
Secret Service, 25, 39
security, 237
    business knowledge in, 78
    career opportunities in, 85, 86
    colleges, 169
    consultants, 10, 77
    contractual, 71, 79
    director, 78
    drug testing in, 80
    entry-level positions in, 76
    following September 11, 2001, 70,
        73, 82
    guard, 73, 76, 77, 296
    hybrid, 71
    Internet, 79
    licensing for, 80
    manager, 83
    mid-level positions in, 77
    officers, 71, 72, 83, 84, 85,
        86, 166
    political trends affecting, 82
    private, 70–88
    proprietary, 71
    requirements for, 79
    statutory policy involved in, 72
    technicians, 10
    top-level positions in, 78
security guard, 73
    advancement of, 296
    private, 76, 77
Security Management, 222
security officers, 71, 72, 83, 84, 85,
    86, 166
    fringe benefits for, 84
    promotions for, 84
    public and private, 71, 72
    responsibility of, 166
    salaries of, 83
    training, education and
        experience of, 85, 86
Security Police (Marine Corps; Air
    Force), 30
self-assessment, 133
self-esteem, 143
September 11, 2001, 37, 129, 284
    animal rescue following, 38

firefighters responding to, 42
security issues following, 70,
    73, 82
sequential reaction to loss and change,
    209, 210
service industries, future growth in, 8
service learning, 114, 124, 125
sheriff-coroner system, 36
sheriffs, 21
    deputy, 56
sheriff's departments, volunteer service
    in, 169
Shore Patrol (Navy), 30
sit-ups, 135
Sixteen Personality Factors (16PF), 158
smoking, 141, 247
social issues, increasing complexity
    of, 13
social workers, 57, 58
Society of Human Research
    Management, 198
special district police, 21
special weapons and tactics (SWAT)
    teams, 34
spelling skills, 174
squat thrusts, 135
St. Paul, Minnesota, Police
    Department, testing by, 155
standing broad jump, 135
state corrections, 61
state department of natural resources
    (fish, game and watercraft), 23
state employment office, 223, 235
state fire marshal division, 23
state highway patrol, 23
state investigative agencies, 22
state judicial systems, 54
state law enforcement agencies, 22,
    23, 32
state patrol, 23
stenotyping, 55, 56
strength tests, 135
stress
    dealing with, 258, 259
    fitness and, 138
    six keys to stress-free living, 138
    Type A personality and, 138
    upside of, 139
stress interview, 258, 259, 261
stress questions, 264, 274
Strong Interest Inventory, 157
substance abuse counselors, 57
Superintendent of Documents, 11
support system, 208, 232
surveillance, high-tech equipment
    for, 76

Technological Revolution, 5
technology skills, 7, 34, 92
teleconferencing interview, 262
telephone interview, 242, 243
terrorism, 24, 73, 284

test anxiety, 146, 297
testing, 146–164, 252, 269
    knowledge, 147, 148, 149, 162
    memory, 151
    observation, 151
    physical fitness, 128–145, 162
    polygraph, 159
    preparation for, 150, 162
    promotions, 296–299
    psychological, 154, 162
tests
    essay, 153
    integrity, 158
    multiple-choice, 152
    strategies for, 151
    true/false, 152
thank-you letter, 270, 274
Thematic Apperception Test (TAT),
    156, 158
Toffler's three waves theory, 4, 5
*Top 100: The Fastest Growing Careers
    for the 21st Century,* 9
township police, 21
traffic record, 96
transition curve, 211, 212
Transportation Security Administration
    (TSA), 25

treatment programs, 59
tribal law enforcement agencies, 22
trunk extension test, 134
trunk flexion test, 134

Uniform Crime Reports (UCR), 26
uniformed guard force, 30
union jobs, 269
U.S. Army, nutrition program of, 139
U.S. Computer Emergency Readiness
    Team (US-CERT), 26
U.S. Customs Service, 25
U.S. Fire Administration, 42
U.S. Forest Service, 29
U.S. Mint, 29
U.S. Office of Personnel
    Management, 32
U.S. Park Police, 29

values, 178
values journal, 99
vertical jump, 135
Victims of Child Abuse Act, 28
Victims of Crime Act (VOCA), 28
videoconferencing interview, 262
vocational counselors, 57
voice writing, 55, 56

volunteer work, 92, 102, 106, 180
    after job loss, 310

war on drugs, 61
wardrobe engineering, 244
Watson-Glaser Critical Thinking
    Appraisal, 157
Wickersham Report, 13
women, hiring of, 31
Wonderlic Basic Skills Test, 158
word processing skills, 174
work
    balancing with life, 319
    brief history of, 4
    changing world of, 5
    expectations about, 92
    hard truths about, 309
    importance of, 2
    myths about, 307, 308, 309
    satisfying needs, 3, 4
    survival and, 319
    world of, 2–15
workforce
    gender composition of, 6
    growing population and, 6
workplace know-how, 171
writing skills, 173, 227, 239